The Other World

FIFTH EDITION

The Other World

Issues and Politics
of the Developing World

Joseph N. Weatherby

Emmit B. Evans, Jr.

Reginald Gooden

Dianne Long
California Polytechnic State University, San Luis Obispo

Ira Reed
Trinity College, Washington D.C.

Longman

New York • San Francisco • Boston
London • Toronto • Sydney • Tokyo • Singapore • Madrid
Mexico City • Munich • Paris • Cape Town • Hong Kong • Montreal

Vice President and Publisher: Priscilla McGeehon
Executive Editor: Eric Stano
Senior Marketing Manager: Megan Galvin-Fak
Production Manager: Douglas Bell
Project Coordination, Text Design, and Electronic Page Makeup: Clarinda Publication
    Services
Cover Designer/Manager: Nancy Danahy
Cover Photos: *Clockwise from left:* Copyright © AP/WideWorld; Copyright ©
    AP/WideWorld; Copyright © PhotoDisc, Inc.; Copyright © PhotoDisc, Inc.
Manufacturing Buyer: Al Dorsey
Printer and Binder: The Maple-Vail Book Manufacturing Group
Cover Printer: Coral Graphic Services, Inc.

Library of Congress Cataloging-in-Publication Data

The other world: issues and politics of the developng world / Joseph N. Weatherby
[et al.].—5th ed.
    p. cm.
  Includes bibliographical references and index.
  ISBN 0-321-08879-4 (pbk.)
    1. Developing countries. I Weatherby, Joseph.

D833 .O74 2003
909'.09724—dc21

                                                                2002067638

Please visit our website at http://www.ablongman.com

ISBN 0-321-08879-4

1 2 3 4 5 6 7 8 9 10—MA—05 04 03 02

Contents

PART *I*

Global Issues in the Other World

CHAPTER *1*

The Other World   1

CHAPTER *2*

The Old and the New: Colonialism, Neocolonialism, and Nationalism   23

CHAPTER *3*

Political Economy 61

CHAPTER *4*

Women and Development 91

PART **II**

Other World Regions

CHAPTER **5**

Latin America   **108**

CHAPTER **6**

Sub-Saharan Africa   **180**

CHAPTER *7*

Asia   239

CHAPTER *8*

The Middle East and North Africa   281

CHAPTER **9**

Prospects for the Future   340

Preface

*Washing one's hands of the conflict between the powerful
and the powerless means to side with the powerful.*

PAULO FREIRE

$\mathbf{M}$uch of our perception of the world is from an American perspective. We tend to focus on events in our country, those in other Western nations, and until recently on U.S.-Soviet relations. Yet, despite the military, political, and economic power of the United States, we account for only 5 percent of the world's population. Clearly, most of the world exists outside of our country. Indeed, this Other World has become crucial in understanding the larger world in which we live.

This book aims to help students grasp some of the main dimensions of contemporary global issues in the Third World, which we term the "Other World." It is intended to present that part of our world that is considered non-Western in its orientation. To appreciate the Other World in today's international climate, we need to know more about its geography, culture, traditions, and political and historical development.

The Other World is a primer on Third World issues, with an interdisciplinary focus. We make no apology that this book is what it appears to be: a descriptive background to selected world issues. It is descriptive because we emphasize basic information on geography, culture, and political tensions in the Other World. The book targets general education students rather than the specialist. Our position is that these students are better served by a book that emphasizes specific issues, events, and places in a clear, jargon-free way, rather than by one written for political science majors and graduate specialists.

We also hope that our analysis will be welcomed by readers who are looking for a supplementary textbook to use in international relations, geography, and comparative government courses in which coverage of the Third World is needed. Our point of view is that at the beginning of the twenty-first century, the focus of world politics has shifted away from an East-West dimension to a North-South dimension.

Two traditional approaches dominate the study of global politics: the comparative approach and the area studies approach. The former addresses the political situation in selected countries with an emphasis on their values, institutions, levels of modernization, and types of governments. A deficiency of this method is that it often fails to provide an overview of the geographical areas in which the separate states are located. However, comparative studies are dominant in the social sciences because of their ability to account for similarities and differences among political communities.

The second approach, area studies, centers on the study of geographic regions. This perspective focuses on a region's general characteristics, including geography, climate, economics, political and social structures, culture, religion, and history. Instead of contrasting the differences among states with dissimilar backgrounds, this method promotes an understanding of the peoples and countries in geographical proximity to one another.

This book combines both perspectives. First, it gives an overview of issues relevant to the understanding of contemporary problems common to the Other World. Second, it provides regional coverage of Latin America, Africa, Asia, and the Middle East and then describes the similarities and differences within these regions. Third, it traces events and issues in selected countries in each region.

All of the chapters have been rewritten to take into account the effects of changing conditions as the people of the Other World enter the twenty-first century. We have attempted to keep the topics as relevant and up-to-date as possible. Time does not stand still, so we apologize in advance for any illustrations that may have become dated because of the rush of events.

NEW TO THIS EDITION

- New Chapter 4, Women and Development, written by Dianne Long, examines the role of women in "the other world." It replaces previous edition Chapter 4 (Conflict Resolution). Some elements of the previous Chapter 4 are included in this edition in Chapter 2, The Old and the New, and in Chapter 3, Political Economy.
- New discussion about multinational corporations appears in Chapter 3, Political Economy.
- Chapter 6, Sub-Saharan Africa, has been substantially rewritten and updated by Ira Reed.
- A completely new chapter on Asia (Chapter 7) by Joe Weatherby has been substituted for the previous edition's chapter on Asia.
- Includes discussions about the September 11, 2001, terrorist attacks on the United States.
- New review questions, key terms, and useful Web site listings have been added at the end of each chapter.

It is our hope that the readers of *The Other World* will gain a new understanding of the major issues that affect much of the world's population. If we are to comprehend the political turmoil in the Middle East or the food crisis in Africa, we need to be aware of the dynamics of life in those regions. Finally, we believe that issues in the Other World do not respect borders and that global interdependence will be a fact of life in the future.

All of us involved in this book benefited from the comments made by the following reviewers: Lucy E. Creevy, University of Connecticut; Robert C. Dash, Willamette University; Lyman H. Heine, California State University, Fresno; Waltraud Q. Morales, University of Central Florida; Quintan Wiktorowicz, Rhodes College.

We believe that this text is stronger because of the help of others. Jane Weatherby provided aid in overcoming the technical difficulties of this project. Sarah Elliott worked long hours to generate information found on many of the charts. Others who helped with proofreading and sympathy include John Culver and John Nickerson. The following friends generously loaned photographs to us from their personal collections: Richard Kranzdorf, Randal Cruikshanks, Domingo/Lendarts, Earl Huff, and Forrest. A special thanks goes to Anita Castro who guided us through the editorial stages. We also received help from others at Longman including Eric Stano and Doug Bell. Trish Finley at Clarinda Publication Services was indispensable in helping us to get our text ready for publication. Our copyeditor was Julie Blum. Because of the number of coauthors, we each have the luxury of blaming the others for whatever errors remain.

A chapter-by-chapter test bank with multiple-choice, true-false, and long- and short-answer questions is available to adopters. This test bank is available in hardcopy. To order it, please contact your Allyn & Bacon/Longman sales consultant.

Joseph N. Weatherby
Emmit B. Evans, Jr.
Reginald Gooden
Dianne Long
Ira Reed

About the Authors

JOSEPH N. WEATHERBY

Joseph N. Weatherby has been a professor of political science at California Polytechnic State University since 1968. In 1977 he was an invited visiting scholar at Wolfson College, The University of Cambridge, England. He has been awarded a summer Fulbright to the Middle East, an *NEH* Fellowship in Middle East Studies at The University of Michigan, and a Joseph P. Malone Fellowship in Arab and Islamic Studies. He is the author of *The Middle East and North Africa: A Political Primer* published by Longman in 2002. At Cal Poly, he has chaired the academic senate and received the university's outstanding teaching award. He holds B.A. and M.A. degrees from Baylor University, Texas, a foreign trade degree from The American Graduate School for International Management, Arizona, and a Ph.D. in political science and Middle East Studies from the University of Utah.

EMMIT B. EVANS, JR.

Emmit B. Evans has been a faculty member in the political science department at California Polytechnic State University since 1990. He has conducted research in Kenya, Mexico, and at the Scripps Institution of Oceanography and was the executive director of a rural community development organization in the southwestern United States for 10 years. His teaching and research interests are in the areas of comparative development administration, world food politics, and contemporary global issues. He is a former Peace Corps volunteer, having served in East Africa. He earned a Ph.D. degree in political science from the University of California, Berkeley.

REGINALD GOODEN

Reginald Gooden was born in Camaguey, Cuba, and spent his early years in Cuba and Panama. He has taught classes in inter-American relations and political philosophy at California Polytechnic State University since 1970. At Cal Poly he has chaired the academic senate. He has also served on The California State University Chancellor's Advisory Committee on General Education. He has been a member of the C.S.U. Academic Senate since 1985 and is their representative to the C.S.U.

Academic Council on International Programs. He completed his undergraduate work at U.C.L.A. and earned his Ph.D. degree in political science from the University of California, Santa Barbara.

DIANNE LONG

Dianne Long teaches political science and public administration at California Polytechnic State University in San Luis Obispo, California, where she has been a member of the faculty since 1982. Her teaching and research interests center on public policy and administration, particularly antipoverty programs and urban sprawl. A former Peace Corps volunteer in Central Africa, Dr. Long continues her writings on the nature of Third World peoples and politics. As a contributor to two chapters in *The Other World,* she brings to the text a perspective on issues affecting women, environmental change, and technological adaption. She holds a Master of Public Administration degree and a Ph.D. degree in political science from Michigan State University. She serves as chair of the political science department at Cal Poly and was the administrator of the Masters of Public Administration program at Michigan State University.

IRA REED

Ira Reed has been on the political science faculty at Trinity College, Washington, DC, since 1983; he previously taught at Mount Vernon College and Georgetown University. He teaches primarily comparative politics courses, including introductory classes and those focusing on Africa, developing areas, Russia and East Europe, and Western Europe, as well as courses on American politics, U.S. public policy, weapons and peace, political courage, democratization, and political futures. He serves as program chair in political science and has twice served as chair of his college's Academic Coordinating Council and five times as chair of the college Rank and Tenure Committee. He has published in *The Journal of Third World Studies* and has frequently presented papers at the annual meetings of the American Political Science Association, the Third World Studies Association, the World Future Society, and other national and regional associations. He holds a B.A. in political science from Virigina Tech and a Ph.D. in government from Georgetown University.

Introduction

There is nothing more difficult to take in hand, more perilous to conduct, or more uncertain in its success, than to take the lead in the introduction of a new order of things. Because the innovator has for enemies all those who have done well under the old conditions, and lukewarm defenders who may do well under the new.

NICCOLÒ MACHIAVELLI

The Other World is a place of dynamic change. Change is multifaceted: It can be simple or complex, positive or negative, of short- or long-term consequence, welcomed by some, opposed by others, and anticipated or unforeseen, as well as a combination of all of these factors.

Political geographers argue that the international system will soon undergo the most profound change since the modern state system was created. The number of recognized states may even double within the next quarter century. These changes will be the result of trends that are already observable in the Other World. New states are being created as the last colonies become independent. Others are being established as nations break away from already existing states to form additional entities. Finally, new states are also evolving out of the turmoil resulting from both the collapse of the Soviet Union and the end of the cold war. Geographer George Demko succinctly described this process when he observed, "The current changes in the political and economic geography of the world are as significant as what the world went through after the Treaty of Westphalia."[1]

Twentieth-century conflicts were largely fought by nation states over ideologies. Many analysts believe that disputes in the early twenty-first century will focus on the struggles for clean air, water, and energy. These struggles will become part of more fundamental clashes of civilizations. As early as in 1993, Samuel Huntington identified this process when he wrote, "Civilization identity will be increasingly important in the future, and the world will be shaped in large measure by the interactions among seven or eight major civilizations. The most important conflicts of the future will occur along the cultural fault lines separating these civilizations from one another."[2] Geographically, most cultural/religious fault lines will involve parts of the Other World.

This textbook focuses on the process of change in the Other World. As used here, the term *Other World* has a broader meaning than the more commonly used expression *Third World.* The Other World includes both underdeveloped and developed states that because of geography, history, or culture have similar interests and perceptions.

As in the fourth edition, *The Other World,* Fifth Edition, is divided into two parts. The first part comprises four chapters that address global issues of a general nature, including colonialism, economic development, and a new chapter on the changing role of women. Each of these chapters is introductory in nature. They are written for those with little previous exposure to Other World issues. An Issues for Discussion section has been added to each chapter in Part I. It is hoped that these topics raise provocative questions that can be used for classroom discussion. In most cases, the authors have made no attempt to offer solutions to these questions.

The second part presents surveys of the Other World regions involved in change. To make meaningful comparisons, we have organized this part geographically into chapters on Latin America, Africa, Asia, and the Middle East and North Africa. Each regionally focused chapter contains material on geography, people, government, economics, and history. Case studies involving key countries are featured throughout this part. These chapters also contain Flashpoints, which provide background material on issues and conflicts. The chapter on Asia is entirely new, the chapter on Africa has been substantially rewritten, and the other area chapters have been completely updated. The concluding chapter summarizes the main points of earlier chapters and offers a look into the Other World in the century ahead.

Before beginning this study, the reader should recognize that all people make assessments of others that are based on their own cultural biases. For example, we know that a person's color is not a behavioral or cultural characteristic. Nevertheless, because most of the people in the Other World have dark skin and most of the people in the developed world have white skin, cultural and behavioral stereotypes are common. People in the developed world often assume that darker skin is a symbol of backwardness. At the same time, the colonial experience has caused people in the Other World to view white skin as the representation of evil exploitation. If we are to make any headway in understanding others, we must attempt to avoid such stereotypes.

It is not necessary to be Western in order to be modern. For over 100 years, Western cultural imperialism has conditioned us to assume that westernization and modernization are the same. They are not, as any person on the streets of Jeddah, Hong Kong, or Seoul can point out. To understand the process of change that is taking place in the Other World, the reader must accept this fundamental fact.

The breadth of subjects covered in these chapters required us to make generalizations, although we have attempted to be specific where possible. At the same time, we hope that we have provided the reader with a useful introduction to the major political issues facing the Other World.

Joseph N. Weatherby

NOTES

1. Robin Wright, "The Outer Limits," *Los Angeles Times*, 25 August 1992, p. H4.
2. Samuel P. Huntington, "The Clash of Civilization," *Foreign Affairs* 72, no. 3 (summer 1993): 25.

CHAPTER 1

The Other World

Dianne Long

I am a citizen, not of Athens or Greece, but of the world.

SOCRATES

Socrates was a man of wide vision and understanding, a "citizen of the world" who knew about the great Babylonian, Assyrian, and Egyptian empires that had dominated "the world" long before his time. But his world included only the Mediterranean regions and the area we now call the Middle East. He would have had little awareness or knowledge of the Far East and the complex civilization of the Zhou dynasty that was in existence during his lifetime. Even if he had some fragments of information about China, it is certain that the Mayan civilization, flourishing on the other side of the world, was totally unknown to him.

Like Socrates, we have all seen the maps and globes that represent our world. But we tend to have limited perspectives based on our small knowledge of much of the world and its peoples. Many of us are not aware that the United States makes up less than 5 percent of the world's population. Almost one-fifth of the human race is Chinese, 17 percent live in India, and hundreds of millions of others live in states that have only recently gained their independence. Almost all of the 80 million people added to the world's population in 2000 live in the developing world.[1] The developing world comprises more than two-thirds of the world's states, the vast majority of which are economically less developed and less industrialized than the Western economies.

The world of ancient Greece consisted of a small portion of what we now call Europe, Africa, and Asia and included less than a million people. Today we know that almost 6 billion people inhabit five massive continents. Sophisticated communications and complex social, economic, and political interactions increasingly link them into a "global village." These linkages bring Americans into increasing contact with those parts of the Earth about which we have little knowledge or awareness—the "Other World."

This chapter looks at Other World definitions and characteristics. The following chapters consider colonial domination, economic development, and conflict resolution. The final chapters consider the major regions and suggest issues we face in this century.

DEFINING THE OTHER WORLD

The shaded areas on the map shown in Figure 1.1 identify the regions that various writers refer to as the "have-not," "underdeveloped," "developing," "less-developed," "South," "nonindustrialized," or "Third World" countries. Although political scientists, economists, and geographers do not always agree about which specific countries make up this area, the term *Other World* refers to most of the countries in Latin America, Africa, Asia, and the Middle East. These countries include more than three-quarters of the world's population, yet our daily references to them tend to include little more than sparse observations about a cultural orientation or a few generalizations about national politics.

The term *Third World* arose in the Western industrialized community, during the years when it referred to itself as the First World and to the Soviet republics and satellites as the Second World. The term *Third World* has historically been used in reference to those states that are characterized by limited development of industry, economic structure, and international trade, and have had persistent, sometimes overwhelming, socioeconomic problems. The Third World countries often lack stable political structures and have characteristically been dominated by First or Second World countries.

The discussion in this text includes some developed countries that, because of location, history, or culture, are distinct. For example, Kuwait, South Africa, and Israel attract special attention because of their regional importance and relationships with powerful sponsors outside their areas.

THE CHANGING WORLD

The world today is rapidly changing. Western concepts and traditions of political systems based on competing parties dependent on popular support have been arrayed against the centralized systems of radical socialism in the Soviet sphere. In recent years, however, the USSR has fragmented, and many of its constituent and satellite countries are remodeling themselves to fit into the Western system. At the same time, many states of Western Europe are moving even more closely together into an economic entity called the European Union. Germany has reunified into a single state, which includes both the Western element and the formerly Communist element and is clearly included within the European Union. Some of the countries of Eastern Europe are undergoing changes as well; however, old

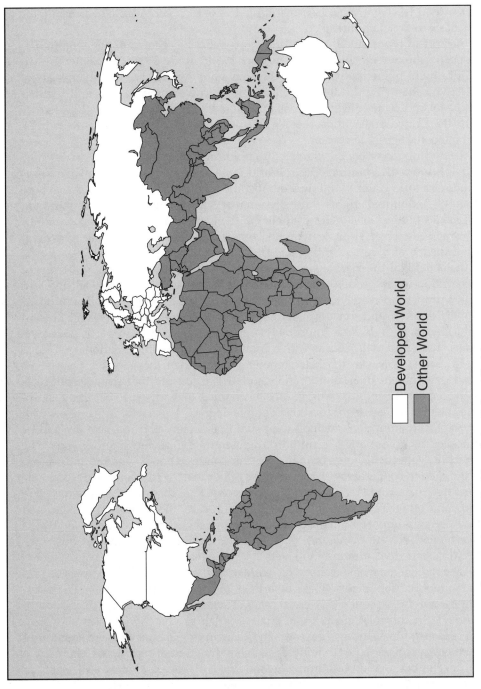

FIGURE 1.1 The Developed World and the Other World

Developed World
Other World

ethnic rivalries have emerged, resulting in conflict and bloodshed, as in the Croatia-Serb-Bosnia political crisis.[2]

Terrorism rooted in ethnic and religious belief has grown exponentially. The tragedy of the destruction of the New York World Trade Center on September 11, 2001, brought home the realities of the "have not" world that is unhappy about U.S. involvement in Middle East affairs. Support for some nations and regimes like Israel and economic embargoes on others like Iran have incurred hatred toward the United States and other Western powers. That hatred finds its expression in hostile acts of terrorism.

Clarifying major concepts related to political and economic frameworks may be helpful to understanding Other World issues and differences. Many countries in today's world claim to follow a democratic and capitalist model in which concepts of individual rights and free-market assumptions have importance. *Democratic* assumptions include a belief in the equality of political and economic rights possessed by all people in the society. *Capitalism* assumes private ownership of production and trade combined with a largely unrestricted marketplace based on the belief that the market is self-regulating and should be free of government intervention unless it fails. The individual is assumed to maximize self-interest; to own property privately; and to compete with others to achieve efficient production, distribution, and consumption of goods and services. Both economically and politically, the individual is important. People are free to own property, start businesses, trade, and make profits with minimal government intervention.

In reality, however, markets sometimes fail. When they do, the people demand government intervention and regulation to ensure that suitable products are available at tolerable prices. In most economies that appear to be capitalist, socialist elements are present to a considerable degree.

Socialist assumptions include the belief that society and markets need to be controlled by government to minimize abuses by the powerful and greedy. The society or "collective" holds property for "the common good," and individuals are encouraged to cooperate with one another rather than to compete. Socioeconomic structures such as the mail system, the phone system, roads and waterways, railroads and other transportation systems, health care, the education system, and other elements important to the economic life of a society may be controlled by the government. Private ownership of homes and businesses is tolerated but regulated according to community interests.

The radical form of socialism, called *Marxism,* is based on the writings of Karl Marx and Friedrich Engels, who saw human history as a struggle between the exploiting and the exploited classes. In Marxist states, the government plays a dominant role in controlling economic affairs, which produces the political system called *Communism.* Today, however, the dismantling of the Russian version of Marxism has coincided with widespread abandonment of traditional Marxism in the developing world. Communism, modified in various ways, still exists in North Korea, China, Cuba, and Marxist-led Eastern European states.

In reality, neither the socialist nor the capitalist model seems to produce optimal results. As a result, no economy is purely capitalist or socialist and today, mixed economies prevail. In such economies, there are places where government intervention is deemed appropriate. For example, government often is responsible for national defense and providing of services to victims of poverty, but private firms provide consumer goods and services. Mixed economic systems require political frameworks that not only encourage markets to develop but also allow regulation when markets fail. They provide opportunities for, as well as safeguards against, private individuals and groups that control communications, transportation, banking, and other vital parts of the political economy.

As ideologies blur and international agreements bring industrial states closer, it is difficult to predict the political and economic changes that will occur. The evolution into a global economy causes changes in the power relationships. These changes may lead to increasing international conflict as nations form regional trading blocs driven by the pursuit of profit rather than by political ideology. Control of labor and raw materials may become the principal source of conflict in the post–cold war era as First World nations and trading blocs compete with one another and as developing nations and masses attempt to resist increasing domination. The 1991 Persian Gulf war indicated the kind of conflict that may characterize the new world order. The Iraqi attempt to establish strong leadership of the Arab world by its invasion of Kuwait threatened the supply of oil to, and therefore the economic stability of, the United States, the European Union, and Japan. It appears that the Soviet Union acted to protect Iraqi interests in the cold war. In response, the United States was able to persuade the Soviet Union, and most members of the United Nations (UN), to accept using massive military force to end Iraq's occupation of Kuwait.[3] Since then, Arabs and Africans continue to support Saddam Hussein, and Western assumptions of a developing world as sharing political and ideological values appear to be mistaken. Such misperceptions are compounded by policymakers who fail to understand that the power of ethnic rivalries and staggering socioeconomic inequalities are factors in the view of Other World countries who have little to lose by undertaking aggressive behavior.

UNDERSTANDING THE OTHER WORLD

The consideration of economics, technology, and political structures is important for understanding the world's peoples. Geography is also a significant factor. The view of the Earth from the first *Apollo* spacecraft revealed it as a small marble of three colors: the blue of oceans, the brown of continents, and the changing swirls of white clouds that envelope its climates. The Earth's topographical and geographical features, in continuous dynamic balance with its climates, have influenced much of the destiny of the peoples occupying these fragile lands and traversing its seas. What the *Apollo* photos do not show is the proliferation of national divisions and boundaries. They do not show sharp economic or cultural differences between areas. Nor can we ascertain quality of life.

This discussion of the developing Other World is descriptive and explanatory. Our approach supports the "diverse dependency" school of thought, which we observe as the social, political, and economic conditions in various geographic locations, and we see them as components within the context of a continuously developing international economy. It suggests that these parts of the world are partially integrated into a global political economy, discussed here as the "global village." In fact, there is *one* world of developing international political economy, with different states occupying different and changing places in the first, second, and third sectors of the international political economy.

Modern social systems are specialized and interdependent. Much of this specialization occurred in the modern world as a result of the Industrial Revolution at the turn of the nineteenth century, when the factory and the workplace away from home became characteristic and symbolic of modern life. More complex and intricate machinery and processes were invented, driving us into a world where computers urge us to act at a faster pace. Today, the spread of technology, especially in communications, is accelerating the pace of change.

In 1945, when the UN was founded, 31 of its 51 members, or 61 percent, could have been described as "developing" states. Since then, the UN has grown to include 189 members.[4] Most new members are developing states (see Table 1.1). Their entry into the UN has shifted the balance of influence and voting power in the General Assembly from Western to non-Western control.

For many new states, the move from colonial status to independence was gained through political and social upheaval. However, as discussed in later chapters, ethnic and regional loyalties are still strong and impede the development of national unity in many of these states.

Today, violent conflict prevails in about 25 different locales in the world and involves millions of people. Because of these conflicts, there are over 14 million refugees displaced from their homelands. More than two decades after the U.S. military withdrawal from Southeast Asia, battles still occur in the Vietnam-Kampuchea-Laos area. Tensions also continue between India and Pakistan. The war between Iran and Iraq during the 1980s was one of the more bitter conflicts in recent years, taking more than 1 million lives. The Iraqi occupation and annexation of Kuwait became a global crisis. Sporadic fighting is endemic among other countries in the Middle East, as well as in the former states of the Soviet Union. In addition, the Afghanistan conflict has pushed people across borders in Pakistan where they live in holding camps in cold temperatures at near starvation. Afghanistan is a principal source of refugees (over 2.5 million in 1999). Another principal source is the Palestinians (almost 4 million).[5]

Africa is also a troubled continent, where civil strife exists in almost every country. Diverse ethnic groups divided by language, culture, and ancient rivalries vie for power and wealth. The crossroads of Africa, the Congo, is beset by such chaos and bloodshed that trade routes and economies are being severely disrupted. Military conflict between Ethiopia and Somalia has continued for years, as has the military and economic disruption in Uganda, Angola, Mozambique, South Africa, Sudan, Somalia, and their respective neighbors. In Latin America, struggles continue in Guatemala, El Salvador, Honduras, Peru, Chile, and Ecuador. UNICEF, the UN agency dedicated to helping the world's young people,

TABLE 1.1   ROSTER OF THE UNITED NATIONS

The 189 Members of the United Nations as of September 2001,
with the Years in Which They Became Members

Member	Year	Member	Year	Member	Year	Member	Year
Afghanistan	1946	Congo, Democratic		Indonesia	1950	Mozambique	1975
Albania	1955	Republic of	1960	Iran	1945	Myanmar	
Algeria	1962	Congo	1960	Iraq	1945	(Burma)	1948
Andorra	1993	Costa Rica	1945	Ireland	1955	Namibia	1990
Angola	1976	Côte d'Ivoire	1960	Israel	1949	Nauru	1999
Antigua and		Croatia	1992	Italy	1955	Nepal	1955
Barbuda	1981	Cuba	1945	Jamaica	1962	Netherlands	1945
Argentina	1945	Cyprus	1960	Japan	1956	New Zealand	1945
Armenia	1992	Czech Republic	1993	Jordan	1955	Nicaragua	1945
Australia	1945	Denmark	1945	Kazakhstan	1992	Niger	1960
Austria	1955	Djibouti	1977	Kenya	1963	Nigeria	1960
Azerbaijan	1992	Dominica	1978	Kiribati	1999	Norway	1945
Bahamas	1973	Dominican		Korea, North	1991	Oman	1971
Bahrain	1971	Republic	1945	Korea, South	1991	Pakistan	1947
Bangladesh	1974	Ecuador	1945	Kuwait	1963	Palau	1994
Barbados	1966	Egypt	1945	Kyrgyzstan	1992	Panama	1945
Belarus	1945	El Salvador	1945	Laos	1955	Papua New	
Belgium	1945	Equatorial		Latvia	1991	Guinea	1975
Belize	1981	Guinea	1968	Lebanon	1945	Paraguay	1945
Benin	1960	Eritrea	1993	Lesotho	1966	Peru	1945
Bhutan	1971	Estonia	1991	Liberia	1945	Philippines	1945
Bolivia	1945	Ethiopia	1945	Libya	1955	Poland	1945
Bosnia and		Fiji	1970	Liechtenstein	1990	Portugal	1955
Herzegovina	1992	Finland	1955	Lithuania	1991	Qatar	1971
Botswana	1966	France	1945	Luxembourg	1945	Romania	1955
Brazil	1945	Gabon	1960	Macedonia	1993	Russia	1945
Brunei		Gambia	1965	Madagascar	1960	Rwanda	1962
Darussalam	1984	Georgia	1992	Malawi	1964	Saint Kitts and	
Bulgaria	1955	Germany	1973	Malaysia	1957	Nevis	1983
Burkina Faso	1960	Ghana	1957	Maldives	1965	Saint Lucia	1979
Burundi	1962	Greece	1945	Mali	1960	Saint Vincent	
Cambodia	1955	Grenada	1974	Malta	1964	and the	
Cameroon	1960	Guatemala	1945	Marshall		Grenadines	1980
Canada	1945	Guinea	1958	Islands	1991	Samoa	
Cape Verde	1975	Guinea-Bissau	1974	Mauritania	1961	(Western)	1976
Central African		Guyana	1966	Mauritius	1968	San Marino	1992
Republic	1960	Haiti	1945	Mexico	1945	São Tomé	
Chad	1960	Honduras	1945	Micronesia	1991	and Principe	1975
Chile	1945	Hungary	1955	Moldova	1992	Saudi Arabia	1945
China	1945	Iceland	1946	Monaco	1993	Senegal	1960
Colombia	1945	India	1945	Mongolia	1961	Seychelles	1976
Comoros	1975			Morocco	1956	Sierra Leone	1961

(continued)

TABLE 1.1   ROSTER OF THE UNITED NATIONS *(CONTINUED)*

*The 189 Members of the United Nations as of September 2001,
with the Years in Which They Became Members*

Member	Year	Member	Year	Member	Year	Member	Year
Singapore	1965	Swaziland	1968	Turkey	1945	Uzbekistan	1992
Slovakia	1993	Sweden	1946	Turkmenistan	1992	Vanuatu	1981
Slovenia	1992	Syria	1945	Tuvalu	2000	Venezuela	1945
Solomon		Tajikistan	1992	Uganda	1962	Vietnam	1977
Islands	1978	Tanzania	1961	Ukraine	1945	Yemen	1947
Somalia	1960	Thailand	1946	United Arab		Yugoslavia	1945
South Africa	1945	Togo	1960	Emirates	1971	Zambia	1964
Spain	1955	Tonga	1999	United		Zimbabwe	1980
Sri Lanka	1955	Trinidad and		Kingdom	1945		
Sudan	1956	Tobago	1962	United States	1945		
Suriname	1975	Tunisia	1956	Uruguay	1945		

SOURCE: United Nations, 2001.

held a World Summit for Children in 1990. Leaders of 70 countries addressed the problems of children as both victims of and fighters in war, as well as the brutal exploitation of child labor. The summit's participants reflected on the millions of starving or undernourished children, the millions who receive no formal education, and the many forced to scratch out a living on city streets.[6]

The current situation in Afghanistan highlights the troubling circumstances of the population. Afghanistan has occupied a favored invasion route since ancient times. Foreign empires ruled over tribal peoples until the mid-eighteenth century. Although the country achieved statehood since that time, Afghanistan has remained a tool of her more powerful neighbors. As an example of this, most of the turmoil and human suffering that currently exists is the result of more than 25 years of outside interference that has totally destroyed any political legitimacy within the country. The Afghanistan of regional warlords, each backed by a rival neighbor, has created a situation of instability in central Asia. Whether the weak regime that has emerged in Afghanistan can eventually take its place as a contributing member of the new states in this part of the world is an unanswered question. The Afghan question is discussed in detail in Chapter 7.

CHARACTERIZING THE OTHER WORLD

The great diversity of the peoples and cultures of the Other World means that it is impossible to speak of any significant uniformity among them. The generalizations below, however, describe common features of many of these countries.

1. Dependence on Western powers;
2. Delayed modernization;
3. Population explosion; and
4. Unequal distribution of wealth.

In general, then, the Other World faces a wide variety of significant problems. Our task in this book is to outline the major themes and give specific examples.

Dependence on Western Powers

Most Other World countries have historically been colonies of major Western powers. Their economic, educational, religious, and political systems are now heavily influenced or dominated by their histories and resulting patterns of neocolonialism. Although nominally independent, emerging countries usually maintain economic and political ties with their former colonial masters, preserving many of the established patterns of commerce, politics, and daily life. Such patterns, however, tend to perpetuate the dependence of the new nation on its former rulers. Political and economic institutions designed to extract resources from the colonies are slightly modified and carried into the post-independence era. These institutions, now occupied by indigenous politicians and business leaders, still primarily serve the interests of the industrial powers. These political and economic elites depend on First World governments and corporations for power and position. Dependency exists in varying degrees. Some are still almost completely dependent on other powers, whereas others are moving away from dependency. In the 1990s, private capital from the West flowed into emerging markets of the Other World. Western capital rose from $44 billion in 1990 to $265.7 billion in 1997.[7] Asia and Latin America, participating heavily in the ups and downs of investment, brought about upheavals in global economies, which affected the financial markets of the United States and Western nations. At the same time, massive financial flows from the West have outgrown regulatory frameworks and have had such negative effects as increased ecological damage and threats to local cultures as their traditional values and strengths become displaced by Western consumerism.

Inflation (rising prices without corresponding increases in goods and services) creates additional hardships. Many peoples not only have low incomes but also find that inflation decreases the value of what little they have. In attempting to support and stabilize economic development, Other World governments have borrowed heavily from First World banking institutions. Latin American nations alone owe more than $500 billion to banks in the United States, Western Europe, and Japan.[8] Large debt levels constitute a risk of general economic instability in the entire world.

Delayed Modernization

Sanitation of food, water, and environment is a crucial factor in human health and only one-third of the Other World has access to adequate sanitation. Facilities for adequate disposal of human wastes are especially inadequate in rural areas, where 2.3 billion people live. In India, for example, fewer than 10 percent of the population have toilets. Poor sanitation in urban areas is a serious threat to public health because bacteria, viruses, and parasites in human wastes contaminate public drinking water.[9]

Although communication linkages are growing, Other World peoples have little access to telephones, publications, television, and the Internet. In China, for example, only 4.5 telephone lines exist for every 100 people compared to 60 lines per 100 people in the United States. Cellular phones are quickly catching on worldwide as a flexible resource to a community, even with those who are illiterate. In Cambodia, over 60 percent of phone users subscribe to cellular phones. The Internet is primarily a tool in industrial countries—home to 90 percent of subscribers.[10] Internet use, however, is catching on, particularly in China and India. Some use it for telecommuting and educational services, and others for protesting human rights and environmental violations and maintaining cultural ties.

Although developing countries have been slow to industrialize, auto production in the 1990s set new records. Latin America and Asia are areas sited for new car factories, and General Motors is investing $2.2 billion in new car plants in Poland, China, Argentina, and Thailand.

Most developing states have high rates of illiteracy and a shortage of experienced and skilled teachers, technicians, managers, scientists, and engineers. Moreover, the limited number of technologists is usually isolated in a few population centers in each country. Industrialized nations have four times as many managers and technicians per capita. Some countries, such as South Korea, now have intensive training programs to assist in the development of exports and industrialization. Many other countries, however, are unable to mount such training programs. Sometimes they are unable to pay wages appropriate to certain levels of training (e.g., to physicians), so that the danger of a "brain drain" to the higher-paying rich countries always exists.

Management and technological know-how are critical to industrialization and modernization. Because of a lack of capital and appropriate technology, developing countries have difficulty installing and maintaining sanitation systems, energy systems, transportation and communication networks, national security, and government services. The potential for agricultural and industrial progress is also curtailed. Even when financial and technical aid is imported in these areas, there is often little capability to maintain systems and provide inventories of replacement parts and equipment. Technological projects depend on efficiency, punctuality, organization, centralization, and productivity, but often these values conflict with those that are culturally dominant in the developing areas of the world. Local autonomy and interdependence, individual community status, decision by consensus and traditional tribal authority, and personal cooperation are usually more highly regarded than industrialized, organizational values. This situation produces conflict within a larger traditional developing society. On the other hand, erosion and displacement of values may bring chaos to previously stable and self-sufficient Asian, African, Middle Eastern, and Latin cultures, leading to serious social and psychological disruptions. Development raises very fundamental ethical questions about meddling in peoples' lives. One thing is certain: once change has been introduced to a developing country, there is no going back.

Population Explosion

It took 2 million years for the world's population to reach 1 billion, but it took only 100 years to reach the second billion. Today, the world's population is exceeding 6 billion and is growing still. Each year, 90 to 100 million people are added. If the present rate continues, over 9 billion people will populate the Earth by the year 2050. The greatest majority will live in the Other World, where the population is growing at two to three times the rate of the population in the industrialized world. Some of the dramatic increases are due to better sanitary conditions and medical technology in some areas, which have led to improved infant survival and increased longevity.[11]

Birthrates and poverty are closely linked. In poverty-level cultures, families live in the dilemma between the need for many workers and the risk of too many mouths to feed. The larger the family, the less each person's share of the family's resources. The poorer the family, the more likely the adults will find it desirable to

Population Control: Two young girls enjoy a holiday goat cart ride in China where the population growth rate is controlled by the state.

SOURCE: *Forrest*

add new family members as future caretakers and workers. Poor societies are dependent on children, adolescents, and young adults to care for the elderly and to support family unit economies. In addition, in poor families, inadequate nutrition and medical care may lead to low birth weights and infant deaths. The higher the likelihood of early death or disability, the more likely new workers must be born into families to ensure that the work gets done and there are providers for the elderly. When the fittest survive to learn traditional skills and values, and when those survivors stay in the clan and village to provide for all, including the very young and very old, the pattern of life continues. However, if young workers find it desirable to move from farms to cities, or if drought or war diminishes food supplies, life hangs on a thread for the children and the elderly left behind in rural areas. In many nations, food production has increased with improvements in farm management and crop techniques. Without an adequate infrastructure to allocate and distribute these increased supplies, more food does not necessarily mean more food on the tables for the bulk of the population.

Disease continues to reduce populations. The number of people living with human immunodeficiency syndrome (HIV)/acquired immunodeficiency syndrome (AIDS) worldwide is estimated to be 34 million, with the largest number living in sub-Saharan Africa and Asia. Over 15 million of these are adult women and 1.3 million are children. As this disease continues to spread, primarily through sexual contact, the world awaits a cure.

Unequal Distribution of Wealth

The most compelling similarity among developing states is the severe poverty of most of their people, who generally live at a subsistence level. Over half of the world's population survives on an annual per capita income of $800 (U.S.) or less. Haiti, for example, is one of the most impoverished countries in the Western Hemisphere. Its per capita gross domestic product (GDP) is approximately $350 (U.S.). Poverty can be measured by more than income or per capita GDP, however. In Haiti, almost one-third of the population is under 15 years of age, about 80 percent is illiterate, and life expectancy is 53 years. By contrast, the per capita annual income in the United States is over $17,000, 9 out of 10 people are literate, and life expectancy is over 70 years.[12]

The World Bank issued a major study of the world's poor in mid-1990. The report, issued as the World Bank's annual *World Development Report 1990: Poverty,* states that some progress toward overall economic growth has occurred since the 1960s. Fewer people are falling below the poverty line in countries like China and Indonesia, and increases in life expectancy have occurred in the Middle East, Asia, and Latin America. These gains can be attributed to foreign aid and productive use of labor, and increased basic social services in education, healthcare, and family planning for the poor. Still, 1.1 billion people—one-fifth of the world's population—have annual incomes of less than $370, the amount at which the World Bank draws its poverty line.[13] People below this limit are deemed unable to have access to adequate food, shelter, and other necessities of life. The World

Bank study shows a decline by nearly one-third in the number of the world's poor by the year 2000. Conditions in Africa, however, continue to run contrary to the worldwide decline in poverty. Africa's share of the world's poor has doubled from 16 percent to 32 percent in the last decade.[14] That continent faces intractable problems such as high population growth; weak basic economic infrastructure; and wars that have devastated Liberia, Angola, Namibia, Mozambique, Ethiopia, Somalia, and the Sudan. Over 43 percent of the population south of the Sahara lived in poverty in 2000.

THE CHANGING SOCIAL STRUCTURES

For several centuries the books written by world travelers have described the strange and interesting peoples of other lands, but these books were not widely read. A generation ago, however, Americans and Europeans experienced a growing flood of interesting magazines, illustrated with pictures of exotically clothed or unclothed people of color going about their daily lives and religious activities in ethnic costumes and settings. The magazines were paralleled by a profusion of documentary films. All of these visual images have tended to emphasize the unfamiliar. They appear in strong contrast to the usual informative publications that depict white or light-skinned people in Western attire and activities.

The people of the Other World have less opportunity to see the magazines and movies that depict them, but they have more and more opportunity to learn about the Western world and its ways. What can be said about the tensions and clashes that arise in both directions? What observations can be made, especially about women and cultural minorities?

The Family as a Basic Social Unit

In traditional cultures throughout the Other World, the family has always been the basic social unit. People are born, nurtured, and taught identities, values, and skills within families. Even rulers think of extended clans and larger political organizations as "my family." The larger ethnic or national family determines one's place in the world and one's most fundamental loyalties.

All is not well for women, however. The society and family may value males over females, leaving females abandoned, neglected, or ignored. The unspoken act of infanticide has more female victims than males. Orphanages in countries such as China and Pakistan are full of female children who have been left for adoption. Even if girls are nurtured within the family, they may not be allowed to continue in school or have access to job training or other avenues to economic life. In some Muslim countries, women's activities are restricted to the household with little venturing into the town or marketplace without a male family escort.

Traditional cultural values are threatened by the intrusion of foreign ideas, customs, and dress. Exposure to Western people, institutions, and media introduces such influences as Christianity, democracy, dating, rock music, denim jeans, and use of alcohol. Such changes are not easily tolerated. Even the veneer of modern dress is not accepted in some cultures. In many areas of Africa and the Middle East, Muslim women on the street continue to cover their hair, and sometimes their faces, as religion and custom dictate. They struggle to maintain their deepest beliefs and secure patterns. In other places, women become uncertain about new attitudes. Ethnic dress may persist while sometimes covering denim jeans or mini-skirts. Young people, who are especially drawn to new ways, are fearful of repercussions from those opposed to their changing status and role in society.

In today's world, extended families are being torn by brutal and sudden political changes in the surrounding world. Many people have become refugees. This uprooting of peoples into other lands not only fragments family and economic life, but presents an even more desperate condition for women, who must try to survive and nurture others while being hampered by food shortages, polluted water, lack of shelter, and possessing few basics for sustaining human life.

Isolation, Poverty, and Victimization

The cohesion of families and clans is being eroded by new patterns, such as the migration of large numbers of adult males to distant cities, mines, oil fields, and other locations of apparent economic and individual opportunity. Most of them hope to provide for the families who are left behind, and they earnestly try to do so. They find, however, that supporting the distant family while also maintaining themselves is more difficult than they had expected. After complications arise as a result of new involvement, effective close communication with the original family may become impossible. The absence of adult males shifts all of the family and community responsibilities to the women. They and their children also become more vulnerable to cultural conflict and to victimization and abuse. More than one billion people, mostly women and children, lack the ability to meet their basic needs. Although enrollment in primary school has grown to 70 percent of the population in developing countries, many women remain illiterate and unskilled. In some countries of Africa and Asia, more than three-quarters of the women between the ages of 20 and 24 have no formal education. Without literacy and the ability to earn income, women are marginal members of society. Regional conflict has made it difficult to grow crops, keep farm animals, and produce crafts and household products for sale or barter.

Faced with poverty, and sometimes abandonment, some women and children are forced to take up prostitution, with its risks for HIV/AIDS infection. The largest growth in HIV/AIDS is seen in Africa, where more than one-half of all victims can be found. It is a shame that HIV-infected males in Africa are raping female children as young as three and four years old, believing they will magically escape further health deterioration. The misguided hope for a cure by raping virgins has only accelerated the disease and caused untold suffering. Other circumstances bring HIV/AIDS home. Men who have lived away from home often engage in unsafe sexual behavior. Upon return, they infect their wives, who in turn carry the virus to unborn children. The spread of the HIV virus and AIDS is of crisis proportion in much of Africa south of the Sahara and in Southeast Asia, where birth control and AIDS prevention are not common practices. Other World women and children suffer a higher incidence of health problems, particularly with the breakdown of traditional nutrition and health practices, the continual exposure to unsafe water supplies, and loss of community and family support systems.

Western versus Traditional Ways

Westernization has brought new opportunities that are certain to be attractive to youths. Some young people are not content to maintain traditional ways. Yet they may not be well prepared to succeed in the new ways either. Western-oriented education becomes very important and very competitive. Those who succeed tend to be males who are the most energetic and assertive, the best and the brightest. But success has its price. Established patterns of subsistence farming and hunting break down and are replaced by new knowledge of property and economic structures. Trends toward democratization appear, but they erode such institutions as male-oriented local decision making. Males who leave the village are unlikely to return home. The women and those males left behind find that they have greater burdens.

Some trends in democratization are more symbolic than real. For example, the 1979 Convention on Eliminating All Forms of Discrimination Against Women, guaranteeing equal rights to men and women, was signed by 25 countries in sub-Saharan Africa. However, in some of those countries, and in most Other World countries, patriarchal societies continue. They provide stability,

The Old and the New: A cricket cage seller markets a traditional Chinese good luck symbol (left). Folk dancers at the Great Wall hope to perform for foreign visitors attending the Chinese Olympic Games (right).

SOURCE: *Joe Weatherby*

continuity, and economic opportunity, but they also deny women social, legal, political, and economic equity. In practice, access to information on basic human rights and to programs directed toward changing the condition of women is severely restricted.

The United Nations Fourth World Conference on Women and the Non-Governmental Organizations (NGO) Forum on Women convened in Beijing, China, in September 1995. It created a platform for action to improve the status of women. Although over 30,000 activists and politicians addressed the common problems women face, these participants could not fully subscribe to equality between the sexes.

In a time when gender relations are changing, women are caught in the stress of trying to preserve what is necessary for family and cultural life while at the same time clamoring for change. Articulating increased impoverishment and powerlessness, their cry is becoming more shrill at international meetings and global conferences. World leaders find it difficult to ignore pleas for greater participation in political and economic life and a greater say in social policy.

THE DILEMMA OF THE OTHER WORLD

Everywhere national, cultural, and political systems are shifting in response to complex internal and external pressures and conditions. In the Other World, however, change is occurring at a speed never before seen and in a context of inadequate structures and resources, while leaders express uncertainty about development goals and management strategies for handling chaos.

When the United States became independent in 1776, the world was changing, but it was changing slowly. Events happened and news spread at the speed of sailing ships and a foot's pace. As things changed, the fundamental patterns of rural and city life evolved slowly. However, in the developing world, centuries of change have occurred in only 30 years or less. A person whose grandparents had never traveled more than 10 miles from their birthplace may now be on a jet flight to London or New York. While the father plows with oxen, a brother may be operating a diesel tractor, and a sister may be learning the intricacies of world economies. Countries are being pulled rapidly in one direction or another by contending political, social, and economic forces over which they have little control. Deeply felt religious values and beliefs that gave stability to people's lives in the past are crumbling, to be replaced by new and alien philosophies.

Furthermore, as regional wars flare and military power threatens a region, it is difficult for the world to ignore the impact on stability, world security, and international trade. New patterns of alliances, cooperation, and conflict originate from the human experience and interplay among politics, geography, culture, history, economics, and human behavior. The problems and issues that challenge us are discussed in the chapters that follow.

SUMMARY

The Other World is marked by dependence on Western powers, delayed modernization, population explosion, and unequal distribution of wealth. The rapid social and economic changes have been hard on some populations. Women, minorities, and the poor suffer more than others in the sea of change as social and economic structures change. Although improvements have been made, war, human rights violations, and poverty act to disrupt the lives of many.

ISSUES FOR DISCUSSION

1. Will the world population explosion crush us all?

Predictions about population growth have been alarming. Demographers have projected astounding growth rates for the world—particularly for the Other World. Recently, however, they lowered their estimates by 4 billion people. New trends show a global stabilization with a target population of 9.4 billion people by 2050 instead of the 11.9 billion originally anticipated. What accounts for this lowered projection?

One answer is global conflict, in which thousands die annually across the troubled nations of the world. Yet another is the increased number of AIDS/HIV deaths, which are growing dramatically. Human casualties also result from changes in the Earth's climate, with the resultant disasters and failures of food supplies. Another answer is social change, such as family planning practices that significantly contribute to slow population growth. For example, China in the early 1970s had one of the highest population growth rates in the world. At almost 1 billion people, making up one-fifth of the world's population, China introduced stringent family-planning policies. The "later, longer, fewer" campaign of 1972, for example, focused on lowering the birthrate from six children for each woman to one. By 1979, fertility had fallen to 2.7 children, and the one-child policy led to even further reductions, especially in cities.

Social change causes disruption in other areas of life. In China, the pattern of one child in cities and two children in rural areas has caused shortages in services for the aged, because fewer young adults are available to care for their parents. In addition, preference for male children, increased longevity of the elderly population, and fragmentation of the extended family have fractured the society. Are these family-planning policies desirable?

2. Will the Other World be able to afford equality regardless of gender and race?

Boutros Boutros-Ghali, former secretary-general of the United Nations, noted in his address "An Agenda for Peace—June 1992" that democracy requires respect for human rights and fundamental freedoms—especially for the minorities and the more vulnerable groups in a society, women and children.

Until World War II, international law did not intervene when sovereigns treated their subjects inhumanely. Detention, arbitrary arrest, torture, and execution were commonplace. The UN adopted an international bill of rights, the Universal Declaration, in 1946 to promote and protect individuals from government abuse. Nevertheless, sanctions and incentives appear to be discretionary, and there seems to be little change in abuses cited in the daily news. The condition of women and minorities has not improved significantly. But the social stability needed for economic growth demands the empowerment of the poor. If social stability is a requirement of economic growth, will social change be encouraged? Will governments act to improve financial and administrative capacity to protect the weak and prevent the strong from engaging in exploitation?

3. Should the West intervene when abuses occur in the Other World?

It is not easy to generalize about ethnic and religious differences among peoples. Geographic and historic diversity divides people into separate and conflicting ethnic and religious groups, each with its own customs and traditions.

In some areas of the world such groups are mixed together and have managed to co-exist. But some contemporary national boundaries include populations that are in long-standing conflict with each other. Also, some ethnic/religious populations live on both sides of national boundaries. Examples are seen in the Middle East. Turkey, Iraq, and Iran are contiguous, but in Turkey there is a dominant population of moderately religious Muslims and a minority population of Kurds. The Kurds live on both sides of the border with Iraq. Kurds are Sunni Muslims, but in Iraq they are a minority in a country dominated by Arabic Shia Muslims. The Sunni Muslims have been in conflict with the Shia Muslims since the seventh century. At the other end of Iraq is Iran, which has a Persian, not Arabic, culture with a very conservative government dominated by Shia Muslims. However, in the area where Iran has a boundary with Afghanistan and Pakistan, there are many Sunni Muslims in all three countries. Some of these countries also contain populations of Armenians, Jews, Assyrians, and Zoroastrians straddling national borders. Each country has its own traditions and laws affecting religious belief and practice. They range from tolerant to aggressively intolerant.

Different examples are observable in India and Pakistan, which have high proportions of females. Women have little value and are regarded as financial burdens on families, who must provide wedding gifts (dowries) to shift the financial responsibility elsewhere. The murder of female babies and young wives by poisoning, burning, and neglect is frequent but officially hidden. In contrast, many Chinese villages have alarmingly few females of marriageable age because of abortions and infant deaths. In some geographic areas of India and China, ethnic cleansing of religious and ethnic minorities is systematically practiced, though rarely reported.

Among the Bedouin people of Saudi Arabia, family honor is esteemed and cultural codes are very important. The father is central to the family and society, and both young men and women are expected to obey family wishes. Marriages are arranged to protect desert wells and to cement relationships between families. Although Bedouins have moved to cities in large numbers, rather than following the nomad life of the desert as they have for centuries, traditional values have changed little. Family honor is valued, and women are excluded from modern production. This exclusion has served to trivialize women's decision-making role and minimize their influence within the society.

Since the creation of the United Nations in 1945, over 100 major international or ethnic conflicts have left 20 million dead. The United Nations was powerless to intervene because proposed interventions were vetoed in the Security Council—300 such vetoes occurred. During recent years, following the cold war, such vetoes have ceased, and demands for United Nations action have accelerated dramatically. Thus, it seems when conflicts arise, nations depend on others to intervene.

As some parts of the world clamor for global governance, there are also increasing expressions of nationalism. Other World peoples are establishing sovereignty under ethnic, religious, social, or linguistic identities. This fragmentation of the previous nation-state system causes a vacuum of international power and effectiveness, thus threatening economic and social well-being in various geographic areas. How can we protect human rights and preserve national autonomy?

4. Can poor people still prosper when a wage economy is introduced?

Over one-half of the world's people exist in subsistence economies. To many, the coming of a wage economy and the elimination of subsistence are positive features of modernization. With wages, it is argued, greater possibilities exist for improving family conditions and for trade with other peoples.

As men in previously subsistent societies begin to earn cash wages, however, they do not always spend them in ways that benefit the family. They may buy alcohol or attractive merchandise. At the same time, women continue to have little access to resources. Women often are prevented from owning land, entering into contracts, or engaging in business enterprises. Over time, women's traditional contributions to family survival are discounted. Activities such as planting and harvesting crops, gathering forest products, husbanding of food supplies, crafting clothing and household products, and caring for children and elderly family members, seem to have less value than cash wages. These activities are not only discounted by wage-earning men in the family but also by government statisticians and economic experts unaccustomed to costing out women's work.

World Bank studies show deterioration in children's nutrition even though wages and purchasing power have increased through development projects. When cash crops such as coffee, bananas, tobacco, cotton, cocoa, or specialized foods are introduced, the disparity between wages and child nutrition worsens. Both men and women tend to focus on earning cash. Women work on family cash crop lands instead of in family gardens, which provide food for the table and food to sell at market. As families seek to maximize acquiring cash, the best lands are used for that purpose and only deteriorated soils are used for family gardens. Thus, women work harder, but families do not always benefit. What should be done to relieve this situation?

5. At the end of the twentieth century, does the world seem to be a small or a big place?

Some see the world as a global village, tied by communication links, international corporations, and trade links that propel ideas and products across oceans to overcome cultural, class, and linguistic barriers. The ability to fax a photo, link up with a friend many time zones away, and extract local currency with a hometown bankcard gives the impression that the world is a small place indeed. Jet travel makes almost all parts of the world accessible for tourism and trade. Products like corn flakes and jeans are available in many remote shops worldwide; however, problems also have no boundaries. Pollution, supply shortages, job losses, and crime know no borders.

Yet as the diversity of peoples, places, and products increases, cultural conflicts and international complexities also increase. Cultural expressions distance one group of people from another. Rural infrastructure, that is, bad roads and unreliable communication, makes it difficult to move out of large cities. The period needed to clear a check at an out-of-town bank introduces a time warp. The availability of medical treatments, educational facilities, and public health regulations to ensure clean water and a safe food supply may be lacking. Do such gaps make the world seem a big place? If impressions vary so greatly, does the world appear small instead?

Review Questions

1. Will the world population explosion crush us all?
2. Will the Other World be able to afford equality regardless of gender and race?
3. Should the West intervene when abuses occur in the Other World?
4. Can women still prosper when a wage economy is introduced?
5. Does the world seem to be a small or a big place?

Key Terms

- **First World**—Western states, primarily the U.S. and Europe.
- **Second World**—Former states of the Soviet Union.
- **Third World**—States with limited development, primarily in the Southern Hemisphere.
- **Capitalism**—A system of private ownership of property, with little or no government intervention, with emphasis on the individual.

- **Socialism**—A system of collective ownership of property with considerable government intervention, with emphasis on the common good of all.
- **Communism**—A system with extreme government control, the most radical of which is called Marxism.
- **Diverse dependency school**—An approach to studying the world by looking at social, political, and economic conditions in various places.
- **Global village**—A term to describe one developing international economy.
- **United Nations**—International governing body established with 51 countries in 1945 has increased to 189 countries today. Members are dedicated to reducing global conflict.
- **Modernization**—Introduction of systems for sanitation, communication, industry, transportation, management, and technology.

Useful Web Sites

http://www.worldbank.org
http://www.un.org
http://www.thirdworldnews.com
http://www.oneworld.org
http://www.ctwo.org

Notes

1. R. Famighetti, *The World Almanac and Book of Facts 2001* (Mahwah, New Jersey: K III Reference Corporation, 2001), pp. 866–867 for population figures.
2. Ibid., 760–859 for description of important events by country.
3. Ibid.
4. Ibid., 865–868 for a brief sketch of the UN.
5. Ibid., 799–800.
6. United Nations. *Human Development Report 1998* (New York: Oxford University Press, 1998), presents data on the have's and have-not's with special attention to women and children.
7. World Bank. *World Development Report 1999/2000* (Washington, D.C.: World Bank, 2000), p. 72.
8. Ibid., 81–82.
9. Ibid., 220.
10. Ibid., 266–267.
11. *World Almanac 2001* (New York: Newspaper Enterprise Association), p. 860.
12. World Bank. *World Development Report 1997* (Washington, D.C.: World Bank, 1997), pp. 843–845 and *World Development Report 1999/2000* (Washington, D.C.: World Bank, 2000), pp. 250–257.
13. Ibid., 24–25.
14. Ibid., 236–237.

A Student Guide to Useful Reference Materials on the Other World

Most college and university libraries maintain government documents with reports on countries and the issues that concern them. Documents are available in paper form, and they are available on the World Wide Web, where governmental agencies have Web sites and newspapers have ongoing news briefs and articles covering global issues. The many reports published by the UN are invaluable, particularly the *Statistical Yearbook* and *Demographic Yearbook.* Some autonomous UN agencies that maintain data on specific issues include the World Health Organization (WHO), the Food and Agriculture Organization (FAO), the International Monetary Fund (IMF), and the International Fund for Agricultural Development (IFAD).

The *U.S. Statistical Abstract* has data on U.S. aid to foreign states, trade statistics, and other information. The State Department also publishes annually a *Status of the World's Nations.*

Several other useful sources include the *Political Handbook of the World,* ed. Arthur S. Banks (New York: McGraw-Hill, 2001); *The State of the World Atlas,* ed. Michael Kidron and R. Segal (New York: Simon & Schuster, 2001); Charles L. Lewis and Michael C. Hudson, *World Handbook of Political and Social Indicators* (New Haven, Conn.: Yale University Press, 2001); and *DPG Student Atlas of the World* (Guilford, Conn.: Dushkin Publishing Group, 2001).

Also, many countries publish their own statistical abstracts on a regular basis. General information can be obtained in any quality almanac, such as *The World Almanac,* published annually by the Newspaper Enterprise Association (New York).

CHAPTER 2

The Old and the New: Colonialism, Neocolonialism, and Nationalism

Joseph N. Weatherby

We the English seem, as it were, to have conquered and peopled half the world in a fit of absence of mind.

JOHN ROBERT SEELEY, 19TH CENTURY HISTORIAN

It is easier to conquer an empire than it is to keep it.

JOSEPH CHAMBERLAIN, BRITISH COLONIAL SECRETARY

The West has been involved in colonial activity for almost six centuries. No area of the world has managed to avoid being affected completely by this experience. Places as diverse as Gibraltar and the Falkland Islands are still areas of contention.[1] The dismantling of the major colonial empires held by the Western powers has been one of the key political developments since World War II. The postwar period has also witnessed the rise of both neocolonialism and nationalism as major features of the Other World. This chapter discusses Western colonialism, neocolonialism, and the Other World's reaction to those events, that is, nationalism.

COLONIALISM

Few subjects in international politics evoke as much emotional reaction as colonialism. Most people have a general idea of what the term means, but attempts to establish a definition agreeable to all are frustrating. It is unnecessary to trace its inconsistent use to determine that its meaning is in the eye of the beholder. To avoid confusion, however, some of the more important aspects of colonialism need to be described.

In earlier times, the term *colonialism* simply described a country's foreign settlements, or colonies. Writers in the complex world of the later twentieth century have used *colonialism* interchangeably with the word *imperialism* to describe the extension of control by one state over another. Used in today's context, both of these terms have an anti-Western bias.

Colonialism and imperialism have slightly different meanings. Colonialism is a relationship in which a group of people located in one country is subject to the authority of the people of another country. This authority can be exercised through direct control by the dominant country, as in the most typical form of colonialism, or through indirect influence, as in neocolonialism. *Neocolonialism* is the process by which rich, powerful, developed states use economic, political, or other informal means to exert pressure on poor, less powerful, underdeveloped states. In both direct colonialism and indirect neocolonialism, the dependent community can be made up of an indigenous people, immigrants, or a combination of the two. Imperialism, however, is the act of acquiring or holding colonies or dependencies. Thus, whereas colonialism describes a relationship between the dominant and the dependent, imperialism is the process of establishing that relationship.

Through the years, the terms *imperialism* and *colonialism* have provoked a wide array of emotional responses. Western countries in the last generation of the Victorian period rationalized that colonialism was a beneficial process that would help to bring a "backward" Other World into the light of the modern age. Their leaders often argued that the highest calling of society was to extend the benefits of Western civilization to its "black, brown, and yellow brothers" in the rest of the world. Sir Winston Churchill put it this way, "The act is virtuous, the exercise invigorating, and the result often extremely profitable."[2]

In addition, Westerners were certain that they were destined by history to act as the trustee for a less fortunate colonial world. It was in this spirit that President William McKinley justified the annexation of the Philippines on the grounds that the United States would bring Christianity to the islands. For many westerners, the expression *white man's burden* was both a challenge and an honor.[3]

Today, colonialism no longer implies honor. There is little doubt that the Other World considers it a disparaging word. Using this contemporary tone when speaking of the American and French experience in Vietnam, General Giap said, "The Americans were on the side of the colonialist—the American generals are not very good students of history. Dien Bien Phu paved the way for us to defeat not only the French but later the Americans and now to defend our country against the Chinese."[4]

HISTORY OF COLONIALISM

Many critics charge that colonialism is both a recent development and a result of the expansion of exclusively Western power into the less technically advanced areas of the world. If judged by its definition, it is apparent that colonialism is neither new nor exclusively Western in origin. History abounds with examples of one people exercising control over others. Even the history of Western Europe has been colored by the invasions of Huns, Mongols, and Turks. Most of the world's peoples have been guilty of practicing some form of domination at some time in history.

For almost all of the last 600 years, the West has played the leading role in the colonial drama. In Western colonialism's early stages of development, Portugal and Spain were the major European participants. They were so powerful that in 1494 a papal settlement, the Treaty of Tordesillas, divided the colonial world between them. Under the terms of this agreement, the Portuguese had largely a free hand in Africa, Brazil, and parts of Asia, and the Spanish were free to conquer the rest of the Americas and the Pacific. Soon the colonial fever had spread to the Netherlands, England, and France, each of which carved out great empires of their own in the sixteenth and seventeenth centuries. All of these European actors converged in the Americas, in general, and the Caribbean basin in particular.[5]

Speaking romantically of this period of Christians, conquistadors, and buccaneers, William Lyle Schurz has written,

> The conquest was a thing of superlatives and the men who took part in it were supermen. For never has sheer human will and force of personality accomplished so much through the efforts of so few on so vast a stage. The conquerors not only gave a new world to Castile, their discoveries and conquests resulted in a worldwide social and economic revolution that radically changed the whole pattern of life in Europe and its overseas dependencies.[6]

The first phase of Western colonialism ended in 1781 at Yorktown, Virginia, when American rebels won their independence from the British. At that time, many people in England and other parts of Europe believed that colonies were no longer worth the effort required to hold them. This view was confirmed by the early nineteenth-century withdrawal of the Spanish and French from many areas in Latin America.

Because of perceived needs created by the industrial revolution, colonialism evolved into a new phase during the second half of the nineteenth century. Markets and minerals became the drive that led Europeans to establish new colonies throughout the Other World. During this period, many states attempted to acquire colonies. Although the old imperial powers were in the forefront of the new colonizing activities, they were soon joined by Italy, Germany, Japan, and eventually the United States.

Maps at the end of the nineteenth century showed Britain with an empire that included Hong Kong (1841) in the east, India (1661) in South Asia, and African holdings almost too vast to contemplate. France's empire included Algeria (1830),

Tunisia (1881), and Indochina (1884). In the twentieth century, France would acquire Syria (1920), Lebanon (1920), and part of Morocco (1912). Although Spain lost its American empire by 1898, it still maintained modest colonial enclaves in North Africa (1470–1580), West Africa (1860), Fernando Po (1778), and Guinea (1844). Portugal's empire included the ancient enclaves of Macao (1557) and Goa (1510) along with the more profitable colonies of Angola (1484) and Mozambique (1498).

Lesser colonial powers included the Netherlands, Belgium, Germany, Italy, and the United States. The Netherlands controlled the Dutch East Indies (1610–1641). Belgium's king owned the Congo (1884), now called Zaire, until 1908, when he ceded the territory to the people of Belgium as a colony. The Italians were established in the horn of Africa (1889), and in this century they carved out an empire in Libya (1911). The Germans held major colonies in southwest Africa (1884), New Guinea (1884), and Tanganyika (1885). The United States acquired the Philippines, Cuba, and Puerto Rico through its victory over Spain in the Spanish-American War of 1898. In this century, the United States leased the Panama Canal Zone (1903), purchased the Virgin Islands (1916), and gained control over the Pacific Trust Territories (1947).

Although few people realized it at the time, traditional colonialism was a dying movement when the twentieth century began. Spain's day in the imperial sun was already over, and the decline of the other powers was soon to follow. As if by apology, even those colonies acquired by Western states in the early years of the century were called "protectorates," a legal fiction, instead of colonies.

When the end finally came to traditional colonialism, it occurred with swift finality. Germany lost its African possessions with its defeat in World War I. Italy and Japan were forced to follow the German example at the end of World War II. In the aftermath of World War II, most of the former possessions of England, France, Belgium, the Netherlands, and the United States won their independence. The impact of independence on the Other World can best be understood if one considers that these territories included, among others, India and Pakistan (1947), the Dutch East Indies (1949), French North Africa (1956–1962), the Belgian Congo (1960), and the Philippines (1952). Today, only a few quaint anachronisms remain to remind the world of almost 600 years of Western colonial rule (see Figure 2.1 on page 28). Examples of these out-of-the-way places include St. Helena, Reunion, Madeira, and Aruba, which are still administered by France, the United Kingdom, Portugal, and the Netherlands, respectively.

As an epitaph to this period, it should be pointed out that the peoples subjected to colonial rule in the nineteenth century were both non-Western and nonwhite. Although this feature of colonialism was not important at the time, it has allowed contemporary critics in the Other World to present their grievances with the West in racial terms.

It is interesting to note that the former Soviet Union largely escaped criticisms of this type. Even though it contained vast amounts of territory and encompassed millions of people, the Soviet empire was masked by a Marxist ideology to which many in the Other World were sympathetic. To them, the stigma of colonial racism was to be applied only to Western powers. Now that everyone knows how

Nassau, Bahamas: Independent since 1973, this strategic colony was established by the British in 1729 to threaten Spanish colonies in the Caribbean. British Nassau was also used as a base for Confederate blockade runners during the American Civil War. Lord Dunmore built Fort Fincastle in 1763 to protect Nassau from attack.

SOURCE: *Joe Weatherby*

Russians treated non-Russians in the former Soviet republics, it is clear that this position was incorrect.

MOTIVES FOR COLONIALISM

In view of both the long period and the large number of Western nations involved, it should not be surprising to learn that colonies were established for a variety of reasons. Many of the stated reasons for establishing colonies were only

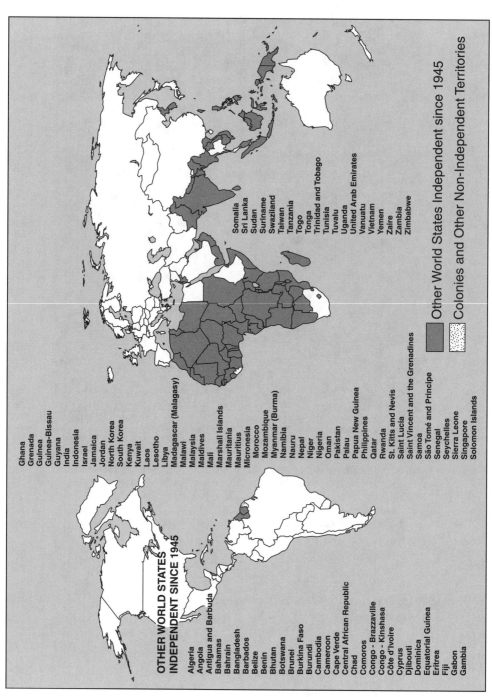

**OTHER WORLD STATES
INDEPENDENT SINCE 1945**

Algeria
Angola
Antigua and Barbuda
Bahamas
Bahrain
Bangladesh
Barbados
Belize
Benin
Bhutan
Botswana
Brunei
Burkina Faso
Burundi
Cambodia
Cameroon
Cape Verde
Central African Republic
Chad
Comoros
Congo - Brazzaville
Congo - Kinshasa
Côte d'Ivoire
Cyprus
Djibouti
Dominica
Equatorial Guinea
Eritrea
Fiji
Gabon
Gambia

Ghana
Grenada
Guinea
Guinea-Bissau
Guyana
India
Indonesia
Israel
Jamaica
Jordan
North Korea
South Korea
Kenya
Kuwait
Laos
Lesotho
Libya
Madagascar (Malagasy)
Malawi
Malaysia
Maldives
Mali
Marshall Islands
Mauritania
Mauritius
Micronesia
Morocco
Mozambique
Myanmar (Burma)
Namibia
Nauru
Nepal
Niger
Nigeria
Oman
Pakistan
Palau
Papua New Guinea
Philippines
Qatar
Rwanda
St. Kitts and Nevis
Saint Lucia
Saint Vincent and the Grenadines
Samoa
São Tomé and Principe
Senegal
Seychelles
Sierra Leone
Singapore
Solomon Islands

Somalia
Sri Lanka
Sudan
Suriname
Swaziland
Taiwan
Tanzania
Togo
Tonga
Trinidad and Tobago
Tunisia
Tuvalu
Uganda
United Arab Emirates
Vanuatu
Vietnam
Yemen
Zaire
Zambia
Zimbabwe

Other World States Independent since 1945

Colonies and Other Non-Independent Territories

FIGURE 2.1 Countries That Have Received Independence since 1945

cover-ups for the real motives. Still, there must have been powerful incentives to induce nations and generations of adventurers to risk hardship and death to establish and hold colonies.

If we look back over the history of this period, we can identify at least five main purposes that led the Western states to establish colonial empires. The participants neither simultaneously nor universally subscribed to these motives. Their importance varied by both the Western country involved and the land selected for occupation. Any list, however, should include the crusading ideal, the economic incentive, the military motive, outlets for surplus population, and the prestige purpose.

Religious and Cultural Motives

Certainly, the desire to spread the Christian faith induced the nations of Western Europe to establish colonies in the Other World. This movement had its birth in the successful reconquest of Spain and Portugal from the Moors in 1492. It was a natural extension of this proselytizing zeal to follow the footsteps of the retreating Moors into Africa and from there to conquer a new world in the Americas. For these Iberians, the introduction of Catholicism was as important as the accumulation of resources in their early colonies. At the time when a continent's wealth was to be had in the Americas, the religious crusade was also vigorously pursued. Today, centuries after both the gold and the colonies have disappeared, Latin America's Roman Catholic population, second in size only to Europe's, stands as a legacy to the serious purpose of the religious crusades of Spain and Portugal.

The cultural motivation was also important, affecting both the colonizers and the colonized. One has only to visit former colonies along the North African coast to see the cultural impact of the English, French, Italians, and Spanish, which has survived long after their departure. The Spanish, Portuguese, and French each believed that the highest gift they could bestow was their language, their culture, and their religion. This cultural "gift" was part of their colonial policy until almost the end of their overseas adventure.

The special emphasis on the importation of culture meant that the indigenous culture of the colony was not considered worthy enough to be maintained. In many places, the native culture virtually died out. Modern Egyptians, referring to the French contact with their country in 1798, say with cynicism that the French were in Egypt for only 3 years, but if they had been allowed to stay for 15, Egyptians would "say their prayers in French." Similarly, Muammar al-Qaddafi, the anti-Western leader of Libya, has ruefully remarked, "Any personal action on our part springing from our personality or from our values is cast into doubt, and we ourselves have begun to doubt. That precisely is how colonialism has affected us."[7]

Economic Motives

Religious and cultural colonialism often went hand in hand with economic colonialism. From the very beginning of the Western colonial experience, colonies were seen as a business and the aim was to produce a profit. The desire to become rich was certainly in the mind of almost everyone who dared to tempt fate by joining in any colonial enterprise. Colonies were always used for the profitable import and export of goods by the mother country. In the nineteenth century, economics became the spur that led to the redrawn maps of the Other World.

One might ask if colonies were actually profitable. The answer depends on the time in history, the location, and the conditions in the colony. For example, in the latter part of the eighteenth century, the French colony of Saint Domingue (now the Dominican Republic), whose economy was based on a slave-powered sugar monopoly, was so lucrative that British claims to vast territories in Canada were considered for possible exchange. Today, almost 200 years after independence, the French have gone; the great plantations are no more; there is a worldwide surplus of sugar; and the same territory, now known as Haiti, is the poorest country in the Western Hemisphere. The boom and bust of this plantation legacy was repeated in Brazil with natural rubber and in other parts of the world with cotton, tobacco, and coffee. At times, colonies held by Belgium in the Congo; the Netherlands in Indonesia; France in Indochina; and Britain in Africa, China, and India were very profitable.

It is easy to summarize some of the reasons that made colonies economically desirable for the mother country: They furnished food, minerals, and even human labor. In return, the mother country supplied the dependent territory with finished products. This arrangement, often monopolistic, gave the mother country's industries preferential trading opportunities unavailable to others. It should be remembered that economic colonialism was not exclusively a one-way street. The countries most successful with their colonies were able to strike a balance between their own desire for economic advantage and the needs of their subject peoples.

Strategic Motives

Following in the footsteps of those who carried the flag for gold and gospel were others who saw the need to protect the mother country's investments. These colonies were established to support more valuable possessions, such as the Spanish occupation of the Caribbean islands to protect and support the mineral-rich colony of New Spain (Mexico). In the nineteenth century, Britain adopted a foreign policy based on the establishment of a world empire dependent on control of the seas. To be successful, the British had to establish a string of strategic colonies—including such diverse outposts as Hong Kong, Aden, Malta, Gibraltar, and the Falkland Islands—for the defense of major colonies and for refueling and repairing the fleet. The importance of strategic colonies to the survival of the British Empire was reaffirmed at the beginning of World War II, when Winston Churchill said that if the Spanish had attempted to neutralize Gibraltar he would have been forced to seize the Canary Islands to keep the sea lanes to Australia free from German U-boats.[8]

Another type of strategic colony was established to serve as a defense for the mother country itself. The British Crown's 1000-year association with the Channel Islands, located just off the French coast, has provided a first line of defense against a second Norman Conquest of the home islands. In the same way, much of Spain's North African enclave empire was established to guard against a repetition of the Moorish invasion of the Spanish mainland.

Finally, some strategic colonies were established by nations pursuing a world balance of power. The value of these colonies is understandable only when analyzed in the context of the great-power politics that existed at the time they were established. For example, the nineteenth-century German occupation of the Marshall Islands and Nauru was probably motivated more by international politics than by hopes for economic gain. Certainly, the visit of the German gunboat *Panther* to Agadir in 1911 provoked Allied fears of German power that led to the Franco-Spanish partition of Morocco in 1912. In that incident, France and Britain invited Spain to occupy northern Morocco to prevent the possible establishment of a German military presence in North Africa, which might upset the balance of power in Europe. It should be clear that the importance of strategic colonies cannot be evaluated by normal standards for other colonies. They may have been costly to hold, as in the case of the Falklands, and their importance lay primarily in their ability to help maintain or safeguard other interests of the mother country.

Strategic colonies have been the most difficult to deal with in the age of decolonization. Many of them had little or no economic worth. Often they were established and settled by the mother country as territories carved out of another land. In Gibraltar, Ceuta, and the Falklands, establishing military bases also involved the expulsion of the indigenous population and resettlement by immigrants considered loyal to the imperial authorities. Today, in the face of Other World pressures for independence, it is questionable which party has the right to make the decision that determines a colony's future. Should it be determined by the territory's current residents or by the descendants of the original inhabitants? The question is more complex than it appears: Spaniards have lived in Ceuta since the fifteenth century, Italian immigrants have inhabited Gibraltar since the beginning of the eighteenth century, and Scots have resided in the Falklands since the early nineteenth century.[9] If one accepts the notion that ancient claims to colonial lands may be pursued in opposition to the present inhabitants, it raises the specter of calls for resettlement in many areas of the world. Yet this is precisely the argument advanced by those who wish to see colonial territorial fates based on historic ties rather than current reality.

Before ending this discussion, we should not overlook those strategic enclaves where the people have no wish for separation from the mother country. One example of this type of colony is Gibraltar, which has been in British hands since it was taken from Spain almost 300 years ago. Originally maintained to protect the trade routes to British East Africa and South Asia, Gibraltar has lost its strategic purpose. With the 1997 British withdrawal from Hong Kong, the Spanish government renewed the call for a return of the 1,396-foot-high rock to Spanish rule. As José Rodriguez-Spiteri of the Spanish foreign ministry stated in June 1997, "There are lessons to be learned from Hong Kong that could be applied to Gibraltar."[10] The Spanish then suggested a co-sovereignty agreement with the Gibraltarians retaining British ways in an autonomous Spanish state. The 27,000 Gibraltarians however, have repeatedly opposed any efforts to join Gibraltar with Spain. The

British problem is that the two issues are not comparable. On the one hand, the British held 90 percent of Hong Kong on a 99-year lease. Legally, that land reverted back to China when the lease expired in 1997. Britain was forced to hand over Hong Kong at the end of the lease regardless of the views of the residents.

The case for a British Gibraltar is different: The Treaty of Utrecht in 1713 awarded Britain sovereignty over Gibraltar in perpetuity. Should territories such as Gibraltar be returned against the will of the inhabitants merely because the land is contiguous to a larger state?

The issue is complex, and postwar solutions to similar disputes are inconsistent. Usually the colonial power has attempted to arrange the best deal possible for the inhabitants before agreeing to abandon the colony. This was the case with the British withdrawal from Hong Kong. They negotiated a promise from China to let Hong Kong maintain internal autonomy for 50 years in a policy called "one China, two systems." Portugal and China then agreed to a similar arrangement regarding Macao. However, the British were willing to fight a war with Argentina in 1982 to maintain their control over the Falkland Islands. The future is still unclear for places like Gibraltar, where the residents are not Spanish and do not wish to become Spanish. Whether Britain would go to war to defend Gibraltar as they did in the Falklands is an unanswered question. It is clear that the British are prepared to do anything short of war to protect the stated interests of the residents of Gibraltar.

Finally, it should be noted that over the years many strategic colonies have developed both artificial economies and large populations. If suddenly granted independence or absorbed by surrounding territories, these enclaves and their inhabitants would not be able to survive. The mother countries are often forced to maintain and support them long after the empires they were designed to protect have disappeared. Some of the Pacific and Caribbean islands are examples of this type of misfortune, and many of the flashpoints featured throughout this book illustrate the disputes that occur over their fates.

Surplus Population Motive

At different times, the argument that colonies would serve as outlets for a mother country's surplus population has been advanced to justify colonial enterprises. In the past, Britain and France sent convicts, debtors, and other undesirables to Australia and the Americas; and as late as the 1930s, the Japanese talked about relieving their population problem by sending surplus people to Manchuria. Although immigration has often been used as an argument for expansion, it is difficult to find cases in which the exportation of a surplus population was the primary motivation for establishing a colony.

It is easier to find cases in which immigration was used to justify territorial expansion—for example, the nineteenth-century territorial expansion of the United States and Russia. Some critics of Israel's past settlement policy have charged that Jewish immigration into the West Bank of the Jordan was encouraged by the government to justify the expansion of Israel's borders, in much the same way as American and Russian immigration justified the expansion of nineteenth-century borders to the Pacific. *The Evening Standard* of London spared no words in making this charge.[11]

The statement by Mr. Ariel Sharon that he is planning to bring another one million Jews to Israel will further stir the witch's brew of Middle Eastern politics. The paper further states, "To the Palestinians, talk of Israeli leaders of a million additional immigrants raises the prospect of more settlers or settlements on illegally occupied land."

Prestige Motive

Probably the most enigmatic motivation for colonization was the establishment and maintenance of colonies as symbols of greatness. If one looks at the world's remaining colonies, it is evident that many are still held for the purpose of prestige. Spain continues to hold the North African enclaves of Ceuta and Melilla long after the justification for them has ended. These colonies have little economic value, and their existence weakens Spain's own claims to the British-held enclave of Gibraltar. However, to Spain, these small possessions form a link to a glorious overseas tradition. For modern Spaniards, the crusading ideal, the empire, the civil war, and the tradition of military service in Africa far outweigh any political and economic liabilities that these colonies may bring. Because of the rise of anti-colonial feelings throughout the Other World, few other powers continue to maintain colonies purely for prestige, although it may partially explain the French role in Martinique and Guadeloupe and the British hold on the Falklands.

THE LEGACY OF COLONIALISM

Sir Winston Churchill expressed a justification for traditional colonialism when he wrote:

> To give peace to the warring tribes, to administer justice where all was violence, to strike the chains from the slaves, to draw the richness from the soil, to plant the earliest seeds of commerce and learning, to increase in whole peoples their capacities for pleasure and diminish their chances of pain—what more beautiful or valuable reward can inspire human effort.[12]

Most of the Other World has achieved independence during the last 50 years. Since the colonizers inevitably justified their empires with the claim that they were bringing the benefits of Western civilization to a backward world, it is appropriate to assess the results of their efforts.

Government

The primary interest of the colonial powers was economic, and the quality of preparation for independence varied. In many places, the British left a class of native civil servants who were prepared to keep the machinery of government running after the British had gone. However, where the evacuation was not amicable

Ceuta: In Christian hands as early as 1415, this fortress town has been a Spanish possession on the coast of Morocco since 1578. The mountain above Ceuta and the Rock of Gibraltar are called the Pillars of Hercules.

SOURCE: *Joe Weatherby*

or where the mother country's own civil servants had governed, little native expertise existed after independence. This sad state prevailed in many of the colonies of France, Belgium, and Portugal. When Belgium recognized the independence of the Congo in 1960, there were fewer than a dozen university graduates in the country. The highest position held by Patrice Lumumba, the Congolese leader, had been postmaster general.[13] Even under the best of conditions, the bureaucratic transfer from colony to independence was not easy. More often than not, coups, corruption, and dictatorships—not Western-style democracy—were the legacy of colonialism.

Education

One of the claimed benefits of colonialism was access to modern education. Since the beginning of the nineteenth century, Other World students have studied in Europe and America, and Western schools teaching modern science and mathematics have been established throughout the Other World. Unfortunately, the results of Western education have not met initial hopes and expectations. There have been generations of Western-trained elites who are not accepted in the West and who are viewed with suspicion in their own countries. It was said in the nineteenth century that the Ottomans sent their best young people to Paris to learn to become soldiers and engineers. Once they learned French, they read the writings of Hobbs, Locke, and Rousseau instead of artillery manuals. These young people then returned home as "Young Turk" revolutionaries dedicated to the overthrow of the Ottoman Empire. This destabilizing process has been repeated thousands of times in many countries in the last 150 years. For example, many members of the first cabinet established in Iran after the Shah was deposed in 1979 were Western-trained and held Western passports. For years, these leaders had been working from exile in Europe and America for the downfall of the Shah. Many other Western-trained elites have become anti-Western as their education has given them the perspective to see the hypocrisy of Western policies when applied to their own countries. These elites become disenchanted when they realize they would have better spent their time studying the foreign policies of Britain, France, and the United States than utopian Western philosophers. Their disillusionment with the motives of the West has been matched only by their dissatisfaction with conditions at home. Overeducated for the economy, unable to adjust to their own country, and resentful of the West, many of these educated elites have become a major source of instability in the Other World.

Economics

The economies of the Other World are invariably tied to the needs of the developed world. Agriculture in the former colonies is oriented to crops like coffee, tea, and sugar, and industry is oriented to the export of raw materials. For example, after independence from France, the Algerians found that one of their major industries was the cultivation of grapes for wine, a beverage that they were forbidden by their Muslim religion to drink. To compound the problem, the postcolonial French had developed new sources for grapes so there was little market for Algerian wine. The Algerians were forced to destroy many of their vineyards and replant with crops more suited for domestic consumption. The Algerian experience has been repeated as a sad economic fact of postcolonial life throughout much of the Other World.

Health

One of the undeniable legacies of colonialism has been the extension of modern health practices to areas in which they had not been available. Even where the healthcare needs of the impoverished still overwhelm the available clinics, the situation has improved during the past three decades. Western-initiated improvements in medical care, hygiene, and clean water have dramatically increased life expectancy everywhere in the Other World. The result is that adults are living longer and fewer infants are dying. Unfortunately, these advances have outstripped social practices geared to a more brutal age. The result is a population explosion in the Other World that threatens to destroy any chance for people to enjoy the material gains of the twentieth century. Egypt, which only 100 years ago had no population problem, now has a growth rate that requires an increase in water storage capacity equal to the construction of a new Aswan High Dam every 10 years, just to irrigate enough land to feed its people. With no change in social policy, Other World countries, such as Egypt, are leaking lifeboats, the inhabitants bailing water but doomed ultimately to sink in a sea of humanity. In one way or another, the population explosion, brought on in part by modern health practices, threatens the future of almost every government in the Other World.

Stability

Unlike nations in the West, many states of the Other World have failed to achieve internal unity. The boundaries of most are the result of balance-of-power decisions rather than any desire by Westerners to create states containing the seeds of geographic or cultural unity. The result is a postcolonial world that has few of the economic, social, or political elements generally thought necessary to establish stable governments.

The colonial experience must be judged to have had a generally negative impact on the peoples of the Other World. Although significant material benefits have been inherited from the West, they are offset by the economic, social, and political problems that are the legacy of colonialism.

NEOCOLONIALISM

Today, the great colonial powers of the past no longer occupy the center stage of world affairs. The fate of the world is not determined by traditional colonial powers like Spain, Portugal, Holland, or Belgium. Since colonialism was a primary force in the affairs of nations for nearly six centuries, this question can now be asked: Is colonialism dead or is it merely reappearing in a new form? If traditional colonialism is the only type to be considered, it must be concluded that this era of history has probably come to a close.

The second half of the twentieth century has been characterized by the arrival of almost 100 Other World states on the international scene. This rapid evolution of colonies into sovereign states has led to a situation in which many former colonies now fall under the influence of "new" imperial powers.

The old imperial powers laid the foundations for the Other World as it exists today. They drew the arbitrary boundaries that continue to be a source of conflict. They developed an economic system geared to the provision of needed products for the developed world. They created a leadership caste, which now perpetuates an unfair economic system that exploits the majority for the benefit of the few. The result was the creation of a new colonial system that allows one-fourth of the world to acquire 80 percent of the world's resources.

Fifty years after formal independence, much of the Other World is characterized by hunger, poverty, overpopulation, political instability, and economic dependence. Most of these problems are the legacy of a colonial world that emphasized economic return to the mother country with little regard for the needs of the indigenous inhabitants. Much of the economic, cultural, political, and social institutions of the Other World still serve the interests of the developed world, which is the successor to colonial rule. The economic imbalance between rich and poor, the production of crops for export while children go hungry, and the exportation of bulk raw materials while luxury consumer items are imported are only some of the many problems of the new dependent relationships that have evolved between the developed world and the Other World. As previously stated, the leading colonial powers during the great period of Western expansion were also leaders in world politics. Since World War II, the major neocolonial states have shaped most political events. Today, the United States, Germany, and Japan play dominant roles in the economic affairs of many Other World states. These neocolonial powers and their older allies, Britain and France, are now the developed world's political leaders. In this context, traditional colonialism is dead, but neocolonialism is very much alive.

What Is Neocolonialism?

Neocolonialism differs from traditional colonialism in at least two respects. First, there is no official acknowledgment of colonial ties because the subordinate government has established legal independence. Unlike traditional colonialism, the control exerted here is indirect. Second, this influence is exercised through the interaction of the dominant nation's banking, business, cultural, and military leaders with the Other World's elites. This process results in relationships that are dependent on the wishes of the dominant power. The political, military, and economic requirements of the controlling state drive the relationship between the two entities, whereas the needs of the subordinate country are of secondary consideration. Today, the Other World has become a dumping ground for consumer goods and military hardware exported from the developed world. Often these imports must be paid for with borrowed funds, which mortgage the future for people in the Other World.

Little America: Two typical street scenes in the walled American compound at Dhahran, Saudi Arabia.

SOURCE: *Joe Weatherby*

TABLE 2.1   A 2001 COMPARISON OF THE GROSS SALES OF SEVEN MAJOR AMERICAN CORPORATIONS WITH THE GDP OF SELECTED OTHER WORLD STATES

Corporation	Sales in $ Billions	Equals Approximate GDP
Wal-Mart	203	Saudi Arabia plus Uganda
General Motors	168	Egypt
Ford Motor Co.	146	Nigeria
IBM	75	Morocco
Mobil	72	Israel
Chrysler	61	Myanmar (Burma)
Philip Morris	54	Singapore

SOURCE: Adapted from *The World Almanac and Book of Facts, The 21st Century World Atlas; Millenium Edition,* and *The Washington Post.* Gross domestic product is defined as the market value of all goods and services that have been bought for final use during a year. The GDP covers all workers and goods employed within a nation's borders.

The influence exercised by a dominant power over a dependent state ranges from the activities of multinational corporations to the approval of international bank loans. In an independent world market, it is not unusual for the value of an American corporation's sales to exceed the gross domestic product (GDP) of a medium-sized state. Many Other World states are particularly vulnerable to multinational economic pressure (see Table 2.1). In this environment, externally provoked domestic economic problems lead to political instability. Other World leaders go along with a neocolonial relationship to survive. For instance, when their economies were in trouble in 1998, the governments of Thailand and Indonesia were forced to make important economic concessions before the United States–backed International Monetary Fund would guarantee the rescue packages considered necessary to stabilize the financial situation. The result was political unrest throughout the region.

In most cases neocolonialism is not driven by malice but by the marketplace. It is not a matter of illegal exploitation, but rather a case of the rich, through superior purchasing power, being able to influence Other World economics. This process occurs because the wealthy can outbid the poor for goods and services. The neocolonial relationship is manifested in at least four unequal associations: cultural, political, economic, and military dominance. Taken together, they constitute a degree of control exercised by the developed world that exceeds anything thought possible during the original fight for independence.

Cultural Domination

Traditional imperial powers proceeded on the assumption that their culture was superior. The Spanish, Portuguese, and French took steps to destroy the indigenous culture of the colonies and to replace it with a culture imported from the mother country. This policy resulted in the total destruction of many societies in the Other World. Although they took a more benign view, even the British spoke of "the lesser breeds." Colonial policies created a westernized upper class throughout the Other World. Two hundred years after independence, Latin American culture is still dominated by Spanish and Portuguese tradition. Thirty years after the French withdrawal from Tunisia, Tunisian elites still speak French. In 2002, the upper-class children of the Egyptian revolution talk of London while they play polo and croquet at the British-founded Gezira Club. These Western-oriented elites have become the transmission lines for foreign cultural domination in the Other World.

Radio, television, advertising, newspapers, magazines, books, and the Internet present a seductive message of Western cultural superiority. From Mexico City to Rabat, from Manila to Lima, young people have been conditioned to want jeans and rock music. Schools that are often patterned after systems from abroad further reinforce this cultural dominance.

In a society of scarcity, such as exists in much of the Other World, the obsession of the elites to create a native version of Western society has caused scarce resources to be diverted from the country's real needs to serve the interests of the few at the top. This practice leaves the developing nations vulnerable to other forms of neocolonial domination.

Political Domination

Much of the Other World is made up of unstable systems of artificially created states, each of which is fearful of its neighbors and therefore continually preparing for war. Thus many developing states seek the aid of other states to achieve political goals that otherwise would be impossible, making them prime candidates for outside influence.

Other World leaders need financial, technological, and military support from the developed world. To get this help, many are willing to submit to varying degrees of outside political influence. In a recent example of this kind of political pressure, the *Times of India* reported the following, "The United States on Saturday pledged more than a billion dollars in economic aid to Pakistan as a reward for its support for the war on terrorism, but it rebuffed Islamabad's attempt to rationalize its Kashmir policy and bring the issue to center stage."[14] Over time, this unequal relationship undermines the popular legitimacy of the government in question, and as a consequence, it forces authorities to continue the arrangement to remain in power.

During the cold war, Western intervention in the political affairs of Other World states was rationalized as a necessity to "contain communism." In the aftermath of this struggle, foreign interventions will be more difficult to justify. In the 1990s there has been less emphasis on maintaining the balance of power and more concern about securing access to Other World markets, resources, and cheap labor. As the twenty-first century begins, these goals are uncomfortably similar to those of the imperial powers of an earlier age.

Economic Domination

Economic neocolonialism may be pursued as the dominant country's formal policy, or it may occur subtly as the result of informal private activities. For example, whereas Western economic aid is clearly policy-driven, the activities of such great multinational powers as Ford, Standard Oil, and General Electric operate largely outside of the control of both the dominant and dependent countries. On occasion, the dominant government and private corporate policies may coincide, but this is not always the case. Such ambiguity makes the Other World charge that there is always a link between the policies of the neocolonial power and the multinational corporation, but this charge is difficult to prove. Some American corporations have used their foreign operations to frustrate their own government's policies on trade. The bottom-line strategy for multinationals is profit, not foreign policy.

The multinationals advocate free-trade policies that enable them to buy as cheaply as possible and sell for the highest price, regardless of where the market is located. They maintain that a policy of free trade will eventually result in the establishment of a system that will provide the greatest good for the greatest number of people.

No matter the intentions, people in the Other World believe that the economic impact of neocolonialism has a negative effect on their independence. In their eyes, the history of foreign trade has been the promotion of activities that work almost entirely to the advantage of the developed world. Its policy of keeping markets open to free enterprise virtually guarantees that it will continue to maintain a stranglehold on the wealth of the Other World. The rules of the game of trade have been made by the developed world and benefit the developed world. Economic neocolonialism is a legacy of this modern system of trade.

Military Domination

Much of the Other World is politically unstable. To survive in this hostile environment, the weak have had to pursue a policy of nonalignment or seek the protection of a powerful ally. After World War II, the United States and the Soviet Union courted these countries in an effort to structure a favorable balance of power. The result was the creation of military client-state relationships that involved most of the Other World. Since that time, the two superpowers have supplied massive amounts of sophisticated weapons to Other World countries. Weapon availability, parts, and training are all indirect methods for major powers to affect the behavior of their clients. The final outcome of the Falklands war (1982) was influenced by the U.S. spare parts embargo, which denied service to equipment supplied earlier to the Argentine Air Force. Without spare parts, the Argentineans were severely handicapped in both the size and the number of air strikes that they could mount against the British. This deficiency was one factor that ultimately helped to turn the tide of battle in favor of the British forces.

The militaries of the Other World form the life-support system for the arms business in the developed world. Arms sales have been significant sources of income and influence for the United States, the former Soviet Union, South Africa, and a number of states in Europe. President Carter did express concerns about U.S. arms policy, however: "We also need to change our weapons production and weapons sales overseas as a basic foundation for jobs in this country."[15]

This kind of military blackmail is often a two-way street. When visiting New York in November 2001, President Musharraf raised the issue of 28 F-16 fighters that had been sequestered in the early 1990s when Pakistan became a nuclear power. By supporting the war on terrorism, as a Muslim state, he hoped to get the United States to release the aircraft to Pakistan.[16]

In the guise of offering a helping hand to friendly nations, developed states are able to tie clients to their arms industry. During the cold war, this policy allowed sophisticated military hardware to fall into the hands of Other World leaders. In many cases, balance-of-power issues took precedence over the consideration of local issues when decisions on arms sales were made. On more than one occasion, leaders of selling countries were shocked to find that client states were fighting each other in local conflicts with the weapons that were intended for use in the cold war—for example, the hostilities between India and Pakistan, and between Iran and Iraq.

The 1990 Iraqi invasion of Kuwait demonstrated the folly of indiscriminate sales of advanced military technology to the Other World. To the surprise and horror of leaders in the developed world, the Iraqis showed that their acquisition of military technology had a level of sophistication that made a military response from the developed world difficult. In the end it took a half-million troops and a war to force the modern Iraqi army to leave Kuwait.

Developed nations have found that once their most advanced military technology is in the hands of a foreign leader, they can no longer control its use in the low-intensity conflicts that occur in the Other World. The development of sophisticated arms industries geared to exports by China, Brazil, South Africa, Turkey, Israel, North Korea, and South Korea has introduced a new dimension to this problem. The end of the cold war and the "build down" of the military forces in the United States and the former Soviet Union threatens to cause a "fire sale" of surplus military hardware, further complicating the issue.

In the wake of the 1991 U.S. victory over Iraq in the Persian Gulf, American arms sales to the Other World exploded. The U.S. government was placed in the embarrassing position of condemning Russian arms sales while, at the same time, increasing sales of its own.

Despite obvious dangers, the major powers continue to actively promote conventional arms sales to the Other World. For example, in May 1998, Vice President Al Gore visited the Lockheed Martin Corporation's Fort Worth, Texas, assembly plant to congratulate the workers on successfully securing a $7 billion F-16 aircraft order from the United Arab Emirates. That one order was worth 2,000 new skilled jobs for the Fort Worth area. In appreciation to the United Arab Emirates, President Clinton then met with Crown Prince Khalifa bin Zayed al-Nahayan, Deputy Commander of the Armed Forces, to thank him personally for the order.[17] It should be noted that this order equaled the approximate 1998 GDP for states like Cambodia, Cyprus, or Nicaragua. If the proliferation of exported weapons continues, the developed world's ability to influence low-intensity conflicts will be greatly reduced.

In summary, neocolonialism, like traditional colonialism, describes a process in which one people exerts power over another people. In the case of neocolonialism, the subject people are legally independent, so the dominant power's influence is indirect. Because the practice of neocolonialism is now so widespread, it must be considered one of the two major influences on contemporary politics of the Other World. The second is nationalism.

NATIONALISM

Like modern colonialism, nationalism is largely a Western invention. With the rise of the nation-state in Europe during the eighteenth century, Europeans abandoned their traditional loyalties to clan, church, and crown.[18] No longer were political leaders successfully able to command large followings purely on the basis of divine right, family ties, or papal decrees. For the first time, Europeans started to confer legitimacy on what was to be called the nation-state. This entity would have authority over a group of people, called a nation, who believed that they had a common cultural identity. Leaders who emphasized this linkage to reinforce the legitimacy of their rule strengthened the sense of identity between the nation and state. Commonly proclaimed symbols of nationhood included racial, linguistic, religious, and historical ties that separated one people from another. In time, the nation's flag, anthem, special days, and other traditions assumed a quasi-religious character that was almost unquestioned. Like the mystics of ancient times, the modern leader who successfully captured these images was able to rule. Today, leaders wrap themselves in the national colors at every opportunity to establish their legitimacy in the minds of the people. Modern nationalism represents the idea that the merger of the nation and the state creates an entity that is more than the sum of its parts. The individual's personal interests are subordinate to the interests of the nation-state. What makes the nation-state different from states of the past is the transference of the people's loyalties, hence legitimacy, to the state instead of to the crown, religion, city, or clan.

Nationalism is based on the notion of exclusivity and, therefore, the superiority of one nation over another. Conversely, one of the features of nationalism is the use of a fear of others to encourage unity. The "foreign devil" is one of the primary motivations for modern nationalism; that is, leaders in both the East and the West portray other leaders as foreign devils to secure popular support for their own policies. The perception of a Saddam Hussein, Muammar al-Qaddafi, Bill Clinton, or Fidel Castro as a foreign devil depends on one's location.

Nationalism in the Other World is part of the legacy of colonialism. As colonial administrators, teachers, soldiers, and missionaries sought to replicate the culture of Europe, they inadvertently planted the seeds of nationalism. Students learning about Magna Carta rights, the French Revolution, and American independence could not avoid drawing parallels between their own situations and the struggles of young Westerners of another age. Nationalism appeared in the hearts and minds of Western-trained elites long before it became the mass movement that it is today. For example, Western-educated intellectuals formulated the beginning of a theory that all Arabs form a single nation. At the time, their purpose was to create unity for a common Arab struggle for independence. Similar nationalists led movements in many Other World locations during the nineteenth and twentieth centuries.

For many years the Marxist-Leninist model was seen by nationalists as an alternative to the Western approach to development, with its neocolonial implications. However, the collapse of the economy in the former Soviet Union has discredited much of this effort in the eyes of many in the Other World. There is doubt about whether the Marxist-Leninist approach will continue to have much influence.

Some nationalists sought to chart a new course between the push-pull approaches of the East and the West. For them, nonalignment was the only way for the individually weak but collectively strong states to avoid the reimposition of colonialism in a new form. During the 1950s, Nkrumah in Ghana, Sukarno in Indonesia, and Nasser in Egypt effectively used the East-West rivalry to play off one side against the other. With the end of the cold war, Other World nationalists will have little to bargain with when they are forced to deal with the developed nations. It is questionable whether nonalignment will be a viable policy for them to pursue in the future.

SUMMARY

After nearly 600 years, Western colonialism has come to an end, and over 100 new nations have gained their independence. Born out of the colonial struggle for independence, these new states are engaged in the uneven process of nation building. The traditional symbols of nationalism may not be universally present. Many countries have yet to meet the criteria necessary for a state as it is recognized in the West. Admittedly, these states have artificial and often illogical boundaries and are divided by political ideology and religion. However, they have a common legacy of colonialism, which unites them. This unity is based on the development of a militant nationalism that is anticolonial, antineocolonial, and anti-Western.

If the hostility to the West is to be reduced, the Western policymakers must strive for a new fairness in dealing with the Other World. Fairness needs to be applied to policies on arms sales, trade, and banking. The present neocolonial practices carried out by the West ensure that extreme poverty will be the fate for millions of Other World people. The poor will continue to pay high prices for what they purchase from the West while being paid low wages for what they produce. The perpetuation of this unfair relationship is simply a license for the West to "strip-mine" the Other World for anything that is of value. As long as this situation persists, the West should not be surprised at the hostility, social unrest, and ethnic rivalry coming from the Other World.

ISSUES FOR DISCUSSION

1. Should the Other World be held to the same labor standards advocated in the developed world? The case for hand-tied oriental carpets and the issue of child labor are considered.

For every person living in the United States there are approximately 21 people living elsewhere. The majority of these people live at a subsistence level in the Other World. The circumstances of their existence dictate conditions of work that often seem harsh and immoral to Westerners. Is it possible or even fair to hold the Other World states to the same labor standards that have taken 200 years to evolve in the industrialized West?

There is a saying that the wealth of a society can be measured by the age at which the young must go to work. In oriental carpet factories stretching from Morocco across North Africa and South Asia to India and Nepal, the age of children working at the looms is young indeed. Ranging from as young as four to their mid-teens, thousands of young girls work for up to 14 hours a day in the carpet factories. Fine, hand-tied oriental carpets are produced by children because their hands are considered to be faster and they are more patient in their work than adults.

Oriental carpets are highly praised and find a ready market in the homes and offices of the United States and Europe. Almost all of these carpets are manufactured for export. Few Westerners understand or care to hear about the pain and suffering that is involved in the production of these beautiful, expensive works of art.

The defenders of child labor in the Other World point out that carpet factories and other industries are not unlike the nineteenth-century textile mills and mines that helped to create the wealth of modern Europe and the United States. To them, these harsh conditions are a temporary but necessary part of the development process. Other World businesspersons are outraged when they hear reformers in the West calling for boycotts of their goods simply because they were produced with the help of child labor. They are quick to point out that labor reform is simply another way for the West to restrict competition in a free-market economy. Other World states compete with the only advantage that they have—the willing backs of their young. To them, the old colonial metaphor still applies: After 200 years of playing industrial poker, the West has acquired enough of the economic chips to pronounce the game immoral and demand that the Other World join in a game of contract bridge.

The dilemma for the Other World is clear. The West is attempting to impose its own moral standards on a world that has very different values. In much of the Other World, a child who helps to support a poor family by working at the wheel or the loom is considered to be a good child. In places where the only advantage

Break Time: Child rug weavers taking a break in a North African carpet factory.
SOURCE: *Joe Weatherby*

that industries have over the West is low labor costs, there is no alternative to child labor if the family is to live.

This same story can be repeated in industries that manufacture products destined for Western markets, including sporting goods, textiles, and shoes. Labor organizations in the West have asserted that as many as 100 million children must work in the factories of the Other World for their families to survive.

The developed world may have seen the elimination of the worst excesses of the nineteenth-century England of Charles Dickens. Cripplers may no longer haunt the slums of Cairo looking for children to turn into the beggars described in the stories of Naquib Mahfouz. Nevertheless, harsh working conditions for children remain throughout the Other World.

Under the circumstances, should the reader boycott the carpets, textiles, sporting equipment, and shoes manufactured in the Other World because of these labor excesses? To do so will deprive millions of poor people of their only hope for a livelihood. Or should the reader assume that, as has occurred with industrialization in the West, conditions for labor will improve in Other World industries as manufacturing gradually improves the standard of living?

2. Should the Other World be required to adopt the ecological standards of the developed world? Can the Other World achieve a balance between environmental concerns and economic needs?

During the nineteenth century, British industrialists were fond of saying that "where there is muck there is brass," in short, dirt and pollution mean profits. By

Pollution: Flowing along the border between Mexico and the United States, the Tijuana River is polluted by the dumping of chemicals from the dozens of *maquiladoras*, or small factories, located on the Mexican side of the border. The people in the foreground are waiting for nightfall to slip across the border in the hope of finding work in the United States.

SOURCE: *Joe Weatherby*

2002, the developed world could afford to lead the rest of the planet in expressing concerns about the environment. Leaders from North America and Europe warned of the possibility of an ecological holocaust if drastic changes were not made to improve the environment. Many of their concerns were focused on the environmental problems found in the Other World.

By coupling their aid and foreign trade requirements to environmental policies, developed states were able to transfer their concerns to the Other World. The convention emerging from the United Nations (UN) conference on environment and development was signed by over 180 states. In support of this effort, the United States started to shape bilateral assistance programs in the Other World designed to encourage energy efficiency, renewable energy, and forest management. At the same time, the Europeans called for Other World producers to switch from environmentally unfriendly crops to new strains such as "green" cotton and "green" jute.

Through long-term planning, real progress has been made in improving the environment in parts of the developed world. The United States has dramatically increased the forestlands on the East Coast through replanting projects. In London, the Thames River is now clean enough to support salmon for the first time in hundreds of years. Clearly, the environment can be improved if people have the will and the wealth to make the long-term choices that are necessary. Most of the changes have occurred in the developed world. The question remains, can these environmental successes be repeated in the developing world and, if so, at what price?

People and states are far more vulnerable to the whims of the marketplace in the Other World. Westerners can afford to recycle cans and bottles while, at the same time, consuming millions of trees to supply paper for their Sunday newspapers and disposable diapers. Their wealth allows them to purchase the trees elsewhere and engage in reforestation nearby. Long-term improvements in the environment of the developed world can occur with little personal cost.

Long-term environmental choices are not readily available to much of the Other World. Subsistence farmers engaged in the "slashing and burning" of the rainforest have few choices if their families are to survive. They can continue to farm in the old way to the detriment of the environment. They can leave farming and try to eke out a living in the great slums of cities like Rio de Janeiro, São Paulo, or Mexico City. They can head north to find work as undocumented aliens in the developed world. Like millions trapped in similar situations elsewhere in the Other World, they do not have the luxury to consider long-term alternatives to their day-to-day existence.

Leaders of Other World states also have few long-term alternatives. Their people demand recognizable improvements in living conditions. The leaders must offer hope for a change for the better or face social unrest. Despite the desire of some to make environmental improvements, rapid development, regardless of the consequences, often seems to be the answer. For example, when Brasilia was established as the new capital of Brazil, it was done to encourage development in the interior, not to preserve the rainforest. Likewise, it may be unreasonable to expect the leaders of other developing states like China, India, and Mexico to place a high priority on environmental protection if it means a substantial delay in economic development. For them the choice is either development or a continuation of neocolonialism.

This issue came to a head in 2001 when the Bush administration withdrew the previous administration's commitment to approve the Kyoto Global Warming Treaty. The idea of holding developing countries to more relaxed standards on air pollution was flatly rejected by the United States. President Bush pointed out that Other World states were not being held to the same standards as those in the developed world. He was quoted as saying, "The world's second largest emitter of greenhouse gases is China. Yet, China was entirely exempted from the Kyoto Protocol. India and Germany are among the top emitters. Yet, India was also exempt from Kyoto."[19]

The United States was recognized as the world's largest emitter of greenhouse gasses. Without American support, the Kyoto was doomed to fail. However, it should be pointed out that other developed states like Japan and Russia also had reservations about the treaty. For the present, the states concerned about the emission of greenhouse pollution had to be content to approve a watered-down version of Kyoto that had nice sounding principles but would do little to clean up the atmosphere. Even this modified treaty failed to receive American support.

Try to look at the issue of ecology from the standpoint of the limited choices that people face in the Other World. Already economically subservient to a marketplace dominated by the developed world, what priority should Other World leaders give to the environment at the expense of their own development?

Finally, what should the developed world commit in the way of resources to the improvement of the environment in the Other World? Are people in the developed world willing to make the sacrifices that may be necessary, thereby lowering their standard of living, to free the funds required to improve the environment in the Other World?

3. Is free trade between the developed world and the Other World a good idea? Should the developed world look at the human cost of this kind of trade? The North American Free Trade Agreement (NAFTA) treaty is a case in point.

There is general consensus that, in the long run, a free market is beneficial to both the developed world and the Other World. It is believed that competition will eventually cause the best products to be produced at the lowest cost for the consumer. Noncompetitive products will be unable to survive in a free marketplace.

Aristotle, in the *Nichomachean Ethics,* wrote, "There is as much ethics in the equal treatment of unequal cases as in the unequal treatment of equal cases." Nowhere is this paradox more evident than along the border between the United States and Mexico. Called *La Frontera,* this 2,000-mile border is a separate nation separated by an artificial boundary. The people living in this region share interdependence based on family, history, and economics. It is here that a collision of the Other World and the developed world occurs. Here, the sweatshops of the United States and the *maquiladoras* in Mexico thrive.

This border is made up of overlapping cultures, economies, and jurisdictions. In Mexico, lax environmental standards and low wages have created a new frontier. The establishment of the border industrial program in 1965, followed by NAFTA in 1994, has aided this process. Many U.S. and Japanese companies have relocated south of the border, establishing manufacturing plants called *maquiladoras* to produce goods that will be sold in the United States.

Although clearly beneficial to the North American consumer, this practice is costly to many others. Since the ratification of NAFTA, Mexico has already attracted $7.7 billion in auto parts factories that have relocated from the United States. It is estimated that an additional $8 billion will be spent on Mexican auto parts manufacturing by the year 2000. Mexican manufactured vehicles exported to the United States have doubled under NAFTA to 800,000 units in 1998. Companies taking advantage of NAFTA to assemble vehicles or manufacturing parts in Mexico include Daimler-Chrysler, General Motors, Nissan, Ford, Daimler-Benz, and Volkswagen. The 1998 United Autoworkers strike against General Motors centered on a belief that Flint workers were losing jobs to Mexican workers.

The pollution coming into the United States from the *maquiladoras* plants is well known. Concerned U.S. residents are filing lawsuits against businesses operating in Mexico for health problems believed to be caused by air pollution drifting across the border.

La Frontera: Frontier sign warning California motorists to avoid hitting people illegally crossing the border from Mexico.

SOURCE: *Jane Weatherby*

These developments are also causing social problems in Mexico. In 1998, an estimated 1 million Mexican workers were employed in the *maquiladoras* system. Literally thousands of people are moving north in the hope of finding work in the *maquiladoras.* This process is overwhelming the social services and causing a decline in the wages of Northern Mexico. In one day, 20 people in Juarez died from drinking contaminated water from an overextended system. It has been reported that the influx of workers seeking jobs in *maquiladoras* had caused a decline in the daily wages from $4.06 a day in 1990 to $3.77 a day in 1998.[20]

On the United States side of *La Frontera* live the poorest of America's poor. There, conditions for some people are not much better than in Mexico. Across the border from Juarez, in El Paso, Texas, as many as 75,000 residents may not have running water and sewer systems. Many of these U.S. residents lost their minimum-wage jobs when their employers, taking advantage of NAFTA, moved their manufacturing operations to Mexico. These Americans still work, but now in the hundreds of small sub-minimum-wage sweatshops that proliferate along the border. These businesses operate along the American side in a lawless atmosphere by subcontracting work for legal manufacturers on both sides of the border.

In an analysis of the latest Census Bureau figures, Eva Deluna, a budget analyst for the Center for Public Policy Priorities, reported that the Texas counties that border Mexico exist, "as a continuing treadmill" of poverty.[21]

Like many places where there is a dramatic collision of wealth and the lack of it, *La Frontera* is an area of uncertainty and confusion. Does this mean that these people should be sacrificed to further the trading interest of the powerful in the short term, in the hope that everyone will benefit in the long run? Should the developed world be concerned that with change there will be winners and losers in tearing down the trade barriers between the developed world and the Other World?[22]

4. Do Other World states engage in imperialism? If so, is this a different form of imperialism than has existed in the past?

Earlier in this chapter, imperialism was described as the extension of control by one state over another. Since 1945, over 100 new states have been created from the ruins of the old empires established by the West. This new world is incredibly complex, making it difficult to generalize about the subject of imperialism.

Are Other World states, who have recently emerged from colonialism, capable of pursuing imperial aims of their own? Most of these states were artificially created by the colonial powers. Are they now simply engaged in the process of sorting out their natural boundaries? If so, is this process imperialism?

If imperialism is engaged in by Other World states, it is a more complex process than the one seen during the period of Western colonialism. This neoimperialism has at least several causes. First, there is the traditional seizure of the territory of others, as in the cases of China's occupation of Tibet, India's occupation of Hyderabad, Indonesia's invasion of East Timor, Libya's attempt to take northern Chad, and Iraq's invasions of Iran and Kuwait. All of these incidents may be described as imperialism in much the same way as was done in the past.

However, other examples of irredentism are more difficult to categorize. Is there a neoimperialism that includes the acquisition of territory because colonialism created artificial boundaries that fail to correspond to the actual ethnic divisions that exist? The desire for ethnic or tribal hegemony is justified in the seizure of territory in large parts of the Other World. Depending on one's viewpoint, this process includes Morocco's occupation of the Spanish Sahara, Somalia's claims to the Oqaden territory of Ethiopia, and the tribal conflict involving Burundi and Rwanda.

Defensive imperialism is also a controversial subject. Is a state justified in taking the land of another for purely defensive purposes? Did Israel become a neoimperialist state because of the establishment of the security zone across the southern border of Lebanon? Did the Vietnamese invasion of Cambodia to put down a hostile regime constitute neoimperialism? Does Syria's occupation of parts of Lebanon, to deter Israel, qualify it to be called a neoimperialist state?

Finally, are anticolonial liberation movements cases of neoimperialism? If so, many Other World states are guilty. Some examples of such actions include India's occupation of the areas on the subcontinent formerly controlled by France, the seizure of Goa, and the support for separatist movements that led to the establishment of Bangladesh. Argentina attempted to establish control over the Falkland Islands before being defeated by the British. If it were not for the British military commitment to Belize, it might soon be occupied by Guatemala, which has claimed this territory in the past.

Will the complex makeup of Other World states in 2002 require a more complex definition of imperialism if it is to have any practical meaning? If it exists, how should neoimperialism be defined? Under what circumstances can Other World neoimperialism be justified?

5. Should the United States continue to distribute foreign aid to the Other World?

Perhaps there is no foreign policy program that provokes more controversy and misunderstanding among taxpayers than the foreign aid program. First, people are confused about the amount of the U.S. budget allocated to foreign aid. Most polls indicate that the American people believe that this program takes up as much as 15 percent of the nation's budget. Although the figures are affected by the definition of foreign aid, most estimates place the foreign aid budget at about 1 percent of the national one. Furthermore, although the United States and Japan are the leading contributors in real dollars, the United States ranks near the bottom of the developed world in the percentage of gross national product devoted to this program.

The issue of foreign aid raises more questions than it answers. Not only is there confusion about actual dollar amounts, but there is little agreement about what should be included. What should an aid program accomplish? Who should benefit from foreign aid? Should foreign aid be limited to serving the interest of the donor? Should these programs target only states that are either democratic or promote free-market economics? Is military assistance legitimate foreign aid? Should foreign aid target the poorest states, or should it go to the more developed states that are in a position to use it effectively? Finally, should aid be given to programs that are morally necessary but economically or politically unproductive?

It may be a surprise to learn that of the approximately $14 billion that the United States sets aside for foreign aid, half is devoted to security or military assistance. The rest of the program is earmarked for economic, humanitarian, and development assistance. However, nearly half of that amount goes to three states: Israel, Egypt, and Russia. This leaves only about $3 billion to be divided among the rest of the Other World.[23] The U.S. example is not unusual. Japan, perhaps the world's largest donor nation, often limits aid to only those states that are potential customers.

Another surprising feature of the U.S. foreign aid program concerns the way in which aid is distributed. The richest part of the Other World gets twice as much aid per head as the poorest. Each year, Israelis get about $1,800 per head of U.S. aid, while the poorest aid-recipient states receive about $1.[24]

Furthermore, a good bit of aid is really a subsidy for American business and agriculture. Whether it is aerospace, defense, construction, automobiles, or Midwestern farmers, many Americans benefit from the foreign aid programs because of the requirement that goods and services must be purchased in the United States. This policy is understandable, because to do otherwise would be to ask the American taxpayers to support the products and services of their competitors.

It has been suggested that the taxpayers' desire to help people in real need might be better served if aid money were directed through international organizations such as the World Bank and agencies of the United Nations. Unfortunately, the track record of these organizations has not proved to be much better than that demonstrated by the unilateral programs. On the one hand, critics charge that the World Bank has tended to support huge development projects that have been harmful to the environment. On the other hand, the UN agencies have become so bogged down with short-term missions of peacekeeping and the feeding of refugees that they have had little impact on the long-term improvement of conditions in the Other World.

One of the fastest growing areas of foreign aid is the funneling of money directly through voluntary bodies such as church groups and other nongovernmental organizations. Arguably, these groups are working in ways that have a better chance to get the aid to those who really need it. At this time, this process is still too diverse and new to be evaluated.

The dilemma for the donor states is clear. Foreign aid was modeled after the post–World War II successes of the Marshall Plan in Europe. That plan was intended to jump-start the war-shattered economies of the time. Fifty years later, foreign aid is a vast system, which after the expenditure of $1.4 trillion has failed to improve conditions in the Other World. A recent evaluation of foreign aid programs in 96 countries by the London School of Economics concluded that they had made little impact.

The questions to be considered here are difficult. What should be the purpose of U.S. foreign aid? Should it be an extension of foreign policy? Should American workers be favored in making purchases for foreign aid programs? Finally, how should the United States structure the foreign aid program to ensure that the dollars are most efficiently spent on those who are in need of help?

6. Can a terrorist be a freedom fighter?

> *There cannot be good and bad terrorists, our terrorists and others. . . . All those who have resorted to arms in order to resolve political disputes, all those organizations, all those structures and individuals who carry out these policies should not be tolerated.*
>
> RUSSIAN PRESIDENT VLADIMIR PUTIN[25]

> *The international community cannot tolerate states which assist and harbor terrorists and use terrorism as an instrument of their state policy.*
>
> INDIAN PRIME MINISTER ATAL BEHARI VAJPAYEE[26]

According to the United States government, in the presidential Executive Order number 13224, terrorism is defined as an activity that:

a. Involves a violent act or an act dangerous to human life, property, or infrastructure, and
b. Appears to be intended,
c. Intimidates or coerces a civilian population,
d. Influences the policy of a government by intimidation or coercion, or
e. Affects the conduct of a government by mass destruction, assassination, kidnapping, or hostage-taking.[27]

A terrorist group is a structured organization . . . of more than two persons, acting in concert to commit terrorist offenses. . . . These offenses are committed with the aim of intimidating and seriously altering or destroying the political, economic or social structures of countries.

EUROPEAN UNION DEFINITION OF TERRORISM[28]

We are not waiting until Arafat decides to take steps against terrorism. . . . We are planning now to bring another one million Jews to Israel.

ISRAELI PRIME MINISTER ARIEL SHARON[29]

According to the *Times* of London, Syrian President Bashar al-Assad recently said that Palestinian "freedom fighters" were not terrorists, they were like the French resistance under Charles de Gaulle. It was Israel, not Syria, that was "prosecuting state terrorism."[30]

At the United Nations where terrorism was the main topic, Arafat accused Israel of practicing 'state terror' against the Palestinian people.[31]

We will direct every resource at our command, every means of diplomacy, every tool of intelligence, every instrument of war, to the destruction of the global terror network.[32]

U.S. PRESIDENT GEORGE W. BUSH

Terrorist expert John K. Cooley has stated, "For bin Laden's Muslim and Arab mercenaries who have already wrecked havoc in societies from Algeria and the Philippines to New York, seem to be regarded by the Bush administration as on a par with local guerilla and terrorist organizations with support from Syria and Iran to North Korea and Indonesia. Having expanded the list of organizations it considers terrorist, the Bush administration seems to think the U.S. should try to destroy terrorist groups everywhere. This is impossible, and a tragic error of judgment."[33]

Who is the terrorist?

The subject of who is a terrorist is as confusing as the preceding statements are contradictory. Were the French, Dutch, Danish, and Norwegian resistance fighters who sought to end the World War II Nazi occupation of their countries terrorists? Were the Russian, Yugoslav, and Greek partisan movements also terrorists? What about the members of the Irish Republican Army and their opponents, the various protestant paramilitaries: Are they also terrorists?

It is certainly true that the followers of Osama bin Laden have taken their ability to organize and create destruction to a level not seen before. However, this "global network" does not imply that all resistance movements are linked or that they have the same energy and the same ideological goals. The subject demands a more comprehensive look. All movements that seek to change the existing order by revolution are not equal, as anyone who looks at the wording of the American Declaration of Independence would have to admit.

Terrorism is a strategy, not a movement. It is a strategy used by the weak against the strong. Terrorism involves the use or threat of violence against innocent people to influence political behavior.[34] It is a strategy of conflict that involves a low risk to the perpetrators. It is inexpensive and it works. Terrorists rely on the intimidating effects of assassinations, random bombings, or airplane hijackings to accomplish their goals. Though similar in some respects, terrorism is not the same as unconventional warfare, counterinsurgency warfare, or clandestine warfare.

Individuals, groups, and some states use terrorism. The decision to do so is mostly the result of having no other realistic chance to affect political outcomes. In the case of the September 11th attack on the World Trade Center, an airplane hijacking became an option because the terrorists knew that after the American military victories over both Iraq and Serbia they could not hope to confront the military power of the United States directly. What the terrorists hoped to do was demonstrate to the Other World the vulnerability of the United States to this kind of strategy. If one looks at the loss of life, the loss of jobs, the general economic damage, including the collapse of the travel industry, one would have to conclude that the terrorists succeeded in the September 11th attack.

What needs to be said is that one should not confuse the organizations that have global reach and engage in terrorism with the hundreds of political movements that may occasionally employ this strategy. Each situation is different. Each movement may or may not have a linkage with like-minded groups that pose a threat to America. For the United States to believe that it has the power to end terrorism as an option in the world is to behave like the mythical literary character Don Quixote "tilting at windmills" without success.

A Reuters Dispatch from Berlin dated November 28, 2001, reported that the German Chancellor Gerhard Schroeder warned the United States against pursuing a broadened war on what were viewed as terrorist states. Referring to talk about Phase II in the war against Arab and Islamic militant groups and states sponsoring terrorism, he was quoted as saying, "We should be particularly careful about a discussion about new targets in the Middle East . . . more could blow up in our faces there than any of us realize."[35]

Can organizations using terror as a strategy be defeated?

Terrorism as a strategy cannot be ended. However, global terror organizations can! Other terrorist groups can be limited and, in time, contained at an acceptable level. The answer is for the established powers to actively engage the grievants in a way that will offer other opportunities for resolving conflicts besides terrorism.

In the case of the Other World, the grievances that lead to the use of terrorism as an option lie in the colonial past, the unresponsive governments, the festering Arab/Israeli dispute, the massive ignorance, the grueling poverty, the total lack of hope among the masses. A solution may be found in the developed world's serious willingness to work to resolve these injustices that cause the anger expressed by peoples of the Other World. To do otherwise is for the West to risk having to fight an endless series of conflicts, always having to decide just who is the terrorist and who is the freedom fighter.

Is the Afghan experience an exception to the rule that there is no unified terrorist movement?

Before the *coup d'etat* and Russian intervention in the 1970s, Afghanistan was considered to be one of the more progressive central Asian states. However, when Russian troops occupied Afghanistan in December 1979, their action was viewed within the context of the cold war as an attempt to breech the containment of communist strategy of the West. American reaction to the Soviet invasion was swift. American athletes were ordered by the American president to boycott the Russian Olympic Games!

As Afghan resistance to the Russian occupation developed, American support for the Muslim rebels developed. The United States saw Afghanistan as a Russian Vietnam. America's friends in the Arab world, especially in Saudi Arabia, were encouraged to furnish money, arms, and volunteers to support the Afghan resistance.

Thousands of zealots were recruited from all over the Muslim world to fight against the Soviets. When the Russians were forced out of Afghanistan in 1988, many of these "freedom fighters" returned to their homelands committed to the ideals of reform through political Islam.

To these Afghan veterans, their societies were corrupted by Western secular values. Their governments were illegitimate pawns of the neocolonial powers. Their leaders were making accommodations with America and Israel to the detriment of the Muslim people, and their religion had drifted away from the teachings of Mohammad. Their former opposition to communism was transferred to the West in general and the United States in particular.

Osama bin Laden had the money and organizational skills to mold these veterans into the revolutionaries that would eventually become Al-Qaeda. He found a safe base of operations in the post-Soviet Taliban Afghan government. For the first time, Al-Qaeda, as a nongovernmental organization, was able to gain a global reach for employing the strategy of terrorism.

The United States military response to the September 11th attack brought down the pro-bin Laden government in Afghanistan. It is doubtful that any other country will risk an American attack by offering bin Laden and his followers the freedom that they earlier enjoyed. While it may be true that groups of his supporters exist throughout the world, they no longer have the organization, money, or military resources necessary to amount a worldwide campaign of terrorism. Still the question remains, can another terrorist organization develop the global reach of Al-Qaeda?

What can the United States do about the Other World's terrorist threat to the West?

After September 11th, the United States took the first step against this threat when overwhelming military force was used to first smash the Afghan base of Al-Qaeda and then drive the Taliban government from power.

In the wake of this victory, American planners should avoid the temptation to apply the Afghan formula against every Other World organization that employs the strategy. This kind of policy could involve Americans in an endless series of conflicts around the world. This kind of policy cannot be sustained over a long period of time.

Instead, the United States needs to make a clear distinction between groups that occasionally employ the strategy of terror on a local level and any organization or group of cooperating organizations with the global reach that pose a threat to the United States or its allies. These terror networks can be defeated. However, the long-term solution to the present unrest emerging out of the Other World will require Western support for real social justice, improved economic conditions, and political reform (see the sidebar on page 57).

Review Questions

1. Describe the differences between colonialism and neocolonialism.
2. What were some of the motivations for traditional colonialism?
3. Were there benefits to the other world gained from Western colonialism?
4. Define imperialism.
5. Define nationalism.

Key Terms

- **Colonialism**—The relationship between a group of people in one country who are subject to the authority of the people in another country.
- **Artificial states**—Former colonies whose borders provide no internal unity because they are the result of balance-of-power decisions made in Berlin, London, and Paris.
- **Population growth**—caused by combination of social practices geared to a more brutal age combined with modern health practices.
- **Neocolonialism**—The process by which developed states use informal, indirect means to exert pressure on politically independent less developed states.
- **Other World nationalism**—It is different from traditional nationalism because it is also anticolonial.

SELECTED MIDDLE EAST TERRORIST INCIDENTS AGAINST AMERICAN TARGETS[36]

- Ambassador to Sudan assassinated March 2, 1973, by Black September Organization
- Iran Hostage Crisis, November 4, 1979–January 20, 1981, by Iranian revolutionaries
- Bombing of U.S. Embassy in Beirut, April 18, 1983, by Islamic Jihad
- Bombing of Marine barracks in Beirut, October 23, 1983, by Islamic Jihad
- William Buckly, Embassy Officer in Beirut murdered, March 16, 1984, by Islamic Jihad
- Malcolm Kerr, President of American University Beirut murdered, 1984, by Iranian and Lebanese terrorists
- Restaurant bombing, Torrejon, Spain, April 12, 1984, by Hizballah
- TWA hijacking, June 14, 1985, by Hizballah
- *Achille Lauro* hijacking, November 23, 1985, by Palestinian Liberation Front
- Egyptian air hijacking, October 7, 1985, by Abu Nidal group
- Bombing of TWA flight 840, March 30, 1986, by Palestinian terrorists
- Berlin discothèque bombing, April 5, 1986, by Libyan terrorists
- William Higgins murdered in Lebanon, February 17, 1988, by Hizballah
- Napes USO attack, April 14, 1988, by Organization of Jihad Brigades
- Bombing of Pan American Air flight 103, December 21, 1988, by Libyan terrorists
- Failed Iraqi attacks on U.S. bases in Indonesia and Philippines, January 18–19, 1991, by Iraqi agents
- World Trade Center bombing, February 26, 1993, by Islamic terrorist
- Attempted assassination of President Bush, April 14, 1993, by Iraqi agents
- Jerusalem bus attack, August 21, 1995, by Hamas
- Riyadh military compound attack, November 13, 1995, by Islamic Movement of Change
- Jerusalem bus attack, February 26, 1996, by Palestinian suicide bomber
- Bet El West Bank attack, May 13, 1996; Hamas suspected
- Saqqara attack, June 9, 1996, by Popular Front for the Liberation of Palestine
- Khobar Towers bombing, Saudi Arabia, June 25, 1996; many Islamic groups claimed responsibility
- Empire State Building attack, February 23, 1997; gunman attacked "enemies of Palestine"
- Israeli shopping mall bombing, Jerusalem, September 4, 1997, by Hamas
- U.S. Embassy bombings in East Africa, August 7, 1998, by Osama bin Laden
- USS *Cole* attack, Yemen, October 12, 2000, by Osama bin Laden
- Twin Towers World Trade Center attack, September 11, 2001, by Osama bin Laden

SOURCE: Adapted from Terrorist Incidents List 1961–2001, Office of the Historian Bureau of Public Affairs, U.S. Department of State, October 31, 2001, The Arabists: *The Romance of an American Elite,* Robert Kaplan, Free Press, New York, 1993.

- **Strategic colonies**—are used to support major colonies.
- **Prestige colonies**—are created to glorify the mother country.
- **NAFTA**—The North American Free Trade Agreement is an arrangement to lower or end tariffs between Canada, the United States, and Mexico.
- *La Frontera*—The 2,000-mile artificial boundary that separates the United States and Mexico.
- **White man's burden**—Call glorifying colonialism taken from an 1899 poem by Rudyard Kipling:

  > *Take up the white man's burden*
  > *Send forth the best ye breed—*
  > *Go, bind your sons to exile*
  > *To serve your captive's need.*

Useful Web Sites

http://www.commonwealth.org.uk/
http://www.arab.net/algeria/history/aa_french.html
http://www.imf.org/
http://www.icj-cij.org/
http://www.wto.org/

Notes

1. For over 100 years, Argentina has claimed the Falkland Islands under the Spanish name Malvinas. In 1982, it fought a war with Britain for control of the islands, which Britain won. Since most maps use the English name, that practice will be followed in this chapter.
2. Valerie Pakenham, *Out in the Noonday Sun: Edwardians in the Tropics* (New York: Random House, 1985), p. 10.
3. The expression "white man's burden" comes from the Rudyard Kipling poem of the same name. A verse is quoted here:

   > *Take up the white man's burden*
   > *And reap his old reward:*
   > *The blame of those ye better*
   > *The hate of those ye guard.*

   Quoted from *Who Said What When: The Chronological Dictionary of Quotations* (London: Bloomsbury Publishing Ltd., 1988), p. 200.
4. William Tuohy, "Viet Nam, A Key Battle Reverberates: Dien Bien Phu Recalled," *Los Angeles Times,* 5 May 1984, p. 18.
5. See W. M. Will, "Power, Dependency, and Misperceptions in the Caribbean Basin," chap. 2 in *Crescents of Conflict,* ed. W. M. Will and R. Millett (New York: Praeger, 1985).
6. William Lyle Schurz, *This New World* (New York: Dutton, 1957), p. 112.
7. See Muammar al-Qaddafi, "Third Way," in *Islam in Transition: Muslim Perspectives,* ed. John Donohue and John Esposito (New York: Oxford University Press, 1982), p. 103.

8. Winston S. Churchill, *Their Finest Hour: The Second World War* (Boston: Houghton Mifflin, 1949), p. 519.
9. Lewis M. Alexander, ed. *World Political Patterns* (Chicago: Rand McNally, 1963), p. 262.
10. Edward Owen, "Give Us Hong Kong Over Gibraltar," *The Express,* Sunday, 22 June 1997, p. 33.
11. "Sharon's Poor Timing," *The Evening Standard* (London) 8 November 2001, p. 13.
12. Pakenham, p. 10.
13. Daniel Papp, *Contemporary International Relations* (New York: Macmillan, 1984), p. 112.
14. Chidanand Rajghatta, "US Pledges $1 Billion Plus to Pak," *The Times of India,* 12 November 2001.
15. See Jimmy Carter, *New Age Journal* (March/April 1990): 52–54, 132–134.
16. Chidanand Rajghatta, *op. cit.*
17. Todd Gillman, "Gore Helps Lockheed Martin Celebrate," *Dallas Morning News,* 16 May 1998, p. A31.
18. The Treaty of Westphalia (1648), which ended the Thirty Years' War in Europe, is the acknowledged beginning of the modern nation-state.
19. "Kyoto Treaty Flawed: Bush, Sridhar Krishn Aswami," *The Hindu* (India) 13 June 2001.
20. "Mass Production," *The Dallas Morning News,* 1 February 1998, sec. H, p. 1.
21. For more information on the industry in *La Frontera,* see Chris K. Raul and Evelyn Iritani, "Asia, Mexico Learn to Work Together," *Los Angeles Times,* 29 May 1995, p. D1.
22. George Moffett, "Foreign Aid on the GOP Chopping Bloc," *Christian Science Monitor,* 22 February 1995, p. 4.
23. "The Question of Foreign Aid," *U.S. News and World Report,* 30 January 1995, p. 32. Also see Stephen Zunes, "The Strategic Functions of U.S. Aid to Israel," *Middle East Policy Journal* IV, no. 4 (October 1996).
24. Ibid.
25. Clara Ferreira-Marques, "Putin Warns Against 'Double Standards' on Terrorism," Reuters Release, Moscow, 6 November 2001.
26. Ibid.
27. Executive Order 13224: Blocking property with persons who commit, threaten to commit, or support terrorism. Issued by President George W. Bush on 24 September 2001.
28. "EU Gears up to Fight Terrorism," BBC News Release (U.K.), 20 September 2001.
29. Alexandra Williams, "War on Terror: I Want 1,000,000 More Jews in Israel; Sharon's Battle Cry," *The Mirror* (U.K.), News Section, 8 November 2001, p. 11.
30. Tom Baldwin and Philip Webster, "Blair Loses His Way On the Road to Damascus," *The Times of London,* Home News, 3 November 2001.
31. "Arafat on Board: Hails U.S. Backing for Separate Palestinian State," *The Toronto Sun,* News Section, 12 November 2001, p. 32.
32. "War on Terrorism Two Months Later, The War on Six Fronts," *The Dallas Morning News,* 11 November 2001, p. 31A.
33. John K. Cooley, "In War on Terror Don't Overreach," *The Christian Science Monitor,* U.S. Opinion, 15 November 2001, p. 21.
34. William Tuohy, *op. cit.,* p. 18.
35. "Germany Warns U.S. On Wider Anti-Terror War," Reuter's Dispatch, Berlin, Germany, 28 November 2001.
36. The President's executive order lists more than 50 pages of organizations that have funding frozen because of suspected links to terrorist organizations. This list contains the names of organizations and individuals from all over the globe. A few examples from the executive order are listed here simply to give the reader an idea of the wide

range of organizations: the Al Rashid Trust (Pakistan), Kahane Lives (Israel), Palestine Islamic Jihad (Palestine), The Real Irish Republican Army (Ulster), *The Sendero Luminoso* (Shining Path) (Peru), The Somali Internet Company (Somalia), The Kurdistan Workers Party (Turkey), The Liberation Tigers of Tamil Eelam (Sri Lanka), and several hundred others.

The United States has identified the following states with strong Al-Qaeda influence in the population, including Algeria, Egypt, Pakistan, Saudi Arabia, Afghanistan, India, Indonesia, and the Philippines. They also consider Libya, the Sudan, North Korea, Syria, Lebanon, Iraq, and Cuba as states that give refuge to terrorist organizations.

For Further Reading

Berthon, Simon, and Andrew Robinson. *The Shape of the World: The Mapping and Discovery of the Earth.* New York: Rand McNally, 1991.

Danzinger, James. "The Developing Countries in the Post-Cold War World." Chap. 17 in *Understanding the World: A Comparative Introduction to Political Science.* New York: Longman, 1996.

The Dorling Kindersley World Reference Atlas. London: Dorling Kindersley, 1994.

Gellner, Ernest. *Nations and Nationalism.* Ithaca, N.Y.: Cornell University Press, 1983.

Ghaliand, Gerard, and Jean-Pierre Rageau. *Strategic Atlas: A Comparative Geopolitics of the World's Powers.* New York: Harper & Row, 1990.

Harrison, Paul. "Winner Takes All: Precolonial Societies and Colonialism." Chap. 2 in *Inside the Third World.* London: Penguin Books, 1987.

JeBlig, H. J. *Human Geography: Culture, Society, and Space.* 4th ed. New York: Wiley, 1993.

Lapping, Brian. *The End of Empire.* New York: St. Martin's Press, 1985.

Porch, Douglas. *The Conquest of Morocco.* New York: Alfred A. Knopf, Inc., 1982.

Poulsen, Thomas. *Nations and States: A Geographic Background to World Affairs.* Englewood Cliffs, N.J.: Prentice Hall, 1995.

Snow, Donald. *Distant Thunder: Third World Conflict and the New International Order.* New York: St. Martin's Press, 1993.

Stokes, Gale. "The Underdeveloped Theory of Nationalism," *World Politics* 31 (October 1978): 150–160.

Trainer, F. E. *Developed to Death: Rethinking Third World Development.* London: Green Print, 1989.

CHAPTER 3

Political Economy

Emmit B. Evans, Jr.

Creating an economy that is both socially and ecologically sustainable [is] the central challenge facing humanity as the new millennium begins.

CHRISTOPHER FLAVIN[1]

We whirl headlong into the twenty-first century at a pivotal time in human affairs. On the one hand, we are fast approaching global limits of social and environmental sustainability. A group of 1,670 leading world scientists recently issued a "warning to humanity" urging that we have no more than a few decades to reverse trends that are carrying us toward "spirals of environmental decline, poverty and unrest leading to social, economic and environmental collapse."[2] On the other hand, global changes eroding the power of the centralized political and economic structures that have long controlled human affairs are creating opportunities to build a new, more democratic, and sustainable world.

As described in the preceding chapter, the global systems of production and distribution that have determined the contrasting lifestyles of the citizens of the industrialized West and the Other World were initiated 500 years ago. The first voyage of Columbus in 1492 marked the beginning of patterns of Western domination that have evolved through a series of stages to the globalization of today.

The purposes of this chapter are to trace the evolution of this system of global political economy from mercantilism to capitalism to globalization, to examine the manner in which it inextricably connects all the peoples of the world, and to explore the challenges and opportunities before us as we realize our common future in a rapidly evolving global society.

POLITICS, ECONOMICS, AND POLITICAL ECONOMY

Politics is commonly defined as the authoritative allocation of scarce values, or who gets what, when, and how. The political process, in other words, determines how those things people value most (such as survival, material goods, wealth, and status) are distributed among a society's, or the world's, peoples. Analysts of the political process have long noted that *power* is the primary factor that determines who gets what and when; an even more concise definition of politics is that it is simply the exercise of power. Power, in turn, is defined as the capacity to control other people's behavior.

There are three types of power: violence, knowledge, and authority. In conflict over the allocation of those things people value, violence is the most fundamental type: Most people place a high premium on avoiding pain and on survival. As Thomas Hobbes observed, when nothing else is turned up, clubs are trumps; the only appeal to violence is violence itself. However, there are limits on the use of violence to maintain political control: Coercion is expensive, violence tends to escalate, and people will not tolerate rule by violence indefinitely. To maintain their regimes over time, political elites must base their rule more on knowledge and authority.

Most political elites attempt to rule through authority, an institutionalized form of power based on the claim that government has the legitimate right to rule. However, the authority of government ultimately derives from its ability to control the forces of violence in society. *Government* is defined as the institution that has the *enforceable* right to control people's behavior. In determining the allocation of scarce values, laws are actually a form of sublimated violence through which the decisions of government are backed by the ability to enforce dictates with a court system and police and military forces.

Governments that last over time also derive much of their power from the control of knowledge. Elites use knowledge power both to control what people know and to create and manipulate images and ideologies they want people to believe. As noted by Niccolò Machiavelli, with time, the rule of lions must give way to the rule of foxes.

Analysts of the political process have also long noted that self-interest is the driving force, or the engine, of government. Those with political power strive to advance their personal interests, serving broader community interests only to the extent necessary to maintain their positions of control. Closely related is the observation that power corrupts, or compels those with the power to determine who gets what to use public resources for private benefit. And absolute power corrupts absolutely.

The logic of the preceding definitions and observations carries one directly to the conclusion that all governments are *oligarchies*, or political systems controlled by a few to further their self-interests. Governments serve political elites either directly, as in communism and fascism, or indirectly through payoffs derived from serving the interests of economic elites, as in socialism and capitalism. If power determines who gets what and if power corrupts, then there is a natural human tendency for those in control of government to use its institutions and processes for personal gain.

In analyzing political and economic affairs, it is useful to think of politics and economics as closely related, interconnected processes. Before the emergence of classical liberalism from the eighteenth-century writings of John Locke and Adam Smith, politics and economics were in fact studied under the single discipline of *political economy*. The artificial separation of that study into fields of political science and economics has been in large part driven by the assertion that there is no necessary connection between politics and economics. The position is that, under a free-market system, government need only be involved in economic affairs to the extent necessary to provide for defense, protect private property rights, and supply some of the infrastructure for the economy.

Wealth and political power are inseparably linked, however. Governments are integrally involved in the economic affairs of most countries, usually serving the interests of the dominant economic group in society. In communist and fascist systems, governmental and economic institutions are formally fused, and political and economic elites are one and the same. In socialist and capitalist systems, nominal separations between governmental and economic institutions are bridged by informal networks of mutual interests between elites and by "revolving door" mechanisms through which individuals circulate back and forth between institutions. The role of political elites in free-market economies is to maintain conditions within which economic elites have the freedom to pursue their interests with a minimum of interference from other interests in society. Freedom here is the freedom to maximize profit through manipulating supply and demand and the psychology of consumer need and preference.

Pause and reflect for a moment on the fundamental connections between political and economic processes apparent in the following definitions.

POLITICS: Who gets what, when, and how
ECONOMICS: The production, distribution, and use of wealth

The perspective of political economy, which views politics and markets as "in a constant state of mutual interaction,"[3] therefore provides a useful analytical tool.

STAGES OF GLOBAL POLITICAL ECONOMY

Mercantilism

Mercantilism was based on the belief that the power and glory of a government was a direct function of the wealth of its monarchy. The goal of a mercantilist political economy was the accumulation of as much wealth in precious metals as possible. The initial voyages of global exploration financed by Spain and Portugal were essentially quests to locate new sources of gold and silver, and the conquests of Other World territories that followed created colonies to implement and maintain the mercantilist system.

Mercantilist political economy was simple and direct. The colonial powers posted governors, military forces, and administrators in the colonies of the Other World to manage and enforce the mining and transfer of precious metals from the Other World to the monarchies of the West. The first global political economy incorporated the peoples of the Other World into a global order as forced labor to produce wealth allocated to the coffers of the royal families of Europe.[4]

Capitalism

The process of industrialization brought two fundamental changes in global political economy. First, it created a new economic elite of industrial capitalists and financiers whose wealth and power grew to outstrip that of monarchs. As a new economic class of capitalists emerged with increasing power, the control of Western governments shifted from royal families to new oligarchies controlled by those with industrial and financial wealth. Second, the economic value of the colonies shifted from precious metals to the raw materials of industrial production and capitalist trade. The colonial military and administrative structures established as a part of mercantilism now served to transfer industrial raw materials and trade goods to benefit a new capitalist Western elite.

FROM COLONIALISM TO NEOCOLONIALISM AND "DEVELOPMENT"

The exploitation of Other World peoples and resources under mercantilism in the initial stages of capitalism was explicit. The Western colonial powers wanted the wealth of the Other World, and used the force of colonial control and administration to extract it. The transition from colonialism to neocolonialism described in the preceding chapter was accompanied by a seemingly new approach to Other World political economy that appeared to change an emphasis on exploitation to a new emphasis on the development of Other World countries. *Development* appeared on the international agenda with the winding down of the colonial era and the explosion of newly independent states in the late 1940s.

For many, economic development was part of the logic of political independence. Industrial economies were an integral feature of the Western states that formed the model for most of the new political entities. And for the masses caught up in the torrent of rising expectations released by the promises of independence, a higher standard of living seemed a right that had been won through the struggle for political freedom. For others, building the economies of the new states presented opportunities to establish more effective forms of domination and control through new and more subtle forms of colonialism.

Development has been a dominant feature of Other World economic, political, and social affairs for the past 60 years. Disagreements over how it should be pursued and, indeed, how the concept should even be defined have been the source of ongoing conflicts that have ranged from discussion and debate to

The Global Marketplace: Fried chicken in China, Pepsi in Qatar, and McDonald's in Saudi Arabia.

SOURCE: *Joe Weatherby*

terrorism and war. It is consequently difficult to understand the contemporary Other World without an understanding of development. Toward that end, in the following pages we consider various definitions based on competing systems of values and beliefs, survey the history of development efforts, evaluate the successes and failures of those efforts, and consider the prospects for development as we proceed into the twenty-first century.

Values, Ideologies, and Development

Attempts to define development in social, economic, or political terms begin on shaky conceptual grounds. Most people think of the concept as an unfolding of events through a succession of states or changes, each of which is preparatory for the next and all of which contribute to some final end. Such efforts are thus exercises in *teleology*, or attempts to explain natural phenomena as being directed toward some final cause or purpose. The assumptions that such ultimate purposes exist and, if they do, that we are intellectually capable of discerning them may be presumptuous from the start.

Human beings are, however, a precocious lot, and doubts about the limits and validity of our knowledge have seldom stopped us from designing grand theories that explain current events in terms of where we are headed. Karl Marx's communist utopia and John Maynard Keynes's capitalist utopia were both built on teleological theories. What people usually do when defining "where we are headed" is describe that future state in terms of their personal values, or where they would *prefer* for us to go. It is at this point that political values and ideologies (or belief systems) become important in defining development.

Development and Conservative Values   A fundamental element in conservative value systems is the belief that one of the keys to human development lies in providing those with special strengths and abilities the *freedom to* pursue their individual interests without constraint. In a dialogue with Socrates reported over 2,300 years ago by Plato in *The Republic,* a Greek sophist named Thrasymachus argued that it is the natural right of the strong to take more than their equal share of what the world has to offer. The strong are morally justified in designing and operating the institutions of government to pursue their interests; "might makes right." Over the intervening years, these ideas, which have become known as the Doctrine of Thrasymachus, have provided the rationale for a variety of conservative ideologies that often argue—in social Darwinist, survival-of-the-fittest terms—that protecting the special positions and abilities of those who have risen above the common masses is necessary for the evolution of the human species and the grandeur of humanity.

Capitalism is a contemporary version of the Doctrine of Thrasymachus. One of its basic tenets is that the most secure avenue to development is provided by supply-side economic strategies that encourage and facilitate the accumulation of capital by the able and adept. According to Keynes, in order to develop, societies must pass through a transnational phase in which human greed and avarice are unleashed by the drive for personal profit to propel us through the "tunnel of economic necessity," wherein a concentration of capital in the hands of a few will create an industrial system capable of producing material abundance.

In the Other World, capitalist ideas and ideals have taken the form of "take-off," or modernization, theories, which hold that the surest way to achieve development is to maximize the opportunities for investment by private firms, most of which are located in the industrialized world. The goal is to create a critical mass of concentrated capital that will support the takeoff of Other World economies into sustained economic growth. A more liberal interpretation of this theory adds that the investment of public funds in physical and human infrastructure is a necessary complement to the private market.

In capitalist economic systems, the primary measure of economic progress used throughout the world is the rate of increase in gross domestic product (GDP, formerly gross national product [GNP]), a quantitative measure that represents the total of all goods and services produced by an economy in a year. In Other World countries pursuing takeoff development strategies, increases in GDP indicate that economic output is expanding and economic development is taking place.

From a conservative perspective, substantial inequality in the distribution of the wealth created by expanding economic output is viewed as natural, necessary, and just. Human beings are viewed as unequal in essence: The poor are poor because of shortcomings *within themselves,* often considered to stem from race, gender, or class. Efforts to improve substantially their lot are not only futile but unjust in that they take from those at the top of society, who have earned their position through their special talents and virtues, and whose unencumbered progress is necessary for human evolution. Although life is unavoidably harsh for the poor, the capitalist utopia does promise eventual material abundance for all. In the short run, relative economic prosperity for the weaker members of society can best be achieved by the creation of jobs through the concentration of capital into large-scale industries.

Development and Liberal and Radical Values Those who hold liberal and radical belief systems take a very different view of the nature and degree of differences among people, which lead to very different definitions of the goals of development and how those goals should be pursued. From this perspective, human beings are considered to be equal in essence: Although a certain level of inequality is natural in any society because of relatively minor differences in health, intelligence, and emotional balance, the tremendous inequalities that exist within societies and among countries are viewed as primarily the result of shortcomings *within political and economic processes and institutions.* Julius Nyerere, a former president of Tanzania, captures this idea when he writes that

> even when you have an exceptionally intelligent and hard-working millionaire, the difference between his intelligence, his enterprise, his hard work, and those of other members of society cannot possibly be proportionate to the difference between their "rewards." There must be *something wrong in a society* where one man, however hard-working or

clever he may be, can acquire as great a "reward" as a thousand of his fellows can acquire between them.[5]

Whereas liberals and radicals agree on the essential equality of human beings, they differ in their solutions to inequality. Liberals advocate peaceful, step-by-step reforms, often based on programs to redistribute wealth from the rich to the poor and to create more equal opportunities for the poor to compete. Radicals believe that, given the resources commanded by world political and economic elites and the manner in which they control existing political and economic institutions, established powers will always be able to keep ahead of and nullify any reform efforts. They argue that justice and equality for all can be achieved only through the overthrow of established political and economic institutions and the rebuilding of individual societies and the international order.

Whether achieved through evolutionary or revolutionary means, definitions of development put forth by liberals and radicals consistently target egalitarian values as the end toward which development should be directed, emphasizing *freedom from* poverty and exploitation. Measures of progress include the degree to which nutrition, health, housing, education, and economic security are available equally to all. Here, equally is not defined in absolute terms, but as "free of extremes": Because of differences in abilities that are free of extremes, some have more than others, proportionate to differences in abilities. Such definitions often include the ideal that society should encourage and facilitate the self-fulfillment and self-realization of all. This ideal is central to the utopia envisioned by Marx, where all would share equally in the resources of society and be free to develop their full potential as human beings. More recent examples carry the same theme: A contemporary writer hopes that "development will become a means to serve people";[6] another argues that "development should be a *struggle* to create criteria, goals, and means for self-liberation from misery, inequity, and dependency of all forms."[7]

As the world is becoming increasingly aware of the devastating and threatening global effects of pollution and resource depletion, environmental goals have been merged with egalitarian values to create concepts such as *eco-development*, or balanced social and environmental development. *Sustainable development* is defined as living within the limits of natural systems while ensuring an adequate standard of living for all, meeting the needs of the present without compromising the ability of future generations to meet their own needs.[8]

Such definitions make a sharp distinction between growth and development. *Growth* is defined as things simply getting bigger, or quantitative increases in economic output. In contrast, *development* is defined as things getting better through qualitative changes, which result in improvements in life for all in harmony and balance with nature. Strategies proposed to pursue such change generally emphasize decentralized efforts controlled by local populations to improve life and habitats at the local level. Supporters are encouraged to "think globally and act locally." *Appropriate technology,* or technology suitable to particular applications and needs even when more sophisticated technologies are available, is often a part of such strategies.[9] An example would be the use of 10,000 workers with picks and shovels instead of 10 Caterpillar tractors to build a system of levees to control the flooding of small, family agricultural plots, thus supporting small farmers and workers who might otherwise be unemployed and preserving topsoil that would otherwise be washed away.

A History of Development Efforts

Competing conservative and liberal or radical value systems gave rise to two different approaches to development after World War II. A few countries, including Cuba, Algeria, Libya, Angola, North Korea, Vietnam, and Cambodia, broke out of the world political and economic order that had been established by the colonial powers and joined the states of the Soviet empire and China to establish development programs ostensibly designed to pursue egalitarian values. With assistance from the major Second World powers, they adopted the ideas and ideals of Marx, Lenin, and Mao to create centralized command economies in which property was communally owned and economic activities were closely orchestrated by socialist and communist party elites.

Most Other World countries remained within the orbit of the old colonial order. With assistance from the Western industrial nations, they adopted development programs grounded in takeoff theory to establish free-market economies guided by capitalist economic policies and practices. Free-market approaches are now coming to dominate most of the world, including the former states of the Soviet bloc and China. To understand the history of development efforts, it is therefore important to explore the ascendancy of the free-market system of international capitalism.

Immanuel Wallerstein employs the concept of political economy in his study of the system of international capitalism, which he terms the *capitalist world-economy*, that has expanded from its genesis in sixteenth-century Europe to drive much of the politics and economics of the globe today.[10] Tracing that expansion, Wallerstein describes how the pattern of international relations among great world powers ranges on a fluid continuum: At one end, there is an almost even balance among powers of roughly equal strength (a rare and unstable condition); in the middle the powers group into two or more camps, with no side being able to impose its will (the usual state of international affairs); at the other end, a single great power is able to dominate (also a rare and unstable condition). He defines the latter end of the continuum as *hegemony*, or a situation in which one single world power is so dominant that it "can largely impose its rules and its wishes . . . in the economic, political, military, diplomatic, and even cultural arenas."[11] Such a condition of hegemony existed when the United Kingdom dominated world affairs from roughly 1815 to 1873 and when the United States came to occupy a similar position of world dominance from 1945 until the early 1970s.

U.S. Hegemony and a New Postwar World Order   The establishment of a hegemony by the United States at the very same time that programs to develop the Other World were launched had a profound effect on the nature of development efforts and the role and position of Other World states in the international political economy. The United States emerged from World War II as the unchallenged dominant power in the world. It was able to use its power to implement a new world order that was carefully designed to serve its interests and the interests of the other former colonial powers in the capitalist world economy. The foundation for this new order was laid through the Bretton Woods agreements, signed by the Allied powers in 1944.

The Bretton Woods system erected three pillars around which the new order was built. The International Monetary Fund (IMF) was established to further cooperation on monetary matters among the countries of the world. Under IMF guidance, the U.S. dollar became the standard against which the value of other currencies was set, and the United States became the banker for the world. The General Agreement on Tariffs and Trade (GATT) was designed to promote world trade. Periodic trade conferences were scheduled to facilitate negotiations among world trading partners with the goal of maintaining "free" trade through low tariffs on internationally traded goods and services. The International Bank for Reconstruction and Development, or World Bank, which was originally created to facilitate investment in Europe after World War II, turned toward stimulating investment in the Other World.

The United Nations was chartered in San Francisco in 1945 as an international governmental organization designed to resolve political and economic conflicts between and among countries and promote world peace and development (see Figure 3.1). Two quasi-legislative bodies comprise the core of the UN: the General Assembly, to which most states (now about 190) belong, and the Security Council. Only the Security Council can take direct military action to enforce its decisions. The Council is composed of five permanent members—the United States, Britain, France, Russia, and China (each of which has the power to veto any proposal of the Council)—and 10 temporary, rotating members (none of which has veto

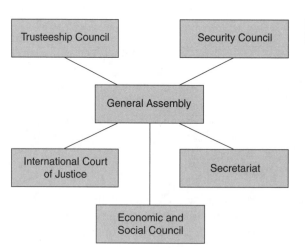

FIGURE 3.1   Core of the United Nations

power). Lacking the power to enforce its decisions, the General Assembly serves basically as a forum for expressing the opinions of member states.

Early Development Efforts   With the success of efforts to rebuild the economies of Europe and Japan fresh at hand, the Western industrial nations launched a flurry of bilateral and multilateral efforts in the 1960s, which was dubbed the "development decade." The stated intent was to propel Other World economies to a point from which they could take off and achieve self-sustaining growth. John Kenneth Galbraith, a Harvard economics professor who had served as U.S. ambassador to India, published a book in 1964 that aptly described these early development efforts as attempts to copy the institutions and processes of the modern industrial powers. "Development," he observed, "is the faithful imitation of the developed."[12] Galbraith noted three characteristics of these attempts: symbolic modernization, maximized economic growth, and selective growth.

Symbolic modernization gave a developing country the appearance of modernity. Airports and four-lane highways were built, tall buildings were erected, and impressive government offices were constructed. Efforts to maximize economic growth were directed at increasing economic output as measured by GNP. Growth strategies emphasized large initial capital investments from the World Bank, from private firms located primarily in the industrial nations, and from First World governments, with the goal of establishing industrial bases that could then be expanded. Domestic rates of taxation and savings were set to promote the fastest rate of growth possible.

Some efforts were targeted at building the infrastructure for an industrial society through the strategy of selective growth. A variety of foreign aid programs, many organized under the umbrella of the Development Assistance Committee of the Organization for Economic Cooperation and Development (OECD), were created to address this need. Electric, water, sewer, and communications systems were installed; loans were made to farmers and small businesspersons; and agricultural education and community development activities were initiated. The "green revolution" of the 1960s and 1970s is a good example of a selective growth strategy. Increases in agricultural production were sought to generate funds for industrial expansion through earnings from export crops and to increase the supply of food in Other World countries. Programs were undertaken to encourage the replacement of family-scale farms, which used native seeds, composting, traditional pest-control methods, and hand implements, with large-scale agribusinesses employing hybrid seed strains, fertilizers, pesticides, herbicides, irrigation, and mechanized farm machinery.

Those who conceived of and measured development in terms of increases in economic output were pleased with the results of these early efforts: With some exceptions, development programs were generating dramatic increases in GNP. However, it did not take long for those who had hoped that the development decade would result in a better standard of living for the masses of Other World peoples to realize that the strategies described above were not contributing significantly to that goal. Benefits were accruing primarily to a few, while living conditions for most were not markedly improving; in fact, for some they were actually declining. Along with Galbraith's book, others with titles such as *False Start in Africa*[13] pointed out that the hollow imitation of Western symbols and an emphasis on supply-side economic policies, industrial development, and Western technologies would not result in the kind of economic and social change that would significantly benefit the many. The almost singular emphasis on building an industrial infrastructure and raising GNP meant that basic essentials such as food, housing, and health services were often neglected in favor of exporting minerals and cash crops to earn foreign exchange, much of which was sent back overseas in the form of profits for foreign corporations or spent on importing luxury goods for indigenous political and economic elites.

A Balance Sheet of Development   We are now in a position to evaluate the accomplishments of more than 50 years of sustained development efforts guided by takeoff theory. Advocates of this approach point with satisfaction to statistics that show that Other World GDP per capita has been growing at higher rates than were achieved by the industrial nations in comparable periods of their history, that life expectancy is increasing faster in decades than it did in an entire century in the industrialized world, and that substantial gains have been made in literacy and access to education. Critics point out that while these statistics accurately reflect the fact that conditions have improved in some ways for many and in many ways for some, they hide the true nature of economic processes that have resulted in tremendous disparities within Other World societies and among Other World countries: More than a third are now so poor and economically underdeveloped that they are placed in a special "Fourth World" category in which development seems impossible.

Statistics compiled by the United Nations and the World Bank provide a useful balance sheet of human development progress. Whereas the estimated share of the world's population suffering from "low human development" fell from 20 percent in 1975 to 10 percent in 1997, some 3 billion people (roughly half the world's population) survive on an income of less than $2 per day, and some 20% of the world's people survive on less than $1 per day.[14] Whereas 80 percent of people in the Other World have access to health services, 800 million still lack basic care and 1.2 billion do not have safe water and sanitation. Whereas immunization efforts for one-year-olds are saving 1.5 million lives annually, 1.58 billion children under five suffer from malnutrition, and 14 million die each year before reaching their fifth birthday. Whereas income per household head grew 4 percent annually in the 1980s, more than 1.3 billion people live in extreme poverty, and income is actually declining in large parts of the world.[15]

After completing a similar evaluation in which he notes that there were more people living in absolute poverty in 1987 than in 1960, Paul Harrison concludes that

> this balance-sheet can only be read as progress if one abstracts from the human realities. In terms of concrete individual experience, there is a greater absolute quantity of human suffering in the world today than

ever before, and all the indications are that it will increase as we approach the millennium. For all the talk and all the action about development, *virtually no progress has been made in the task of eliminating absolute
poverty; indeed, there has been gradual regress.*[16]

Harrison's comments parallel those of an Egyptian who once commented that the
overall effect of development efforts in Egypt was that more people now lived
longer in greater misery.

The links among poverty, security, and population growth are important in
understanding this increase in absolute poverty. Poverty and fertility rates are directly related: The higher the degree of poverty in a society, the higher the rate of
population increase. The instinct to survive dictates that poor families have more
children than wealthier families for practical economic reasons: Children are a
source of security for those living at the margins of survival. More children mean
more hands to help with the difficult tasks of eking a living out of a subsistence
environment; a working child can contribute to household resources by age 6 and
produce more than she or he consumes by age 12. More children increase the
probability that one of them might be fortunate enough to secure an education, a
rare job, and cash earnings to contribute to the family. More children mean a
greater likelihood that someone will be around to help when old age makes it impossible to survive on one's own. High infant and childhood mortality rates mean
that the odds of accomplishing all of these objectives are improved by having
enough children to replace those who die young.

In transferring much of the wealth of the Other World to the industrialized
nations, the forces of colonialism and neocolonialism have substantially contributed to the poverty that is fueling rapid population increases in the Other
World. These global shifts in wealth and family security have also contributed to
declining fertility rates in the First World. Population policies that address fundamental issues of family security, rather than simply encouraging or enforcing
birth control, are the surest way to reduce rates of population growth.

The manner in which the international political economy produces and dis-
tributes wealth is well illustrated by the production and distribution of world food
resources. If the wheat, rice, and other grains produced throughout the world
were distributed equally to all the world's peoples, each individual would receive
3,600 calories per day, well above the average U.S.-recommended daily allowances
of 2,700 calories for adult males, 2,000 for adult females, and 1,300–3,000 for
teenagers. Yet 22 million people die every year from starvation, and 1 billion do
not have enough to eat. The typical Western family of four consumes more grain
(directly and indirectly in the form of meat) than a poor Indian family of 20.[17]

India, where over one-third of the world's hungry people live, is one of the
top cash crop exporters in the Other World. The "green revolution" was instrumental in boosting India and a number of other countries to the status of agricultural exporters. However, the benefits of increased agricultural production in
those countries have often accrued to those wealthy farmers who could obtain
bank loans to purchase the large irrigated farms, mechanized equipment, and

expensive seeds, fertilizers, pesticides, and herbicides required for green revolution agriculture. Many poor farmers in these countries have in the process been displaced, driven to marginal dryland plots or the cities where they are unable to afford the food now produced through expensive farming methods on the lands they once tilled.

Similar consequences have resulted from the acquisition of Other World farmlands by multinational corporations based in the industrialized world. In Brazil, for example, foreign-owned companies, some with holdings in the millions of acres, have displaced Brazilian farmers and shifted the emphasis of agricultural production to export products such as soybeans and beef for fast-food restaurants in the First World. These shifts have created a shortage of black beans, the staple in the diet of Brazil's poor, with a resulting increase in malnutrition.[18]

Brazil provides an especially illustrative example of the balance sheet generated by an economic development process driven by the singular pursuit of increased economic production. In 1964, a military coup established a new government that opened the country to foreign investment by providing an array of attractive incentives and freedoms. In the following 10 years, which became known as "the Brazilian economic miracle," the country's GNP tripled, and Brazilian executives became for a time the highest paid in the world. Meanwhile, the real income of 80 percent of the population declined; the production of basic necessities such as food, clothing, and housing remained stagnant; and Brazil's infant mortality rate became the second highest in Latin America. Foreign-owned corporations gained control of 100 percent of Brazil's tire and rubber production, 95 percent of its automobile production, and 80 percent of its television and radio industry (while 60 Brazilian electronics firms were driven out of business or taken over by foreign firms). Surveying these statistics, a group of Catholic bishops and clerics issued a statement on the condition of the Brazilian people in 1975, concluding that

> the Brazilian miracle has resulted in privileges for the wealthy. It has come as a curse upon those who have not asked for it. The rich become always richer and the poor always poorer in this process of economic concentration. Far from being the inevitable result of natural deficiencies, this tragedy is the consequence of international capitalism. Development came to be defined not in terms of the interests of Brazilian society, but in terms of the profits made by foreign corporations and their associates in our country.[19]

Mexico's more recent "economic miracle" repeats the same pattern. By the early 1990s, strong economic growth had resulted in a dramatic concentration of wealth and a widening gap between the rich and the poor: While 92.4 percent of the population earns less than $5,700 U.S. per year, the top of Mexico's socioeconomic hierarchy is now occupied by seven Mexican billionaires, more than in Britain or Saudi Arabia. And the Mexican government has signed a free-trade agreement with the United States and Canada (the North American Free Trade Agreement) that is encouraging a flood of foreign investment and ownership in the country.

Understanding the Balance Sheet   The preceding balance sheet is not difficult to understand if one considers that the roots of capitalism lie in conservative value systems. Development based on takeoff theory has primarily benefited the strong because it is intended to; the accounting system of the capitalist world economy prioritizes individual gain, not egalitarian values. The history of Other World development is consistent with the 400-year trend of capitalism—an ever-increasing concentration of wealth in the hands of a few, much of which is spent on luxury consumption and speculation rather than being reinvested in any industrial infrastructure that might significantly benefit the many in either the short or the long run.

Through an analysis known as *dependency theory,* liberals and radicals in fact argue that, given the position of the Other World in the international political economy, development that would substantially improve the lives of a majority of the Other World's peoples is unlikely to occur at all. They point out that the designation "Third" World is an accurate description of that position: Although there is really only *one* world of political economy, with all the world's states linked in various fashions to the whole, most of the countries of Africa, Asia, and Latin America occupy tertiary positions on the periphery of the dominant political and economic order. Their primary function, as it was under formal colonialism, is to provide raw materials and cheap labor for the industrialized powers. Other World countries are now dominated by structures of neocolonialism that differ little in substance from the colonialism of the past.

From the perspective of dependency theorists, Other World political systems are particularly dependent on the Western industrial powers. Neocolonialism operates through the collusion of Other World political elites, who have been co-opted into serving foreign interests. Independence means only that political institutions originally established to facilitate and enforce the extraction of wealth from the Other World are now occupied by African, Asian, and Latin American politicians and bureaucrats instead of by expatriate colonial officials. These new elites serve as "brokers," managing the flow of resources from their countries in return for brokerage fees (or commissions) in the form of foreign aid and other payoffs, which they use to maintain their positions of political control and to build their personal fortunes.

The rule of many Other World political elites in the neocolonial era constitutes a contemporary mercantilism in which national political economies are operated to increase the wealth of the rulers.[20] The widespread corruption, or the use of public office for private gain, that pervades Other World politics is a key factor in explaining why the development programs of many countries have done little to improve the lot of the masses. Much of the political instability endemic to Other World political systems stems from the fact that governments operated openly for private gain (or *kleptocracies*) have little legitimacy among, or acceptance by, a significant proportion of the population, in neocolonial times as in the past. The Al-Qaeda movement of Osama bin Laden is one example of an attempt to free a country (in this case, Saudi Arabia) from a corrupt and repressive regime propped up by a neocolonial power (in this case, the United States).

Perhaps more difficult to understand is the fact that those countries that followed communist and socialist development strategies have been only a little more successful in accomplishing egalitarian goals and probably less successful in preserving the natural environment. The inequalities that have developed in these states, although less dramatic than those in the capitalist world, indicate that the tendency of the powerful to serve their self-interests is not unique to capitalism. Economic growth and social inequality is a common pattern, with increases in economic output accompanied by increasing inequality throughout history.[21] The 400-year history of capitalism is an extension of a trend that began 6,000 years ago when humankind first established urban-based civilizations capable of creating wealth in surplus of the resources needed for human survival, a trend accelerated 2,000 years ago when Western civilization emerged in the Greek city-states and legitimized the value of individualistic materialism. While an appreciation of capitalist ideology helps one understand the particular details of the process through which development has come to benefit primarily a few in the capitalist world economy, one must go beyond the level of ideology to the underlying realities of politics, power, and self-interest to understand the universal links between increased economic output and greater inequality.

Increases in economic output, in Mesopotamia or ancient Greece or the Other World of the post–World War II era, go primarily to those groups within a society, and to those states within the international political economy, that are able to control the forces of violence and the institutions and policies that determine the distribution of that output. At this level of analysis, ideologies primarily represent efforts by political elites to use knowledge power to convince the public that the government is being operated in the public interest. While ideologies are useful in defining the goals and values that people of various persuasions believe *should* be served by development, they are relatively insignificant in determining political realities. The actual outputs of governments operating with "competing" ideologies are only marginally different; in this context, one can appreciate the observation that while under capitalism man exploits man, under communism it's the other way around.

GLOBALIZATION

The 1970s marked the emergence of globalization as a new form of global political economy that has evolved to increasingly dominate world economic and political affairs. Globalization is an international regime in which the economic interests of multinational corporations and other nonstate actors (such as the IMF and the North Atlantic Treaty Organization) are coming to supersede the interests and powers of individual states. In the preceding chapter, colonialism was defined as a relationship in which a group of people located in one country is subject to the authority of people in another country. The logic and the drive of the capitalist world economy is now creating a fundamentally different global regime in which all the world's people are increasingly subject to the power of multinational institutions.

Globalization: Disco sign outside the Hard Rock Café in Tai'an, China.
SOURCE: *Joe Weatherby*

National boundaries and loyalties are of little significance in a global economy driven by the exclusive and ceaseless pursuit of profit. In this coming age of postindustrial production, the demand (and compensation) for labor is predicted to decline as a transnational elite seeks custom, designer goods made by specialized producers hired at the lowest wage rates possible from a global labor pool, rather than the standardized products of the mass assembly lines that have provided employment to many in the past.

Riccardo Petrella, a futurist for the European Union, describes how the forces of globalization are separating all the world's peoples into two classes that cut across national boundaries, divided into the "fast" and the "slow" on the basis of access to computer-based information and communications technologies. In this evolving structure, a global upper class of the affluent and privileged living in a high-tech archipelago of hyperdeveloped, walled, and gated city-regions and consisting of less than one-eighth of the world's population is emerging among a global underclass consisting of seven-eighths of the world's population left to fend for itself in a disintegrating social and environmental wasteland.[22]

Colin Leys defines this new international regime as a world

1. Dominated by multinational corporations,
2. Regulated by the IMF, and
3. Enforced by the military might of the United States[23]

In an era characterized by the privatization of government functions, private mercenary armies are also being formed to enforce this new global system. For example, Executive Outcomes, a private South African corporation formed by ex-members of the notorious apartheid-era 32nd Battalion of the South African special forces, offers states and corporations able to afford its multimillion-dollar fees a full spectrum of military services and products. The company fields highly trained combat troops equipped with the latest military hardware ranging from automatic assault rifles to helicopter gunships to fuel–air explosives designed to kill all life within a one-mile radius by sucking oxygen from the air.[24]

The development programs that characterized much of the history of the Other World beginning in the 1940s are being rapidly abandoned under globalization. Since the 1970s, foreign aid programs have been steadily and significantly reduced as Other World countries are directed to pursue their economic development through integrating their economies into the global marketplace. As part of globalization, the functions of the GATT have been assumed by the World Trade Organization (WTO). Established in 1995 and headquartered in Geneva, Switzerland, the WTO has become a powerful multinational force working to set the rules of trade between and among the countries of the world.

CONCLUSIONS

The peoples of the Other World face difficult times in the coming years. The internal affairs of many Other World countries are coming increasingly under the direct control of IMF officials, who are imposing *structural adjustment programs* that change domestic spending patterns to make possible repayments on enormous debts owed to First World financial institutions. These changes often include cuts in health, education, and other social service programs. Much of this debt was incurred during the oil shortages of the 1970s and grew with a rise in interest rates in the 1980s. In African countries, this debt typically amounts to five times annual export income. Many Latin American countries now pay out one-fourth of their export receipts in debt payments on long-term loans, some of which do not even cover interest due. *Privatization programs,* which transfer the control of government services to private, for-profit firms, are further loosening the thin ties that link public resources to public needs.

Power vacuums resulting from the end of the cold war are contributing to spiraling levels of violence in many parts of the Other World. In the decades preceding the fall of the Soviet empire, both the United States and the Soviet Union de-livered a substantial portion of their foreign aid in the form of military assistance. Other World dictators who were willing to wave one flag or another as clients in the ideological contest between capitalism and communism, sometimes adroitly playing one side off against the other, amassed enormous military capabilities. With the cold war balance of power now ended, stockpiles of weapons are fueling disastrous conflicts between and within Other World states. This factor played prominently in the rise of the Taliban in Afghanistan following the defeat of the Soviet Union in 1990, the 1990 invasion of Kuwait by Iraq, and in bloody civil wars and anarchy in Somalia in 1992 and in Rwanda beginning in 1994.[25]

The Politics of Change

Those who hold conservative values can find much to be encouraged by in con-temporary global trends. Globalization heralds a global class apartheid in which the strong are free to pursue their interests unencumbered by any sense of connec-tion with or responsibility to the social commonwealth or the environmental com-mons. In contrast, those who prefer a different future face tremendous challenges. As noted above, power is the primary factor that determines who gets what, when, and how in the world, and it is power that will ultimately determine whether world affairs will continue to be dominated by the goals and values of the capitalist world economy or by alternatives embodied in concepts such as eco-development.

The qualitative changes in societies and in the international political economy necessary to achieve change that would serve egalitarian and environmental val-ues are vast in range and scale. The range of change would have to include politi-cal, economic, and social processes and institutions, for all of these aspects of hu-man organization are inseparably linked. Within this web of interconnections, it is impossible to separate economic development from political development or so-cial development; improvements in the economic conditions of the less powerful could be achieved only through parallel improvements in political and social con-ditions. The scale of change would have to be fundamental, for the processes and institutions that currently determine the use and allocation of the world's resources are deeply and firmly entrenched. Changes of this extent would require radical transformations in the power relationships that hold these systems together.

However, as we proceed into the twenty-first century, there are signs that the centralized Western power structures that have long dominated our affairs are be-ginning to crumble under the pressure of converging crises of overpopulation, en-vironmental destruction, resource scarcity, economic discontinuity, and sociopo-litical decay. These crises may create opportunities for change in chaos not present in more stable times. As the Chinese have long noted, when there is great disorder under the heavens, the opportunities for change are excellent.

E. F. Schumacher observes that whereas some have challenged the ethic of ma-terialism and argued for different priorities throughout history, "Today, however, this message reaches us not solely from the sages and saints but from the actual course of physical events. It speaks to us in the language of terrorism, genocide, breakdown, pollution, exhaustion."[26] Samuel Huntington hypothesizes a resurgence of Confucian, Japanese, Islamic, Hindu, Slavic-Orthodox, Latin American, and African civilizations against a Western civilization now at the peak of its power and global intrusiveness.[27] Samuel Barber describes forces working to diminish the power of the nation-state.[28] And Alvin Toffler argues that we are at one of the greatest turning points in history as breakdown and exhaustion in health, education, transportation, welfare, urban, and ecological systems converge to challenge the centralized power structures that control our societies.[29]

The peaceful revolutions against authoritarian rule that swept the Soviet Union and Eastern Europe at the end of the 1980s and early 1990s provide tantalizing support for these theses, as do mounting signs of institutional collapse and widespread public disenchantment in the Western industrial nations. Significantly, so do democratization and local autonomy movements that are erupting across the Other World, fueled by the irrepressible force of global mass communications. And a proliferation of globally based nongovernmental organizations (NGOs) are working to build a global civic culture and new global institutions capable of controlling the excesses of globalization and directing the forces of global integration toward the common good.[30]

Changing power relations could provide those who envision development as a way to serve people and to create the means for self-liberation with opportunities in the coming years that seemed impossible in the past. If the information technologies that are elevating knowledge to a position as the dominant source of power were dispersed among the world's masses, the resulting diffusion of power could result in the first true democracies the world has ever known. On the other hand, if the new technologies are controlled by a few, we could be plunged into a new Dark Age of orwellian proportions. In the coming decades it is likely that those who control knowledge and the technologies of knowledge will also control wealth, violence, and the institutions of government.

As we proceed through a time of pivotal change in human affairs, the individual actions of each of us will count more than at any time in previous years. For we are all participants, whether as consumers, investors, or political activists, in the international political economy that we share with the peoples of the Other World. Our common future depends on our common efforts to build a more socially and ecologically sustainable world.

SUMMARY

The first global political economy of mercantilism was created as part of the colonial era that began with the first voyage of Columbus in 1492. Mercantilism evolved into capitalism as industrial and financial elites came to control Western governments. Beginning in the 1940s, Other World international relations and domestic affairs were dominated by a concern with development. Driven primarily by the capitalist world economy, development programs guided by takeoff theory resulted in significant increases in GNP/GDP and improvements in the lives of some Other World peoples; they also contributed to increasing inequality and growing numbers of people living in absolute poverty. Whereas takeoff theorists attribute these problems to the necessities of progress, dependency theorists view them as the result of the exploitation of the Other World by the industrial powers and Other World political elites through structures of neocolonialism. Advocates of both schools ground their positions in political ideologies that express fundamental beliefs and values about the way the world should be.

Powerful world trends indicate that takeoff strategies, now in the form of globalization, are likely to continue to prevail as the dominant approach to Other World development, with direct implications for increasing inequality, poverty, and environmental decline and increasing levels of political, economic, and social instability. Other trends indicate the possibility of changes in power relations that could make possible development designed to promote egalitarian and environmental values. We are living at a pivotal time of convergence in human affairs that will have fundamental consequences for the future of the global community we inhabit with the peoples of the Other World.

ISSUES FOR DISCUSSION

1. Can you refute the Doctrine of Thrasymachus?

The Doctrine of Thrasymachus consists of two reinforcing parts. Part I states that it is the natural right of the strong to take more than their equal share of what the world has to offer. This is a philosophical statement, or one that addresses what is considered to be right and wrong, good and bad. Here Thrasymachus asserts the unbridled right of the strong to take from the weak, drawing on their physical strength, intelligence, or any other attribute that would enable them to overpower others. Any means imaginable, including violence and fraud, is morally justified. Part II states that might makes right. Here Thrasymachus addresses how the strong use government to serve their interests by writing and enforcing laws that work to their advantage. The idea that whatever the mighty say is right is right underlies the concept of relative justice—whatever the strong say is just is just, with some laws legitimately applied unequally to different citizens and some laws legitimately applied only to certain groups. For Thrasymachus, justice is whatever is in the interests of the strong.

Liberty, or the *freedom to* pursue one's interests without constraint, and equality, or *freedom from* relative poverty and exploitation, are conflicting values; a society cannot encourage one without sacrificing the other. On the one hand, if citizens are free to pursue private interests without constraint, some will invariably take advantage of others, creating greater inequality in society; on the other hand, efforts to build more egalitarian social orders can only be pursued by restraining personal liberty. The ideas expressed in the Doctrine of Thrasymachus are thus among the most significant in the history of political thinking in that they so unequivocally proclaim the value of liberty. They take us to the core of one of the central dilemmas of political organization: Government policies that restrain liberty stifle initiative, whereas policies that encourage liberty result in exploitation. As the basis for the conservative ideas and ideals that provide the foundations of capitalism, takeoff theory, and the ethic of globalization, they also take us to the heart of what development should be and can be about.

If Thrasymachus is right, it follows that all governments are oligarchies, or political systems operated by a few to serve their interests. While most claim to have been created by God to serve the people, such claims are part of the fraud perpetuated by elites to hide the fact that government is in fact designed to serve the interests of the strong. If the political institutions that control peoples' behavior to allocate societies' scarce values are operated by a few to serve their interests, it further follows that what we call "civilized" life rests on the exploitation of the weak.

Attempts to refute or support the ideas expressed by Thrasymachus are central to political philosophy. Can you refute the Doctrine of Thrasymachus? If so, how? If not, why not? Consider your response from both normative and empirical perspectives: normative analysis is concerned with what should be, or with moral judgments of right and wrong; empirical analysis is concerned with what is, or the way things are in actual fact.

2. What degree of inequality results in political violence and instability?

Two types of scarcity characterize shortages of those things people most value. *Absolute scarcity* exists when there is simply not enough of a given item for everyone to have a share; the "pie" is so small that it can't be sliced thinly enough to give everyone a piece. *Relative scarcity* exists when there is enough of an item to go around, but some receive a small share or no share at all because some take much larger shares.

Most of the goods and values in the world are in relative scarce supply. While the world's resources could support a reasonably comfortable life-style of all of the world's peoples, the fact that some take gigantic shares means that many live in poverty. Worldwide, there are currently 325 billionaires who own more than half the world's population (3 billion people); in the United States, the wealthiest 1% of the population owns more net financial assets (wealth that can be used to create more wealth, such as property, buildings, equipment, stocks, and bonds) than the other 99 percent of the population; in Los Angeles, the 50 richest individuals have as much money as the poorest 2 million.

Relative inequality within countries and across countries is the primary source of political violence and instability. While people will accept absolute scarcity in which all share shortages, political resentment builds when some are seen as taking more than they deserve relative to their abilities. A popular sense of justice holds that one's rewards should be proportionate to one's capabilities.

Money, Sun, and Sand: Since the 1970s Georgetown, capital of the Cayman Islands, has provided a tax-free refuge for the funds of the rich and famous from around the world. The branches of many foreign banks have been opened here to serve these customers.

SOURCE: *Joe Weatherby*

Political analysts have long pondered the degree of inequality that results in political conflict. Plato and Aristotle hypothesized that there is a fivefold difference in abilities among equals, and that political instability results when the difference between the property of the richest and the poorest is more than five times. In other words, some individuals are five times more intelligent, hard working, and emotionally stable than others, and can therefore be expected to accumulate five times more than others in a stable political economy in which one's abilities are proportionate to one's rewards; allocations over that ceiling result in political instability.

From Thomas Jefferson's perspective that "all are created equal," substantiated by modern research showing that the genetic makeup of all human beings is over 99 percent identical, what do you believe to be the actual difference in human abilities? Is it five times, as suggested by Plato and Aristotle? Or 20 times, 50 times, or 100 times? Is the wealthiest man in the world 60 billion times more intelligent, hard working, and emotionally stable than others? If not, how do you explain his wealth?

3. Internationally, how can you best protect yourself in an era of globalization and increasing inequality and conflict?

With 4.6 percent of the world's population, the United States presently consumes 40 percent of the world's resources. With 15.4 percent of the world's population, the other industrialized countries consume another 40 percent. The 80 percent of the world's population living in the Other World is left to live from the remaining 20 percent of world resources.

These inequalities have been cited as one of the sources of the conflict resulting in the attacks on the World Trade Center on September 11, 2001. In his book *Blowback: The Costs and Consequences of American Empire,* Chalmers Johnson posits that in the decade following the end of the cold war, the United States used military force and financial manipulation to help maintain and increase the inequalities described above, and that the twenty-first century may be a time of reckoning for the United States.[31] Specifically addressing the events of September 11 in a *Los Angles Times* Opinion article titled, "The Lessons of Blowback," Johnson argues that in response to the attacks, the United States should

- Recognize that the terrorism of September 11 was not directed against America but against American foreign policy;
- Listen to the grievances of the Islamic peoples;
- Stop propping up repressive regimes in the area;
- Protect Israel's security but denounce its apartheid practices in Palestinian areas; and
- Reform our "globalization" policies so that they no longer mean that the rich are getting richer and the poor poorer.

Johnson concludes that if the United States' only response to the September 11 attack is military reprisal, "the end result will not be 'victory' in a 'war on terrorism' but a further cycle of terrorists attacks, American casualties and escalation."[32]

Considering the implications of the preceding for your own safety and security, what do you feel you can do to most effectively address the increasing level of international violence characteristic of today's world?

4. Domestically, how can you best protect yourself in an era of globalization?

The world orders of colonialism and neocolonialism were generally good to the U.S. middle class. Factories that processed materials drawn from around the world provided high-paying jobs with benefits to generations of workers, spawned a range of support jobs in the professions and the retail and service industries, and provided part of the tax base that built and maintained the country's infrastructure. The new world order of globalization is not so kind. Trends toward the specialized production of custom goods by firms with sites around the world, and with loyalty only to corporate profits, mean that U.S. citizens are increasingly competing in a global labor pool for fewer jobs that pay lower wages with few or no benefits.

Over the past 30 years, globalization has accounted for the shift of millions of U.S. jobs abroad as multinational firms located in the United States pursue greater profits by saving on labor, plant, and environmental compliance costs. Although many of these jobs have been in the garment and automobile assembly industries, they cover the full spectrum of skills and salaries. For example, major U.S.-based computer software companies that pay up to $90,000 per year for top-of-the-line software engineers in the United States can now hire equally well-qualified engineers in China for $6,000 per year. Computer-based satellite communications networks make it possible to link employees from around the world in a global virtual worksite, with full and immediate access to any software or hardware tools needed on the job.

The trend toward a hyperaffluent upper class progressively separated from a growing underclass is well underway in the United States. Three decades of changes in tax, investment, and trade laws have resulted in a greater redistribution of wealth from the middle and lower classes to the rich than at any time in the country's, and probably the world's, history. Steady economic growth has fueled tremendous financial gains for the wealthiest 5 percent of the population while the standard of living of most has declined, despite efforts by mothers entering the workforce and employees working longer hours to compensate for falling household income. The take-home pay of full-time workers declined by 20 percent over the past 30 years, and the percentage of full-time workers with benefit plans dropped from 84 percent in 1982 to 56 percent in 1995. Of the 20 million jobs created in the United States between 1983 and 1993, 50 percent paid less than $20,000 per year, and 28 percent paid less than $13,000.

The United States is also heavily involved in its own structural adjustment program as public funds that formerly supported public services and infrastructure are being diverted to pay the country's debt. As a part of these readjustments, cuts in public funding for education are resulting in skyrocketing increases in college fees: In California's colleges and universities, fees increased 113 percent between 1990 and 1994. The average income of the families that send their sons and daughters to college is rising as cuts in financial aid mean that students from lower-income families are unable to attend.

If current trends continue, it is clear that many in today's college-age generation will not be able to enjoy a quality of life as high as that of their parents. For many in the United States and the Other World, globalization is likely to mean a declining standard of living.

How can you best protect yourself in a global order? Keep in mind that power ultimately determines who gets what in the political process and that the primary sources of power are violence, wealth, and knowledge. What kind of power do you have most access to, and how could you best develop and use it to protect yourself, your family, and your community?

5. Do you owe posterity a sustainable world?

It is estimated that the human species has been on the planet for some 4.5 million years. For the bulk of that time, we had little effect on the natural environment, as our hunting and gathering activities caused only slight disturbances in the self-regulating natural ecologies that we inhabited. We began concerted and determined efforts to dominate and control the environment to serve human ends 6,000 years ago with the first urban-based civilizations, and have since been so successful that our technologies are now overwhelming the natural systems that we evolved with and upon which we depend for our survival. Our impact has become so substantial that we have damaged many of the self-regulating and self-balancing mechanisms that controlled the natural world, creating disturbed ecosystems that can be kept from chaos and collapse only through constant human intervention and manipulation.

Many in the scientific community are now questioning our ability to maintain the necessary balances and equilibriums. The cumulative and long-term effects of pollution, resource depletion, and species and habitat losses seem to be so significantly altering the living world that doubts are being raised about our ability to sustain life as we know it. Unless we dramatically change our stewardship of the earth, our environment will probably become so irretrievably mutilated over the coming decades that future generations could suffer vast misery and eventual extinction.

In response, some ask, "So what? Why should we care? What has posterity ever done for me?" At its extreme, the ethic of globalization in fact includes a nihilistic view that the planet is already so overburdened with population and pollution problems that it is beyond saving and that we should therefore live life to the hilt in the time we have remaining. This view provides another rationalization for the short-term greed that is driving the contemporary global economy.

Do you owe posterity a sustainable world? If not, why not? If so, on what is this obligation based? Exactly what are you willing to give up in your current lifestyle and levels of consumption to make life tolerable and possible for future generations? In pursuit of the goal, are you willing to become more actively involved in the political process? How?

Review Questions

1. Define (a) politics and (b) economics. How are politics and economics related? What is the role of government in the process of economic production and distribution?
2. Describe and explain the difference between colonialism and neocolonialism.
3. Explain the difference between "growth" and "development." Describe and explain the results of more than five decades of programs to achieve "development" in the Other World.
4. Describe the links between poverty and population increase.

5. Define and describe the nature of globalization. What are the implications of current global trends for our natural environment and for social and political stability?

Key Terms

- **Politics**—Who gets what, when, and how; The authoritative allocation of scarce values.
- **Economics**—The production, distribution, and use of wealth.
- **Power**—The use of violence, knowledge, and authority to control the behavior of others.
- **Oligarchy**—Government by the few, in the interest of the few.
- **The Doctrine of Thrasymachus**—(a) It is the natural right of the strong to take more than their equal share of what the world has to offer, and (b) might makes right.
- **Neocolonialism**—Indirect control of Other World countries by First World countries and multinational interests.
- **Brokers**—Other World political leaders who act in the interest of First World countries and multinational interests.
- **Sustainable development**—Living within the limits of natural systems while ensuring an adequate standard of living for all; meeting the needs of the present without compromising the ability of future generations to meet their own needs.
- **Structural adjustment programs**—Domestic spending plans to make possible repayments on loans; often include cuts in health, education, and other social service programs.
- **Globalization**—Emerging international regime in which the economic interests of multinational corporations and other nonstate actors supercede the interests and power of nations.

Useful Web Sites

http://www.oneworld.net/
http://www.oswego.edu/reshaping/
http://www.oxfam.org.uk/
http://www.undp.org/
http://www.wto.org/

Notes

1. Christopher Flavin, "Rich Planet, Poor Planet," in *State of the World 2001*, ed. Linda Starke (New York: W.W. Norton & Company, 2001), p. 5.

2. Union of Concerned Scientists, *World Scientists' Warning Briefing Book* (Cambridge, Mass.: Union of Concerned Scientists, 1993), p. 4.
3. Jeffrey A. Freiden and David A. Lake, *International Political Economy: Perspectives on Global Power and Wealth* (New York: St. Martin's Press, 1987), p. 1.
4. Howard Zinn, *A People's History of the United States 1492–Present* (New York: HarperPerennial, 1995), pp. 1–8.
5. Julius K. Nyerere, *Ujamaa: Essays on Socialism* (Nairobi: Oxford University Press, 1968), pp. 2–3.
6. Charles K. Wilber, ed. *The Political Economy of Development and Underdevelopment* (New York: Random House, 1988), p. 25.
7. James J. Lamb, "The Third World and the Development Debate," *IDOC-North America* (January–February 1973): 20.
8. See "The Cocoyoc Declaration," adopted by participants in the UNEP/UNCTAD Symposium on Patterns of Resource Use, Environment and Development Strategies, Cocoyoc, Mexico, October 8–12, 1974. Reprinted in *International Organization* 29, no. 3 (summer 1975): 893–901; Lester Brown, et al., *State of the World 1991: A Worldwatch Institute Report on Progress toward a Sustainable Society* (New York: Norton, 1991); Jim MacNeill, Pieter Winsemius, and Taizo Yakushiji, *Beyond Interdependence: The Meshing of the World's Economy and the Earth's Ecology* (New York: Oxford University Press, 1991); and World Commission on Environment and Development, *Our Common Future* (New York: Oxford University Press, 1987).
9. See E. F. Schumacher, *Small Is Beautiful: Economics as if People Mattered* (New York: Harper & Row, 1973).
10. Immanuel Wallerstein, "The Three Instances of Hegemony in the History of the Capitalist World-Economy," in *International Political Economy: A Reader,* ed. Kendall W. Stiles and Tsuneo Akaha (New York: HarperCollins, 1991), pp. 427–435.
11. Ibid., p. 428.
12. John Kenneth Galbraith, *Economic Development* (New York: Houghton Mifflin, 1964), p. 3.
13. Rene Dumont, *False Start in Africa* (New York: Praeger, 1969).
14. Quoted in Flavin, *op. cit.,* p. 7.
15. United Nations Development Programme, *Human Development Report 1997* (New York: Oxford University Press, 1997), pp. 27–29.
16. Paul Harrison, *Inside the Third World: The Anatomy of Poverty* (London: Penguin Books, 1990), pp. 465–466 (emphasis in the original).
17. Ibid., p. 276.
18. *Controlling Interest: The World of the Multinational Corporation* (San Francisco: California Newsreel, 1978).
19. Ibid.
20. Robert H. Jackson and Carl G. Rosberg, "The Political Economy of African Personal Rule," in *Political Development and the New Realism in Sub-Saharan Africa,* ed. David E. Apter and Carl G. Rosberg (Charlottesville: University Press of Virginia, 1994), p. 292.
21. Gerhard E. Lenksi, *Power and Privilege: A Theory of Social Stratification* (New York: McGraw-Hill, 1966).
22. Riccardo Petrella, "Techno-apartheid for a Global Underclass," *Los Angeles Times,* 6 August 1992, p. D6.
23. Colin Leys, "Learning from the Kenya Debate," in *Political Development and the New Realism in Sub-Saharan Africa,* ed. David E. Apter and Carl G. Rosberg (Charlottesville: University Press of Virginia, 1994), p. 227.

24. Elizabeth Rubin, "An Army of One's Own," *Harper's Magazine,* February 1997, pp. 44–55.

25. See Robert D. Kaplan, "The Coming Anarchy," *This World,* (13 March 1994), pp. 5–10.

26. E. F. Schumacher, *Small Is Beautiful: Economics as if People Mattered* (New York: Harper & Row, 1973), pp. 293–294.

27. Samuel P. Huntington, "The Clash of Civilizations?" *Foreign Affairs* 72, no. 3 (summer 1993): 22–49.

28. Benjamin R. Barber, *Jihad vs. McWorld: How Globalism and Tribalism are Reshaping the World* (New York: Ballantine Books, 1996).

29. Alvin Toffler, *Powershift: Knowledge, Wealth, and Violence at the Edge of the 21st Century* (New York: Bantam Books, 1990).

30. See George Soros, *Open Society: Reforming Global Capitalism* (New York: Public Affairs, 2000); and Craig Warkentin, *Reshaping World Politics: NGOs, the Internet, and Global Civil Society* (New York: Rowman & Littlefield Publishers, Inc., 2001).

31. Chalmers Johnson, *Blowback: The Costs and Consequences of American Empire* (New York: Owl/Metropolitan Books, 2001).

32. Chalmers Johnson, "The Lessons of Blowback," *Los Angeles Times,* 30 September 2001, p. M1.

For Further Reading

Apter, David E., and Carl G. Rosberg, eds. *Political Development and the New Realism in Sub-Saharan Africa.* Charlottesville: University Press of Virginia, 1994.

Barber, Benjamin R. *Jihad vs. McWorld: How Globalism and Tribalism are Reshaping the World.* New York: Ballantine Books, 1996

Brown, Lester R., et al. *State of the World 2001: A Worldwatch Institute Report on Progress toward a Sustainable Society.* New York: Norton, 2001.

Clapham, Christopher. *Third World Politics: An Introduction.* Madison: University of Wisconsin Press, 1985. *Foreign Policy* 107 (summer 1997), Globalization: The Debate.

Grieder, William. *One World Ready or Not: The Manic Logic of Global Capitalism.* New York: Simon & Schuster, 1997.

Harrison, Paul. *Inside the Third World: The Anatomy of Poverty.* London: Penguin Books, 1990.

Johnson, Chalmers. *Blowback: The Costs and Consequences of American Empire.* New York: Owl/Metropolitan Books, 2001.

Lenksi, Gerhard E. *Power and Privilege: A Theory of Social Stratification.* New York: McGraw-Hill, 1966.

MacNeill, Jim, Pieter Winsemius, and Taizo Yakushiji. *Beyond Interdependence: The Meshing of the World's Economy and the Earth's Ecology.* New York: Oxford University Press, 1991.

Schumacher, E. F. *Small Is Beautiful: Economics as if People Mattered.* New York: Harper & Row, 1973.

Soros, George. *Open Society: Reforming Global Capitalism.* New York: Public Affairs, 2000.

Stiles, Kendall W., and Tsuneo Akaha, eds. *International Political Economy: A Reader.* New York: HarperCollins, 1991.

Tinder, Glenn. *Political Thinking: The Perennial Questions.* 6th ed. New York: HarperCollins, 1995.

Toffler, Alvin. *Powershift: Knowledge, Wealth, and Violence at the Edge of the 21st Century.* New York: Bantam Books, 1990.

Trainer, Ted. *Developed to Death: Rethinking Third World Development.* London: Merlin Press, 1989.

Union of Concerned Scientists. *World Scientists' Warning Briefing Book.* Cambridge, Mass.: Union of Concerned Scientists, 1993.

Warkentin, Craig. *Reshaping World Politics: NGOs, the Internet, and Global Civil Society.* New York: Rowman & Littlefield Publishers, Inc., 2001.

World Commission on Environment and Development. *Our Common Future.* New York: Oxford University Press, 1987.

CHAPTER 4

Women and Development

Dianne Long

Talking about man without talking about woman
is like clapping with one hand.

ANONYMOUS

Visual glimpses of the developing world in Western media often capture the faces, figures, and activities of women. Photos depict the tall Masai women of East Africa with their colorful garb, the Indian women in saris carrying children and water, the formless Afghan women veiled in blue burkas from head to toe scurrying through the marketplace. The developing world cannot truly be understood without discussing women. Yet these photos and the stories accompanying them do not fully tell us about the lives of women in the Other World.

Women play a crucial role in development. Surprisingly little attention has been paid to their important involvement. The primary reason for this lack of attention is the fact that most attempts at development activities have been carried out by male-dominated institutions and reported from the perspective of international bureaucracies that did not recognize women's roles. However, women are an essential link to population control. They carry heavy responsibility for food production, not only for their own families, but also for community marketplaces. They contribute significantly to wage labor, even though wages tend to be very meager. Because they bear responsibility for family health and nutrition, they are aware of how pollution, desertification, deforestation, and pollution affect community health and prosperity. In the developing world, women face many obstacles—political, economic, and social. In various areas of the world, female children are less valued. This leads to high infanticide and child mortality rates. Neglect, violence, multiple pregnancy, poor nutrition, and hard physical labor take their toll on women's well-being. In many areas of the developing world, school enrollments of females and literacy rates are lower than those for males. Individual and economic opportunities for females are diminished throughout life.

This chapter takes note of *four major factors* that affect women in developing countries. They include: (1) the legacy of colonialism, (2) the push for modernization, (3) the evolving of nationalism, and (4) the pervasiveness of globalization. Examining these factors as they affect women adds to our understanding of women's past, present, and future in the Other World.

WOMEN AND THE LEGACY OF COLONIALISM

Colonialism was not a new concept to either the European powers or to the colonies. It was the foundation, of course, of the Roman and Ottoman empires. What was new about colonialism in the eighteenth and nineteenth centuries was the scale of exploitation. This exploitation was largely fueled by the Industrial Revolution that arose in Britain. From approximately 1750 to 1850, it was a period of rapid and profound social and economic change. Britain changed from a traditional agricultural society to the modern industrial one. In particular, the invention of the steam engine in 1769 and the development of steam for power resulted in building of roads, railroads, canals, and cotton textile manufacturing in England. By 1830, it had been established in France, and soon thereafter, industry was a dominant factor in Germany and other countries of Europe. The United States and Russia entered the industrial age. Industrialization produced and required expanded markets, cheap labor, and raw materials, for which the industrial nations turned to the less developed areas of the world, primarily Africa and Asia. *Imperialism,* the extension of rule of one society over another, was a natural consequence.

The precolonial world had a variety of cultural arrangements. Living in clans and extended families, women's lives had been shaped by centuries of local custom and necessary adaptation to change. There is no doubt that they shared power and responsibilities in order to survive. Certainly their human experiences are reflected in every historical and geographic context. Western colonization, however, pushed aside the traditional patterns and introduced new concepts and requirements for private and public gender. They placed primary emphasis upon women's reproductive function and role of rearing and nurturing children. Women's lives were considered to be limited to this "private" or internal sphere of home and children, while men were considered to operate in the "public" or external sphere, managing matters outside the home. Men were seen as having roles that included economic planning and building, settling conflicts, waging war, and bonding with other males for political and economic strength.[1]

European values shaped women's lives. In the sixteenth and seventeenth centuries, Spanish and Portuguese colonizing efforts brought Catholicism and

A Traditional Role for Women: Both Eastern and Western societies have, at times, segregated women from public life. Houses in the old city of Jidda, Saudi Arabia, contain wooden screens that are designed to allow the women to remain private while viewing the street.

SOURCE: *Joe Weatherby*

"macho" attitudes that diminished the roles of indigenous women. In the nineteenth century, a pattern of patriarchy spread throughout industrialized Europe and was introduced into the developing world. In the new industrial world, both politics and economics were considered to be male's concerns, and female power over any part of the sector declined. European cultures put decision making and property into the hands of male heads of household. Women were part of that property. Thus, a patriarchal pattern replaced other customary patterns. England, especially, became a world power. During the rule of Queen Victoria (1837–1901), England was transformed from an island at the edge of Europe to an empire where the sun never set and where the monarch was crowned the Empress of India and ruler of vast areas of Africa and the Pacific. Although the monarch was a woman, power was in the hands of political and industrial men.

Colonial administrators, taking charge of the developing world from a Victorian perspective, ignored the importance of women to community life and to local economies. Men made decisions, held property, and restricted women to subservient roles. In Africa and Asia, women had been primarily agricultural workers. New development introduced into these areas required that men be trained to work for wages in plantations and large-scale farms. The men often resisted and ignored the training, and Colonial administrators often failed to comprehend the weakness of their agricultural programs. Nevertheless, development

Oriental Carpets: Carpet weaving is a common occupation for women in Central Asia, Pakistan, India, and China.

SOURCE: *Joe Weatherby*

established ownership and dominance, men were forced to comply with new conditions, and women were shut out of their traditional subsistence farming. Even where women had strong political and economic roles—as they did in West Africa—their positions in traditional societies were eliminated. They could no longer hold any position of importance, such as clan chiefs, judges, or managers of resources.[2]

Traditional societies had usually held their land in common, not as individuals. Land reform was introduced with colonialism. European powers granted land titles to European entrepreneurs, government officials, and important "native" leaders. The government redefinition of ownership, and land grants, dispossessed women in the "private" economy, and empowered male leaders in the "public" economy. Families were forced to abandon the subsistence farming that had always met family needs. Their land was taken for commercial agriculture. Women, who had always done at least half of the agricultural work, were deprived of their lands and were pushed into smaller and less fertile areas to continue their struggle to feed their families and neighbors. Food supply, distribution, nutrition, and health of women and children suffered. The land that had been community property, farmed for the common good, had become commercial, used for the profit of others.[3]

WOMEN AND THE PUSH FOR MODERNIZATION

There is a widespread belief that modernization, along with democratization, urbanization, and industrialization, will improve women's lives, offering opportunities and rising economic and social status. This belief has not always proved true. Modernization was introduced to agricultural communities to improve production of cash crops. Foreigners developed large-scale plantations and other agricultural businesses. Men—and some women and children—found that they could survive only by going to work for the new owners, usually for low wages and long hours to buy food and other necessities. Commercial agriculture created powerful new requirements. It required advanced technology and training, modern equipment, synthetic fertilizers and herbicides, and the money to buy them. Commercial agriculture provided colonial people with technical training in agricultural methods. Modernization did not trickle down to everyone. Women continued to have smaller garden areas to grow crops for the table. Soils and water supply were at times marginal, and harvests could be disappointing. In some countries, women also went to work on plantations for small wages, while still carrying the responsibilities for house, family, and garden. Caught up in both the deteriorating family economy and modernization requirements, their lives were not improved.[4]

New financing mechanisms were introduced along with changes in agricultural production, distribution, and consumption. Local farmers were required to adapt to the new agricultural industries introduced into the Other World or they were displaced from the land. Trying to maintain themselves, they acquired debt. The World Bank, United Nations (UN), and nongovernmental organizations (NGOs) extended loans to farmers to buy seed, equipment, and fertilizer. Credit was not extended to women. Having no access to either economic resources or to technical training, they were marginalized and excluded. Even in North Africa and Asia, where women farmers first cultivated cotton and rice, women became irrelevant to commercial agriculture.

Forests, along with other natural resources, were placed under new ownership. Extracting timber became a commercial enterprise. Forests had traditionally been the source of firewood for heating and cooking; for fruits, plant products, clothing, and important herbs in medicinal preparations; and for small and large animals for food and other necessities. Now women were excluded from forestlands that had always been crucial to their way of life.

Like other natural resources, mines were claimed for commercial use. Minerals and ores were important materials for shaping farming and household implements. In the new system, tools could only be purchased with hard currency. Without currency, women did without. In many areas of the world, women

Processing Silk: This woman is operating a machine that unrolls the cocoons of silkworms to make thread.

SOURCE: *Joe Weatherby*

had traditionally managed fisheries and brought home the catch to feed the family and sell at market. With colonialism and modernization, commercial companies took the place of women.

Urbanization (the rise of cities) developed from the economic needs of the Industrial Revolution. Factories for production, banks for finance, and offices for government and commercial operations were built. Industrialization required urbanization; urbanization brought with it modernization. Villages developed into cities with electricity, telephone and telegraph communications, water and sanitation systems, contemporary buildings, roads and railroads, and other essentials of modern city life. Jobs were centered in cities, and both men and women migrated to them out of economic necessity. Men took jobs in industry and in low-waged building projects. Women worked in industry too, primarily in textiles and parts assembly for manufactured goods. Where women could not find jobs, they turned to earning wages by domestic labor or prostitution to survive. Apart from traditional families and clan protection, women became even more vulnerable to violence, disease, and isolation.

Modernization was harsh for women. Where once there was food aplenty, now cash crops like tobacco and sugar were grown to support imperialist economies. Commercial forests, mines, and fisheries claimed economic enterprises. In many places, men traveled to far-off plantations, mines, and cities for

Making Quilts: At a factory in Suzhou, China, women stretch silk to make the filling for fine quilts.

SOURCE: *Joe Weatherby*

work, leaving women to tend to home. Family life became fragmented. Young people, male and female, traveled to cities out of economic necessity. Scarcity of food and other necessities increased. Coping with scarcity became a woman's concern.

WOMEN AND THE EVOLVING OF NATIONALISM

The colonial era was disrupted by the economic and political events of the twentieth century: the Great Depression and World War II. Major realignments of power occurred, and many areas of the world experienced an explosion of newly independent states. The spirit of *nationalism,* a political philosophy that holds that the welfare of the nation-state is paramount, spread. Nationalism, however, necessarily treats individual rights and group rights within the society as secondary. Women, in particular, have had to take a back seat to nationalism.

In 1945, 51 nations formed the UN. Since then, many new nations have formed: 189 nations are now UN members—most of these come from the Other World. The original 51 nations of the UN had been in existence for many years and had long-standing political and economic structures, clear geographic boundaries, and an established national identity. In contrast, the new nations created after World War II were created out of the colonial lands with arbitrary boundaries and a legacy of dependence upon colonial powers. Nation building required citizens to take on a national identity to serve as an empowering ideology. This proved difficult in some places where governments attempted to oversee a coalition of various competing cultures. In other places, religious belief and cultural patterns initially helped to forge a new identity. In the North African nation of Algeria, for example, the nationalist effort was imbued with strong family values and Arab-Islamic codes prescribing women's roles. Upon independence from France in 1962, the new rulers of Algeria committed themselves to socialist modernization while attempting to set aside gender concerns in deference to national development. In 1992, however, civil war caused further disruptions. Terrorists and extreme political groups harassed women and created a general uneasiness in the population. A successful union of Islam with culture helped create a national identity for other nations in the Middle East, notably Iran, Iraq, and Lebanon. Palestinians, even without a homeland, also forged a national identity out of a merger of religious and cultural values.

A nation-state comprises many power relations within its boundaries: economic, political, legal, and cultural. The creation of legitimacy is a prime consideration. New nations have reduced and simplified social codes to give them legal force. Modern African nations, for example, used the "rule of law" to gain legitimacy. By law, women gained legal rights to schooling, property, and divorce. In practice, applications of law were sometimes arbitrary and women were denied rights. Many codes continued to emphasize the public-private divide. Modern legal processes emerged as a form of imperialist intervention. Although women worked with men in the struggle for independence, economic opportunity, basic human rights, and the right to vote, women's voices were ignored as new states worked to design new governing institutions. As nations evolved, the battle for human rights—including those of women—was viewed with the suspicion that champions for such causes were collaborating with an imperialist Western enemy.

The case of Afghanistan illustrates this point. The Taliban leadership dominated other tribes, establishing a very conservative religious policy that disallowed the education of women and relegated women to wearing the burka—the blue covering transforming a woman into a shapeless, faceless identity. Women teachers and professionals lost their jobs and were punished for appearing in public without a male protector. Women were confined to their homes. Before the fall of Taliban regime, protest was regarded as treason and could be met with harassment or death. Women have returned to school and to market, and many women removed the burka following the fall of this Afghan government.

In general, new nations have adopted bureaucratic forms of government in which decisions are made at the top of the organization and those below follow orders. These decision structures have served male interests. New governments pushed women aside and intruded in both private and public lives. Although patterns of opposition from women were different from one geographic space and one historical time to another, any resistance caused new social conflicts. In the end, women and the state viewed each other with suspicion.

The lack of a middle class necessary for running a democracy made governing difficult. Thus it is not surprising that in some nations, only women from the upper classes have been able to represent women's issues. In China, India, Pakistan, and the Philippines for example, political women came from the upper economic educated stratum of society. They knew little of the struggle of poor women. Their individual successes were dependent upon pragmatic male support in political parties and state government. Gender-specific issues, such as prenatal care, contraception, and women's property rights were discouraged. During the last two decades, women have begun to enter local politics and legal disputes to represent their interests.

In the process of formation, new nations oftentimes were incapable of providing needed basic welfare services and educational programs. In the Middle East, for example, women voluntarily assume a role in providing these services. In Bangladesh, women have had difficulty finding a presence in decision making for poverty reduction programs. In China, the situation is complex. China is not a new nation, but modern economy is new to it. The state has come to some recognition of the role women play in the economy, but the informal economy is often seen as perpetuating the marginalization of women by maintaining a male-dominated family structure. At the same time, the courtyard economy where women grow crops and make household items for the market provide women with both economic independence and social status.[5]

In new nations, government corruption has often developed as the way of doing business. Both the legal and illegal uses of power operate with little public accountability. Even with clear laws, rulers are often above the law and corruption is a part of everyday living. Some politicians, bureaucrats, and citizens give the law itself a low status. Capacity to enforce law is overshadowed by other interests, and the rule of law is undermined. Protest then replaces petition. Although their visibility makes them open to punishment, women in many parts of the world have come to organize to confront the nation's rulers, its rules, and its pattern of corruption. They have come to address two main issues of our time: nationalism and the oppression of women.

WOMEN AND GLOBALISM

Political independence and economic development are intertwined. Industrial economies, an integral component of the Western nation-states, formed the model for most of the new political entities. For the masses caught up in rising expectations, independence and nation building held great promise. A higher standard of living seemed a right that had been won through the struggle for nationhood. However, these new independent nations were vulnerable to external factors such as international economic and political ties; they were dependent on the outside world for trade, technology, economic aid, and military aid. They were weak in enforcing laws and regulating security. The governments often had little control over factors such as intimidation and corruption.

In many countries, national policies reflect a gender division of labor. Women are held to the low-paying jobs in the public economy or to the nonpaying jobs in service of the family. Poor women are forced to migrate because of economic necessity, not by personal choice. The traffic in prostitution, mail-order brides, and domestic services and slavery conditions in clothing assembly bear this out. In national legal and political systems, women do not have the same legal remedies available as men have, and they may be forced to deal with dangerous circumstances ending in abuse and sometimes death. Furthermore, states have been helpless to control human immunodeficiency virus (HIV)/acquired immunodeficiency syndrome (AIDS) spread through sexual activity as part of sexual tourism, especially in Asia.

Until recently, international organizations and development conferences have not interested themselves in women's lives, but have concentrated on those of men. The Fourth World Conference on Women was held in China's capital, Beijing, in September 1995. Over 50,000 members attended and declared that

Style Show: Chinese women modeling western dresses near Shanghai.

SOURCE: *Joe Weatherby*

women's rights are human rights. The Beijing Declaration and Platform for Action resulted. This platform encourages one hundred countries and UN organizations to make commitments to improve the status of women. They look for important changes in national policies that restrict women's rights, such as changes in inheritance laws and property rights. They ask countries to improve data gathering and set targets for improving the enrollment of women in primary school and improving female literacy. They look for countries and organizations to participate in international development in a coordinated way. The conference messages underscore key concerns. The first concern is that women's rights are human rights. Second, discrimination and violence against women must end. Third, equality for women is an important goal politically, economically, and socially. Fourth, issues of population control and development that include women's voices are global concerns. The platform builds on progress made in previous UN conferences on women—in Mexico City in 1975, in Copenhagen in 1980, and in Nairobi in 1985. Each conference has emphasized the role women have in development and the importance of protecting human rights.

In response to these global discussions, UN organizations, the World Bank, and the U.S. Agency for International Development have focused more attention on women as appropriate recipients of development efforts. These organizations have echoed the concerns of the Beijing conference and its call to action. A key element for many projects is increased school enrollment and literacy for girls as well as boys. Females who are educated tend to marry as adults rather than as adolescents. They have fewer children, they have access to important information on health and nutrition, and they have greater opportunities for better wages in the marketplace. Other international conferences related to poverty

TABLE 4.1   WOMEN'S POLITICAL AND SOCIOECONOMIC STANDING IN THE OTHER WORLD (UNITED NATIONS RANKINGS)

Country	Gender Development Index Rank	Women's Income as a Percent of Men's
Chile	46	22%
Cuba	69	31%
Mexico	66	26%
S. Korea	37	29%
Thailand	40	37%
China	93	38%
India	128	25%
Egypt	111	25%
Zimbabwe	118	38%

SOURCE: UNDP, Human Development Report 1998. New York: Oxford University Press, pp. 133–138.

have also begun to give prominence to those projects that address the status of women and the feminization of poverty. The 1994 International Conference on Population and Development stressed this point in their examination of health and reproductive rights: increasing female education is necessary for population control.

It is increasingly difficult for organizations such as the UN and World Bank to ignore the plight of women. International conferences demand that women's voices be heard and that human rights abuses be addressed. In the 1990s, both the UN and World Bank developed as goals the improvement of the lives of women. In response to pressure from women's networks, international organizations have directed themselves toward improving literacy of women and increasing female enrollments in school. They have also urged nations to dedicate themselves to the same goals. In addition, NGOs have begun to focus on women as being key to economic development efforts. Programs are designed to help women become knowledgeable about contraception and family planning, and to improve nutrition and prenatal care. Women's needs are considered, such as drilling new wells for drinkable water, designing improved cooking methods using little available fuel, and providing small loans to women for starting businesses that market their products and crafts. These early efforts offer much hope.[6]

Women throughout the Other World

Special sections on women appear as Flashpoints in the area chapters of this book.

SUMMARY

The Other World is a difficult place for women. The legacy of *colonialism* stressed patriarchy and ignored the important economic and social roles women played in developing societies. *Nationalization* concentrated power into the hands of a few political leaders who saw women as marginal to the goals of forming a new government. Corruption also made women's lives difficult, as abuses against women often went unpunished. *Modernization* shifted populations to cities and shifted economic life from small farming plots to large agricultural businesses that pushed women into undesirable land. Sustaining human life became more difficult. *Globalization* brought international corporations into decision making regarding both social and economic policy. Economic opportunities have been meager. Women have been required to perform low-wage jobs. Their contributions to family economies have been underestimated. Women also have been subjected to violence, abuse, and trafficking. International conferences, like the one in Beijing, continue to press for change in women's status and to make women's rights an important issue in the human rights struggle.

ISSUES FOR DISCUSSION

1. Is development good news for women in the developing world?

Many think development will benefit all in a society. This is not always true. From the 1950s to the 1980s, women did not receive wage parity with men even in modern developing nations. Per capita income rose dramatically in many places in the Other World, but women continue to lag behind men. In some countries of Asia and Africa in particular, women have significantly less access to resources and to income opportunities. Primary school enrollment and literacy data continue to show a gender gap between women and men, even though many nations and international organizations stress gender equity. In some cultures, women provide the family's basic needs. Men in the family may decide to use earned income for business or personal gain. It is women in much of sub-Saharan Africa who must provide shelter, clothes, school fees, and medical care for themselves and for their children. Men may acquire radios, bicycles, and other objects for personal consumption. Children's nutrition and health actually has worsened in some countries even when per capita income increased. This pattern exists in Guatemala, Belize, Mexico, and India.

Women's work may not always provide economic opportunity. Where jobs are created for women, wages are low and women are forced to work two jobs: one at home and one in the formal economy. Working women in developing countries often put in 12 to 18 hours a day. The World Bank, the largest international aid agency in the world, now promotes economic opportunity for women in its development efforts. Women in Development program (WID) was created in 1977 to ensure that women were part of a project design. The program operated in a male-dominated agency with top-down directives. Later, in 1993, a Gender and Development (GAD) division replaced WID. Feminist critiques were critical. Since then, the World Bank has tried to listen to women's voices in designing its programs.

2. Can women find the opportunity for increased literacy, despite their secondary status in Other World societies?

Almost every international meeting on human rights and the eradication of poverty has targeted increased literacy for women, but the reality is that in many societies, women are not valued. School fees are expensive and young girls and women are needed at home to help with chores or to work in factories and plantations so the family can afford school and job opportunities for boys. Patriarchal attitudes persist and block potential benefits for women.

The UN Population Fund continues to track the close connection between education and fertility. The more education women have, the more likely they are to have small families. In the southern Indian state of Kerala, the fertility rate is low, 2.3 children per woman. Why is it so low when others may have three or four times as many children? Most claim it is because female literacy is 66%—many times greater than other areas of India. In addition, women of Kerala have social and legal status. They can inherit land, and families must pay a bride price to the bride's family when a marriage takes place. In other areas of the developing world, it is common for the bride's family to give money to the groom instead of receiving money. Many experts also believe that women with education appear to look for more equality in marital arrangements and for more economic opportunities for themselves and their children.

3. Can women in developing nations have a voice in government?

Today there are very few women running for political office and serving in legislatures in both the developed and developing worlds. Women's voices have been ignored, and women have been cast to the sidelines. Traditional society suggests that women restrict their efforts to the home rather than to public life. The burden of household management, childbirth, and care for children and the elderly remove women from having opportunities to learn about government offices and policy issues. Certainly low levels of literacy for females in many areas of the developing world play a big part in denying women a voice in government. International organizations have taken up the banner of equality in government and encourage women to become informed and to run for local, regional, and national offices. Feminist voices have collectively made a difference. Participating in meetings and organizations, they pressure for changes in both national and international policies that restrict women.

Economic development and literacy are prerequisites to more political opportunities. Women face a number of obstacles to gaining equity with men. In Asia and Africa, laws are often ignored. Without the ability to have voice or to protect property, women's lives continue to be determined by other persons and by other forces.

Improving the status of women is key to gender equity and to political voice. In Bangladesh, for example, the Grameen Bank gives women small loans to develop businesses. Participants become important parts of a local economy, raising domestic animals, making handicrafts, and growing important agricultural products for the market. They also have begun to pressure for a decision-making role in the life of the villages in which they live.

4. Will women gain control over their own reproductive decisions?

Economic and social development require population control. A major factor in population control is contraception. In the developing world, women often do not have access to information on contraceptive medications and devices, or they cannot participate in decisions to limit families. In addition, religious values, customs, and practices may militate against birth control. Contraception is often unavailable for women. They are encouraged to have more children, especially sons, because sons take care of their parents as they grow older. In some areas of India, for example, over half of the women over 60 years of age are widows. Without a spouse, they are dependent on family members or they are cast into the streets as beggars.

Economic development creates demand for family planning services. Economic security translates into a more equitable role in families and into a lesser need to have so many children to take care of them in old age. About 60% of Grameen Bank members have some kind of family planning. The members have begun to make decisions about their lives, and they have decided to have fewer children and to create a better economic situation for themselves.

5. What role should NGOs play in supporting human rights?

Human rights abuses abound. Women and children are particularly vulnerable. Women in many parts of the world deal not only with the dark side of poverty, natural disaster, and war, but they also face such abuses of human rights as widow burnings, bride killings, torture, rape, and forced prostitution. Should NGOs work in support of women's rights? Or should they leave the job to national and international courts and governments? The UN has committed itself to protecting human rights. However, issues concerning the rights of women are contentious. Traditional legal structures are threatened and legislation to protect rights and lives is slow in coming.

Economic conditions for rural women in particular have worsened in some areas of the world. The impetus to provide better protection and opportunities for women has been lost in regional wars and nationalist struggles. Some cultures and religious groups have criticized these efforts as Western intervention; others find the feminist movement threatening to traditional ways of doing things.

Review Questions

1. Can women in the Other World overcome the legacy of colonialism? Can governments find some way to increase opportunities for girls too?
2. Can women in developing nations find a place in governmental decision making at the local and national levels?
3. Will women ever overcome the dominance of patriarchy so that they can inherit property and enter into contracts? Is there any way to ensure fairness in property disputes?
4. Will modernization continue to displace women?
5. Will globalization help or hurt women in the Other World?

Key Terms

- **Victorian values**—Term describing strict gender roles for men and women during the rule of Queen Victoria of England in the mid and late 1800s.

- **Inheritance laws**—Laws determining who gets what property when a person dies.
- **Literacy**—Ability to read and write.
- **Population control**—Use of government programs to limit family size, usually through education, contraception, sterilization, and/or abortion.
- **Courtyard economy**—Garden production for family use and market sale, usually referring to women's garden production in China.
- **Feminism**—Concept related to women and women's struggle for status and equity with males.
- **Equity**—Concept of fairness, usually comparing those who are able to receive benefits of society and those that do not.
- **Human rights**—Ability to enjoy basic freedoms without undue restraint.
- **Contraception**—The artificial prevention of the beginnings of human pregnancy.

Useful Web Sites

http://www.unifem.undp.org
http://www.caa.org
http://www.womenwatch.org
http://www.feminist.org
http://www.fsk.ethz.ch

Notes

1. See the essays in Uma Narayan, *Dislocating Cultures: Identities, Traditions, and Third World Feminism* (New York: Routledge, 1997).
2. See Mary Poovay, Catherine R. Stimpson, eds., *Uneven Developments: The Ideological Work of Gender in Mid-Victorian England* (Chicago: University of Chicago Press, 1999).
3. This is a simple summary from Georgina Waylen, *Gender in Third World Politics* (Boulder, C.O.: Lynne Rienner Publishers, 1996).
4. A discussion of debt appears in the United Nations Development Programme, *Human Development Report 1999* (New York: Oxford University Press, 1999), pp. 81–114.
5. See Nalini Visvanathan, Lun Duggan, Laurie Nisonoff, eds., *The Women, Gender and Development Reader* (New York: St. Martin's Press, 1997).
6. The World Bank annually provides data and analysis on both program efforts, and on economic indicators. See World Watch Institute and Population Action International, *Entering the 21st Century, World Development Report 1999/2000*, and *Attacking Poverty, World Development Report 2000/2001* (New York: Oxford University Press, 2000; 2001).

For Further Reading

Ahmed, Leila. *Women and Gender in Islam.* New Haven, Conn.: Yale University Press, 1992.

Bayes, Jane H., Tohidi, Nayereh Esfahlani (eds.). *Globalizations, Religion, and Gender: The Politics of Implementing Women's Rights in Catholic and Muslim Countries.* New York: Palgave Macmillan, 2001.

Datta, Rekha, and Kornberg, Judith (eds.). *Women in Developing Countries: Assessing Strategies for Empowerment.* Boulder, C.O.: Lynne Rienner Publishers, 2002.

Edwards, Michael, and Gaventa, John (eds.). *Global Citizen Action.* Boulder, C.O.: Lynne Rienner Publishers, 2001.

Jabri, Vivienne, and O'Gorman, Eleanor. *Women, Culture, and International Relations.* Boulder, C.O.: Lynne Rienner Publishers, 1999.

Kelley, Rita Mae, Bayes, Jane H., Hawkesworth, Mary E., and Young, Brigitte (eds.). *Gender, Globalization, and Democratization.* New York: Rowman & Littlefield Publishers, 2001.

Kumar, Krishna (ed.). *Women and Civil War: Impact, Organizations, and Action.* Boulder, C.O.: Lynne Rienner Publishers, 2001.

Narayan, Uma. *Dislocating Cultures: Identities, Traditions and Third World Feminism.* New York: Routledge, 1997.

Scott, Catherine V. *Gender and Development: Rethinking Modernization and Dependency Theory.* Boulder, Co.: Lynne Rienner Publishers, 1996.

Tulchin, Joseph S. *Democratic Governance and Social Inequality.* Boulder, C.O.: Lynne Rienner Publishers, 2002.

Visvanathan, Nalini, Duggan, Lun, Nisonoff, Laurie (eds.). *The Women, Gender and Development Reader.* New York: St. Martin's Press, 1997.

Waylen, Georgina. *Gender in Third World Politics.* Boulder, C.O.: Lynne Rienner Publishers, 1996.

CHAPTER 5

Latin America

Reginald Gooden

*[Latin] America is ungovernable, the man who serves a
revolution plows the sea; this nation will fall inevitably into the
hands of the unruly mob and then will pass into the hands of
almost indistinguishable petty tyrants of every color and race.*

ATTRIBUTED TO SIMÓN BOLÍVAR BY GABRIEL GARCÍA MÁRQUEZ IN HIS
NOVEL *THE GENERAL IN HIS LABYRINTH*

Latin America, a large portion of the world, is located generally south to southeast of the United States. Traditionally, *Latin America* refers to those countries settled primarily by the Spanish and Portuguese. Portions of this area were also influenced by the British, the French, and to a lesser degree, the Dutch.

Latin America was the first of the Other World regions to experience European
colonialism, and it has been struggling with the consequences of political liberation from Europe for at least a century longer. The countries of the Other World
have had similar experiences in their courses toward independence and in their
struggles for political and economic development. One of the differences between
Latin America and the others is that it shares the hemisphere with a nation that underwent European colonialism but then grew to be the dominant world power.

A major theme of this chapter is the external domination that affects the development of public institutions. At just about the time that most of Latin America
had succeeded in winning independence from Spain and Portugal, the United
States proclaimed the Monroe Doctrine, and the evolution of its various interpretations and applications was keenly felt.

After an initial overview of the geography of the region, specific emphasis
will be given to the legacy of colonization and the subsequent movements for political and economic independence. Along with much of the Other World, Latin
America is still pursuing the path to development and economic independence.

Colonialism gave way to neocolonialism; what these terms mean make up much of the subject matter of this chapter.

Some of Latin America's demographics and social characteristics are contrasted in Table 5.1. In addition to the political and physical maps of Latin America, this table will be useful as various countries are discussed. Three case studies illustrate the different paths to independence taken by Cuba, Mexico, and Brazil. The chapter concludes with the Flashpoints on current troublesome areas and issues.

As we move into the next millennium and the climate of the cold war recedes, the continent faces a promising future at the 500th anniversary of its European discovery by Cristóbal Colón.

GEOGRAPHY

The geography of Latin America is diverse (see Figure 5.1 on page 112) and has presented the region with difficult communication problems, some of which were not overcome until the development of commercial air travel. Even in those places where the mountains did not hinder travel, impenetrable vegetation or treacherous soils did. For example, in the middle of the nineteenth century, when a railroad was being built across the isthmus of Panama, the laborers awoke in the morning to find no trace of the railroad bed they had constructed the previous day; it had submerged into the unstable sand as they slept.

Geologically, an abrupt break in the North-South flow of mountain ranges that characterizes western North America occurs about midway through Mexico. Here a chain of volcanic mountains heads in a West-East direction through southern Mexico, Guatemala, and Honduras and across the Caribbean floor to form Jamaica, southeastern Cuba, Hispaniola, Puerto Rico, and the Virgin Islands. Connecting this region to South America are two chains of volcanic ridges that make up the Lesser Antilles and the highlands of El Salvador, southwestern Nicaragua, Costa Rica, Panama, and western Colombia.

In western South America lie the Andes, which contain some of the highest peaks in the Americas. Located at altitudes of more than 10,000 feet, mountain passes tower 3,000 to 4,000 feet over similar passes in the North American Sierra Nevada and Rockies. Mt. Aconcagua (22,835 feet) is the tallest mountain in the Western Hemisphere. The older highlands of Brazil and Guiana are located on the eastern part of the continent. Between these highlands, heading North, East, and Southeast, respectively, lie the plains of the Orinoco and Amazon rivers as well as the rivers flowing south into the La Plata estuary.

The mountains of Central and South America contributed to the rise and development of the high pre-Colombian civilizations of the Aztecs, Mayas, and Incas in several ways. They offered a variety of altitudes and climates, which allowed for a broadly based pattern of food production. These mountainous soils were not subject to the debilitating leaching action suffered by land in the tropical rainforests. This generous combination of factors was further enhanced by the

TABLE 5.1 CHARACTERISTICS OF LATIN AMERICAN COUNTRIES

Country	Population (millions)	Population Growth Rate (%)	Infant Mortality Rate	Population under 15 Years of Age (%)	Life Expectancy	Urban Population	Literacy Rate	Arable Land	Per Capita GNP ($U.S.)
Caribbean									
Bahamas	0.295	1	18	30	71	88	98	1	20,100
Cuba	11	0.39	8	21	76	75	96	24	1,560
Dominican Republic	8	1.64	41	35	73	64	82	21	5,000
Grenada	0.9	-0.36	11	38	65	37	85	15	3,500
Haiti	7	1.39	96	41	49	35	45	20	1,300
Jamaica	3	0.46	13	30	75	56	85	14	3,300
Middle America									
Belize	0.25	2.75	31	43	71	54	93	2	3,000
Costa Rica	4	1.69	13	32	76	48	95	6	6,700
El Salvador	6	1.87	27	38	70	46	71	27	3,000
Guatemala	13	2.63	45	42	66	39	56	12	3,800
Honduras	6	2.52	40	43	70	52	73	15	2,400
Mexico	100	1.53	23	34	71	74	90	12	8,300
Nicaragua	5	2.2	39	40	69	56	66	9	2,500
Panama	3	1.34	23	31	75	56	91	7	7,300

South America

	Population	Population Growth Rate	Infant Mortality Rate	Population Under 15	Life Expectancy	Urban Population	Literacy Rate	Arable Land	Per Capita GDP
Argentina	37	1.16	18	27	75	90	96	9	10,300
Bolivia	8	1.83	60	39	64	62	83	2	3,000
Brazil	173	0.94	34	29	63	81	85	5	6,100
Chile	15	1.17	10	28	76	85	95	5	12,500
Colombia	40	1.68	23	32	70	74	91	4	6,600
Ecuador	13	2.04	29	36	71	64	90	6	4,800
Guyana	7	-0.1	124	43	64	32	36	2	1,180
Paraguay	6	2.64	35	39	74	55	92	6	3,700
Peru	27	1.75	37	35	70	72	89	3	4,300
Suriname	0.43	0.65	26	32	71	74	93	0	3,500
Uruguay	3	0.77	13	24	75	91	97	7	8,600
Venezuela	24	1.6	26	33	73	87	91	4	8,500
Comparison States									
Austria	8	0.25	5	17	78	65	100	17	22,700
Hungary	10	-0.33	9	17	71	64	99	51	7,400
Ireland	4	1.16	6	22	77	59	100	13	18,600
USA	276	0.91	7	21	77	76	97	19	31,500

SOURCES: Population, Infant Mortality Rate, Population Under 15 Years of Age, Urban Population, Literacy Rate, and Per Capita GDP from *The World Almanac and Book of Facts, 2001.* Population Growth Rate, Life Expectancy, and Arable Land from *CIA World Factbook, 2000.*

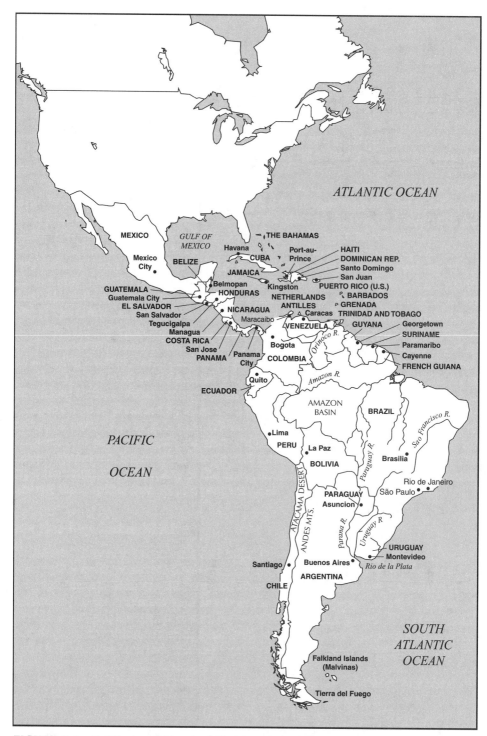

FIGURE 5.1 Political and Physical Characteristics of Latin America

availability of a reliable source of water. In South America there was the added benefit of a substantial source of fertilizer to be mined from the Guano Islands off the Peruvian coast. All of these factors combined to create an environment conducive to the production of food needed to support a large population. These large concentrations of people would later be exploited by the *conquistadores* to mine the gold and silver of the mountains. In fact, the administrative center of the Spanish viceroyalty of New Spain was established at the capital of the Aztec empire, Tenochtitlán, which in time became Mexico City.

PEOPLE

In dealing with an area of hemispheric proportion, we should not be amazed by the cultural and physiological variation among the Amerindians present when the first Europeans arrived. These native peoples ranged in sophistication from very primitive to the highly civilized cultures of the Aztecs in northwest and central Mexico, the Mayas in Guatemala and Yucatán, the Chibchas of the Colombian highlands, and the Incas in the highlands of Peru, Ecuador, Bolivia, and northern Chile. Their control of the environment was sufficient to account for three-fourths of the population of the area at the time of discovery by the Europeans. Those of the native peoples that remained were relegated to isolated and often inhospitable regions, where they sought refuge from the more successful and aggressive cultures.

The arrivals from Spain and Portugal were themselves a rich mixture of cultures and races that had swept across the Iberian Peninsula since the time of the Roman conquest. The Christian reconquest of Spain over the Muslims and the later persecution of the Jewish population promoted an overwhelming degree of fervent proselytizing when the Spanish and Portuguese encountered the pagan populations in the New World.

It is estimated that the native populations suffered a mortality rate of 45 to 90 percent during the first century of contact with the Europeans.[1] This population decline contributed to the forced importation of African slaves. The coastal regions, which grew one of the primary cash crops of the hemisphere, sugar cane, did not have "reliable" sources of native labor. The Indians either died or were able to escape to the interior, which induced the Europeans to bring in Africans as slaves.

Although the dominant religion in Latin America is Roman Catholicism (see Box 5.1), the influence of the African religions of the slaves had an important impact on the region's religious culture. Blending African gods with Christian saints, the African religions produced such exotic rites as *Candomblé* in Brazil and *Voodoo* in Haiti and Cuba.

Diversity and combination are two important characteristics of Latin American people; the third is the high population growth. Africa may have a higher birthrate, but the population growth in Latin America is among the highest in the world because the relative improvement in health standards has reduced the death rate. Today, more children are surviving, and this is producing volatile social and political results. Population pressure is increasing, requiring more producers

BOX 5.1 LIBERATION THEOLOGY

Along with the military and the landed oligarchy, the Roman Catholic Church has been a major influence in Latin America. This triumvirate of power dates to the original conquest of the continent, when the church was given the responsibility of Christianizing the "savages." As in Europe, powerful families would be linked to the ecclesiastical hierarchy, providing sons to serve as bishops, archbishops, and cardinals. Its traditional link with the establishment has generated antagonism between the church and reform movements in the past—often carried to bloody extremes, as with the *cristero* rebellion in Mexico during the 1920s and 1930s. For a long time the church had helped to postpone social unrest by preaching a doctrine of passivity and resignation with one's earthly condition. The Catholic Church is itself now undergoing a dialogue concerning its function. Confronted by the blatant social injustice that typifies the life of most of its membership in Latin America, increasing numbers of priests have accepted different strains of church doctrine, which sympathize with the downtrodden, and have combined them into a coherent philosophy that has come to be known as liberation theology. This new perspective has rekindled hope and enthusiasm as well as stimulated practical consequences in the form of community organization. Expectations and demands usually follow when people come together to discuss scriptural passages. These ecclesiastic communities have in turn provoked vicious counterattacks by groups that feel threatened by the prospects of social and economic reform.

Priests and laypersons have been assassinated or marked for extermination. The murderers are often linked with reactionary members of the establishment, who have seldom been brought to trial and are yet to be convicted and punished by a court of law.

Different interpretations of the responsibilities of the Roman Catholic Church to the needs of the oppressed have created tensions not only within the ecclesiastical hierarchy but also between that church and the political power structure. Cardinal Paulo Evaristo Arns, who served as archbishop of São Paulo, Brazil—the largest archdiocese until it was split into five smaller ones in 1989—created a commotion when he sold the official residence and surrounding park to raise money to pay the church workers caring for the slum dwellers. During the dictatorship (see the case study of Brazil), he documented the widespread use of torture against the opponents of the government.

In Guatemala, Roman Catholic Bishop Juan José Gerardi Conedera was bludgeoned to death with a brick on April 1998, two days after he released a report blaming the military for the preponderance of the 200,000 deaths in that country's 36-year civil war. Almost three years later, June 2001, three members of the military were sentenced to 30 years in prison and Fr. Mario Orantes, the bishop's assistant, was sentenced to 20 years as an accessory in the bishop's murder. The hunt for the killers was prolonged by death threats to those investigating the crime. Witnesses and several judges left the country. During the trial, grenades were thrown into Judge Jazmin Barrios' back yard and drive-by shooters targeted her house.

(In the section on the troubles in Chiapas, Mexico, we will introduce another clerical champion of the poor indigenous peoples, Samuel Ruiz, Bishop of San Cristobal.)

to develop a more productive agriculture. Some countries, like Brazil, have vast unsettled regions and are able to relieve the pressure by promoting colonization of the interior. Unfortunately, when this settlement is done carelessly, an ecological disaster can occur as tracts of primeval forest are slashed and burned. In areas where there is no room for expansion, the population pressure may cause migration from thousands of depleted, unproductive minifarms into the cities. Other refugees cross international frontiers and bloody clashes result—one that occurred between El Salvador and Honduras in 1969 is known as the "Soccer War."

HISTORY

The Colonial Experience

During the fifteenth century, the monarchs of Castile and Aragon were, like their colleagues in other parts of Europe, consolidating power. The system of government used by Queen Isabella to unify her strife-torn realm was later transferred to the New World. To achieve the unification of Spain, the Spanish had to deal with the Moors, Muslim inhabitants originally from North Africa. To the Catholic Spanish, the Moors were infidels. Ferdinand, king of Aragon, and Isabella, queen of Castile, joined forces in a military effort driven by religious beliefs to expel the Muslims from the region.

In both war and diplomacy, Aragon and Castile presented a united front, although in their internal political operations, Ferdinand and Isabella governed independently. Because the first expedition of Columbus was authorized and financed by the queen, the profits of the enterprise accrued to her and her heirs exclusively. As a result, Mexico and Peru were administered as separate territories, combined with the kingdom of Castile, and Isabella had sole possession of the sovereign rights as well as the property rights. Every privilege and all status, economic, political, and religious, came from her; it was on the basis of this arrangement that the conquest and occupation of the New World proceeded.[2]

So exclusive was Isabella's proprietary sense that during her lifetime only Castilian subjects were allowed to emigrate to the new dominions. A subject of her husband's kingdom required a special dispensation, and these were rare until her death, when Ferdinand assumed the regency. Along with the belief that only her subjects should enjoy the advantages of the new discoveries, there was also the fear that non-Castilians would introduce liberties alien to the much stricter and more centralized institutions controlling Castile. The traces of these Castilian institutions are still apparent in Latin America today (see Figure 5.2).

After the initial period, the Spanish monarchs asserted their supremacy more directly. Most of the privileges extended to the original discoverers were withdrawn, and the total political incorporation of the colonies under the sovereignty of Castile was established. This move was to sow the seeds of later defiance. The highest offices of Spanish colonial government were now exclusively filled by *peninsulares*, or those sent to America from Spain. The *criollos*, descendants of the original settlers, who considered themselves to be just as authentically Spanish as

FIGURE 5.2 European Colonialization of Latin America in 1790

the others, were barred from all forms of colonial administration except the *cabildo*, or town council. It was in the town council that the first cries for independence from Spain were uttered in the nineteenth century.

The independence movement in Latin America developed around the *cabildo*, which was the local unit of government. It was the only institution in which the *criollos* were allowed to serve, and as such it became a great source of prestige for American-born Spaniards. A *criollo*, or creole, meant a person of "pure" Spanish heritage who differed only in one respect from a *peninsular*, who could be a relative: The former was born in America and not in Spain.

The Wars for National Independence

The system of centralized government did not produce a smooth operation in the colonies. There were sporadic rebellions and uprisings, but these were not directed so much against the Spanish sovereign as against an oppressive local official. There were also rebellions by the Indian population motivated by reactions against their deplorable situation. In fact, it was the distant, but relatively humane, policies promulgated by Spain that tended to mitigate the abuses heaped on the indigenous people by the colonists. The isolation of the formal seat of power from the daily practical problems of governing engendered the local response of "I obey but do not comply" to the administrative directives arriving from Spain. In effect, the colonists were practicing self-government, but in the tradition of authority flowing from the top down. This system tended to stifle development at the grass roots. These "roots" have yet to take hold in a friendly political environment.

With the early exceptions of the United States in 1776 and Haiti in 1804, the wars of national liberation were not initially guided by the liberal ideas produced by the Enlightenment. In Spanish America, the wars of national independence had their origin in the continuing loyalty to the crown. The anticlerical theme of the French Revolution was opposed by the loyal subjects of the Spanish Crown. The attempt by Napoleon Bonaparte to install his brother, Joseph, on the Spanish throne in 1808 stimulated organized opposition in the form of local juntas both in Spain and America. The word *guerrilla* was coined during this time. In Spanish, *guerrilla* means "small war" and refers to the resistance directed against the occupying French troops by Spanish nationalists.

As part of its colonial relations, Spain had insisted on the doctrine of mercantilism. This theory prohibited trade between the colonies and non-Spanish ports, effectively excluding creole businesspersons from the profits made by the enfranchised merchants sponsored by the Crown. Later, in the nineteenth century, as English and North American traders gained access to Latin American ports, local merchants, who now enjoyed the profits earlier reserved for privileged *peninsulares*, began to uphold the free-trade doctrines of Adam Smith.

The Napoleonic interlude allowed the colonists to enjoy the results of Enlightenment thought and policies such as equal participation in the empire and proportional representation in the Spanish parliament. Others suggested experimenting with constitutional monarchy. Although the *peninsulares* and *criollos* could unite in their nationalistic opposition to France, they soon fell apart over their visions of life in America after Napoleon.

The clash of ideas soon broke out in armed conflict between the royalists and revolutionary leaders such as Simón Bolívar. As a student in Caracas and Europe, Bolívar had been impressed by the liberal ideas of Rousseau and the French *philosophes*. Returning to Latin America, he soon joined those in Venezuela who were plotting independence.

The possibility of reverting to an earlier time again under Spanish domination after savoring some of the fruits of freedom eventually tilted the controversy in Latin America toward independence. By the summer of 1825, the last stronghold of royalist opposition was defeated in Upper Peru. This territory was subsequently renamed Bolivia in honor of the liberator.

The revolutionary wars in Spanish South America were initiated and fought by the middle class in an effort to determine who among them, *peninsular* or *criollo*, would govern. In Mexico the movement took on a different hue. There, from the beginning, the independence movement had the look of class war as the Indians, the mestizos, and the have-nots rose up against the haves. The rebellion began in the provinces, led by a priest named Miguel Hidalgo y Costilla. On September 15, 1810, the ringing of the church bell in Dolores announced the start of the Mexican war of independence. The rebels, armed with farm implements, were soon defeated, and the liberation of Mexico was quelled for the time being.

In Spain, a revolt forced the king to establish a liberal constitution, the anti-clerical tenor of which so appalled conservative Mexicans that they organized a new revolt against Spain. The leader of this movement was Agustín de Iturbide, who had joined earlier with Spanish loyalists to defeat the revolt launched by Father Hidalgo. Iturbide proclaimed three notions that had popular appeal: the exclusiveness of Roman Catholicism, to be the only faith tolerated in the country; the equality of Spaniards and Mexicans; and an offer to the king to reign over an independent Mexico as a constitutional monarch. When the council in Mexico City took its oath to support the liberal Spanish constitution, Iturbide and his followers declared the independence of Mexico. In May 1822, the junta proclaimed him Emperor Agustín I. Glory was short-lived for the 39-year-old emperor. He was executed by General Antonio López de Santa Anna and the liberals in 1824. Mexican conservatives would have to bide their time as the liberals assumed control of the country.

The independence of Brazil took a different course. On November 29, 1807, as the invading French army came in sight of Lisbon, the Portuguese court sailed down the Tagus River on British ships en route to Brazil. After reaching Bahia, the original colonial capital, the royal court moved on to Rio de Janeiro, which was established as the new seat of the empire. This was the only time that a king ruling from America was the head of a European state. The arrival of the Portuguese court stifled the development of the juntas, which had emerged everywhere else in Latin America, where the great distance between the colonies and Spain had promoted local government.

When the French were finally repulsed, the Portuguese demanded the return of their king, Dom João, who reluctantly departed for Lisbon, leaving his son as regent in Brazil. The independence fever persisted in Brazil. Brazilian representatives to the parliament in Lisbon were slighted by not being allowed to participate fully in debates. They remembered the recent days when they were allowed to play a more important role in the creation of policy. In the presence of this mounting resentment against the metropolis, Brazilian independence came rather quietly. The regent became increasingly sympathetic to the Brazilian cause and refused the summons to return to Portugal. On September 7, 1822, the regent heard the news that his liberalizing decrees had been invalidated and that he himself had been judged a Portuguese traitor. He stripped the Portuguese colors from his uniform and declared, "Independence or death. We are separated from Portugal."

His declaration was popularly received, and the regent was installed as the constitutional Emperor Dom Pedro I by the council in Rio de Janeiro. The fact that Brazil had gained its independence without straining the government institutions already in place allowed it to avoid much of the internal strife that was to plague the post-independence political, social, and economic development in the rest of Latin America.

Postcolonial History and the Beginnings of U.S. Involvement

One abiding concern of the Latin American governments for much of the remainder of the nineteenth century was the designs that Europe and the United States had on their newly won independence. The United States has played a greater role in the affairs of Latin America than it has in any of the other areas under discussion in this book.[3] Many of the domestic and foreign policies of the nations of the hemisphere are carried out under *yanqui* influence.

On December 2, 1823, in a message to Congress, President Monroe declared what has come to be known as the Monroe Doctrine. Written by Secretary of State John Quincy Adams, it contains three themes: the noncolonization principle, U.S. abstention from European involvements, and the exclusion of Europe from the Western Hemisphere.[4]

In 1845, war broke out between Mexico and the United States over the annexation of Texas. During the war, the Polk administration indicated to the Californians that nothing would interfere with their entry into the Union if they were to gain independence from Mexico. President Polk invoked the Monroe Doctrine in an attempt to forestall French and British opportunism in California.

During the remainder of the nineteenth century, the United States limited the extent of the Monroe Doctrine to North America. Not until the advent of the Spanish-American War at the turn of the century, and the beginning of a boundless sense of "manifest destiny," did Latin America have further real cause to worry over *yanqui* intentions.

The policy of the United States assumed a more aggressive posture during the twentieth century. The "Roosevelt Corollary" to the Monroe Doctrine represents the policy in its most expansive phase. President Theodore Roosevelt's interpretation held that the United States should prohibit incursions by foreign creditor nations into the hemisphere by undertaking preemptive invasions and occupations of those Latin American countries that failed to honor their debts. Using this inflated view of its self-appointed role, the United States justified military intervention in many of the states of the Caribbean and Central America. This arrogance stimulated vociferous opposition throughout Latin America and created such deep suspicion on their part that they would not agree to a collective defense treaty until 1947.

With the development of the cold war in the late 1940s and the accompanying goal to contain communism, there was a tendency to suspect leftist and reform governments in Latin America. The Johnson Doctrine, pronounced in 1964, went so far as to promote the destabilization and overthrow of Marxist governments even if they had been popularly elected.

ECONOMICS

Several social and political phenomena occurred as the economy developed during the twentieth century. One was expansion of the middle class (professionals, shopkeepers, and small businesspersons) who serviced and profited from the export of raw materials and the import of finished goods. These people, not members of the landholding stratum, were concentrated in the cities. The other major change was the development of a more astute urban working class, resulting from the waves of immigrants, mostly from southern Europe, who were encouraged to come to Latin America to work in the new industries.

The presence of a large urban labor force coinciding with severe economic conditions made for a very unstable social milieu. The establishment and the traditional economic doctrine were discredited as a result of the Depression, and the people were willing to accept the stability proffered by a new military leadership. The result was the reemergence of the *caudillo,* the traditional "man on horseback," who had been such a common political landmark in earlier times. Unlike the early postindependence days, however, the new *caudillo* voiced a populist doctrine. Populism supplemented his military connection and mobilized mass support among the members of the working class, who were now tamed and incorporated into the political system. The influence of these leaders, Juan Perón in Argentina, Getúlio Vargas in Brazil, and Lázaro Cárdenas in Mexico, is still important today.

After World War II, Latin American countries ran up against a new reality: To remain competitive with a reindustrialized postwar Europe, they would have to match its new and sophisticated production methods. The most modern developments were occurring in Europe and the United States, and to obtain them Latin America had to produce the necessary foreign exchange. It could do so only by reverting to the sale abroad of its traditional export commodities, and a new cycle of "colonial" economy reemerged. Extreme examples are the so-called banana republics of Central America, who were so dependent on the North American market and shippers for their well-being that they had to place themselves at the dis-

Jamaican Bananas: This field worker carries bananas destined to be exported.

SOURCE: *Joe Weatherby*

posal of large corporations like the United Fruit Company. Added to these problems was the fact that the latest technology tended to be capital intensive. That is, it reduced the need for human labor, which is what Latin America had (and continues to have) in surplus. Reducing the size of the local labor force by using capital-intensive production methods compounded the problem because it reduced the demand for domestic products as it decreased employment.

Three Views on Development

Why is Latin America as a whole still considered underdeveloped? Several explanations have been offered to describe this phenomenon.[5] The most traditional explanation holds that there is no qualitative difference between Latin America and the other "advanced" nations of northern Europe and Japan. Development is just a matter of degree, and Latin America has not as yet launched itself. Advocates of this theory split into conservative and liberal camps. The conservative position often heard in the United States is that Latin America needs to create the proper climate for foreign investment. The foreign investments conservatives have in mind, in these cases, are generated by private funding. Such an approach works to the advantage of wealthy investors in the United States.

The liberal view argues for public investment. This view speaks of the need to develop an infrastructure, including transportation, communications, and power-generating systems, before the economy can be self-sustaining. Because the development of the infrastructure is so expensive and because everybody benefits, not just the industry that will be using the particular resource, it is felt that such projects should be public undertakings and the type of venture to which foreign governments could contribute. This was the kind of rationale that was heard during the mid-1960s in support of the Alliance for Progress. Of course, another reason given to support the Alliance was the urgency to provide an alternative to the rising popularity of the Cuban revolution and the temptation for many reformers to turn to radical and violent solutions to the problems facing their countries.

The second and more recent view goes under the name of dependency theory. Unlike the older perspective, dependency theory is pessimistic about the prospects for the evolution of healthy socio-politico-economic development in Latin America because its economies depend on external systems. The economics of the various Latin American countries have evolved as the result of a system that is driven by exports. To the degree that an infrastructure has been developed, its primary function is to transport the resources of the nation beyond its boundaries to foreign lands, thereby neglecting local needs. According to this theory, Latin America will never develop under these conditions. This view sees no improvement until the area, and all of the Other World for that matter, breaks out of the dependency mold. Because the problem is structural in nature, breaking out is equivalent to overthrowing the system. The United States has not been receptive to such "solutions" since Castro's experiment in Cuba. These two theories underlie much of the controversy about what needs to be done in Latin America today to achieve the lifestyle of the so-called developed nations.

The third answer to the lack of development is not economic in nature but, rather, explains the situation in historical terms. This theory claims that Castile, unlike many of the other countries in Western Europe, was particularly centrist in its political administration. In contrast with England, Castile lacked a "true" feudal system, did not have a Protestant and nonconformist religious tradition, and lacked the entrepreneurial establishment that caused England to be considered "a nation of shopkeepers." Even in those countries, like Mexico and Cuba, that had a true revolution (as opposed to the interminable round of palace coups endemic to the area), the end result was a centrist, authoritarian government. The three factors contributing to the rise of liberalism in North America were lacking in the Castilian political and economic tradition.

As mentioned in the previous section, this tradition of governmental centrism seems to be on the wane as Latin American governments experiment with reduced state involvement in the economy. We will be looking at specific examples of this trend when we turn to the case studies of Mexico and Brazil. The trend toward less government in the marketplace is there in other countries as well, with the exception of Cuba. Whether the hardships that reduced government subsidies in employment, food staples, transportation, and fuel are compatible with democratic government remains to be seen. The initial stages of economic neoliberalism were instituted by the military dictatorships of the 1970s, or, in the case of Mexico, by the dominant political party under the administrations of Miguel de la Madrid and Salinas de Gortari.

GOVERNMENT

In the 1970s, one could count the "free" governments of Latin America on four fingers: Mexico, Costa Rica, Colombia, and Venezuela. The major countries of South America—Argentina, Brazil, and Chile—had military-installed bureaucratic, authoritarian regimes. Authoritarian government also occurred in Uruguay, which had formerly been referred to as the Switzerland of South America because of its democratic tradition. The exception was Peru, which initiated a peculiar variation in that it was not controlled by the traditional power groups. Its government was able to institute some minor revolutionary reforms, including extensive land redistribution. Peru's experience resembled to a lesser degree the revolutionary governments of Mexico and Cuba of the 1920s and 1960s, respectively.

The bureaucratic-authoritarian regime was a phenomenon of the 1970s and 1980s and is distinguished from the tradition of authoritarian governments in Latin America by several characteristics. Military officers were not in charge of the different government agencies; instead, these offices were filled by career bureaucrats. The working class was eliminated from directly influencing policy because political parties and labor organizations were curtailed or prohibited altogether. The government favored the establishment and, to some degree, the middle class because groups from these sectors were in the best position to define policy and protect their interests as the influential bureaucrats came from their ranks. This condition resulted in an acute case of bureaucratic or military myopia, which interpreted all problems as technical in nature and reducible to an administrative solution rather than negotiation. This kind of government provided the appearance of stability so satisfying to foreign investors, and often succeeded in attracting business from abroad. In time, however, it aggravated and finally alienated the members of the domestic middle class. They may have originally welcomed the military "solution" to the rising social chaos, but in time felt threatened by the growing entry of foreign investment challenging their economic status.

As the tenuous base of support for the military from the middle sectors eroded under the economic strain of reentry into the neocolonial economic mode and growing economic indebtedness, the ruling groups exercised several options. One was to call for a constitutional convention and return power to the people, as the Brazilian military did in 1985 after 21 years in power. Another was to increase repression and attempt to suppress dissent, as happened in Chile under General Augusto Pinochet until the military returned to the barracks in March 1990 after 16 years of military dictatorship. In Argentina, the military attempted to divert rising discontent and defiance through a nationalistic diversion that led to the invasion of the Falkland Islands. Argentina was defeated in this 1983 war with England, and the country was so humiliated that the military lost all ability and will to continue the repression. It is inconceivable that regardless of their level of incompetence, the military rulers intended the outcome they obtained.

Conflict Resolution through Regional Organization: The Organization of American States

The notions of nonintervention and the sovereign equality of all states, along with the principles of mutual security, peaceful settlement of disputes, and a commitment to democracy and human rights, combined in three separate treaties to establish the Organization of American States (OAS). These treaties are the Inter-American Treaty of Reciprocal Assistance (Rio Treaty), 1947; the Charter of the Organization of American States (Charter of Bogotá), 1948; and the American Treaty on Pacific Settlement (Pact of Bogotá), 1948.

The Rio Treaty, which provides for collective defense under the provisions of Article 51 of the United Nations (UN) Charter, is seen as a regional arrangement, although the treaty makes no mention of this fact. This omission led to much controversy because all of the disputes in the area have a regional origin. According to Chapter VII of the UN Charter, every effort at achieving a peaceful settlement of regional disputes shall be exhausted before they are referred to the Security Council.

Problems arose between the United States and the other members of the OAS because North American administrations tended to interpret communist "intrusion" into the area as "external" aggression to be repulsed by the full force of "collective measures" (usually initiated and led by the United States). The Latin American states are usually more restrained in their interpretation of the "threat," seeing it as local in origin and protected against unsolicited interference by well-intentioned neighbors by the fact that all members of the organization have officially upheld the principle of nonintervention.

Because of the superior political, military, and economic power of the United States in comparison with all of the other members of the hemisphere together, another problem arises. Is the OAS a collective security arrangement in any authentic sense, or is it merely a convenient aggregation of states through which the United States can give a collective cast to its own unilateral decisions? It is often the case that in major controversies, such as the Dominican intervention in 1965, there is a struggle between the "Colossus of the North" and the other members of the OAS about which international organization should deal with the crisis. The United States likes to keep a crisis within the confines of the OAS and, hence, under its control; many of the other hemispheric nations would like to take it to the UN, where the United States can be balanced by Russia and the other major powers in the Security Council.

Given the differences in power between the United States and Latin America, why did not the latter reject the OAS as nothing more than a convenient apparatus for the United States to reimpose the Monroe Doctrine in a multinational disguise? The answer seems to be that the OAS is better than nothing or, worse, a return to the bad old days of unilateral *yanqui* intervention. Its existence at least confirms the legal equality of all states, a tenuous acknowledgment perhaps, but a straw that small states can grasp in disputes with larger states. Furthermore, because substantive policies must gain a two-thirds majority before adoption by the organization, it acts as a brake on actions contemplated by the United States. Thus, the OAS persists because it is of mutual benefit to the member states. The end of the cold war and Canada's recent membership in the organization should improve its effectiveness and economic development.

During the controversy between the Reagan administration and the Nicaraguan Sandinistas, the sister nations of the OAS asserted their independence from U.S. domination. The effort was led by President Oscar Arias Sánchez of Costa Rica, which borders Nicaragua to the south, who was fearful of being drawn into the conflict as had Honduras to the north, which was being used as a staging area for the *contras* in their effort to overthrow the Sandinista regime. Gaining the support of the other nations of Central America, President Arias was able to have his Peace Plan adopted in March 1988. It called for ceasefire, amnesties for the belligerents, peace negotiations, and the cessation of external support for the combatants. It also entailed the presence of the UN to guarantee the peace and future elections. With the Soviet threat diminishing, the balance was shifting away from concern with hemispheric security to the promotion of democracy.

In the summer of 1991, at its meeting in Santiago, Chile, the OAS resolved to take a more active role in promoting democracy in the hemisphere. This resolve was partly the result of Latin American displeasure with the recent U.S. invasion of Panama, but it also followed that all of the members at least nominally represented democratically elected regimes for the first time since the OAS was founded. Latin American democracies have an interest in telling the military not to interfere and were quick to adopt economic sanctions against Haiti in October 1991, when that country's military deposed the popularly elected Jean-Bertrand Aristide. In April 1992, the OAS met to denounce the termination of the democratic process in Peru by President Alberto Fujimori and the military. The organization sent a delegation headed by Secretary General João Baena Soares to convince the president to reverse the course that his "frustration" with the legislature had precipitated. As with Haiti and Panama, the OAS is in a difficult position; it is now on record as opposing undemocratic turns by governments, but it knows that the imposition of economic sanctions will hurt the innocent more than the guilty.

For example, after the initial effort by the OAS to restore Aristide had been vitiated by the insistence of the Bush administration (1989–1993) that Haitian plants associated with American corporations be exempted from sanctions, pressure finally had to be applied by the UN. The Security Council approved a blockade of the Haitian side of the island of Hispañola by the U.S. Navy on October 18, 1993. However, many of the Haitian elite profited from the embargo because they controlled smuggling and gained from the increased cost of gasoline on the black market. More pressure was needed to resolve the standoff between the

Haitian generals and the international organizations. The U.S. administration froze the American-held assets of the supporters of the military and suspended flights out of Haiti. The UN approved a resolution authorizing the use of force. President Clinton was able to overcome partisan politics in the United States by approving a last-minute attempt to reach an accord through the mediation efforts of a peace delegation comprising former President Jimmy Carter, Senator Sam Nunn, and retired General Colin Powell. They convinced General Cedras to accept a peaceful solution and withdraw from power. Simultaneously, President Clinton had dispatched an invasion force to Haiti. Those troops were already airborne as the discussions were concluding on September 19, 1994. To everyone's relief, the force was able to land on the island without opposition. As one can see, however, attempts to support democracy through the OAS test the patience of the oppressed.

Again, the impasse between the dedication to democratic governments echoed in the OAS resolutions and the "self-coup" (*auto golpe*) staged by President Alberto Keinya Fujimori in Peru illustrates the ironies hidden in what would appear to be obvious forces in collision: democracy and dictatorship. When Fujimori took office, the Peruvian economy was in shambles. Inflation was soaring out of control, and the previous socialist administration of President Alán García Pérez had defaulted on the country's external debt. Adding to the turmoil were the depredations of two guerrilla factions—the more notorious being the Shining Path (*Sendero Luminoso*), led by a former philosophy professor, Abimael Guzmán Reynos, who espoused a Maoist ideology.

Terrorists compound the economic problems of the countries in which they operate. Assassinations and destruction of property increase the price of doing business. Workers who fear extermination migrate, especially those in the middle class who are most often targeted by guerrillas and have the skills and means to seek employment elsewhere. Also, resources that go into buying protection, such as walls, insurance, police, and military, could more productively be spent on trucks and tractors. Terrorists are linked to the narcotics trade, which is used to finance their operations and introduces another avenue for corruption into the institutions and relations of a society.

Four different attempts to stabilize the economy had failed before Fujimori's inauguration. There are social and economic costs associated with stabilization plans, and each failure makes it more difficult to convince those that suffer that they should try again.

Frustrated by the legislature and what he perceived to be a corrupt judiciary, Fujimori instigated his coup d'état. The grip on the police and military was relaxed, and Peru rose in the ranks of those countries that are among the worst offenders of human rights. He instituted a severe economic reform (fujishock) along the lines prescribed by Washington and the IMF, which brought down the rate of inflation. Guzmán was captured and given a life sentence in September 1992. This outcome dimmed the exploits of the Shining Path. Fujimori then assuaged the ire of the democracies abroad by inviting them to supervise the election for a constitutional convention to be held later that year. The new constitution enhanced the powers of the president and allowed Fujimori to succeed himself in office. The relative stability associated with his administration led to his reelection in 1995 in a race against former UN Secretary General Javier Pérez de Cuellar (1982–1992). Not satisfied with two terms, Fujimori then fixed it so that he would win the April 2000 presidential election.

Within a year of securing the office for an unprecedented third term, the first of the "Vladivideos" emerged in March 2001. These were videotapes taken by Fujimori's intelligence chief, Vladimiro Montesinos, of officials, politicians, television stars, media moguls, generals, Supreme Court justices, and other well-known figures, plotting against the government. Hidden cameras had recorded these compromising activities for the purpose of holding the transgressors to their bargains. By November 2000, Fujimori's administration had collapsed and was replaced by interim President Valentín Paniagua.

Fujimori, who was attending an economic conference at the time, decided he would reclaim his Japanese citizenship and remain in Japan. Vladimiro Montesinos slipped out of the country but was eventually discovered hiding in Venezuela and brought back to Peru where he will stand trial. The Peruvians have demanded the extradition of Fujimori but so far, Japan has refused to comply, giving his dual Japanese citizenship as a rationale.

Another presidential election was held in April 2001, which required a runoff election in May between former President Alán García and the ultimate winner, Alejandro Toledo, a former shoeshine boy and the first Peruvian president of indigenous descent. After securing scholarships as a youth, he completed his formal education by receiving a Ph.D. in economics from Stanford University. He campaigned on the promise of achieving "capitalism with a human face." Peru will present him with a challenge. The fact that the Fujimori regime dismantled many of the political institutions may make it easier to achieve progress. On the other hand, the decade of corruption associated with the former administration may have enough residual influence to thwart reform. Ensconced in the high-security naval prison at the port of Callao, Montesinos misses his beachside mansion and the Jacuzzi he had installed in his office, but has been accused of using his cell phone to foment difficulties for the Toledo administration. As a lawyer for drug barons in the 1980s, Montesinos was quick to discern which judges, prosecutors, military, and police agents were malleable and which bankers were willing to launder funds. Awaiting trial for weapons smuggling to the guerrillas in Colombia, he can still pull enough strings to embarrass opponents. His former collaborators remain in strategic positions in the armed forces and the media.

The causes of violence persist in Peru and there is still devastating poverty and a chasm separating the poor from the economic and political elites. Authentic democracy will be postponed until these structural problems can be mitigated, but progress in that direction is more likely through greater opportunity for popular participation.

CASE STUDIES

MEXICO

Poor Mexico, so far from God and so near the United States.
JOSÉ DE LA CRUZ PORFIRIO DÍAZ

Under the leadership of Benito Juárez, Mexico experimented momentarily with republican institutions and a new constitution in the mid-nineteenth century. The period is known as the Reform. Out of this brief republican interlude Porfirio Díaz emerged, a man cast in the mold of the traditional Latin American dictator. Under his influence (1877–1911) the country underwent its first round of economic development, but the costs of progress were excruciating for the majority of the population.

Díaz and his administration came under the spell of the doctrines of the French philosopher Auguste Comte, who argued that social integration and development would occur if social scientists were in charge of state planning. A group of self-proclaimed social technicians surrounded the Mexican dictator and opened the country to thorough exploitation by foreigners. In four years railroad track increased fivefold as soon as Díaz granted the concession to external interests in 1880. Foreign trade increased by a factor of nine, and the United States became Mexico's chief trading partner.

Despite such progress, the Mexican middle class was excluded from decisions and became increasingly resentful of the foreigners, who flaunted a rich European lifestyle. The forces that would soon erupt into one of the few revolutions in Latin America gathered momentum with the exile of Díaz in 1911. These forces are personified by some of the famous leaders who emerged from that period: Emiliano Zapata, head of the peasant movement, who demanded land and the restoration of traditional communal holdings; Venustiano Carranza, who represented the landed oligarchy and was favored by the administration of President Woodrow Wilson; and Francisco ("Pancho") Villa, in command of what amounted to an agrarian proletariat that comprised cowboys, small ranchers, and agricultural workers from the northern state of Chihuahua. Mexico remained in turmoil until the presidency of Álvaro Obregón (1920–1924), who began a tradition of the peaceful devolution of power of Mexican presidents in the twentieth century. He also appreciated the need to reign in the turbulence unleashed by the revolution. There were hundreds of associations, armed bands, and ideological groupings that had to be organized and brought to heel if Mexico was to acquire the status of a civil society. The effort to legitimize the revolution found its expression in the formation of an official political party by President Plutarco Calles. This creation was initiated by the revolutionary elite and was imposed from the top down. Like many other political organizations in Latin America, it provided a structure through which the major social, political, and economic forces in the state could seek expression. It also provided a means by which they could be controlled by the establishment.

Elected in 1934, Lázaro Cárdenas is the most admired president in the hearts of the Mexican people and is seen as the embodiment of the revolution. He distributed 44 million acres of land to the dispossessed, almost twice as much as had all of his predecessors. Not all this land was turned over to individuals; much of it went into communal holdings that contained hundreds of families. One of his most popular acts, and one that fueled a sense of national pride, was the nationalization of Mexico's petroleum resources.

Although defeated in the July 2000 presidential election by the PAN (*Partido Acción Nacional*) and its candidate Vicente Fox, the National Revolutionary party as it was originally named, is still a formidable political organization in Mexico. As its current name implies, this is the organization that institutionalized the Mexican Revolution of 1910. It underwent several transformations and today is known as the Institutional Revolutionary party (PRI). As presently organized, it comprises three major sectors: labor, peasants, and a segment of the middle class and bureaucracy. Structuring the dominant political party so as to represent social sectors is consistent with the doctrine of corporatism. The notion that society is analogous to an organism has had prior advocates. The idea reemerged with vigor in Europe during the 1920s and 1930s, where it was given expression again in the doctrine of Italian fascism. The ideas crossed the Atlantic and found a friendly environment in such states as Mexico, Brazil, and Argentina. Normally, it is the state apparatus that organizes itself into sectors representing management, workers, and often, the different professions and trades, but because the PRI, for the last seven decades, has been synonymous with the state in Mexico, the party emerged as the final arbiter of all sectors constituting the society. The PRI is the dominant force in Mexican politics and until recently, the presumed winner in any partisan contest. This status is changing, and the transformation is contributing to the rise in social unrest presently occurring.

The president of Mexico had extraordinary power. Not only did he exercise all the traditional powers of a Latin American chief executive, but he was also the chief arbitrator of conflict among the groups constituting the sectors of the dominant party, as well as the chief determiner of who was to succeed himself in the presidency.

Since the 1970s, the sectors in Mexico's ruling party experienced increasing tension because of the growing pressures brought on by the need for development and repayment of the nation's debt. The strain tempted the party leadership to opt for a solution reminiscent of the Porfirio Díaz days and was represented outwardly by a succession of presidents from the technocratic and financial areas of the government bureaucracy. In the 1988 presidential election, Carlos Salinas de Gortari received 50.7 percent of the votes. In earlier times, that would have been an impossibly slim margin. Irregularities with the ballots were never resolved. His closest rival, and the person who claims to have been denied the victory through fraud, was not the candidate from the traditional opposition party of National Action (PAN), located on the right of the political spectrum. Rather, Cuauhtémoc Cárdenas, son of the revered Lázaro Cárdenas,

A Mexican Election Poster: Power to the people with Rafael García Vazquez.

SOURCE: *Joe Weatherby*

who bolted in opposition from the party his father helped to establish, led a leftist attack on the PRI under the banner of the emerging Democratic Revolution party (PRD).

President Salinas de Gortari instituted election reforms. These contributed to PAN victories in Baja California, Guanajuato, and Chihuahua. He also continued the process begun by his predecessor of moving the country's industry out of public control and into the private sector. These reforms have arrested the rate of inflation and increased economic growth. In 1993, Canada, the United States, and Mexico established a free-trade area for North America. Proponents of this extended market see it as a boon to the development of the larger region. If, in addition, the price of petroleum were to climb again, Mexico would be in a better position to address the narcotics trade, which continues to irritate relations with the United States. (See the sections on the Chiapas uprising and narcotics traffic for a more specific treatment of these issues.)

Another source of friction between the two countries is the flood of undocumented aliens from Mexico and Central America. Many of these people are fleeing stagnant economies or political repression at home. Their desperation makes them easy victims of abuses by predators along their journey to the United States. While residing in the United States, the fear of exportation often perpetuates their exploitation. President Vicente Fox, the victorious PAN candidate resulting from the reforms of the electoral system orchestrated by the PRI's President Ernesto Zedillo, has made the resolution of this source of conflict between the two nations a prime goal of his administration.

As many as three million Mexicans live in the United States illegally and the Fox administration wanted to reach an accord with the Congress of the United States that would grant them legal status by the end of 2001, but the terrorist attack on September 11 postponed the occasion. The opposition to this proposal counters that such an arrangement would be unfair to those who have complied with the law in obtaining legal status. The issue has been put on hold as a result of the terrorist attack on the United States.

Aside from the commitment to improve migration across the border separating the United States from Mexico, the new Fox administration has shown a more convincing pursuit of drug trafficking between the two countries. The corruption associated with the seven decades of PRI rule—and probably the major reason behind the defeat of the PRI as several generations of Mexicans had grown impatient with its policies—may be interrupted momentarily. There is presently more cooperation with the United States in pursuing narcotrafficking and the hope is that the Fox administration will make inroads into the ground lost to the drug cartels. Estuardo Mario Bermúdez, the new antidrug chief, said that the two countries are intensifying exchanges between police and prosecutors so that each side can learn how the other's system operates. The United States has increased funding for training from $4 million in 2000 to $10 million in 2001. On April 5, 2001, a 15,185-pound load of marijuana (the largest seized) hidden in a truckload of television sets was confiscated. A drug-sniffing dog alerted the officials. To protect the informer, the name and breed of the dog was not revealed.

BRAZIL

> *God is a Brazilian.*
> ANONYMOUS

Brazil's transition to national independence was relatively peaceful. Brazil had no military tradition and, therefore, avoided the phenomenon of dictatorial rule until much later. The army did not become a factor until it emerged as the result of a prolonged war initiated by the dictator of Paraguay in 1865. In 1889 the military declared the end of constitutional monarchy and the beginning of republican government. Since then, the military has been a dominant player in Brazilian politics.

As with the rest of Latin America, Brazil had a single-crop economy for most of its colonial history. Originally the crop was sugar, which was the force behind the establishment of slavery. Sugar plantations were concentrated in the northeast and had generated as much as one-third of Brazil's foreign exchange. Later, the dominant crop became coffee, which was grown in the southern highlands, and produced half the country's trade. The shift in crops from sugar to coffee also represented a geographic change in the economic fortunes of the respective areas. In modern times, the northeast has become one of the most depressed regions. Tremendous demographic pressure is exerted on the other areas as emigrants from the northeast populate the shantytowns overlooking large urban centers such as Rio de Janeiro. These economic refugees also trek into the formerly impassable jungles of the interior, following recent inroads by teams of bulldozers. Consequently, an important ecosystem in the midst of a tropical rainforest has now been breached and laid open to wanton exploitation of resources and the indigenous tribes.

Today, the government is focusing on underdeveloped regions of the fragile Amazonian ecology as a source of energy. Brazil relies on dams to provide 90 percent of its electricity. A drought in 2001 required the population to reduce its energy consumption by 20 percent, which added to the financial problems we will address later on. To cope with the demands of a population of 170 million whose consumption of energy has grown at a rate of 5.3 percent a year, the current government is planning the construction of the world's third largest dam on the Xingu River. In what some claim to be the largest excavation project since the Panama Canal, two channels a quarter of a mile wide and seven miles long will be carved out of the Amazon jungle to connect sections of the Xingu river for the purpose of reducing the area to be flooded, which has been projected to cover a mere 155 square miles. It is claimed that the project, to be completed by 2008, will generate 11,000 megawatts at a cost of $6.6 billion. Critics claim that aside from the environmental damage, the dam will displace indigenous populations and settlers, and will impede navigation. Furthermore, during the five-month Amazonian dry season, the water flow would lower the hydroelectric output to a yearly average of 5,000 megawatts instead of the more optimistic forecast.

The economic depression of the 1920s and 1930s compounded the political and social problems of a single-crop economy. Exercising a traditional role, the military stepped into the turmoil and installed a man who would influence Brazilian politics into the twenty-first century: Getúlio Vargas, a politician from the southern state of Rio Grande do Sul.

Vargas was quick to override the traditional autonomy of the states, which were organized around political machines led by local bosses. He replaced the governors with interveners and succeeded in augmenting the power of the federal government, which reached its apex on November 10, 1937, when Vargas proclaimed the New State, designed a new flag, and declared the new motto to be "Order and Progress." Order and progress was the battle cry of positivism, a doctrine imported from France that emphasized science and technology as the means of solving social problems. Earlier the doctrine justified revamping the curriculum of the military academy to emphasize science and engineering. Faith in the technological solutions promised by positivism continues to tempt military officers despondent over the apparent insurmountable problems facing their country.

During Vargas's tenure in the 1940s, the labor unions were brought under government control. Brazil achieved more stability, while remaining an authoritarian state. However, in the euphoria following the defeat of the Axis powers in World War II, it became harder to justify the dictatorship. Vargas attempted to widen his popular support by espousing a populist rhetoric and promoting anti-monopolistic policies with the intent of reducing foreign involvement in the domestic economy. This course alienated him from influential policymakers in the United States, and the army asked him to resign in 1945. He retired to Rio Grande do Sul and was elected a federal senator later in the year. Five years later, in 1950, he again won the presidential election. Although his program was moderate, the inflation rate would not abate, the balance of trade grew increasingly unfavorable, and the administration in the United States was having a difficult time convincing itself that it should assist Brazilian development with public funds.

Vargas was attacked from the left and right. The left denounced him for becoming a lackey of foreign exploiters, and the right claimed that his policies alienated Brazil from its allies. An assassination attempt on one of his vocal detractors was traced to a member of his own security guard. Although Vargas was innocent, the corruption that had begun to swirl around him must have depressed him to the point that he committed suicide. This act resulted in his martyrdom, and those who had exploited the issue of corruption against him soon found themselves on the defensive.

The legacy of Vargas continues to influence Brazilian politics. After a series of caretaker governments, President-elect Juscelino Kubitschek was allowed to assume office in January 1956. The vice president, João "Jango" Goulart, who was elected independently, won by a larger margin. Neither of them was able to win by more than a plurality. There was an attempt to deny them office by the anti-Vargas interests, but the major force in the military prevailed to support the constitution.

During the remainder of the 1950s, Kubitschek pursued a policy of economic development. The construction of a new national capital in Brasília was his lasting contribution in focusing development inward. But the great effort for economic advancement also brought rising inflation, which had to be addressed with unpopular programs. Adding to the problem was the fact that economic development resulted in a growing urban workforce, which grew in political sophistication as well as in numbers. Agricultural workers had become more active politically by organizing in "peasant leagues" to deal with their problems. These factors became a point of concern to the urban middle class, the landlords, and the military, which saw the leagues as threats to their social position.

Into this heated political atmosphere entered Jânio da Silva Quadros, who had risen quickly in the politics of the pivotal state of São Paulo. He offered a more positive program than the conservatives and at the same time avoided the rampant populism that alienated the middle class. The vice president was, again, "Jango" Goulart. The eccentric Quadros abruptly resigned from the presidency in an attempt to force the legislature's hand. This act precipitated a *coup d'état* by the military, which was troubled over the fact that the vice president was visiting the People's Republic of China.[6]

Carnival Participants in the Brazilian Colonial Capital of Bahia: A float depicts the IMF as "Uncle Sam" with the slogans hunger, misery, exploitation, violence, and oppression emblazoned on his jacket.

SOURCE: *Domingo/Lenderts*

The military relented after 16 months, but the Brazilian situation continued to deteriorate by the time João Goulart was allowed to assume the presidency. Attempting to deal with the economic impasse, President Goulart promoted a plan that sought to reduce inflation while simultaneously boosting growth. This plan devastated the economically vulnerable, further aggravating their discontent. Increasing acts of insubordination in the military worried the generals, and the agricultural establishment was resentful over an agrarian reform program that did not compensate them adequately for expropriated land. In the United States, the Johnson administration (1963–1969) was prepared to assist the Brazilian military with the intervention of naval and airborne forces if necessary.[7]

The recent Cuban revolution was too vivid in the minds of the Brazilian middle class, and when the military took control on March 31, 1964, they sighed with relief. Suspending democratic practice provided the stability needed to force the reforms that the technocrats felt would develop the country. After several years there was talk of the "Brazilian miracle" as economic growth attained the heights of the Kubitschek era; meanwhile, the shantytown dwellers were ground down into further poverty.

After 21 years of dubious accomplishments, the "legalists" in the military were able to convince the hardliners to allow the people to choose between slates of candidates approved by the military to start the return to democratic government. In 1985, Tancredo Neves was elected president. He was denied the victory but not because of the military. On the eve of his inauguration he underwent abdominal surgery from which he never recovered. The vice president, José Sarney, struggled in vain to correct the nation's economy.

Brazil currently confronts economic and development problems similar to those facing many of the countries in the Other World. The United States and the International Monetary Fund (IMF) have continually stressed the need to "privatize" the economy by reducing government ownership of industries and services to encourage foreign investment and competition and diminish inflation. A country of tremendous natural resources, Brazil suffers the consequences of their poor distribution. One percent of the population owns over 50 percent of the wealth. It is a country with 12 million landless and impoverished peasants and an estimated 1.24 billion acres of arable land, two-thirds of which is owned by 5 percent of the population, which in turn farms only 15 percent of the total. Nevertheless, these powerful individuals are capable of defeating any attempt at effective land reform. Years of drought and rural hardship have driven millions to seek refuge in the urban areas, where they add to the inflationary pressure by causing the government to spend more on social services.

This was the political context in 1989 when Brazilians directly elected their president for the first time since 1960. Fernando Collor de Mello, the candidate of the center-right National Reconstruction party, beat Luís Inácio "Lula" da Silva of the Worker's party by a vote of 53 to 47 percent. Faced with the highest foreign debt in the Third World at the time ($115 billion) and an inflation rate that was projected to be 1,900 percent for 1990, Collor instituted reforms that collided with da Silva and the military. Collor offered to privatize state-owned industries and, simultaneously, to address the external debt by exchanging ownership of the former for reduction in the latter. This move created some consternation with the more nationalistic members of the armed forces. His reorganization of the economy resulted in the layoff of 350,000 government workers. Fear of unemployment resulted in protests and strikes by workers, which further destabilized the economy and promoted greater recession.

With his popularity waning, Collor suffered the additional indignity of having his brother denounce him for misappropriating campaign funds. Collor resigned from his office on December 28, 1992, to avoid certain impeachment by the legislature. A sad day for President Collor was a memorable one for Latin American democracy as a chief of state, forced to resign, was followed in office by his constitutional successor.

Though honest, the new president, Itamar Franco, did not have an economic recovery plan. He eventually appointed Fernando Henrique Cardoso to fill the vacant post of finance minister. In an earlier time, Cardoso was driven from his post as a professor at the University of São Paulo by the military dictatorship. During his exile, the sociologist collaborated with Enzo Falleto to write one of the basic texts on "dependency theory," called *Dependency and Development in Latin America.*

From 1985 to the present, Brazil has gone through five different currencies. The 1980s were regarded as the "lost decade." Per capita gross domestic product (GDP) in 1990 was what it was in 1980, the last year of the "economic miracle."

The new finance minister, Fernando Henrique Cardoso, installed the *Real Plan*, and inflation declined from 50 percent per month to around 3 percent. The plan was launched early enough in the approaching presidential campaign so that candidate Cardoso could reap the benefits of its apparent success. Most important, the leading opposition candidate, again, "Lula" da Silva, thoroughly frightened the political and economic establishment to such an extent that they backed Cardoso with every means at their disposal. Cardoso won the election with 53 percent of the votes cast, with a margin of more than two to one over da Silva.

As President Cardoso was inaugurated in January 1995, and Brazil's social problems persisted, Amnesty International reported the slaughter of thousands of "street children" at the hands of death squads. In the countryside peasant leaders and environmental organizers were murdered with impunity. The 1994 Home Box Office film (*The Burning Season*), starring the late actor Raul Julia, portrayed the exploits and assassination in 1988 of unionist-environmentalist Chico Mendes. Between July and October 2001, seven leaders of regional labor, religious, or environmental groups were killed. The most recent victim was Ademir Federicci, the director of the Movement for the Development of the Trans-Amazon and Xingu. He had been warned by an illegal logger whose operations he had reported to the authorities, that it was time for "Dema," as he was known affectionately, to start searching for some wood for his own coffin. His opposition to the aforementioned dam and confrontations with gangs of hijackers and car thieves preying on travelers on the Trans-Amazonian Highway had supplied him with many enemies. The intersection of the Trans-Amazonian Highway with the Xingu River is Brazil's equivalent to the earlier North American "Wild West." Judges do not linger after receiving their first death threat. The area is controlled by powerful interest groups intent on profiting from the development that will surround the Belo Monte Hydroelectric Complex.

President Cardoso succeeded in stabilizing the *real*. That accomplishment brought him the popularity needed to amend the constitution in order to allow him to campaign again for the presidency. He triumphed over "Lula" for a second time on the promise that his administration would not devalue the *real* and plunge the country into another inflationary cycle.

Fernando Henrique Cardoso's second term has not been a pleasant one. From the start (January 1, 1999), he has faced a yawning fiscal deficit. The man who preceded him as president, Itamar Franco, is now the governor of Minas Gerais and started the year by declaring a 90-day moratorium on the payment of his state's debt to the federal government. Minas Gerais is an industrial powerhouse that has suffered economically as a result of the global downturn. This has had the collateral effect of raising unemployment with a resulting decline in government revenues. The effect of the economic downturn has been to postpone the goal on the part of the president, a sociologist, to address the nation's mounting social problems after stabilizing the *real*.

One of the six federal republics in the Western Hemisphere, Brazil will differ somewhat from the majority that are unitary in organization. Even so, Brazil presents us with a microcosm of the economic problems faced by many of the other developing countries discussed in this book. Some 2,800 laid off workers at the Ford plant in São Paulo showed up willing to work for less. These are skilled workers and the backbone of the country's labor movement. In order to defend the currency, the government raised interest rates as high as 50 percent, thereby contributing to the recession. Cardoso was on the horns of a dilemma. Should he go back on his campaign promise to control inflation or let the *real* float and hope that the resulting devaluation would encourage exports and arrest the decline in foreign exchange?

His economic problems were compounded by the fact that he had previously secured a $41.5 billion loan from the IMF on the commitment to reduce the fiscal deficit. This was to be accomplished by raising taxes and charging taxes on pensions. If the government were to arrange more favorable interest terms for Minas Gerais, it would have to do the same for all 27 states, and that would endanger the budget deficit and create further difficulties with the IMF. President Cardoso governs with a legislative coalition that includes as one of the three most important members, Governor Franco's party, the Brazilian Democratic Movement (PMDB). Cardoso cannot afford to alienate such an ally if he hopes to institute fiscal and social reforms.

The United States encouraged the IMF loan because Brazil is one of its largest trading partners in South America and feared that a deep recession there would engender falling economies throughout the hemisphere. The fiscal requirements imposed as a condition for receiving an IMF loan and the demands of the people in a transitional democracy are difficult to reconcile in good times and unrealizable in bad times. Violent strikes erupted. Perhaps because there was no longer the threat of Communism, there has been no talk of a military coup.

The Cardoso administration blinked. In January 1999, barely two weeks into its second term, the currency was devalued. Overnight the *real* lost 20 percent of its previous value. By the end of the month, the *real* floated at about 1.44 to the dollar. Inflation, brought under control by Cardoso's *Real* Plan, soon revived as the price of flour for bread rose by 16 percent. The hope was that the ensuing rise in Brazilian exports and increase in foreign exchange would allow a decline in interest rates and further stimulate the economy. By lowering the price of steel, however, steel manufacturers in the United States have accused Brazil of "dumping" and asked the Bush administration for protection. Apparently, developing nations are vulnerable in many ways. Leaving the earlier import substitution model for participation in a global economy is not an easy transition. One can understand why Brazil is not impatient to leave its advantage in MERCOSUR (southern common market) for a more competitive role in the Free Trade Area of the Americas (FTAA) projected for the future.

The *miseraveis* (those living in misery) in a country of 170 million are about 25 million in a nation with one of the worst distributions of wealth in the hemisphere. If conditions worsen, the capital flight from Brazil will be unavailable to address the country's human needs for social programs, agrarian reform, health and education, and for attacking all the other manifestations of poverty. Although the changes initiated by Cardoso have improved things somewhat, the situation where 10 percent of the population makes an estimated 44 times that of the poorest 10 percent continues.

With an energy crisis resulting from a severe drought and the explosion and collapse of an off-shore drilling platform, the return of inflation, and his popularity plummeting, President Cardoso's hopes for social reform during his second administration are decamping. The September 2001 attack on the United States and its economic recession has had an adverse effect on the economies of the southern cone. This prompted a growing backlash against the IMF, making it easy for nationalistic critics to denounce policymakers responsible for implementing its austere measures as *entreguistas* (sellouts or traitors). Support for privatization of the economy has dropped from 75 percent of those polled in 1990 to below 30 percent in 2001. Ten months away from the next presidential election in October 2002, foreign investors wonder as to whether Cardoso's Brazilian Social Democratic Party and its centrist coalition of parties will be able to retain control of the government and the commitment to liberal economic programs or if "Lula" and the Labor Party will finally arrive.

CUBA

It is my duty . . . to prevent, through the independence of Cuba, the U.S.A. from spreading over the West Indies and falling with added weight upon other lands of Our America. All I have done up to now and shall do hereafter is to that end. . . . I know the Monster, because I have lived in its lair—and my weapon is only the slingshot of David.

JOSÉ MARTÍ

Cuba, the largest of the Caribbean islands, looms larger yet in the eyes of current North American policymakers. The island was late in severing colonial ties with Spain. Although the Cubans had initiated several independence movements throughout the nineteenth century, the final attempt came on the eve of the twentieth. A mysterious explosion that sent the American battleship *Maine* to the bottom of the Havana harbor in 1898 provoked an uninvited North American intrusion into Cuba's war of independence. As a result of the North American intervention and the Spanish defeat, Cuba became a U.S. protectorate for the next 35 years.

Cuban pride was trampled when Cubans were forced to accept the provisions of the Platt Amendment in exchange for nominal independence. The amendment stipulated, among other things, that Cuba could not enter into substantial foreign agreements without approval by the United States. It ceded to the United States the right to intervene to maintain a "stable government" and the right to "acquire and hold the title to land for naval stations." Cuba was forced to incorporate the amendment into its constitution before the United States would agree to remove occupying troops. This passage provided the justification for intervention in Cuban affairs by the United States from 1906 to 1920. In 1934, the treaty was abandoned as part of President Franklin D. Roosevelt's "good neighbor policy"; however, the naval base at Guantánamo is still under U.S. control. Until the revolution of 1959, Cuba was seen as an extension of the United States. Its economy was so integrated with that of its northern neighbor that it was treated as another of the 50 states.

The development of the sugar cane industry in Cuba is a good illustration of how the cultivation of an exclusive crop can affect a nation's economic status. By the middle of the 1800s, Cuba was producing close to one-third of the world's supply of sugar, in part because of the labor of over one-half million blacks transported against their will from Africa. Sugar soon came to dominate the island economy during the time of the American protectorate. The mills dwindled in number as the smaller agriculturists were bought out and an increasing amount of land was given over to sugar production. These larger operations came under American control, and the development of the island's infrastructure was planned to exploit the transportation of the main cash crop. By 1928, Americans owned over two-thirds of the island's sugar production,[8] a situation that contributed greatly to the anti-American tenor of Cuban nationalism during the overthrow of the dictator Gerardo Machado in 1933.

Because sugar cane requires infrequent replanting, the demand for labor comes only for three months during the harvest; the remainder of the year is referred to by Cubans as *tiempo muerto*, or "dead time." As there was nothing much to do around the sugar mills most of the year, and the small farms had been bought up and given over to producing cane, a growing rural proletariat emerged, which would drift into the urban areas in search of employment.

In 1903, Cuba and the United States worked out a reciprocal trade agreement that gave sugar a 20 percent reduction from existing U.S. tariffs in exchange for a 20 to 40 percent tariff reduction for Cuban imports from the United States. Because sugar was to become the source of 80 percent of Cuba's foreign exchange, this relationship increased dependence on the United States. This and other arrangements contributed to Cuban prosperity in the good years. Its own economy and politics, however, became susceptible to the plotting of the American sugar lobby, which had its own interests to protect. When the Great Depression racked the United States, the social and political devastation was felt in Cuba as well.

The leftward potential of the groups that overthrew the dictator Gerardo Machado in 1933 was thwarted by Washington's refusal to accept the provisional presidency of Ramón Grau San Martín. Instead, the United States sided with Sergeant Fulgencio Batista, who had led the rebellion in the army that contributed to Machado's downfall. The politics that dominated the next 26 years was a struggle between an ineffective reforming element and the forces backing Batista. It was an era of rampant corruption and abuse of power.

On the eve of the 1952 presidential elections, Batista staged a coup and captured the executive office. This act stimulated a romantic and vain attack on the Moncada Barracks by Fidel Castro and a group of 165 youths on July 26, 1953. The attack was a disaster. Fidel and his brother Raul were lucky to avoid the fate of half of the party, which ended in casualties, capture, and death. In an effort to terminate military reprisals against any comrades associated with the attack, the Castro brothers surrendered and were sentenced to 15 years in prison.

Good luck always followed Fidel Castro. In an attempt to appease the opposition, Batista declared an amnesty and the Castro brothers were released in 1956. They were exiled to Mexico, where the future revolutionaries were joined by others in training for the overthrow of Batista. Later that year a band of 82 revolutionaries sailed for the island. The landing was another disaster. The popular uprising that was to erupt on their arrival never materialized. After several days of mishaps, all that survived from the invasionary expedition were 12 *guerrilleros* (guerrilla fighters) who managed to slip into the Sierra Maestra Mountains, where they would remain pretty much unnoticed until their interview by Herbert Matthews of the *New York Times* the following year.

The interview gave "the bearded ones" the exposure they needed to mobilize the latent anti-Batista sentiment throughout the island. Every revolutionary act would elicit a repressive countermove by Batista, which in turn only stimulated further disobedience and subversion until his support dissolved and he fled from Cuba on New Year's Eve, 1959.

What accounts for Fidel's subsequent rise? Unlike other revolutions in Mexico or China, the Cuban revolution emerged after a relatively brief period of conflict. The corrupt politics of the previous half century had thoroughly discredited the establishment. There was no one to compare in stature with the popular and charismatic revolutionary hero. The *Partido Socialista Popular* (PSP), which was the name under which the Cuban communist party operated, had been slow to back the *guerrilleros* in the Sierra Maestra, joining in the revolutionary movement only at the last minute. The PSP was also suspect because of its long alliance with Batista and its contribution to the organization and maintenance of workers' support during his regimes. So why did Fidel become a communist?

Any authentic reform of the Cuban political and economic structure would have to break the U.S. control of the sugar economy. That act would also entail a thoroughgoing agrarian reform because sugar production was the foundation of the system. The alternative would have to be a socialist or some other economic system with strong central direction from the state. The question was, would it be Cuban or Soviet socialism?

Washington's imperialist reaction to Castro's revolution darkened the atmosphere. Boycott and sabotage during the Eisenhower administration were followed by the unsuccessful Bay of Pigs invasion in 1961 and assassination plots against Fidel sanctioned by the Kennedy administration. Castro had to consolidate the revolution, and to do so he availed himself of the only antibourgeoisie apparatus in existence at the time, the PSP. He remained the revolutionary dictator and was quick to move against any regular party leader who wanted the institution to take the lead and govern. He drew on the communist party and Soviet advisers to replace the fleeing technicians and professionals dissatisfied with the increasing socialist direction of the revolution.

The growing indigenous opposition to socialism rejected assistance from those who had exiled themselves and were plotting a counterrevolution, with the aid of the Central Intelligence Agency (CIA), from afar. The abortive Bay of Pigs invasion had the effect of terminating the internal opposition because it had now become equated with the external counterrevolutionaries in the eyes of the people who had joined in defending the nation. This event gave Castro the support he needed to discredit and eliminate the opposition.

For a time in the 1960s, Fidel sounded independent of the Soviet Union. He denounced the traditional communist parties throughout the hemisphere as reactionary. He squandered Soviet support on pet economic projects and played host to revolutionary leaders from the Other World at a Tricontinental Congress in an attempt to gain the leadership of the "nonaligned" nations. But his support of the Soviet invasions of Czechoslovakia in 1968 and Afghanistan in 1979 and the Russian suppression of the free labor movement in Poland in more recent years indicates how dependent on the Soviet Union Cuba had become for its survival. Many believe that Cuba was more dependent on the Soviet Union than it was on the United States in the pre-Castro years. Others began to hope that Fidel's luck would be changing.

At a time when the Soviet bloc is a distant memory and the two Germanys are reunited, it is tempting to speculate as to when Cuba will go in the same democratizing direction. This is unlikely as long as Fidel Castro remains in control. Socialism did not enter Cuba in the wake of an occupation by the Soviet army. Communism was introduced by an extremely popular leader as a way of freeing his country from a half century of *yanqui* domination and as a means by which he could solidify his control of the revolution.

The Soviet Union supported Cuba with from $5 to $6 billion in assistance in 1989, but as of the Council for Mutual Economic Assistance (COMECON) meeting in January 1990, Russian trade henceforth would be based on market price and hard currency. In the span of a year, sugar exports to the island's primary buyers fell by 50 percent. Despite all of the efforts at agrarian reform, Cuba was as dependent on sugar then as before the revolution. Russia could no longer afford to subsidize the island's petroleum needs.

Cement plants came to a halt. Power would be rationed at night. Farm machinery and other essential vehicles were sidelined for lack of gasoline, and there was talk of bringing back the use of oxen. A deal with China resulted in the importation of two bicycle factories. The hope was that they could persist until the Juragua nuclear power plant could be finished. Costing $1.1 billion so far, the island's biggest industrial project also came to a halt. The Russians were demanding $200 million in cash to continue; there was a $300,000 monthly payroll, and $200 million more was needed for financing. In September 1998, Fidel Castro announced during the Fifth National Congress of Committees for the Defense of the Revolution that work on the Juragua would be suspended indefinitely. The project had been suspended in 1992, but talk of restarting could be heard on occasion. Washington is fiercely opposed to having a nuclear plant less than 200 miles off the Florida Keys. Castro insists that the facility being built in Cienfuegos uses a different technology from the Chernobyl nuclear reactor. Why, he asks, is the United States willing to assist North Korea and not Cuba?

From one of the bright spots in the Other World in terms of quality of life for the worker, Cuba has taken a plunge. The end of the cold war has devastated the

Cuban economy. Prostitution, a social scourge associated with the "capitalist corruption" of the prerevolutionary past, is rampant once again as both men and women attempt to procure the hard currency which affords access to exclusive shops where the Cuban *peso* is not accepted. A many-layered economy has emerged and the top level is reserved for those who have access to foreign currency. The consequence is that many who are employed in menial occupations such as hotel workers, and cab drivers, who frequently come in contact with foreigners, or those who are lucky enough to have friends and family on the outside who can send them dollars, enjoy a better economic status than others such as doctors or teachers who make substantial contributions to the society through their labor but lack the external contact. This latter status engenders a degree of racial tension because whites are more likely to have access to foreign remittances than the blacks. As Andrew Zimbalist comments, "Cuba has become a class society, defined by access to hard currency through work, politics, or family abroad."[9]

A series of embargoes imposed by the United States have contributed to the post–cold war economic decline. The origins of these embargoes date from the Kennedy administration in the early 1960s. Cuba was able to subvert their effects by allying with the Soviet bloc, but with the collapse of the Soviet Union in the late 1980s, circumventing economic pressure from the United States has been more difficult, starting in 1992 when the residual assistance in the Soviet pipeline dribbled out.

That year, the Cuban Democracy Act (also known as the Torricelli Bill) took effect. The statute had the effect of increasing the costs of goods transported into Cuba by prohibiting foreign-based subsidiaries of U.S. companies from trading with the island. It allows private groups to send food and medicines but forbids ships entering Cuban ports for the purposes of trade from U.S. port facilities for 180 days. This restriction annoys our allies by extending the influence of the United States beyond its territory. It authorizes the president to declare any country providing assistance to Cuba ineligible for aid under the Foreign Assistance Act of 1961, ineligible for assistance or sales under the Arms Export Control Act, and ineligible under any program providing for the forgiveness or reduction of debt owed to the U.S. government. It stipulates other restrictions as well, but these were enough to cause Fidel Castro to make some economic accommodations in order to attract foreign capital.

The Cuban administration allowed the use of farmer's markets where farm products could be sold directly to the public. This was a reversal of an earlier attempt along the lines of increasing food production during the middle 1980s which had been abruptly terminated by Fidel because he felt that the policy was breeding *"petite capitalistas."* Another example would be the permission of *paladares* or small private in-house restaurants with a maximum capacity of 12 seats to be served exclusively by members of the household. These limited establishments pay a 50 percent tax on revenues after deducting 10 percent for costs. In addition to proving that their purchases were from legal sources, they pay a monthly license fee of $375 and an additional 1,500 *pesos* to the government.[10] One has to be desperate to start a business under those conditions.

In an effort to accumulate foreign investment, Cuba has modified its economic doctrine to encourage the development of tourism. Even so, the ideological mooring of the economy places it in a competitive disadvantage with other Caribbean resort areas. In an attempt to accumulate foreign exchange, the government requires that investors hire Cuban labor and pay the Cuban government in foreign currency. The government then pays the Cuban worker in *pesos* at the Cuban rate. This maneuver allows the government to make a profit on the exchange rate between what the government is paid in foreign currency and what it pays its citizens. Unfortunately for Castro, labor is less expensive in other similarly inviting locations along the shores of the Caribbean.

Economic development in Cuba has been stymied further by the imposition of the Cuban Liberty and Democratic Solidarity (*Libertad*) Act in 1996, following the downing of two private planes flown by "Brothers to the Rescue" in international waters by the Cuban air force. Also known as the Helms-Burton Bill, the statute, in part, codifies the different embargoes on trade and financial relations in effect since the Kennedy administration. It requires the president to produce a plan for providing economic assistance to a transitional or democratic government in Cuba as well as authorizing United States nationals with claims to property confiscated in Cuba (including those who were Cuban citizens at the time of the confiscation) to file suit in U.S. courts against persons who may be "trafficking" in that property (Title III). This latter provision can be suspended by the president for periods of six months at a time if he considers it necessary to the national interest of the United States and if it will expedite the transition to democracy in Cuba. The fourth title of the statute requires the denial of visas to, and exclusion from the United States of, persons who after March 12, 1996 (when the legislation was passed) confiscate or "traffic" in confiscated property in Cuba claimed by U.S. nationals. The president has yet to impose Title III. Nevertheless, it has a chilling effect on foreign investment in Cuba. Proponents of the Helms-Burton Bill argue that attempts to engage Cuba through trade and normalization of relations by other countries has not changed Castro's posture. On the other hand, the U.S. embargo has caused modest modifications.

The execution of General Arnaldo Ochoa—a "Hero of the Republic," the popular commander of the Cuban expeditionary forces in Angola and Ethiopia—on the charges of corruption and drug trafficking sent the powerful message that no one is safe. A move to depose Fidel would not come from above, as such persons have too much to lose without him. Fidel personifies the revolution. Those below would have an extremely difficult time trying to plot against him. Intelligence channels permeate the society in large part because of the need to maintain readiness against the omnipresent threat of an external invasion. The more the United States threatens Cuba, the easier it is for Fidel to rally mass support for the defense of the revolution. The very security precautions that must be instituted against the eventuality of a U.S. invasion are the same ones that prevent the success of any domestic uprising. When Jorge Mas Canosa and the Cuban-American National Foundation (CANF) set up a real estate registry in Miami, Florida, for the purpose of recovering the properties of returning exiles when they overthrow the Castro brothers, they play into Fidel's hand. Such actions serve only to rally the faithful in support of the regime.

Fidel Castro fainted while giving one of his extended perorations during a hot summer day in 2001. He stumbled on August 13, 2001, during a 75th birthday celebration in Venezuela. It is rumored that Raúl, his younger brother and anointed successor, is in worse health. Is the end of the dictatorship in sight? According to William D. Rogers, a former assistant secretary of state for inter-American Affairs, when it is suggested that Fidel is mortal, Cubans respond that even though Castro may fade away, "Castroism will live forever."[11] The October 2001 success of the *Peronista* Party in Argentina indicates that it is possible to have *peronismo* without Perón. In the United States, where the citizens are more inclined to identify with institutions than with personalities, the principles identified with the "New Deal" are still very much alive. Although the two dominant parties in the United States war over the policies of the so-called "welfare" state, many of the social programs tracing their origins to President Franklin Roosevelt and the New Deal are well entrenched. It will be interesting to see how many of the social programs launched by the Cuban revolution will survive his passing. The cult of the personality is strong in Latin America and one can safely predict there will be a *fidelista* party after the demise of the Cuban Communist party.

In Miami, defections by the membership of the once solid CANF have resulted from the more relaxed direction taken by its current leader Jorge Mas Santos, the founder's son. Whereas his father, Jorge Mas Canosa, would have been in the lead of the Miami demonstrations over the capture and repatriation of Elián González, the son has alienated many of the members of the CANF by acting on the awareness that the attitudes of the older exiled community do not resonate with majority opinion in the United States. By courting the Latin Grammy Awards away from Los Angeles, he produced a split within the organization. The older generation of Cuban exiles could not abide the thought that Cuban artists would be honored in their midst. Many of them terminated their association with the CANF and, with others, generated such a commotion that the Grammy event was returned to Los Angeles for security reasons.

Support for normalization of relations with Cuba seems to be making other inroads as well. The island is no longer a military or an ideological threat, given the discredited nature of the Soviet economic system. Instead, the problems Cuba may present are another influx of refugees attempting passage to the Florida mainland and the establishment of another point of narcotics shipments into North America. How can the United States best contend with these possibilities?

Along with the rest of the world, the economy of the Western Hemisphere was sluggish during the latter part of 2001. The civil war in Colombia has not abated despite the imposition of the Colombia Plan (see the section on Colombia), and who knows what direction the Chávez regime will take Venezuela (see section on Venezuela). The current worldwide effort the United States is leading against international terrorism will turn its attention away from hemispheric problems. Would it not be prudent to pursue those policies that would contribute to a stable and democratic Cuba in the future?

Has unilateral isolationism worked anywhere? The Helms-Burton Law, to the degree that it extends the reach of the legal apparatus of the United States beyond our borders, annoys our allies with our arrogance and makes it more difficult to pursue an effective policy of coalition-building in pursuit of international terrorism following the September 11, 2001, attack on the World Trade Center in New York and the Pentagon in Washington, DC.

It is unlikely that life in Cuba will ever return to what it was before the revolution. There are many among the exile community who fought to bring that about and were subsequently alienated by the direction taken by Castro. It is unlikely that Fidel will change; the question is whether the normalization of relations will be conducive to a less disruptive transition. U.S. policy currently insists that Castro comply with demands that would effectively remove him from power before we relax the embargo. That does not seem realistic. An occasional game of baseball between the Cuban national team and the Baltimore Orioles is not going to reduce human rights abuses. Selective isolation, which some advise, will not work so long as the regime is threatened with security matters and maintains total control over the situation in Cuba. To suppose that we can support the opposition groups without the regime's indulgence is unrealistic.

We do not have to like a government in order to deal with it. There are too many examples where we do that already. The Cuba policy of the United States should be guided by what benefits the United States and if it cannot achieve that today, then, by whatever are the best means for achieving it in the future.

LOOKING AHEAD

Contemporary Latin America continues to reflect its long colonial experience. The political institutions developed in that part of the hemisphere were extracted from a strong central administration, mitigated only by the great distance between the colonies and the seats of empire. On top of that experience have been layered the ideologies of liberalism, positivism, socialism, and Marxism. Regardless of the fact that these influences tug at cross-purposes, the prevailing result has been some sort of highly centralized government. Whether the chief executives are garbed in civilian or military dress, their authority and power eclipse all other political institutions associated with liberal government.

Nevertheless, change is in the air. The prospects for economic development in the region are still positive. Latin Americans are willing to experiment again with regional integration. Earlier efforts toward establishing free-trade areas and common markets in the 1960s floundered. At that time countries were not willing to transcend national interests for the sake of the greater good. The mutual trust required for such an experiment to succeed deteriorated as military regimes pursued their separate agendas.

Staggered by an enormous foreign debt and fearful of the consequences of European economic integration, Latin Americans are now more receptive to

Democracy in Action: The Legislative Assembly of Costa Rica has members elected by proportional representation for four-year terms. The president and vice-president are also elected.

SOURCE: *Reginald Gooden*

economic cooperation. The nations of the southern cone (Brazil, Argentina, Paraguay, and Uruguay) signed the Treaty of Asunción, which established MERCOSUR (southern common market). Modeled on the 1959 Treaty of Rome, which erected the framework for the European Common Market, MERCOSUR intends the reduction of tariffs, along with other restrictions on trade, over time. At the other end of the hemisphere, Canada, Mexico, and the United States launched the North American Free Trade Agreement (NAFTA) on January 1, 1994. The countries of the isthmus are attempting to revive a free-trade area, as are the 13 English-speaking countries that make up the Caribbean Commonwealth (CARICOM).

MERCOSUR celebrated its 10th birthday in 2001 and has enjoyed remarkable success. Trade and investment among the members has expanded, enticing the participation of Chile and Bolivia in the free-trade area. Roads, gas pipelines, and electricity grids are being integrated. The growing comity among the members has had the beneficial effect of staving off attempted coups in Paraguay. The arrangement will be tested as a result of the worldwide recession of the millennium and the rather desperate state of the Argentine economy that finds itself currently the victim of a recession that has lasted 40 months. High unemployment places a burden on government spending for social needs at a time when revenues have fallen off. In an attempt to forestall inflation, Argentina pegged its peso to the dollar. This precludes her from devaluing her currency. To achieve an equivalent effect, it unilaterally abolished duties on imports of capital goods from outside MERCOSUR and raised tariffs on consumer imports to 35 percent, and in so doing, violated the common external tariff of 14 percent on capital goods and a common foreign-trade policy among the members.

Domingo Cavallo, the former Argentine Economy Minister, claimed that the adjustment was "temporary." It may well be, as his government has since lost any say in the matter. In an attempt to meet the requirements imposed by the IMF, which loaned the country $5 billion and another $3 billion on the condition that it adopt cutbacks in public expenditures as a way of avoiding default on the $132 billion public debt, his policies severely diminished popular support for President Fernando de la Rua's ruling *Alianza* coalition of centrist and social democratic parties. During the midterm elections of October 2001, the *Peronistas* (or *Justicialista* party) captured both houses of the legislature. The Argentine people grew restless with the policies imposed to cut deficit spending. Food riots and looting erupted across the country, causing the police to respond with rubber bullets; five Argentines lost their lives initially, the government declared a state of siege December 19, 2001, and Economy Minister Domingo Cavallo resigned at midnight. The next day, President Fernando de la Rua resigned. There is no vice president; he had resigned earlier. The Congress elected Adolfo Rodríguez Saá to serve as interim president, but he resigned when the riots would not abate, to be replaced by Eduardo Alberto Duhalde a former *peronista* governor of the province of Buenos Aires, who claims he will govern as the head of a coalition government of "national salvation." A critic of what he called "exhausted" free-market economic ideas, and a populist of the *peronista* school, it remains to be seen how he extricates Argentina from its economic morass.

After an epoch of import-substitution industrialization (ISI) and its associated macroeconomic devices for protecting domestic industries, government subsidies, public ownership, and intrusive economic programs, what had caused the receptive mood in the hemisphere for free trade, international competition, privatization, and serious attempts at installing those policies that would rein in galloping inflation? To a great degree it was a response to the economic debacle of the 1980s (known as the "lost decade"), coupled with the demise of the Soviet model and the need to change their ways if they were to obtain a sympathetic ear with the international lending organizations.

Flying to Mexico to celebrate the ratification of NAFTA by the U.S. Congress, Vice President Al Gore announced that his country would host a summit meeting of the Western Hemisphere leaders in 1994. The summit, which was held in Miami in December 1994, was attended by 34 heads of state. In the discussions leading up to the event, the Latin American and Caribbean nations stressed their interest in a free-trade area encompassing the two continents. Having just finished a difficult ratification fight over NAFTA, the Clinton administration recommended the addition of less such controversial topics as narcotics trafficking, government corruption, equality for women, and the environment in development. All of these topics found their way into the list of principles that emerged on December 11, 1994.

Nine days after the summit, Mexico devalued the peso and the rosy days of the "tequila sunrise" were followed by the "tequila hangover." What was expected to be a 15 percent devaluation of the overvalued Mexican currency soon had the peso in free fall. Contributing to the skittishness of the foreign investors were a string of unsolved assassinations of high officials in Mexican society and the peasant uprising in Chiapas. Mexico, one of the few governments in Latin America that had maintained a semblance of civilian-led stability during the period of the "dirty wars," which racked so many of its neighbors, appeared to be just as fragile and was no place to risk an investment. Soon, all investments in Latin America were suspect, and the other countries suffered collateral economic damage. What happened?

The 1990s were an economic improvement over the 1980s. Average growth in the area between 1985 and 1989 was 1.5 percent, not the 3 percent since 1990. To this was added the announcement that the countries were liberalizing their economies, controlling inflation, privatizing state industries and resources, and opening their economic systems to foreign investment, coupled with diminished controls on repatriation. Liberalization of trade along with foreign investments stimulated an increase in imports. Lacking the sophistication and capacity to compete internationally, Latin American exports fell behind imports. The difference could be masked momentarily by the influx of capital investment, as well as portfolio investments held in Latin American stocks and bonds, which looked more inviting at a time when the United States was paying low interest rates. In contrast to Asia, where the foreign money was used mainly for investment, in Latin America it was going toward consumption. This is understandable given the economic doldrums of the 1980s. The influx of foreign money increased the value of the local currency, and this had the happy effect of cheapening imports; however, it also made exports more expensive, thus distorting the balance of trade even further.

The expectation that the U.S. Federal Reserve would be raising interest rates caused portfolio investors to pause. Even more significant, however, were the domestic problems emerging in Mexico. When the *técnicos* decided to correct the value of the peso while all the other alarms were going off, the system crashed. Money managers in New York, London, and Tokyo, watching the peso sink on their computer screens, withdrew their volatile portfolio accounts. Nobody wanted to hold pesos under those conditions and so the sell-off devalued the currency even more. The Clinton administration responded by floating Mexico a loan. The Zedillo administration repaid the loan in less time than expected, but only because it put the Mexican population through an economic wringer. These severe economic dislocations, coupled with corruption and violence, have turned much of the citizenry against the traditional political establishment and produced the victory of the PAN presidential candidate Vicente Fox in 2000.

Throughout Latin America it will take longer to address the structural problems we have been discussing. Latin America has one of the worst distributions of wealth in the world. The macroeconomic reforms imposed by the lending institutions are having an excruciating effect on the majority of the population. Investment in education, health, and food is essential but can come about only through fundamental restructuring of the societies. The more the effort to address the social imbalance is ignored, the more uprisings in Chiapas, Guerrero, Venezuela, and, now in Argentina, we will see.

The moderate success that the three members of NAFTA have enjoyed in increasing trade among themselves has spurred others of the hemisphere to pursue the goal of an FTAA. This was the purpose behind the economic summit held in Quebec, April 2001. Amidst rowdy demonstrators and billows of tear gas, 34 Western Hemisphere nations (Cuba excluded) agreed to convene again the following May to draw up the specific details of how they would reduce barriers to trade so as to extend the principles embodied in NAFTA throughout the hemisphere. Some, like Costa Rica, are ready now. Brazil, the largest economy in South America and the leader of MERCOSUR, is hesitant, believing that even by the end of 2005, the date projected for the implementation of FTAA, its merging industries will not be able to compete with the United States.

There are other difficulties facing the adoption of an FTAA. Many U.S. farmers are unenthusiastic about meeting competition from sugar and citrus fruits. These, and other domestic interests, are not inclined to give President Bush the "trade-promotion authority" (formerly known as fast-track authority) it withheld from President Clinton in 1994. Without the ability to present Congress with a "take-it-or-leave-it" FTAA, it is doubtful that the bill would survive a death by multiple amendments.

✳ FLASHPOINTS ✳

VENEZUELA

The panorama of the Indian huts built on stilts in Lake Maracaibo so reminded Alonso de Ojeda of Venice, that he called the area "A Little Venice." For a while after its discovery by Columbus in 1498, the territory remained a Spanish colonial backwater devoted to raising livestock until cacao production was introduced early in the 1600s. Depletion of the native populations as the result of conflicts with the colonists and infection by exotic European diseases, led to the introduction of African slaves to work the crop. Today's dominant mestizo population in Venezuela is the result of interracial marriages dating from those early times.

During the time of the wars of independence from Spain, control was in the hands of the Spanish oligarchy. Returning to Caracas in 1807 after studying abroad, Simón Bolívar resolved to liberate his country. Installing General Francisco de Miranda as head of their army, the *criollos* promulgated the constitution of the Venezuelan Republic. This initial act of separation was soon followed by a devastating earthquake that demolished Caracas and resulted in the death of 20,000–30,000 people in the country. People were convinced this was a sign of God's displeasure, and their resulting contrition and social disruption allowed those upholding Spanish interests to restore control. The independence movement waned for a while until Ferdinand VII, reinstalled as the Spanish monarch with the departure of Joseph Bonaparte, revoked the more liberal policies of the Spanish *cortes*. After a period in exile during which time he was provided with safe harbor in Jamaica and Haiti, Bolívar returned to the struggle for independence.

After a prolonged contest with the Spanish army, the liberation of northern South America was successful and Bolívar was elected President of Gran Colombia with Francisco de Paula Santander as Vice President. Bolívar, the more centrist of the two, left Santander in charge while he continued with the wars of independence in Peru. Santander, impressed with the government of the United States, wanted to install a federal government with a limited executive. Upon his return from the successful liberation of Peru, Bolívar clashed with his vice president, providing the basis for contending governmental styles that were to wrack the politics of the area for the remainder of the nineteenth century, and which would in due course set up the conflict discussed in the section on Colombia.

In 1830, Venezuela seceded from Gran Colombia. The "Liberator" would die soon after of tuberculosis and Gran Colombia would continue to fall apart into what is today Ecuador, Colombia, and Panama.

Venezuela interests us because of the emergence of its current executive Hugo Chávez Frias. From the time of its independence, the political history of Venezuela has been one of turmoil with an occasional brief period of democratic experimentation. The period of the warlords, or *caudillos,* made it easy for Great Britain to join the eastern part of the country to what is Guyana today. In 1899 the dictator Cipriano Castro initiated a line of military rulers that imposed stability for the next forty years. It was in 1904, during Cipriano Castro's reign, that President Theodore Roosevelt appended his "corollary" to the Monroe Doctrine. The German, Italian, and British navy had blockaded the Venezuelan ports demanding restitution of their loans. The United States, emerging as an incipient world power after its victory over Spain, declared that it would not countenance the occupation of a Latin American country by a foreign power. To avoid such a prospect, the United States would engage in preemptive occupations and take charge of governing the "delinquent" republic until it learned to behave in accordance with the standards of "civilized" society.

Juan Vicente Gómez followed Castro and contracted to deplete the debt to its European creditors by contributing a percentage of the wellhead price of the newly developed oil resources. Oil became the country's leading revenue source, and by 1950, Venezuela was third in production behind the United States and the Soviet Union. Much of the wealth was exported, but enough remained in Venezuela to improve the infrastructure of the country and enlarge the size of the middle class. 1928 saw the establishment of the student movement and the federation of the nascent labor unions as well as the gestation of future political leaders such as Rómulo Betancourt and Raul Leoni.

World War II and the politics of the "united front" among the Allies against the Axis powers allowed for cooperation between liberal and Communist groups in the hemisphere. With the end of the war and the subsequent inception of the cold war, attitudes toward the Communists changed and the United States was willing to support regimes that would maintain stability in the hemisphere during a time of rising social unrest. Such was the relationship that developed between the United States and the dictator Marcos Pérez Jiménez during the 1950s. Pérez Jiménez represented stability, and stability made the country safe for investments while oil lubricated the boom years of the 1950s in Venezuela.

During this time, the opposition to the dictatorship grew and called for a general strike in January 1958. In the ensuing conflict, 300 students died. Pérez Jiménez soon departed for Miami and a military-civilian junta took charge. Resentment against the United States for harboring the dictator caused Richard Nixon's motorcade to be stoned when the vice president visited Caracas later that year. Rómulo Betancourt and his political party, Acción Democrática, narrowly won the election that December. Later that month, Fidel Castro and his *26 de julio* movement was to overthrow the dictator Fulgencio Batista in Cuba.

In January 1961, John F. Kennedy and the Democratic Party replaced Eisenhower and the Republicans in the White House. As relations with the Fidel Castro regime deteriorated, the United States was eager to find an example of evolutionary rather than revolutionary ways of bringing about human rights, democracy, and social stability in Latin America. Rómulo Betancourt and the evolutionary example of Venezuela were to be the model promoted by the United States. The discovery of a cache of arms in Venezuela linked to Cuba and associated with an attempt to overthrow his democratic government caused Betancourt to lead the effort, resulting in the expulsion of the government of Cuba from the Organization of American States in 1962.

For the next 30 years, Acción Democrática (AD) and the Christian Democratic Party (COPEI) rotated in office and with each year the politics of the country grew more corrupt. A decline in oil prices resulted in economic devastation and the need to impose the neoliberal economic measures favored by Washington and the IMF. President Carlos Andrés Pérez and AD instituted economic reforms resulting in the privatization of many of the state-owned companies, the holding down of wages, and the removal of trade barriers. These policies increased the hardships of the population, engendering mass rioting in February 1989. An estimated 1,000 lost their lives in the aftermath of *El Caracazo*, the name given the uprising.

AD and COPEI, the two dominant parties, have lost the support of the underclasses and those bearing the brunt of the country's economic problems. Discontent within the army spawned a revolt in February 1992, led by Lieutenant Colonel Hugo Chávez Frias. Although jailed, Chávez was identified as the most popular leader in the nation at the time.

His popularity continues to alarm the traditional elites. A study by the Catholic University in Caracas stated that in 1997, 67 percent of the population earned less that $2 per day, which was an increase from 35 percent 22 years earlier. Thirty-six percent earned less than $1 a day, up from 13 percent during the same period.[12] This state of misery has expanded the popularity of Chávez's MVR party. The initials stand for the Fifth Republic Movement (*Movimiento V República*—a reference to a continuation with the Fourth Republic which followed Venezuela's separation from Gran Colombia in 1830 and contains an additional allusion to Chávez's identification with the *Libertador*, Simón Bolívar) and suggests a mixture of nationalism based on the supposed lack of autonomy imposed by the adoption of neoliberal reforms, as well as the rejection of the corruption associated with the *puntofijistas*—a reference to the 1958 pact of Punto Fijo which initiated the process establishing the Venezuelan two-party system. Jailed as a result of the attempted coup, Chávez was pardoned in 1994 by President Rafael Caldera, an ex-COPEI president, who had won election with a center-left coalition called *Convergencia* on the promise that he would reverse the neoliberal program initiated by the former administration.

In 1996, President Caldera announced that he had no alternative other than continuing with the IMF protocol. This provided the basis for Chávez's victory in December 1998. He won with 56.2 percent of the vote and announced the need for a constitutional referendum upon his installation in February 1999. The referendum was approved by 81.7 percent of the votes in April and the *Chavistas* captured 125 of the 131 delegates to the convention. The new Constitution of the Bolivarian Republic of Venezuela was approved in December and Hugo Chávez Frias was reelected president July 2000, in accordance with the new constitution. In addition to adding the modifier "Bolivarian" to the official name of the republic, the new document enhances the power of the executive by extending the term of office from five to six years with the provision for reelection. The president is now assisted by a vice president who can be questioned by the Assembly and removed. If that were to happen to three vice presidents in succession, the president can then dissolve the National Assembly. The former Senate has been eliminated, leaving Venezuela with a unicameral legislature. Democracy has been broadened by providing for recall of elected officials and the use of the referendum in legislation. Critics, located primarily within the upper and middle classes, fear the potential for demagoguery on the part of President Chávez. Upon taking office, he instituted Plan Bolívar

2000 that extended the use of the military to engage in nation building. When one examines the new constitution within earshot of Chávez's authoritarian rhetoric, it can induce alarm and unpleasant memories of the bad old days of military control of the polity.

The phenomenon of Hugo Chávez Frias bears watching because there are many other countries in Latin America where the promise that neoliberal economic reforms would defeat poverty and elevate living standards has brought disappointment, and the public is growing impatient with its recent transition to democracy. The GDP, which is an average, may be improving in some of these countries, but the gap between the rich and poor continues to widen.

In his own country, a high rate of crime and unemployment are eroding his popularity. Chávez claims that his is a "peaceful revolution" and contrasts his approach with the *auto golpe* launched by Alberto Fujimori, who is presently languishing in Japan hoping to avoid extradition to Peru on criminal charges. As hard times persist in Venezuela, however, Chávez seems to be resorting to the tradition of defying the United States to gain popular support. The policies of the IMF, the World Bank, and the so-called "Washington Approach" become handy whipping boys as the cause of people's misery. Venezuela has led the resistance among the Organization of Petroleum Exporting Countries (OPEC) nations to American recommendations that the organization increase petroleum output. He became the first head of state to visit Saddam Hussein in 2000. He flaunts his friendship with Fidel Castro. He maintains communications with the rebel groups in Colombia and refuses to allow the United States to fly over Venezuela in pursuit of counternarcotics activities. He may revise his sympathies toward the Colombian insurgents as more of his citizens become the victims of rebel kidnappers.

NARCOTICS TRAFFIC

When you have a corrupt chief of police you fire him. When you have a corrupt chief of the army, he fires you.
GONZALO SÁNCHEZ DE LOZADO (FORMER BOLIVIAN PRESIDENT WHO FINISHED HIS TERM)

As long as the demand for drugs exists, it will be difficult, if not impossible, to stifle the sources of supply in Latin America. The supply of cocaine has economic as well as cultural and political bases in Bolivia, Colombia, and Peru. Culturally, the native populations of Bolivia and Peru have traditionally relied on chewing coca leaves to relieve the fatigue, thirst, hunger, and cold that are endemic to life in the bleak environment of the Andean altiplano. Lake Titicaca, located at one end of this intermountain plateau, has an elevation of 12,508 feet above sea level. The medicinal and religious uses of the coca leaf date back to the Inca civilization, and the cultivation of the plant is allowed by contemporary Peruvian administrations at controlled levels. In the Yungas region of Bolivia there are currently 30,000 acres in coca cultivation for the purpose of satisfying the traditional Andean ritual and medicinal needs.

The economic value of coca production is significant. It was estimated that in the 1980s, Bolivia supplied over one-third of the U.S. market for cocaine. This amount results in a gross income of about $3 billion, which represents a figure six times that of the country's legal exports. Family farmers growing coca on plots of less than 3 acres have an average annual income of $2,600 as opposed to the $650 their neighbors would earn for avocados and oranges, the most profitable legal crops grown in the Chapare region of Bolivia. The primary exports of Colombia (coffee and petroleum), Peru (copper and petroleum), and Bolivia (tin and natural gas) have been declining; and when one adds the falling standard of living associated with the austerity programs imposed by the international lending agencies, it is difficult to see how an impoverished people would choose the traditional way of doing business over the more lucrative one of producing and transporting cocaine.

The United States argues that all countries should share the burden of eradicating drugs. Critics counter that if the foreign demand did not exist, the problem would take care of itself. This dialogue points out conflicting approaches. On the one hand, the problem is one of economic development; that is, improving a country's balance of trade by increasing its exports. Such an approach is expensive because it involves the transformation of an entrenched socioeconomic structure at a time when these countries are faced with a large foreign debt. According to Bolivia's former finance minister, "If narcotics were to disappear overnight, we would have rampant unemployment. There would be open protest and violence." According to Peter Andreas, the United States Drug Enforcement Administration (DEA) estimates that Mexico earns more than $7 billion a year from the drug trade. The office of the prosecutor general in Mexico estimated that roughly 200,000 were employed by the drug economy in the late 1990s.[13]

Attempts at convincing the *campesinos* to grow legitimate crops have failed for lack of sufficient extension services, infrastructure, and demand for their legal produce. Many of these small agriculturalists are living on the margin and cannot afford to risk their resources on risky crops. Speaking before a United Nations Conference against Transnational Organized Crime in December 2000, former Bolivian president Hugo Banzer claimed, "If there's not concrete assistance to Bolivia, there is the risk that many people will begin to plant coca again."[14] On the other hand, it is tempting to see the problem of narcotics as merely a matter of eradicating a troublesome crop and delivery system. This approach looks easier but engenders indigenous opposition because Latin American politicians can play on latent anti-American feeling by defining it as another example of U.S. intervention.

Mexican officials were incensed that the United States violated the sovereignty of their country by paying bounty hunters for the delivery of Humberto Alvarez Machaín, a physician alleged to have been in charge of overseeing the torture death of DEA agent Enrique Camarena in 1985.

In an address to about 400 senior Hispanic police officers at a luncheon during the summer of 1998, General Barry R. McCaffrey, the former director of the Office of National Drug Control Policy, talked of the $2 billion failure in stopping drug smugglers. Aside from involving the U.S. military in surveillance, he talked of resorting to new technologies as a means of detection. The trouble with that approach is that law enforcement agencies, which are hierarchically structured, are up against smuggling networks that are loosely organized and capable of reacting quickly to the tactics of the lumbering police powers, which are slowed down by diplomatic formalities, frustrating notions of national sovereignty, and nationalistic dignity.

Meanwhile, the smugglers are trying to provide a product that is relatively cheap to produce and in high demand. The "narcs," on the other hand, are trying to eliminate consumption by blocking the traffic or at least interdicting it to such an extent that it will drive the price beyond the user's ability to pay. This results in a volatile combination of intentions. By raising the price, the profit is inflated. A gram of legal pharmaceutical cocaine costing about $17 to produce ends up bringing $140 on the illegal market. Pilots and skippers are willing to take a chance in exchange for the high salary a shipment of several tons would bring.

The tragic results of the drug trade in Colombia are well known. The Medellín cartel pursued a deadly game of intimidating the government by assassinating officials, political candidates, and journalists. The "extraditables," those at risk of extradition to the United States, tried for some time to reach a compromise with the government. They offered to curb their local violence in exchange for criminal trials at home, where "justice" might be more lenient than in the United States. In 1991, the alleged kingpin of the Medellín cartel, Pablo Escobar, arranged a plea bargain with President César Gaviria Trujillo whereby he surrendered himself in exchange for asylum in Colombia—to the chagrin of the Bush administration. After staging a successful jailbreak during the summer of 1992, he was cornered and killed by a special drug enforcement unit on December 2, 1993.

Closer to home, the link between narcotics traffickers, politicians, and officials of the Mexican government have combined to produce what some term a "narco democracy." Narco tyranny would be a better description of a vicious association of people who have produced an awesome collection of well-connected cadavers. The victims include the Roman Catholic cardinal of Guadalajara, a federal police commander, the Tijuana police chief, the former state attorney general of Jalisco, the general secretary of the PRI, and that party's presidential candidate. The crimes remain unsolved.

The rise of narcotics violence in Mexico is attributed by some to the relative success of our interdiction of the conduit between Colombia and Florida. The squeeze caused the barons of the Cali and Medellín cartels to employ the smuggling channels already in place from California to Texas. The transfer of contraband along the United States-Mexican border goes back before Prohibition and has been passed down among families engaged in the trade. American agents have devised a rule of thumb that claims that the payoff is $1,000 per kilogram of cocaine. The loads flying into central Mexico no longer rely on single-engine, propeller-driven Piper Cubs and Cessnas. The vehicle of choice today is the 727 and other jets capable of carrying 10 tons. There was a scandal in Zacatecas involving a shootout between the federal transportation police and the federal judicial police over possession of a plane that was so overloaded it had blown out its tires upon landing. The judicial police won, and the cargo disappeared. Because of its distinct packaging, it was discovered a few days later, making its way through the American drug market. The vast sums of money generated by drug traffic require laundering as well as protection. In no time at all are the guardians of law and order compromised and corruption rises to the top, where assignments are made to the lucrative exchange points for a fee.

Mario Ruiz Massieu, brother of the slain Francisco Ruiz (general secretary of the PRI), who had been married to Adriana, the sister of former Mexican President Carlos Salinas, was the former deputy attorney general and anti-narcotics chief. A search of his assets showed ownership of homes in Texas and Acapulco and deposits of $9.4 million—$1 million for each month he had served as chief narcotics investigator. He apparently committed suicide September 19, 1999, while under house arrest in New Jersey, rather than be extradited to Mexico to face charges of money laundering and graft. Implicated in the charges along with him were former Mexican President Salinas, his siblings, Raul and Adriana, and father, Raul Salinas Lozano. Brother Raul has been the only one convicted and is serving a 27-year sentence.

The corruption does not remain below the border. Members of San Diego street gangs were transported into Guadalajara for the gun fight that took Cardinal Juan Jesús Posadas Ocampo's life. A senior banker at American Express Bank International of Beverly Hills was convicted of laundering $30 million. The concern now is that access and transport to the United States will be made easier with the implementation of NAFTA.

The worrisome trend is the militarization of the narcotics control effort. As the quotation from the former president of Bolivia at the heading of this section suggests, governments are relying increasingly on the armed forces because the police have become so corrupted. But what guarantee is there that the army is any less susceptible to temptation? Andreas claims that the $500 million narcotraffickers spend on bribery a year is twice the annual budget of the Mexican attorney general.[15] General Jesús Gutierrez Rebollo, appointed by the Zedillo administration as General McCaffrey's counterpart in Mexico's war against drugs was subsequently arrested on charges of working for Alfredo Navarro Lara, the leader of the Juárez cartel. The army became suspicious when he moved from his modest dwelling into a lavish apartment in Mexico City provided by Amando Carillo Fuentes, one of the major drug smugglers at the time. The general was sentenced to 32 years in prison.[16]

A decade after the cold war, during a time when the institutions of the hemisphere are concentrating their energies on economic development and solidifying the transition to democracy, the United States is contributing to the augmentation of military establishments in the name of eradicating illegal drugs. We did that once before in the name of eradicating Communism. With the return of the Canal Zone to Panama and the closing of Howard Air Force Base there, the United States has established a Forward Operations Location (FOL) on the Pacific Ocean in Ecuador at Manta Air Base nearby the Colombian conflict zone (see section on Colombia). Should the growing skirmishes between the Colombian military, the FARC (Colombian Revolutionary Armed Forces), and the paramilitaries impinge on the U.S. surveillance operations in Ecuador, it may be difficult for the United States to remain within the restrictions placed upon our "observers" by the Clinton administration's Plan Colombia.

Peter Zirnite tells us that the U.S. is providing intelligence and military assistance to Peru and Colombia, two countries with an atrocious record of human rights violations in the hemisphere.[17] The interdiction and surveillance reduced coca production in Peru by 70 percent in the last five years, but not without the death of the innocent wife and infant daughter of a Baptist missionary whose Cessna seaplane was shot down by a Peruvian airforce jet. Unfortunately, production moved into Colombia where it doubled in 2000.[18]

ZAPATISTA UPRISING IN CHIAPAS, MEXICO

The contentious period in mid-nineteenth century Mexico, *La Reforma*, was a struggle between forces that identified themselves as liberal or conservative. Much of the dispute had to do with the role of the Roman Catholic Church. The liberals, led by Benito Juárez, wanted to reduce the influence of the church and passed a law, the *Ley Lerdo*, that required all corporations to sell their lands. The state could now go after the church, one of the largest landowners in the country. This law was later incorporated into the liberal constitution of 1857. During the dictatorship of Porfirio Díaz, the original intent of *Ley Lerdo* was subverted and the constitutional provision was used instead to divest the indigenous agriculturists of their communal lands. This resulted in a system of peonage, as the now-landless peasants were forced to work for the large landowners whose properties had just multiplied.

It was from this sector that Emiliano Zapata, the revolutionary leader from the state of Morelos, emerged. Proclaiming the *Plan de Ayala* in November 1911, he denounced Francisco Madero, the man responsible for the overthrow of the dictator Díaz. Madero was himself a large landowner and indicated no interest in addressing the problems of the landless peasants. The new Querétaro Constitution, adopted in 1917, empowered the state in ways that preceded the radical ideas of the Russian Bolsheviks. Article 27 detailed the basis for land reform: It restricted the purchase of land by foreigners and reaffirmed the tradition of *ejidos*. Although subsequent administrations paid lip service to land reform and engaged in minimal attempts at redistribution, the agrarian problem was not seriously addressed until the Lázaro Cárdenas administration (1934–1940). Reinforcing the agrarian basis of the revolution, Cárdenas distributed 44 million acres, which was twice the amount provided by the preceding administrations. Rather than breaking the land into minuscule subsistence plots, he relied on the tradition of communal landholding. He also provided the necessary support services to sustain his program. These holdings, which could include hundreds of families, were also provided with schools, hospitals, and agriculture credit.

This being the case, why did the peasants embarrass the Salinas administration on New Year's Day, 1994, by staging an uprising, capturing towns in the southern Mexican state of Chiapas, and demanding agrarian reform and political democracy? Was not this the administration that had pledged itself to honest elections? How could it be that the Ninth Congressional District, which included the town of Ocosingo, now occupied by members of the Zapatista Army of National Liberation (EZLN), cast a 100 percent vote for the PRI in the 1991 federal elections? It was clear that no party could capture 100 percent of the votes in an honest election.

Perhaps better endowed than other rural areas, Chiapas in many ways represents rural Mexico. It is an area rich in resources. The region contains fertile farmlands, pastures, and forests, as well as petroleum. The mountains along its eastern border drain the clouds laden with moisture that float in from the Gulf. That water irrigates the dense Lacandón rainforest, which controls its flow downhill to where it spins the turbines that produce three-fifths of the electricity empowering all of Mexico. The oil and the power plants belong to Mexico, but most of the population of Chiapas does not share in the common wealth. Article 27 of the 1917 constitution mentions "equitable distribution of the public wealth," but in the town of Ocosingo, only one-third of the homes have electricity and that proportion decreases as one travels into the countryside.

By various means, the rich few have acquired most of the land holdings over the years. These few wealthy families have been allied with the politicians and army and employ forceful tactics in dealing with that portion of the indigenous population that objects to their demands. They have always controlled the judges and frustrated legal attempts to stop them.

Now they can change the law to their liking, as the Salinas administration did in modifying Article 27 of the constitution to allow the subdivision and sale of common lands. The move to do so resulted from the liberalization of the Mexican economy, which cut back on agricultural subsidies while increasing the privatization of state industries and foreign agricultural competition in the wake of NAFTA. One hears the argument that liberalizing the economy will improve everyone's standard of living and that it will be more profitable to develop mechanized, export-oriented agricultural products for U.S. markets and import the cheaper beans and grain grown in the fields of Canada and the United States. However, if the peasants do not have access to credit and the means to compete in export crops, they will sell off their lands. As population pressure on diminishing agricultural land increases, peasants will invade the lands of the ranchers and provoke retaliatory strikes by the owners with their private armies or with the cooperation of the state's armed forces. The National Solidarity Program (PRONASOL), launched by President Salinas to ameliorate some of these problems, distributed generous amounts of resources, but these usually filled the pockets of the local bosses.

The regional elites resort to extreme measures in dealing with the native populations and others who have the audacity to organize peasants, workers, or even meetings. These violent measures have provoked the bishop of San Cristobal de las Casas into forming a human rights center to document the abuses. Governor Patrocinio González Garrido, a Salinas relation, responded by jailing two priests. This treatment of the native population is not something new: The Zapatistas did not emerge overnight. In 1980, after numbing delays while waiting for the legal system to resolve titles to lands that they had claimed, the Indians began to occupy these holdings. The landowners were furious and demanded that the authorities take positive action to remove the intruders. A priest mediated a dialogue between the squatters and the governor. At the appointed time, however, instead of the appearance of the governor, General Absalón Castellanos and his troops massacred the Indians.[19] The general, whose holdings amounted to 77 square miles and 10,000 head of cattle, had a personal message to give to the squatters. Ironically, portions of the general's ranch intrude into lands granted by former President Cárdenas to the community of Las Margaritas. Instead of becoming the target of an investigation, the general became governor of Chiapas from 1982 to 1988.

When the Zapatistas demanded the replacement of the PRI by a more democratic government, they were rejecting the combination of forces in the PRI intent on perpetuating their exploitation. The same governor of Chiapas, Patrocinio González Garrido, was then appointed President

Salinas's secretary of government in 1993. The year before the 1994 presidential election, his responsibility would be to prepare for and supervise, among other things, the election. Maybe this explains how the polls showed total support for an administration the people of the district rejected.

The movement launched by Francisco Madero, which erupted into the Mexican Revolution, pursued the ends of effective representation coupled with the associated notion of no reelection. To that was added the Zapatista demand of agrarian reform. The PRI, the party whose name institutionalizes the Mexican Revolution, could be expected to provide Mexicans with its goals. The neo-Zapatistas remain unconvinced.

Just before Christmas in 1997, 45 unarmed peasants, mostly women and children, were massacred by a paramilitary group linked to the ruling PRI in the town of Acteal in the Chiapas highlands. Under the pretext of attempting to keep the indigenous people from killing each other, the government violated a previous understanding by inserting more troops in the area. Two years before the massacre, during a failed attempt to capture *Subcomandante* Marcos and the rest of the Zapatista leadership, the army broke the truce between itself and the EZLN that had been fashioned after the initial uprising. This resulted in the enactment by the Congress of the Law of Dialogue, which froze their relative positions, while peace talks proceeded. The Congress and the EZLN then signed the San Andrés Accords in 1996 recognizing the rights of the indigenous communities to select their own leadership and control the natural resources in their territories. The accords, however, have not been upheld. Powerful logging, oil, and cattle interests, which control the PRI in the area, are opposed to the accords and have successfully stymied their compliance. These interests are the ones suspected of hiring *pistoleros* (thugs) to do the dirty work of terrorizing the Zapatista supporters so as to isolate them and leave them exposed and vulnerable to subsequent elimination. Unfortunately, this strategy will not address the original causes of the rebellion in Chiapas, Guerrero, or anywhere else in Mexico it may happen next. Nevertheless, the Zapatistas have survived and were successful in replacing seven decades of PRI control with the election of Governor Pablo Salazar Mendiguchia during the same wave of change that elected Vicente Fox president in July 2000. A former PRI senator, Salazar ran as the candidate of an eight-party opposition coalition that includes the PAN and PRD. The two men have pledged to comply with the 1996 San Andrés Accord ignored during the previous Zedillo administration.

President Fox made a special reference to Chiapas during his inaugural ceremony, indicating special concern for the fate of the indigenous people of Mexico. Soon after, federal troops were reduced in Chiapas and Zapatista sympathizers, jailed for political reasons, were released from prisons, but provisions of the San Andrés Accord that would extend greater autonomy to the indigenous people remain unresolved. President Fox has advanced a vision for the development of southern Mexico through Central America that he calls Plan Puebla-Panama. In it he foresees spending $10 billion in infrastructure that would lead to the economic development of the area's potential. The indigenous peoples are skeptical. A long history of victimization makes them suspicious of such a plan. They are more comfortable with their Mayan culture as "people of the corn," content to tend their limited farming plots and reject the prospect of themselves as hourly laborers at a *maquiladora.*

The intent to implement the San Andrés provisions received a further setback with the resurgence of the PRI, which won the majority of the municipal and congressional races in Chiapas in October 2001. During his address to the Congress during the previous month, rambunctious PRI members derided Vicente Fox's campaign pledge by holding up a sign stating: "I will Resolve the Chiapas Conflict in 15 Minutes, Bla, Bla, Bla." The dominant forces in Chiapas do not appear receptive to sharing their interests.

ENVIRONMENT

The concern for *sustainable development,* which is another term for protection of the environment, was one of the principles incorporated in the declaration of the Summit of the Americas, which took place in Miami, Florida, in December 1994. This concept, reconciling the notions of economic development and protection of the environment, had to overcome the following obstacles to gain currency. The first major international discussion of environmental issues took place in Stockholm in 1972. This was a conference sponsored by the United Nations on the Human Environment. Although the agenda was diverse, the major focus was on the deteriorating effect of development on the environment. The developing countries, for which concern about industrial pollution is dwarfed by their hopes of catching up to the industrial powers, denounced the talk of environmentalism as an attempt to deny them their place in the sun.

Twenty years later when the United Nations Conference on Environment and Development (UNCED) met in Rio de Janeiro, Brazil, the conferees were in accord that the solution to environmental problems could only result from the resources provided by economic growth. By then, the language of "sustainable development," which had appeared in an earlier 1987 report on "Our Common Future" (also known as the "Brundtland Report") published by the World Commission on Environment and Development, had become popular.

The question then became: How is sustainable development best achieved? One approach emphasizes the free market as the most efficient method. Its proponents would rely on corporations which, they claim, have the resources to invest in environmentally sensitive techniques and produce a more immediate impact on the GDP. This would in turn provide the economic resources for addressing the social investment needed to deal with education, public health, and other items of social infrastructure essential in achieving economic growth. The advocates of this view would also tend to limit the amount of state involvement in directing development, leaving the formation of policy to emerge from the interplay of nongovernmetal organizations.

Contrasting with the free market approach is one that would entrust development to the local population. This more modest "grass-roots" approach would encourage local capital accumulation and questions the "efficiency" of a market-driven development. Also, the revenues from the development would gravitate to the local area, resulting in a greater benefit to the small producer. Development would proceed at a slower pace and have a less formidable impact on the environment. The United States favors the former approach, but Latin American nations can find allies among the Scandinavians to support the latter.

Examples of both approaches can be found in Latin America and reflect the interplay of factors such as government bias, the degree to which a private industry owns a resource, and to what level the population is informed and a participant in the decision. The Mexican forest policy illustrates the transition from the "grass-roots" to the "market-friendly" approach.

In Mexico, as in many of the Latin American countries, the forests are where the marginal agriculturalists reside. The *latifundios* and cattle ranches have been cleared of forests. The forest, or jungle, still remains to be developed and in Mexico much of this land is in *ejidos.* Until the country entered into NAFTA and the General Agreement on Trade and Tariffs (GATT), its forest policy was determined primarily by domestic considerations. The group in charge of making that policy during the 1970s and 1980s was associated with then Secretary of Agriculture Cuauhtémoc Cárdenas. A member of the PRI at the time, Cárdenas was supportive of the *ejidatarios,* who under existing law held usufruct rights to over 80 percent of the nation's forests,[20] and a sustainable timber policy that benefited the local communities. Given the hierarchical, clientele-type political system associated with the Mexican state, that policy was the result of the balance of forces in control of the PRI. When the economic policies of the party shifted in the 1980s and 1990s under the leadership of Miguel de la Madrid (1982–1988) and Carlos Salinas (1988–1994), a split developed between the proponents of neoliberalism and the old guard populist-nationalists. Cuauhtémoc Cárdenas left the PRI to organize the PRD, and the development of forest resources changed to conform to the open market doctrine embodied in NAFTA.

Carlos Salinas installed his group of pro-market technocrats, and the forest law was rewritten to promote large-scale corporate plantations over the native silvan management. It terminated assistance to the *ejido* projects by stopping financing, extension assistance, and market protection. The hitch with a top-down government such as Mexico's is that it permits no authentic space where opposing interests can ventilate their opinion and have a fair chance to influence policy. As mentioned in the discussion of the rebellion in Chiapas, the issue persists as to whose interests are to be served. The Zapatista rebels have no historical basis for trusting the establishment and are leery of schemes such as the current Puebla-Panama Plan espoused by Vicente Fox to develop southern Mexico, which they believe will leave them without land and at the mercy of the multinational corporations.

The Commission for Environmental Cooperation (CEC) established by the North American Agreement for Environmental Cooperation (NAAEC) was the result of pressure on the Clinton administration by groups in the United States critical of NAFTA. They were alarmed that NAFTA would produce exploited labor and environmental degradation. To protect against such an outcome, they forced a side agreement on the three nations. Among its responsibilities, the CEC is to "foster the protection and improvement of the environment ...," "promote sustainable development ...," and "strengthen cooperation on the development and improvement of environmental laws, regulations, procedures, policies, and practices.[21]

The CEC was established to placate American critics of NAFTA. Canada and Mexico were reluctant to accede. NAFTA is the embodiment of the neoliberal notion of free trade. What is the likelihood that the CEC would be invoked against policies detrimental to the environment resulting from free trade? That would appear to happen only if one of the North American members' ox was being gored by the practices of another. If, however, the forest practices brought on by the free market were to degrade the environment of the host country as the result of its own invitation and encouragement, would the CEC be the likely agency to correct the situation?

Costa Rica has put environmental protection to work for it. Once referred to as a "banana republic," Costa Rica has in more recent times been called a "hamburger republic." The designation results from the practice of destroying forests to provide the pasture necessary to supply the North American fast food industry with beef. Central America has been the United States' third most important source of imported beef after Australia and New Zealand since mid-century. In their study of disappearing primary forest over the last 50 years, Steven Sader and Armond Joyce estimate that Costa Rica lost an average of a quarter of a million hectares per year in the seven-year stretch from 1977 to 1983.[22]

With the decline in beef consumption and the resulting herd reductions in Costa Rica, is that pastureland now available for reforestation? Land anywhere is going to be used to address human needs. Corporations such as Chiquita Banana, Dole, and others project an increased demand for bananas emerging from Eastern Europe. Unused pastureland will be coveted for plantations. This will lead to a different cycle of environmental abuse according to some. As more and more land is brought into banana production, workers benefit from the employment along with the local economy (although most of the revenue leaves the country in the pockets of the international corporations) until the demand drops off. When demand falls off, unemployed workers (many of them from Nicaragua and Panama) will resort to subsistence agriculture on the only land available to feed their families, the forest reserves, which Costa Rica is trying to reestablish.

Costa Rica has made a virtue of reforestation. With its natural beauty, spectacular volcanoes, and resplendent flora and fauna, it has become an ecotourist's Mecca. Scientists have established research laboratories in the forests where they are discovering medicinal uses for many of the preserved species. The idea is to find practical uses for the forest beyond its intrinsic aesthetic value.

It is estimated that around 20 percent of the species of plants in the world can be found in Brazil, spread throughout the Amazon, the Atlantic rainforests, the Pantanal wetlands, and the central plains. This diversity has stimulated the emergence of "bio-prospectors," such as António Paes de Carvalho, a former biophysics professor, who trek the lush countryside with a computer and diagnostic instruments analyzing the flora for its medicinal potential. His company, Extracta, then sells these genetic treasures to foreign pharmaceutical companies. Brazilian science is becoming more and more sophisticated, but the country, as do other developing nations, lacks the financing to benefit fully from its natural endowment. Lacking the companies that have the global infrastructure to test, market, and sell the final product, it has to settle for a small portion of the profit. Another issue results from patent rights. Without a guarantee that there will be a return on the investment, it would be difficult to fund the discoveries that, in turn, people in the developing world cannot afford to use. It takes a country with the resources of the United States to prevail upon a multinational pharmaceutical corporation to provide, for example, the antidote to anthrax, at a reasonable price.

Critics are in an uproar about one scheme that would sell "carbon" bonds to those industrial nations that are threatening the atmosphere with carbon dioxide emissions they have not devised the technology to control. Until they do, Costa Rica will offer certified tradable offsets (CTOs), which they sell at $10 per bond in exchange for one ton of carbon dioxide their forest will affix. This is how the country intends to raise the funds to reforest what they have lost as well as connect the reserves so that they become more than islands of cloud or secondary forests in a sea of agricultural land.

The enterprise of CTOs was launched as a pilot experiment in 1996 sponsored by the United Nations Conference on Trade and Development (UNCTAD). This policy became part of the Kyoto Protocol in 1997, whereby 36 industrial nations (excepting the United States and Russia) committed themselves to reducing emissions.

After rejecting the Kyoto Protocol, the Bush administration is looking for an alternative that would appease his critics and mitigate the degree of pollution in North America. As new power plants come on line, the air quality will only worsen. The electricity sector in the United States emits about 25 percent of all the nitrogen oxide discharged, about 35 percent of carbon dioxide, and 70 percent of sulfur dioxide. It has been proposed that the members of NAFTA cooperate on a "cap and trade" agreement that would place a limit on emissions and arrange it so that those industries emitting less than their allocation could sell the difference to those exceeding theirs. The players (Canada, who is committed to the Kyoto Protocol; the United States, who refuses to participate; and Mexico, who is exempt because of its status as a developing nation) are on different tracts but have a common interest in improving the air they breathe. The most one can expect from this combination would be a voluntary arrangement motivated by environmental sensitivity and the resulting public approbation. A pilot program organized under the name of The Chicago Climate Exchange that includes the cities of Chicago and Mexico City as well as the Manitoba Hydro and Cinergy, which produces gas and electricity, is committed to reduce the emissions of the participants by 5 percent below 1999 levels over five years.[23]

Demand for tropical products in the United States is going to influence the land use in Central America as tropical forests are converted into furniture or the biodiversity of the natural forest is transformed into the biomonotony of a banana plantation. If, as we have seen in the Chiapas example, ranchers increase their cattle herds, thereby crowding the indigenous population off the land, the natives can either migrate to the cities, where they become an urban problem and later perhaps one for the Immigration and Naturalization Service (INS, or *migra*), or to the Lacandón forest. There they will slash and burn and in time destroy or remove the nutrients, which in a rainforest are locked up in the biomass. The depleted forest will no longer be able to arrest the falling rain, and erosion will silt up the streams, affecting the wildlife and in time interfering with the reservoirs and the generation of power.

In Haiti, 63 percent of those employed are rural workers laboring on land that is denuded, exhausted, and no longer able to support the population. Their earnings account for 28 percent of the GDP. Coffee is the leading export crop. Haiti cannot afford to degrade its agricultural base any further, and it has no other option but to engage in sustainable development.

Another threat to the environment results from American efforts to eradicate the raw material for illegal drugs. Aside from militarizing rural Latin America, Plan Colombia intends to reduce half the existing area of illicit crops by 2003. It is estimated that these crops are expanding by about 20 percent a year and account for about half of Colombia's annual deforestation.[24] Most of the destruction of the plants will result from the aerial spraying of the chemical herbicide glyphosate (Roundup) made by Monsanto.

Banana Warehouse: The Del Monte Banana Corporation produces products for the U.S. market.

SOURCE: *Reginald Gooden*

The herbicide is not selective as to illicit crops and has been blamed for destroying other flora as well as causing eye, respiratory, skin, and digestive ailments of the fauna in the vicinity.

Narcotics and the environment are linked in another way and that is the capture and sale of animals, some of which are on the endangered list. It is estimated that after illicit drugs and arms, traffic in illicit animals is the third highest source of smuggling income in the world. Many of these species come from the Amazon region. Those in the drug trade use their established connections to traffic in animals and their parts and organs, which are often in demand for their purported medicinal benefits.

Violence is also associated with those who protect the environment in Latin America. As we have already witnessed in Brazil, so too in Mexico. Digna Ochoa, a 37-year-old civil rights lawyer, who had defended Zapatista rebels and had already survived one assassination attempt, was shot to death. A note was left stating: "You have been advised. This is not a trick." She had defended two peasant environmentalists, Rodolfo Montiel and Teodoro Cabrera, who had gained recognition for working against deforestation in Guerrero, Mexico.

VIOLENCE IN COLOMBIA

On August 7, 1998, Andrés Pastrana, the presidential candidate of the Conservative party, was inaugurated. Pastrana claimed that he would put an end to what has become Latin America's longest civil war. He campaigned as the candidate that would bring peace, halt drug corruption, and reactivate the economy. Soon after his victory, he met secretly with the rebel leaders of the *Fuerzas Armadas Revolucionarias de Colombia* (FARC), or the Colombian Revolutionary Armed Forces. They and the other revolutionary group the *Ejército de Liberación Nacional* (ELN), or the Army of National Liberation, had denounced the former president, Ernesto Samper, a member of the Liberal party, as illegitimate because of his connections with narcotic traffickers. Starting on the Monday of his inaugural week, the two revolutionary groups, which collectively go by the name *Coordinadora Guerrillera Nacional* (CGN) or National Guerrilla Coordinator, launched a combined attack on half the provinces, leaving many wounded, an estimated 70 dead, and scores of troops missing and presumed captured. Asked if the peace talks with the FARC had proved futile, Pastrana answered that this turmoil was directed at the outgoing Samper. For a long time the North American press has been claiming that the CGN are allied with the *cocaleros* or coca-growing peasants. Why would the guerrillas demonstrate such animosity to a presumed ally? Recall that Ernesto Samper's problems with the Clinton administration started when his rival in the 1994 presidential campaign, Andrés Pastrana, accused him of financial ties with the drug cartels. On the basis of recorded conversations between Samper and the wife of a narcotics peddler, revealed by his political rival, the Clinton administration distanced itself from Samper and decertified Colombia as being an ally in the drug war.

The long history of violence in Colombia starts with Simón Bolívar's victory over the Spanish loyalists. Frustration with the area's incapacity to achieve civic harmony prompted the quotation attributed to the Liberator with which we start the chapter. Bolívar wanted to see a strong executive elected for life. His comrade in arms, General Francisco de Paula Santander, became what is today Colombia's first president. He championed a decentralized federal system with a reduced role for the Roman Catholic Church. This became the basis for the Liberal party doctrine. Opposition to this view characterized the Conservative party and the two forces fought each other for the remainder of the nineteenth century. In the process, they made different areas of the country into their respective strongholds; the Conservatives controlling what is today Medellín and the Liberals controlling the area east and north of Bogotá.

A split within the Liberals led by Gabriel Turbay on the right and the nationalist-populist Jorge Eliecer Gaitán on the left allowed the Conservative Mariano Ospina Pérez to win with less votes than those amassed by the two Liberals in 1946. Gabriel Turbay died the following year, and Ospina Pérez began attacks against the Liberals. This started that bloody period in Colombia known as *la violencia*. In 1947 the *gaitanistas* (the followers of Gaitán) swept the congressional elections and left no doubt that Eliecer

Gaitán would win the presidential election in 1948. That year, the Ninth Inter-American Conference meeting in Colombia produced the Pact and Charter of Bogotá, thereby concluding the work started in Rio de Janeiro the previous year (1947) establishing the OAS. Fidel Castro was present with a delegation of Cuban university students to meet with Gaitán, but the meeting never happened. On April 9, 1948, Gaitán was assassinated. The assassin was mobbed, beaten to death, and his corpse was dragged to the presidential palace by the crowd shouting "Death to the assassin." "Death to Gómez." Laureano Gómez, who had been jailed to placate the United States for his fascist views during a previous administration, was now the foreign minister hosting the nascent OAS conference. Bogotá erupted into riot, burning, and looting, and the convulsion became known as *el bogotazo.*

The strife between the rival parties continued in earnest, and in a desperation move reminiscent of Hobbes' "state of nature," members from both sides asked for deliverance at the hands of the military dictator Gustavo Rojas Pinilla. He ruled from 1953 to 1957, when the Liberal Lleras Camargo met with his counterpart Laureano Gómez. Together they agreed on a constitutional reform known as the National Front, allowing the Liberals and Conservatives to alternate in office at all levels of government for the next 16 years. The elites thereby had concluded an understanding; unfortunately, even though women were given the right to vote, too many of the concerns of the majority of the population were not addressed.

The 1960s were a time of uprisings in Latin America, and the United States was anxious that other Cubas not arise; so it countered with a carrot—the Alliance for Progress—and a stick—the School for the Americas, in which the U.S. military gave instruction on countersubversion. Attempts by the Alliance to institute agrarian reform in Colombia floundered on the political maneuvering of the *latifundistas.* Thwarted in their attempts to bring about their vision of a more equitable society and motivated by the example of Fidel Castro and Ernesto "Che" Guevara in Cuba, young students and a sympathetic priest named Camilo Torres, took up arms. The official candidate of the National Front in the April 19, 1970, election was the father of the current president, Misael Pastrana. The excluded groups united in the Popular National Alliance to oppose his candidacy by nominating former president Rojas Pinillas, who lost by two points. The cry of fraud rent the air, and dissatisfaction with the traditional political process engendered the organization of two rebel groups, the FARC and the April 19 Movement (M-19).

As a result of a subsequent peace initiative, both of these groups suspended their armed conflict with the government and sponsored legal political parties. The M-19 garnered brief success, capturing 28 percent of the vote for the special constitutional election in 1990. The Patriotic Union (UP) sponsored by the FARC in 1985 achieved limited influence by winning 14 seats in Congress in 1986. Their numbers were soon diminished by the assassination of over 3,000 of their leaders and supporters, including two of their presidential candidates. The only UP senator winning an election was killed the day he took office, and his successor was forced into exile under threat of death. The experience discouraged further legal political participation.

It is easy to see why Colombia is presently considered the most violent country in the hemisphere. The guerrillas prosper because they have the support of the peasantry. Most commentators would agree that the peasants' situation has deteriorated in the last two decades. The opening up of the markets associated with the implementation of neoliberal economic policies has had a severe effect on the economics of the small landholder. The 2,299,804 small farms represent a mere 15.6 percent of the total arable land. Of these, over four-fifths are considered minifarms. The trend in Colombia is toward ever-larger *latifundios.* The world coffee price has declined, high production costs resulting from the overvaluation of the peso, and a parasitic infestation of the crop has made it very tempting to switch to growing coca and poppies. Official statistics indicate that the FARC operates in over half the territory. In 1985 they operated in 173 municipalities; in 1997 that had increased to 1,071. Yet, it would be inaccurate to characterize them as narcoguerrillas, as some have tried to do. The Colombian military has used that ploy with success in extracting military assistance from the United States.

The guerrilla groups, combining their strategy under the umbrella of the CGN, are well armed and possess sophisticated ordinance. Initially, they supported themselves by robbery and kidnapping for ransom; now they raise revenue by taxing the narcotics operation in the areas they control. They, however, are not the narcotraffickers. The CGN merely supervises the commerce and is preferred by the *cocaleros* to the *narcotraficantes* because it maintains order and protects them from the murderous agents of the cartels.

The large landowners have always resorted to violent methods in resolving their disputes with the peasants. In control of the political apparatus, they traditionally have had access to the military and police in helping them settle disputes or, should these not be available, their own paramilitary forces or *sicarios* (assassins).

The violence is self-sustaining because, as Nazih Richani has elaborated, it has reached a "positive-sum, economy of scale."[25] A military impasse has been achieved by the belligerent factions and a "symbiotic" balance of sorts has resulted. The guerrillas provide protection for the *colonos* (small-to-middle-size agriculturalists). The violent arena reduces the price of land, which is then purchased by the newly rich narcotraffickers looking for a means to launder their money. The military, in turn, is able to receive growing proportions of the national budget. The CGN collects a "war tax" on corporations, *latifundistas,* and ranchers. The military, in the areas in which they set up their drug extermination operations, extract a "tax" in the form of multiple bribes, which the *cocaleros* find more onerous than that paid the CGN.

Narcowealth has gone into the purchase of four to six million hectares (a hectare is about 2.5 acres) used primarily for cattle grazing. The new ranchers naturally join with the established ones in opposing the agrarian reform espoused by the CGN. The military benefits by receiving salary supplements for hazardous duty in the "red zones." Retired military personnel can secure lucrative consulting fees by training paramilitary forces—often composed of former soldiers. As one can see, the military and paramilitary are allies, and, hence, there is no control over the latter who have engaged in grisly massacres of suspected guerrilla sympathizers. Groups with such names as *Monchecabezas* (decapitators) have terrorized the population in an attempt to isolate the CGN from its supporters.

In January 2000, President Clinton asked Congress for "emergency spending" for Colombia. The aid, collectively referred to as "Plan Colombia," arrived that August, providing $1.32 billion for counterdrug activities in the Andean region. About 80 percent of the $862 million earmarked for Colombia will focus on assistance for their military and police forces in the form of equipment and training, making that country the third largest recipient of U.S. military aid after Israel and Egypt. The funds will enhance the efforts of the Colombian counternarcotic battalions operating in the area controlled by the FARC. In return, Colombia is committed to eliminating all of the country's opium and coca production by 2005. Congress limited the number of American service personnel involved and restricted their activities to training only. However, they accompany the Colombian forces in their forays and it will not be long before one or more GIs will be wounded or killed, tempting the government of the United States to escalate the nature of its involvement, especially during a time that the Bush administration has committed the country to the task of eliminating terrorism. Colombia lives in terror; in 2000, there were 3,707 kidnappings (an average of over 10 a day)[26] carried out by members of the guerrilla factions and the paramilitaries, and extending into Venezuelan territory. Although the paramilitaries kidnap less, their victims tend to disappear. This raises the question: As the revenues from the elimination of the poppies and coca decline, will these groups resort to even more kidnappings? The terror unleashed by the paramilitaries has arrived at the point that in September 2001, the U.S. State Department designated the United Self-Defense Forces of Colombia (AUC) as a Foreign Terrorist Organization and the target of economic and political sanctions.

The conflict has moved into northern Colombia and spread into the area bordering on Panama, where land is available and drug shipments moving north find a natural aperture. Here, it is clashing with other concerns. Not only is the violence spilling over into Panama, who has renounced its own military as a result of its former problems with dictators, but cattle ranching is moving into an area they had hoped to keep environmentally pristine. The

Colombian army is demanding roads to more efficiently combat the guerrillas, which would promote even more development. Meanwhile, Panamanians are clamoring to reinstate their discredited armed forces.

In the north, the ELN, the smaller of the two guerrilla groups, declared a unilateral Christmas truce to last from December 18 to January 6, 2002, during which time they will refrain from kidnapping, and bombing oil pipelines and transmission towers, so long as they are not molested by the armed forces or the paramilitaries.

FEMINISM

When women working in the garment industry in the free-trade zone of the Dominican Republic making sub-subsistence wages are asked about the men working in the zone, they said they felt sorry for them, even though the men's wages were higher, because "Just imagine! The wage they pay in the zone is not a wage for men." It is not a wage for women either. The women are the preferred workers because they are less likely to unionize, to fidget during long hours at the sewing machine, are better at the delicate work the garment industry requires, are more reliable, and are less likely to inebriate themselves during the weekend and call in sick on Mondays. These desired feminine traits should be worth a higher wage than their male colleagues. Why the bias?

Although gender discrimination is not peculiar to Latin America, there are historical events that contribute to its Latin flavor. In early colonial times, most "marriages" consisted of Spanish males and indigenous females. It was a case of the conqueror and vanquished and did not leave much room for sexual equality. Each eyed the other with suspicion, and women had few resources available to them in the case of an especially brutal spouse. Aside from immersing themselves totally in spiritual escapism, they might employ the resources of magic in trying to bring about a more favorable relationship. They were in charge of food preparation, and this provided them with ample opportunity to experiment with different potions and, even, poison.

Given this background, it may be easier to make sense out of the twin phenomena of *machismo* and *marianismo*. *Machismo* is an exaggerated expression of maleness. The term is derived from the Spanish term for male, *macho*. "*Es muy macho*—he is very virile" would be taken as a compliment by most men, especially *latinos*, but it would entail different expectations. As one's socioeconomic status and level of sophistication improve, the exhibition of *machismo* usually diminishes so as to completely vanish. We are referring to a type of male behavior that, alas, is still prevalent to such a degree as to be noticeable and given a name. It exhibits an inflated ego, which is easily affronted—even by the slightest gaze. Offense can result from a misinterpreted look that can escalate into deadly violence as each party projects onto the other and magnifies the other's disrespectful glance. It is accompanied by arrogance and the attending refusal to admit error. This rite makes arguments interminable because each combatant refuses to cede the last word. Each *macho* takes pride in his sexual prowess and the quantity of offspring he can sire—a positive confirmation of his virility. Aside from his mother and immediate female relatives, no woman is beyond his amorous blandishments. He takes pride in cuckolding his neighbor and jokes with his drinking partners as to the striking resemblance between his neighbor's offspring and himself. To be the victim of such a prank himself would demand the death of his neighbor and his own wife, as nothing else would stop the laughing behind his back. Women in such an environment are playthings, whose purpose is to cater to him, and whom he in turn will jealously husband.

We have approached the topic of feminism in Latin America in a roundabout way. *Machismo* leaves very little room for *feminismo*. The latter view, which stipulates gender equity, will have to emerge from the ashes of *marianismo*, or the image of woman as a long-suffering and forgiving mother and dutiful wife akin to the exalted symbol of traditional womanhood, the Virgin Mary. In Roman Catholic Latin America the statue of Mary is everywhere. Some representations of the Madonna resemble the indigenous features of the native population, and one in particular, the Virgin of Guadalupe, is the patron saint of Mexico. Subordinated for so long to a second-class status in a patriarchal society with little chance for escape, perhaps the only refuge available would be through identification with Mary and the comfort that might bring. The more difficult a woman's relation with males and the trials they burden her with, the more glorious, presumably, her condition in the next world. This present life is a test and successful passage will improve her status in the life to come. *Marianismo* and *machismo* are mutually reinforcing attitudes, and it is unlikely one will give way without the other doing likewise. So far the way out of this debilitating syndrome has been education and the evolving sense of self that accompanies the raising of consciousness.

Gender role attitudes will accompany women's changing self-image, and that will bring about empowerment and a growing independence from men. Studies by Patricia Whiteford et al. show that education is the main influence in changing women's conjugal role and reproductive attitudes in a less restrictive direction.[27] This change will not evolve easily. For example, in the area of reproductive rights, the Roman Catholic culture of Latin America will not tolerate abortion. The only exceptions are Cuba, Guyana, and Puerto Rico, where abortion is available on demand. At the other extreme are Chile, Colombia, and El Salvador, where abortion is forbidden. In between, exceptions are made for "social and socioeconomic reasons" (in the former British colonies of Belize and Barbados), "to preserve a woman's health and in the case of fetal deformation," "to save a woman's life," and "in the case of rape and incest." This means that abortions are performed illegally and under unsanitary conditions and produce a contrast between Cuba, with 39 maternal deaths per every 100,000 live births, versus averages of 160 and 220 in Central and South America, respectively. Approximately 800,000 Latin American women are admitted into hospitals yearly as a result of complications of botched abortions. In the waning days of the Pinochet dictatorship in Chile, Jaime Guzmán, a lawyer and affiliate of Opus Dei, amended the 1980 Constitution so as to criminalize therapeutic abortions claiming that women faced with martyrdom or immorality should choose the former.[28] Luis de la Barreda, president of Mexico's Human Rights Commission, is quoted as saying: "The question is not whether we agree or disagree with abortion, because whether or not it is legal, women have abortions, as statistics everywhere demonstrate. Rather, the option is choosing life or death for women. Maintaining the punitive laws currently in effect means choosing death."[29]

Other expressions of violence against women, at least, are being addressed. The hemisphere prides itself on being the first to establish an international commission on women. In 1928, after being rebuffed on previous occasions, the Inter-American Commission of Women (CIM—its acronym in Spanish) was established at the Sixth International Conference of American States meeting in Havana, Cuba. Its general mission is to improve the status of women by increasing their access to politics, promote legislation that would provide gender equity, improve the image of women displayed by the communications media, and improve their condition in prisons.

Education manifests in various ways and the repression visited upon the societies of Argentina, Brazil, Chile, Guatemala, and El Salvador during the period of the "dirty wars" engendered a different expression of womanhood than that of the long-suffering Mary. Beginning with the *Madres* of the Plaza de Mayo in Argentina and spreading to the *CoMadres* in El Salvador and the *CONAVIGUA* widows in Guatemala, the women of "disappeared" relatives organized to protest against state despotism. In the process, they have lessened the distance between the public and private spheres by indicating that state violence in the guise of covert executions and disappearance of family members is but another form of the personal violence against women through rape and spousal abuse. The *CoMadres* began as peasant women individually searching the jails, morgues, and body dumps of El Salvador for their lost ones. By the mid-1970s, through the help of the Catholic Church, they began organizing and gathering other urban mothers in their demonstrations, and petitions to the authorities. Soon they were joined by the mothers of soldiers, objecting to the forced recruitment of their young sons. These boys would be captured by the guerrillas and upon supplication by their mothers would be released by the Farabundo Martí Front of National Liberation (FMLN) to the International Red Cross that would, in turn, release them to the army where they would be executed as guerrilla sympathizers.

The two groups of mothers found common ground in their mutual opposition to military abuse. The organizational skills exhibited by the women had been developed through their participation in the *comunidades de base* (base communities) sponsored by the liberal reform priests mentioned earlier in the box on Liberation Theology. The group's concerted purpose also allowed the women to transcend the residual class distinctions separating people in Latin America. Many of these women were in turn tortured and raped by the authorities in an attempt to silence the movement.[30]

The latest of the hemispheric efforts to improve the status of women has been the Inter-American Convention on the Prevention, Punishment, and Eradication of Violence Against Women ratified June 9, 1994, in Belem do Para, Brazil. It defines violence against women as "any act or conduct, based on gender, which causes death or physical, sexual or psychological harm or suffering to women, whether in the public or the private sphere." Achieving the lofty goals of this convention will take time. The next step will be to create in each state the legal resources that will provide the protection.

Review Questions

1. Why are not some of the countries in Latin America further along in their economic development?
2. What factors conspire to prolong the illegal traffic in drugs?
3. Account for the persistence of centralized government in Latin America.
4. Why are the United States and Cuba finding it so difficult to overcome their differences?
5. Employing examples from your reading, account for the endurance of violence as a way of pursuing political, social, and economic ends in Latin America.

Key Terms

- **Criollo**—A person of Spanish descent born in the Americas and prohibited by Spanish policy from occupying the higher levels of the colonial bureaucracy. The local initiative for the independence movements came from these people who had less attachment to the metropolis.
- **Peninsular**—The relative of a *criollo* who would be allowed to serve in the higher levels of colonial administration.
- **Cabildo**—The town council; a minor administrative post, open to participation by *criollos* and the place where colonists were given the opportunity to engage in a degree of self-government. It became the training ground for autonomy and the launching point for cries of independence from Spain.

- **Caudillo**—Literally, the "man on horseback." The history of Latin America is littered with what amounts to "war lords" who seize political power through extra-legal means and govern by force of their personality, inhibiting the institutionalization of the political process.
- **ISI**—Import-substitution industrialization is an economic doctrine which promotes the notion of a self-sufficient national economy. The disruption of trade resulting from the second world war helped to establish the policy. Since then, it has become apparent that the policy would have a difficult time succeeding in the face of the limited markets associated with most of the Latin American economies and the external competition from the more advanced nations. The policy has been eclipsed in recent times by the notions of "free trade," promoted by the United States and the International Monetary Fund.
- **Personalismo**—The politics associated with the charisma of the *caudillos* such as Fidel Castro, Juan Domingo Perón, Getúlio Vargas, and Lázaro Cárdenas, whose forceful personalities and popular appeal inhibit the evolution of political institutions that can establish themselves and provide for a more structured and stable political environment.
- **Fidelistas**—The followers of Fidel Castro.
- **NAFTA**—The North American Free Trade Agreement is a treaty initiated in 1994 establishing a free trade area among Canada, Mexico, and the United States. It represents an attempt to promote the economic policy of free trade in contrast with the protectionism, tariffs, and quotas associated with import-substitution industrialization. Other countries of the hemisphere are experimenting with regional free-trade areas such as that among Brazil, Uruguay, and Argentina (MERCOSUR) in the southern cone. The current talk, led by the United States, is to establish a hemisphere-wide free-trade area known as the Free Trade Area of the Americas.
- **Guantánamo Bay**—A United States naval installation on Cuba's southern Caribbean coast which the U.S. obtained from Cuba as a condition for removing American troops after the Spanish-American War. This base, which is currently housing prisoners taken in the battle against the Taliban and Al-Qaeda terrorists, has been a source of irritation to Cuban nationalists. The lingering resentment associated with the memory of U.S. meddling in Cuba's war of independence provides a receptive environment for Castro's anti-*yanqui* fulminations.
- **Organization of American States**—The OAS emerged after World War II with the establishment of the Rio Treaty in 1947 and the 1948 Treaties of Bogotá. It took the nations of Latin America over a century after their independence to trust the United States to the point of joining it in an alliance to protect the security of the hemisphere as well as promote democratic institution. With the waning of the cold war, the emphasis of the organization has changed from security to advancing democracy and human rights. These issues are now threatened with the problem of narcotrafficking.

Useful Web Sites

http://www.cia.gov/cia/publications/factbook/geos/br.html
http://www.cia.gov/cia/publications/factbook/geos/mx.html
http://lanic.utexas.edu/la/mexico/
http://lanic.utexas.edu/la/cb/cuba/
http://www.cia.gov/cia/publications/factbook/geos/cu.html
http://www.cubamapa.com/
http://www.oas.org/EN/PINFO/gsindice.htm

Notes

1. Nicolas Sánchez-Albornoz, *The Population of Latin America,* trans. W. Richardson (Berkeley: University of California Press, 1974), p. 86; in *Latin America: Perspectives on a Region,* ed. Jack W. Hopkins (New York: Holmes and Mier, 1987), p. 11.
2. C. W. Harring, *The Spanish Empire in America* (New York: Harbinger, 1963), p. 5.
3. Abraham F. Lowenthal, ed., *Exporting Democracy: The United States and Latin America; Themes and Issues* (London: Johns Hopkins University Press, 1991).
4. Samuel Flagg Bemis, *The Latin American Policy of the United States* (New York: Norton, 1967), pp. 63–66.
5. For a straightforward contrast of many of the contending theories about economic and political development, see Ronald H. Chilcote, "Theories of Development and Underdevelopment," chap. 7 in *Theories of Comparative Politics: The Search for a Paradigm.* (Boulder, CO: Westview Press, 1981). Other helpful sources would be Howard Wiarda, ed., *Non-Western Theories of Development: Regional Norms Versus Global Trends.* (Fort Worth, TX: Harcourt Brace College Pub., 1999); see also Hernando de Soto, *The Other Path: The Invisible Revolution in the Third World,* trans. June Abbot (New York: Harper & Row, 1985), for a critical study of the causes for economic stagnation in his country by a Peruvian businessperson. De Soto describes the internal roadblocks to development, such as the interminable formal requirements imposed on newcomers by the economic establishment. For example, an effort to establish a typical one-owner garment factory required 10 months and a loss of net profits equivalent to 32 times the minimum living wage, as well as 11 permits. The owners were asked for bribes 10 times to "expedite" approval, but they paid only the two, without which the project would have been killed. Enormous resources are being squandered daily in much of Latin America because of the control associated with the old economic order. In his more recent study, *The Mystery of Capital: Why Capitalism Succeeds in the West and Fails Everywhere Else* (New York: Basic Books, 2000), de Soto hypothesizes that the lack of development in the "other world" is attributable to the notion that global capitalism cannot succeed without local capital. The orthodox remedies of global capitalism—balanced budgets, free trade, stable currencies, and foreign investments—are not everything; local development is essential for success. What frustrates local development in much of the "other world" is legal access to property. The majority of the population does not have title to shacks that constitute their dwellings. Their very shelter is precarious and without title they lack the equity which would extend the foundations of an economic system beyond the minority presently comprising the elites. If access to property were simplified, development would follow. It would be helpful to read de Soto along with authors such as Claudio Veliz, Lawrence E. Harrison, and

Samuel P. Huntington (*Culture Matters: How Values Shape Human Progress,* [New York: Basic Books, 2000]), who remind us of the contribution made by culture to a nation's economic progress. For an uncritical view of neoliberal economics, see Paul Craig Roberts and Karen Lafollette Araujo, *The Capitalist Revolution in Latin America* (New York: Oxford University Press, 1995). Antidotes for this enthusiasm can be found in James Petras, "Alternative to neoliberalism in Latin America," *Latin American Perspectives* 24, no. 1 (January 1997) or Alan Tonelson, *The Race to the Bottom: Why a Worldwide Worker Surplus and Uncontrolled Free Trade Are Sinking American Living Standards* (Boulder, Colo.: Westview Press, 2000).

6. Thomas Skidmore, *Politics in Brazil, 1930–1969: An Experiment in Democracy* (New York: Oxford University Press, 1967), p. 206.

7. Jan Knippers Black, *United States Penetration of Brazil* (Philadelphia: University of Pennsylvania Press, 1977).

8. Hugh Thomas, *Cuba: The Pursuit of Freedom* (New York: Harper & Row, 1971), p. 557.

9. Susan Kaufman Purcell and David Rothkopf, eds., *Cuba: The Contours of Change* (Boulder, Colo.: Lynne Rienner Publishers, 2000), p. 13.

10. Ibid., p. 22.

11. *New York Times,* "Cuba on the Morning After," 16 August 2001.

12. Fred Rosen and Mo-Marie Burt, *NACLA: Report on the Americas* 33, no. 6 (May/June 2000): 15.

13. Peter Andreas, "The Political Economy of Narco-Corruption in Mexico," *Current History* 97 (April 1998): 160.

14. Ben Kohl and Linda Farthing, "The Price of Success: Bolivia's War Against Drugs and the Poor," *NACLA: Report on The Americas* 35, no. 1 (July/August 2001): 37.

15. Op. cit., p. 162.

16. *New York Times,* 7 June 1998, sec. 1, p. 14.

17. Peter Zirnite, "The Militarization of the Drug War in Latin America," *Current History* 97, no. 118 (April 1998): 166.

18. Sebastian Rotella, " 'You Fly, You Die' Approach to Drug War Faces Scrutiny," *Los Angeles Times,* 25 April 2001, p. A-1.

19. Andrew Reding, "Chiapas Is Mexico: The Imperative of Political Reform," *World Policy Journal* 11, no. 1 (spring 1994).

20. Edwardo Silva, "The Politics of Sustainable Development: Native Policy in Chile, Venezuela, Costa Rica and Mexico," *Journal of Latin American Studies* 29, pt. 2 (May 1997): 481.

21. Stephen P. Mumme and Pamela Duncan, "The Commission for Environmental Cooperation and Environmental Management in the Americas," *Journal of Inter-American Studies and World Affairs* 39, no. 4 (winter 1997–98).

22. See reference in Marc Edelman, "Rethinking the Hamburger Thesis: Deforestation and the Crisis of Central America's Beef Exports," in *Crossing Currents: Continuity and Change in Latin America,* ed. Michael B. Whiteford and Scott Whiteford (Upper Saddle River, New Jersey: Prentice Hall, 1998), p. 394.

23. *Financial Times* (London), 14 December 2001, 2nd ed., p. 12.

24. Maria D. Alvarez, "Forests Under Fire," *NACLA: Report on the Americas* 35, no. 1 (July/August 2001): 29.

25. Nazih Richani, "The Political Economy of Violence: The War-System in Colombia," *Journal of Inter-American Studies and World Affairs* 39, no. 2 (1997): 37–81.

26. Marc Cooper, "Plan Colombia," in *The Nation* (March 19, 2001), quoting David Buitrago, legal director of País Libre, a nonprofit that fights kidnapping.

27. Patricia Whiteford, E. W. Morris, and Michael B. Whiteford, "Education and Changing Roles in a Transitional Society: The Case of Rural Costa Rica," *Journal of Developing Societies* 2, no. 1 (April 1986): 89–102.
28. Lu Rayas, "Criminalizing Abortion: A Crime Against Women," *NACLA: Report on the Americas* 31, no. 4 (January/February 1998): 25.
29. Ibid., p. 26.
30. For a collection of these accounts, see Jennifer Schirmer, "Seeking of the Truth and the Gendering of Consciousness," chap. 2 in *"Viva": Women and Popular Protest in Latin America,* ed. Sarah A. Radcliffe and Sallie Westwood. London, NY: Routledge, 1993.

For Further Reading

Aronson, Bernard W., and William D. Rogers. Co-Chairs. *U.S.-Cuban Relations in the 21st Century: A Follow-on Chairman's Report of an Independent Task Force Sponsored by the Council on Foreign Relations.* New York: Council on Foreign Relations, Inc., 2001.

Atkins, G. Pope. *Latin America in the International Political System.* 3rd ed. rev. Boulder, Colo.: Westview Press, 1995.

Bhagwati, Jagdish. *The Wind of the Hundred Days: How Washington Mismanaged Globalization.* Cambridge, Mass.: The MIT Press, 2000.

Cardoso, Fernando H., and Enzo Faletto. *Dependency and Development in Latin America.* Berkeley: University of California Press, 1979.

Celarier, Michelle. "Privatization: A Case Study in Corruption," *Journal of International Affairs* 50, no. 2 (winter 1997): 531.

Cockcroft, James D. *Neighbors in Turmoil: Latin America.* New York: Harper & Row, 1989.

———. *Latin America: History, Politics, and U.S. Policy.* Chicago: Nelson-Hall, 1996.

Cubitt, Tessa. *Latin American Society.* 2nd ed. New York: Longman Scientific and Technical, 1995.

Domínguez, Jorge I., and Rafael Hernández, eds. *U.S.-Cuban Relations in the 1990s.* Boulder, Colo.: Westview Press, 1989.

Dorner, Peter. *Latin American Land Reforms in Theory and Practice: A Retrospective Analysis.* Madison: University of Wisconsin Press, 1992.

Gilpin, Robert. *Global Political Economy: Understanding the International Economic Order.* Princeton: Princeton University Press, 2001.

———. *The Political Economy of International Relations.* New Jersey: Princeton University Press, 1987.

González, Victoria, and Karen Kampwirth. *Radical Women in Latin America.* University Park, Penn.: Pennsylvania State University Press, 2001.

Harrison, Lawrence E. *The Pan-American Dream: Do Latin America's Cultural Values Discourage True Partnership with the United States and Canada?* New York: Basic Books, 1991.

Korzeniewicz, Roberto Patricio, and William C. Smith. *Latin America in the World-Economy.* Westport, Conn.: Greenwood Press, 1996.

Lawton, Jorge A., ed. *Privatization Amidst Poverty: Contemporary Challenges in Latin American Political Economy.* Miami: North South Center Press, 1993.

Lowenthal, Abraham F., and Gregory F. Treventon, eds. *Latin America in a New World.* Boulder, Colo.: Westview Press, 1994.

MacDonald, Gordon J., Daniel L. Nielson, and Marc A. Stern. *Latin American Environmental Policy in International Perspective.* Boulder, Colo.: Westview Press, 1997.

Mainwaring, Scott, and Arturo Valenzuela, eds. *Politics, Society, and Democracy: Latin America.* Boulder, Colo.: Westview Press, 1998.

Meller, Patricio, ed. *The Latin American Development Debate: Neostructuralism, Neomonetarism, and Adjustment Processes.* Boulder, Colo.: Westview Press, 1991.

Molineu, Harold. *U.S. Policy toward Latin America: From Regionalism to Globalism.* 2nd ed. Boulder, Colo.: Westview Press, 1990.

Morley, Samuel A. *Poverty and Inequality in Latin America.* Baltimore: Johns Hopkins University Press, 1995.

O'Donnell, Guillermo. *Modernization and Bureaucratic-Authoritarianism: Studies in South American Politics.* Berkeley: Institute of International Studies, University of California, 1973.

Pastor, Robert A. *Whirlpool: U.S. Foreign Policy toward Latin America and the Caribbean.* Princeton, N.J.: Princeton University Press, 1993.

Petras, James. "Alternatives to Neoliberalism in Latin America." *Latin American Perspectives* 24, no. 1 (January 1997): 80.

Petras, James, and Morris Morley. *Latin America in the Time of Cholera: Electoral Politics, Market Economics, and Permanent Crisis.* New York: Routledge, 1992.

Purcell, Susan Kaufman, and David Rothkopf. *Cuba: The Contours of Change.* Boulder, Colo.: Lynne Rienner Publishers, 2000.

Radcliffe, Sarah A., and Sallie Westwood, eds. *"Viva": Women and Popular Protest in Latin America.* London and New York: Routledge, 1993.

Randall, Laura, ed. *The Political Economy of Latin America in the Postwar Period.* Austin: University of Texas Press, 1997.

Roberts, Paul Craig, and Karen Lafollette Araujo. *The Capitalist Revolution in Latin America.* New York: Oxford University Press, 1997.

Silva-Michelena, José A., ed. *Latin America: Peace, Democratization & Economic Crisis.* United Nations University. Studies on Peace and Regional Security. London: Zed Books, 1988.

Skidmore, Thomas E., and Peter H. Smith. *Modern Latin America.* 2nd ed. New York: Oxford University Press, 1989.

Smith, William C., and Roberto Patricio Korzeniewicz, eds. *Politics, Social Change, and Economic Restructuring in Latin America.* Boulder, Colo.: Published by the North-South Center Press at the University of Miami and distributed by Lynne Rienner Publishers, Inc., 1997.

De Soto, Hernando. *The Mystery of Capital: Why Capitalism Triumphs in the West and Fails Everywhere Else.* New York: Basic Books, 2000.

Stein, Stanley, and Barbara Stein. *The Colonial Heritage of Latin America.* New York: Oxford University Press, 1970.

Thiesenhusen, William C. *Broken Promises: Agrarian Reform and the Latin American Campesino.* Boulder, Colo.: Westview Press, 1995.

Tonelson, Alan. *The Race to the Bottom: Why a Worldwide Worker Surplus and Uncontrolled Free Trade Are Sinking American Living Standards.* Boulder, Colo.: Westview Press, 2000.

Trouillot, Michel-Rolph. *Haiti: State against the Nation: Origins and Legacy of Duvalierism.* New York: Monthly Review Press, 1990.

Tulchin, Joseph S., and Andrew I. Rudman, eds. *Economic Development and Environmental Protection in Latin America.* Boulder, Colo.: Lynne Rienner Publishers, 1991.

Veliz, Claudio. *The Centralist Tradition of Latin America.* Princeton, N.J.: Princeton University Press, 1980.

Wiarda, Howard J. *American Foreign Policy toward Latin America in the 80s and 90s: Issues and Controversies from Reagan to Bush.* New York and London: New York University Press, 1992.

———, ed. *Non-Western Theories of Development: Regional Norms Versus Global Trends.* Fort Worth, Tex.: Harcourt Brace College Pub., 1999.

CHAPTER 6

Sub-Saharan Africa

Ira Reed

Seek ye first the political kingdom and all other things will be added unto you.

KWAME NKRUMAH

Viewed at the beginning of the new millennium, these words from one of Africa's leaders in the post–World War II generation seem quaint or naive. Independence from colonial rule did not bring "all other things." As emphasized in this chapter, Africa's problems have multiplied in the past decade. In addition, foreign interests now appear to be focused elsewhere in the world. The political instability, economic decline, social unrest, and environmental degradation that became commonplace in most of the states of the region will not quickly improve, despite some hopeful developments.

From 1957 to 1980, more than three dozen African colonies achieved independence, some peacefully and others violently. Despite the different roads taken, a common theme ran through these new states in their early years: hope, excitement, deliverance.

This early enthusiasm struck a responsive chord in the West. Some leaders were genuinely supportive of the new order. British Prime Minister Harold Macmillan declared that "the winds of change" were blowing through Africa and would have to be accommodated. Youthful President John F. Kennedy embraced the notion of a Peace Corps, with Africa a major recipient of hundreds and then thousands of practical idealists. Furthermore, it was believed that the East-West conflict would be fought in the Other World, and the battle for the hearts and minds of the people of Africa was seen as an important objective.

If this earlier period was one of optimism and gains in Africa, then the 1980s was one of pessimism and losses. In fact, the period has been described as "the lost decade." Although there are success stories and some recent encouraging signs, the overall situation is disheartening. It is true that the 1990s witnessed a modest increase in participatory political systems. Furthermore, as will be seen in the Case Studies and Flashpoint sections of this chapter, several of the wars in Africa have abated or ended. However, many countries continue to be under either military rule or strict civilian governments in which democracy, at least as we understand it in the West (e.g., freedom of speech and press, competitive elections, and an independent judiciary), is significantly restricted or nonexistent. In a few states or areas within states, warlords have taken over and governments of any sort have ceased to exist.

By virtually any index, the economic situation has worsened. Per capita income, already the lowest in the Other World, actually declined during the 1980s to rise little in the 1990s. (For recent figures, see Table 6.1.) The international monetary debt of most African states soared. Unemployment or underemployment continued its upward climb. Most agricultural products and minerals are fetching lower world prices than 15 or 20 years ago, causing even those states possessing significant oil deposits, such as Nigeria, to face periods of declining prices. Many millions simply do not get enough to eat.

Nor is the picture any brighter in other areas. The population explosion continues unabated with a few significant exceptions, and is again far higher than in the rest of the Other World. Food production has not kept pace with population growth, and despite rising food imports, the average African has less to eat now than in 1980. Environmental degradation increases yearly, and the underlying support systems sag under the onslaught. More and more species are endangered as impoverished humans encroach on their habitat, sometimes killing the animals for profit. Similarly, the quality of education is in serious straits, and new health problems such as acquired immunodeficiency syndrome (AIDS) dwarf older ones, some of which have been curbed or eliminated, while others, such as malaria, ebola, and tuberculosis, have burst anew among the population.

The history and geography provide some clues to the causes of this unhappy situation. A discussion of the political, social, and economic realities within and beyond Africa today provides additional explanations. The case studies illustrate the dilemmas the peoples of Africa are facing. The chapter concludes with Flashpoints on current trouble spots. (Discussion of the five North African states bordering the Mediterranean is included in chapter 8.)

GEOGRAPHY

Africa, second in size only to Asia, has some of the world's mightiest rivers and abundant mineral resources. Nevertheless, the region has more than its share of natural impediments to development, including its relative isolation from other areas of the world. The Atlantic Ocean is located to the west of the continent and the Indian Ocean to the east. Prevailing wind patterns on the west coast minimized maritime contacts between Africans and Europeans until the fifteenth or

TABLE 6.1 AFRICA

Country	Population (thousands)	Population Growth Rate (%) (1992–2000)	Infant Mortality Rate (per 1,000 live births)	Population under 15 Years of Age (%)	Life Expectancy (years)	Urban Population (%)	UNDP (United Nations Development Program) Literacy Rate (%) (1992)	Arable Land (%)	UNDP Per Capita GNP ($U.S.)
Northern									
Algeria	31,194	1.7	42	35	70	60	62	3	1,490
Egypt	68,360	1.7	66	35	63	45	51	3	2,850
Libya	5,115	2.4	26	36	75	87	76	1	6,700
Morocco	30,122	1.7	49	35	69	55	44	21	3,200
Tunisia	9,593	1.2	30	30	74	65	67	19	5,200
Western									
Benin	6,396	3.0	95	48	50	42	37	13	1,300
Burkina Faso	11,946	2.7	105	48	47	18	19	13	1,000
Cape Verde	401	1.0	43	44	69	61	72	11	1,090
Côte d'Ivoire	15,981	2.6	13	32	45	48	95	8	6,700
Gambia	1,367	3.2	74	45	53	32	39	18	1,000
Ghana	19,534	1.9	75	42	57	38	64	12	1,800
Guinea	7,466	2.0	124	43	46	32	36	2	1,180
Guinea-Bissau	1,286	2.4	107	42	49	23	55	11	1,000
Liberia	3,164	2.0	98	43	51	44	38	1	1,000
Mali	10,686	3.0	117	47	47	29	31	2	790
Mauritania	2,668	2.9	75	46	51	56	38	0	1,890

Country									
Niger	10,076	2.8	111	48	41	20	14	3	970
Nigeria	123,338	2.7	68	44	52	43	57	33	960
Senegal	9,987	2.9	58	45	62	47	33	12	1,600
Sierra Leone	5,233	3.7	123	45	45	36	31	7	530
Togo	5,018	2.7	75	46	55	33	52	38	1,670
Eastern									
Burundi	6,054	3.2	98	47	46	9	35	44	740
Djibouti	451	1.5	98	42	51	83	46	0	1,200
Ethiopia	64,117	2.8	123	47	45	17	35	12	560
Kenya	30,339	1.5	59	43	48	32	78	7	1,550
Madagascar	15,506	3.0	88	45	55	29	46	4	730
Malawi	10,385	1.6	131	45	38	24	56	34	940
Mauritius	1,179	.9	16	26	71	41	83	49	10,000
Mozambique	19,104	1.5	115	43	38	39	40	4	900
Rwanda	7,229	1.1	112	43	39	6	60	35	690
Seychelles	79	0.5	16	29	70	63	84	2	7,000
Somalia	7,253	2.9	126	44	46	27	24	2	600
Sudan	35,079	2.8	69	45	57	35	46	5	930
Tanzania	35,306	2.6	94	45	52	32	68	3	730
Uganda	23,317	2.7	89	51	43	14	62	25	1,020
Zambia	9,582	2.0	91	48	37	40	78	7	880
Zimbabwe	11,342	.3	61	40	38	35	85	7	2,400
Middle									
Angola	10,145	2.2	126	43	38	34	40	2	1,000
Cameroon	15,422	2.5	75	43	55	48	63	13	2,000
Central African Republic	3,513	1.8	101	43	44	41	60	3	1,640
Chad	8,425	3.3	114	48	50	23	48	3	1,000
Congo, Democratic Republic of	51,965	3.2	97	48	49	30	77	3	710

(continued)

TABLE 6.1 (Continued)

Country	Population (thousands)	Population Growth Rate (%) (1992–2000)	Infant Mortality Rate (per 1,000 live births)	Population under 15 Years of Age (%)	Life Expectancy (years)	Urban Population (%)	UNDP (United Nations Development Program) Literacy Rate (%) (1992)	Arable Land (%)	UNDP Per Capita GNP ($U.S.)
Congo, Republic of	2,831	2.2	98	43	47	62	75	0	1,500
Equatorial Guinea	474	2.5	89	43	54	47	78	5	1,500
Gabon	1,208	1.1	81	33	50	81	63	1	6,400
São Tomé and Príncipe	16	3.2	51	48	35	46	73	2	1,100
Southern									
Botswana	1,576	.8	59	41	39	50	70	1	3,600
Lesotho	2,143	1.7	77	40	51	27	71	11	2,400
Namibia	1,771	1.6	65	43	42	30	76	1	4,100
South Africa	43,421	.5	52	33	51	50	82	10	6,800
Swaziland	1,083	2.1	100	46	40	26	77	11	4,200

SOURCES: Infant Mortatlity Rate, Population Under 15 Years of Age, Urban Population, Literacy Rate, and Per Capita GDP from *The World Almanac and Book of Facts, 2001*.
Population Growth Rate, Life Expectancy, and Arable Land from *CIA World Factbook, 2000*.

sixteenth century. With the Sahara Desert in the north, it is easy to understand why overland transportation from Europe and North Africa was and is spotty. The Kalahari Desert in the southern part of the continent is an additional obstacle.

Africa's great rivers—Nile, Zaire (Congo), Niger, Zambezi, and Orange—all have cataracts, sand bars, or other obstructions, which also undermine rather than enhance communications. The continent's smooth coastline, and thus its lack of natural harbors, has been another problem, although today coastal cities such as Dakar, Lagos, Luanda, and Dar es Salaam are highly important.

Most of the region's interior is flat or gently undulating. The major exception is the great Rift Valley system in eastern Africa, which runs north to south for hundreds of miles and features deep trenches, 20 to 50 miles wide, dug into the Earth. Inactive volcanoes, frequent Earth tremors, and occasional earthquakes occur in the area. Lake Victoria is the largest lake in Africa, and Mount Kilimanjaro is the continent's highest mountain, 19,340 feet above sea level.

Whatever the focus, African geography runs the gamut from scarcity to abundance. Although temperatures are generally high, rainfall, when abundant, gives rise to lush vegetation; more often, the absence of rainfall contributes to a parched landscape. Varying soil quality also helps produce rainforests, savannas, or deserts. Mineral resources follow the same oscillating pattern. Some areas in central and southern Africa are uniquely blessed, whereas other locales are virtually void of substances valued in the modern world (see Figure 6.1 on page 186).

The complex interaction of temperature, rainfall, population growth and distribution, and soils is of crucial significance in Africa today. The human habitat was once more hospitable. Thirty-five hundred years ago what is now the Sahara was green. Just 40 years ago the Sahel, which includes the area lying just south of the Sahara, was able to sustain a population of perhaps 20 million. Today, famine is an ever-present danger. Millions of nomadic herders, traders, and small farmers have been turned into refugees trying to eke out a living in an increasingly unforgiving environment.

As a result, both the farmer, whose land becomes more difficult to till, and the herders are forced to move to overcrowded cities. Nouakchott, for instance, the capital of Mauritania and on the edge of the Sahel, has grown from 20,000 people in 1960 to more than 735,000 today. Many of its people barely survive; some starve. The same might be said of Khartoum, the capital of Sudan, some 3,000 miles away. In the last few years, eastern and southern Africa have been affected in a similar way. In fact, the encroaching desert, aided by drought, has affected some two dozen African states. In 1998, the flooding Nile meant that hundreds of thousands of people near Khartoum were victimized both by an absence of rain and a deluge of water.

In the past, Africa's strategic importance rested on its mineral wealth in the central and southern parts of the continent and its geographic "chokepoints" on the perimeter of the region. High-tech industries of the West relied on platinum, chrome, and vanadium, which are found almost exclusively in Africa. Gibraltar, the Suez Canal, Bab el Mandeb, and the Cape of Good Hope at the southern tip of the continent were strategic areas of interest to both East and West. With the end of the cold war, both the economic and geopolitical standing of the region declined.

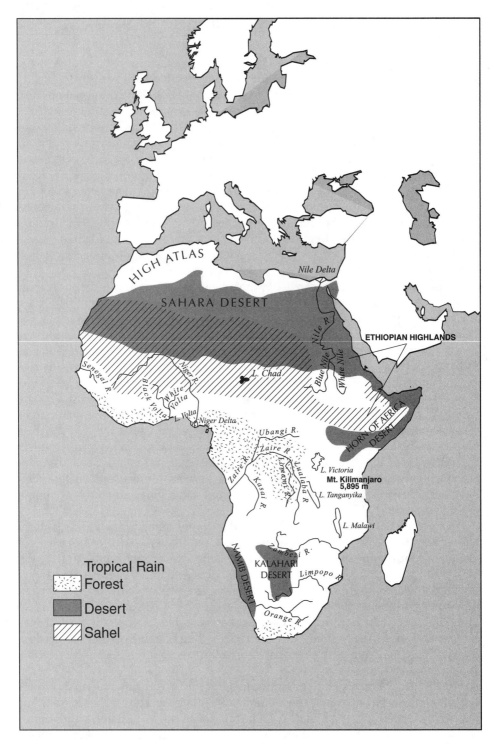

FIGURE 6.1 The Physical Geography of Africa

PEOPLE

Africa's people have been divided by many factors including race, ethnicity, religion, country, and class. The importance of race was established as early as the fifteenth century. Later, it was tied to class when positions in society became dominated by Europeans. Because of the colonial legacy, the belief that one race is superior or inferior to another still has considerable significance in Africa. The emphasis on race was clearest in South Africa, where apartheid, a form of separate development based on race, was officially proclaimed by whites in 1948 and rescinded only in 1990.

Race still remains important in many other African countries. In several former French colonies, there are almost as many Europeans now as there were at independence more than three decades ago. There, as elsewhere, Europeans have many of the most prestigious and best-paying jobs. Often, being white gets one a better seat in a van or truck or allows one to be waved through a checkpoint while others with a darker skin must wait. For the present then, Europeans, a name often given to all whites, still enjoy a high social status and lifestyle far above that of most of the indigenous population.

Between the Europeans and the Africans on the ladder of success are the Indians of East and South Africa and the Lebanese of West Africa. Both groups are major forces in retail and wholesale merchandising and in the economy generally. Because of their positions, both are also targets of protest from those below them on the ladder.

When discussing language, ethnic groups, cultures (and subcultures), and religions, the key concepts are diversity and complexity. There are, conservatively, many hundreds of different ethnic groups. (Because of the negative connotations of the words *tribe* and *tribalism*, the terms *ethnic group* and *ethnicity* have replaced them.) Thus, there are many hundreds of distinct languages and cultures. Although some groups number in the millions of members, others have only hundreds. The sheer number of such groups throughout Africa makes this dimension unique to the continent. Ethnic divisions are a powerful force today. Ongoing struggles in such diverse states as Angola, Burundi, Congo, Ethiopia, Kenya, Liberia, Mauritania, Nigeria, Rwanda, and Sierra Leone may be explained, in part, by deep-seated ethnic divisions.

African religions, again diverse and complex, have generally accommodated external religions, accepting some aspects and modifying others. Christian missionaries, who preceded colonial officials, remained after their government's departure. Although numbers are hard to confirm, there is a consensus that the number of people embracing either the monotheism of Christianity or Islam in some form is growing rapidly. The Roman Catholic population, for instance, has grown considerably in the last decade to more than 120 million, and Pope John Paul II has visited the continent no fewer than 12 times. Local customs and beliefs, however, have challenged Rome's pronouncements; indigenous churches therefore abound. Islam has been an important political factor in many countries in the Sahel, the Horn of Africa, spreading deeper into Central and West Africa also, and militant fundamentalist movements have made inroads.

Most people in the West give their primary support to the nation-state, but such a commitment is rare in Africa. Race, ethnicity, and religion have historical and deep-seated appeals that compete with the nation-state. With a large majority of Africans still continuing to live in the rural areas, developing support for the nation-state is a challenge. Only rarely do state and ethnic boundaries coincide. Nationalism is further hampered by the small size and population of many of the countries, as well as their lack of resources.

A belief in a shared past or shared future, in myths or traditions, in joint economic or social institutions, or in a common culture is in short supply on the national level. Rarely is there a common indigenous language. In fact, in most African states, the official language is a European tongue. In conflicts between personal, family, village, or ethnic ties on the one hand, and a national perspective on the other, the larger focus usually loses. National leaders and others in the intelligentsia have the media at their disposal in their call for increased support for the state, and expanding education for children and adults helps. Nevertheless, developing a broadly based nationalism is proceeding slowly.

As in the former Soviet Union and Eastern Europe, class formation is expanding and perhaps sharpening. With few exceptions, the emergence of a small elite class, often tied to one ethnic group, has become the norm. For the time being, a comfortable lifestyle is beyond even the aspirations of the great majority. With the move to privatization described in the section on economics, some will improve their lot dramatically, but many others will become more embittered as life passes them by.

At the beginning of the twentieth century, the continent of Africa had fewer than 100 million people. Its population now is more than 800 million. During the 1970s and 1980s, the population growth rate increased to more than 3 percent a year. Different sources say that the region's annual population increase is about 2.7 percent. At most, that means a doubling in 25 years, but some factors, including population control policies and the ravages of AIDS, might curb this rate in certain areas.

The birthrate in sub-Saharan Africa has declined slightly in the last generation, but the death rate has declined more. By 1995, the gap had become immense, with an annual birthrate per thousand of 43.1 and a death rate of 14.9! More specifically, the infant mortality rate declined by almost 40 percent between 1970 and 1994. With fewer babies dying, there will be one less reason for parents to want more children. Births per married woman in the region declined only from 6.7 in 1960–1965 to 5.8 in 1998. Botswana, Kenya, Côte d'Ivoire, Tanzania, Djibouti, Guinea, and Zimbabwe have achieved varying degrees of success at population control. Kenya, which a decade ago was averaging close to 4 percent growth per year, the world's highest, is now well under 3 percent, and average family size there declined from eight in the 1970s to 5.4 in 1998. These declines must continue. Widespread government programs enacted there since the late 1970s have reduced childbirth rates in Kenya by one-third. Even with consideration of declining birthrates and increasing deaths from AIDS in some regions, Africa's population is still projected to double in less than three decades.

Only 18 percent of married women between the ages of 15 and 49 used family planning in Africa in 1998; only 12 percent of married African women used modern contraceptive methods. Information and distribution systems for population control are stunted. Some governments still believe family planning will curb the economic potential of their states. In most countries, the status of women is low and their sex education lags behind that of men. The religious admonition calling for large families is another factor driving population growth.[1] It is feared that unless fertility rates soon decline far more than they have, the continent's life-support systems will be overwhelmed and the mortality rate will increase. Over the last 30 years, economic growth has barely kept pace with population growth. Life expectancy at birth in sub-Saharan Africa in 2000 stood at only 50 years, by far the lowest in the Other World. Of the 35 nations categorized as having "low human development" in the 2000 United Nations (UN) Human Development Index, a widely recognized measure of the quality of life that combines life expectancy and educational statistics, 29 are sub-Saharan African, including the lowest-ranked 24 nations.

HISTORY

Africa's history before the arrival of the Europeans was rich, varied, and complex. It involved many types of political systems, social structures, and economic patterns. It also involved considerable interaction with the peoples of North Africa, the Arabian Peninsula, and even China. Africa has been called "the cradle of human history," "the cradle of mankind," and "the first habitat of man." These phrases apply, because the oldest human remains, dating back at least 3 million years, were found in eastern Africa. Nevertheless, many people did not think Africa had a history because, to them, history was based on written language. This bias has now been corrected. In certain areas south of the Sahara, written Arabic was in use 1,000 years ago. More important, we now realize that oral traditions, archaeological exploration, comparative linguistics, art styles, ethnography, radio carbon dating, and a host of other tools can provide a rich history, predating the written word.

The domestication of cattle is 6,000 to 7,000 years old in Africa. Working with metal and iron, planting crops, and engaging in long-distance trade are occupations that go back millennia as well. In fact, there is much discussion today about how much Egypt, often referred to as the cradle of civilization, was influenced by areas further south. The KhoiKhoi (Hottentots), San (Bushmen), and Twa (Pygmies) had long inhabited much of central and southern Africa until incursions from West Africa around the eleventh century began to reduce their spheres.

African kingdoms of great size and wealth predate the European colonial presence by many hundreds of years. Some of the best-known empires—Ghana, Mali, and Songhai—which together lasted over 1,000 years, were in the western Sudan, south of the Sahara. Here, Islam made its presence felt, especially among the rulers of Mali and Songhai. Great Zimbabwe in southern Africa, with its imposing stone structures, reached its apex in the fifteenth century.

By the eighth century, Arab traders had brought Islam to the Horn of Africa, from which it gradually spread south and west. The Arab presence, however, went back much further, especially along the east coast. In succeeding centuries, traders pushed into the interior, although African culture remained dominant throughout. The Arab influence was great, however, from the formation of towns along the Indian Ocean to the rise of Swahili as the most important language in the region. The arrival of the Portuguese, with their superior military power, at the end of the fifteenth century signaled the rapid decline of Arab culture in the area.

Until the latter half of the nineteenth century, there were few Europeans in sub-Saharan Africa, especially in the vast interior. Despite their small numbers, they had a profound and lasting impact on African life. The institution of Western-style slavery cost the continent anywhere from 12 to 50 million men, women, and children. (See the Flashpoints section.) In the seventeenth and eighteenth centuries, slaves were the major export from the west coast of Africa.

By 1850, the European presence in Africa had existed along narrow coastal strips for over 350 years. The Portuguese in the fifteenth and sixteenth centuries, the Dutch in the seventeenth century, and the British in the eighteenth and first part of the nineteenth centuries had been dominant because of sea power. By about 1850, newfound European attention to the "Dark Continent" coincided with turbulence in several parts of Africa and resulted in greater penetration of the interior than ever before. The European objectives in Africa included raw materials to feed the Industrial Revolution, new markets, promising investments, naval bases, the renewed drive to "save souls," and a multifaceted quest for new knowledge.

THE COLONIAL EXPERIENCE

Despite the increasing presence of the Europeans, 90 percent of the continent was ruled by Africans until the last two decades of the nineteenth century. The European powers had not thought the benefits of occupation were worth the costs. As the foreigners jockeyed for power and prestige on the continent and around the globe, the situation quickly changed. The European states moved to establish a series of colonies in the region, and the possibility that the new competition would result in war was seen as a real danger. From October 1884 to February 1885, a conference to discuss the future boundaries of Africa was held in Berlin, at which almost all of the important European powers (but, tellingly, no Africans) were represented. The decisions reached there—and elsewhere in Europe in the remaining 15 years of the nineteenth century—established the basic political map of the continent to this day.

Africa was artificially divided to suit the objectives of the colonial governments. Preexisting ethnic, linguistic, and cultural units were ignored. The maps in Figures 6.2 and 6.3 are only 11 years apart, but the contrast is striking. Throughout Africa, closely knit people speaking the same language were suddenly separated.

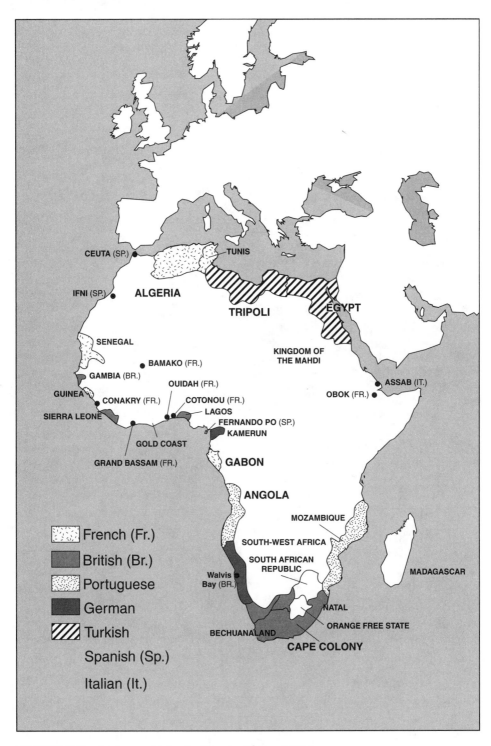

FIGURE 6.2 European Colonization in Africa, 1884

French (Fr.)
British (Br.)
Portuguese
German
Turkish
Spanish (Sp.)
Italian (It.)

CEUTA (SP.)
TUNIS
IFNI (SP.)
ALGERIA
TRIPOLI
EGYPT
SENEGAL
KINGDOM OF
THE MAHDI
BAMAKO (FR.)
GAMBIA (BR.)
GUINEA
OUIDAH (FR.)
CONAKRY (FR.)
COTONOU (FR.)
ASSAB (IT.)
OBOK (FR.)
SIERRA LEONE
LAGOS
FERNANDO PO (SP.)
GOLD COAST
KAMERUN
GRAND BASSAM (FR.)
GABON
ANGOLA
MOZAMBIQUE
SOUTH-WEST AFRICA
SOUTH AFRICAN
REPUBLIC
MADAGASCAR
Walvis
Bay (BR.)
NATAL
ORANGE FREE STATE
BECHUANALAND
CAPE COLONY

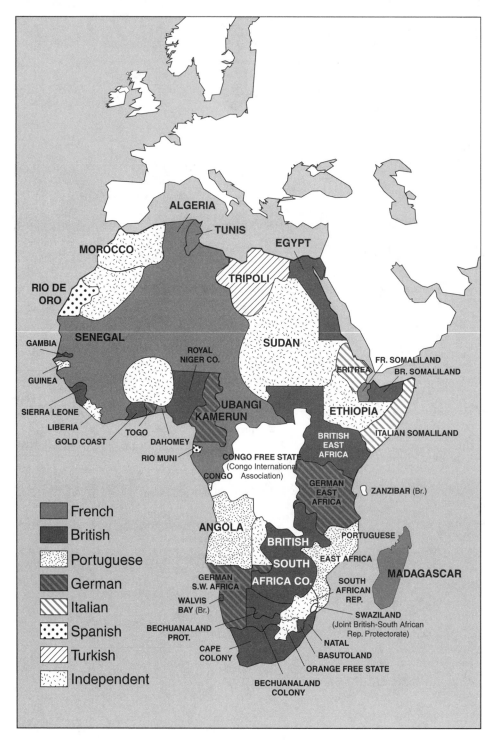

FIGURE 6.3 European Colonization in Africa, 1895

It was from these diversions that future generations' secessionist movements and border claims, known as *irredentism,* would spring.

The heyday of European colonial rule in Africa lasted for only 50 or 60 years; however, those few decades changed the face of the continent forever. The impact of colonialism depended on the type of rule instituted, the presence or absence of white settlers, and the particulars of the African elite. Most importantly, each African ethnic group had its own political and social system. Each responded to colonial rule in a different way, ranging from willing acceptance to bloody resistance of the outside powers. The Baganda people of East Africa welcomed the European presence. In contrast, the Ndebele-Shona Rebellion (1896–1897) against English-speaking settlers in what is now Zimbabwe, the Ashanti and Fulani resistance against the British in West Africa (1900–1901), and the Maji Maji rebellion contesting harsh German rule in East Africa (1905–1907) all resulted in a strong European show of force followed by occupation.

The British generally practiced indirect rule, a system in which they were removed from day-to-day activities; instead they used the traditional authorities, who were now responsible to them. The other colonial systems employed direct rule, in which the European administrators played a much more extensive role in everyday African life. The British, concerned about costs, emphasized the economic dimension and were more aloof; the French, the leading practitioners of direct rule, were more intimately involved, held out the slight possibility that their subjects might become French citizens, and had a more lasting effect on their colonies.

Whatever the differences, the similarities were more important. The colonial powers' dominance occurred everywhere. Different peoples were divided or united by fiat, and long-time trading patterns were subject to fundamental change as the societies themselves were transformed in a hundred different ways. The indigenous populations suffered altered political arrangements, alien tax structures, forced labor, and directed changes in individual wants and societal norms. By shifting the roles and selection processes for traditional political leaders, the colonial authorities unintentionally sowed the seeds for far greater political changes in years to come. Much of the economy fell under the influence, if not control, of the Europeans, who wished to substitute one or two cash crops or minerals for subsistence farming. Foreign goods and the widespread use of colonial currencies were also introduced. Cities, roads, and railroads were constructed for the benefit of the colonial rulers' administrative and economic interests. This colonial infrastructure tended to divide Africa rather than link it together; even today, the African map reflects the extractive goals of the imperial powers. In addition, the missionary and soldier added their particular persuasions to that of the administrator and merchant. By 1920, only Ethiopia, Liberia, and the Union of South Africa were free from formal European control, and the last was run by a white minority.

The new order scarcely touched the lives of the masses in many of the colonies. The people had little contact with Europeans, except when it was necessary to pay some new tax, live under some new law, or adopt a new plan for local land use. For the majority living in the rural areas, change or adaptation was to be a very gradual thing.

In the Portuguese, German, and Belgian colonies, the rule was far more harsh and the impact was often far more devastating. Villagers were routinely taken, with or without their leaders' approval, to work on roads or other projects. Impressment, however, was the least of it. The Congo Free State, for instance, was the private preserve of the Belgian king, whose control was so inhumane that after about 20 years he was forced to cede his 900,000-square-mile playground to the government of Belgium, which then established an only slightly more benevolent rule over this mammoth colony in the middle of Africa.

The movement to independence can be described in one of two ways: structurally or chronologically. Among the most important structures in the movement, especially to the generation coming of age at the turn of the century, was the church. This institution was part of the white establishment, with its distinction between superior and inferior values, but it was also a source for Western-style education and a breeding ground for future nationalists. Although Christianity first undermined local cultures and traditions, later, independent, indigenous Christian churches came to question colonial government policies. Other institutions of change were located in the fast-growing cities. These included the tribal unions and associations; trade unions or workers' solidarity organizations; the rudimentary mass media; the soldiers and ex-servicemen, who had traveled beyond the colony; and finally, overt political movements. All contributed to the requests for greater responsibility by the local, African elite; to calls for autonomy or power sharing by the growing nationalist movement; and ultimately, to demands for independence, now backed by the masses.

In both World Wars, African troops participated on behalf of their European masters, gaining valuable training and combat experience. They also observed that the Europeans were not invincible. Chronologically, the trickle of restrained nationalism before 1885 became a torrent of calls for independence in the years after World War II. West Africa moved ahead more quickly than East Africa, which in turn led the southern part of the continent. Overall, the British colonies were in advance of the French, who led the Portuguese. Even the British were cautious, however, expecting at most a slow devolution of power. The British anticipated that black parliamentary governments would be established by local leaders, who would be "properly" educated and trained. For the French, those few Africans who gained political power would do so not in African political structures, but as overseas representatives in the French National Assembly in Paris. The other European powers believed that any growth of political consciousness would change the status quo and thus was unthinkable.

When World War II began in 1939, no one would have guessed that independence for most of the African colonies was only a generation away. Despite the depression of the 1930s, colonial rule appeared immutable. Certainly, there were the firebrands who agitated for greater rights for Africans, but they were few in number and cautious in method, despite an occasional protest or even riot at a particular location.

The war, however, had a tremendous effect on all parties. Tens of thousands of soldiers saw action beyond the continent. They returned home with newly honed skills and ideas and settled in the cities rather than returning to their homes in the rural areas. They became a part of the mass independence movements that were destined to sweep the continent. The new militancy was fueled by large numbers of students returning to Africa from overseas, the demands of an increasingly urbanized population, and a new generation of political leaders. The battered European powers, meanwhile, were simply hoping to hang on at home and had little interest and few resources for the colonies, thousands of miles away.

Africans under French rule were ready for a new day. Early in the war, General Charles de Gaulle had promised greater local autonomy (but not self-government) and increased rights for the peoples of French West Africa (FWA) and French Equatorial Africa (FEA) if they supported him in his battle against Vichy France and Nazi Germany. Similarly, in 1941, U.S. President Franklin Roosevelt and British Prime Minister Winston Churchill promised in the Atlantic Charter "to respect the right of all peoples to choose the form of government under which they will live." At the end of the war, the newly founded UN called for self-determination, and the two emerging superpowers—the United States and the Soviet Union—both supported changes in the existing colonial order.

The beginning of the end for colonial rule began with a railway workers' strike in FWA in 1946, followed by disturbances over economic issues in the Gold Coast, a presumed model British colony in West Africa, in early 1948. This latter protest, in which ex-servicemen played a major role, spread to the other British colonies in the area. In those postwar years, a new law and a new constitution in Paris also accelerated change throughout FWA and FEA. In the years that followed, Africans that lived thousands of miles apart, spoke hundreds of different languages, and were subjects of several colonial powers took up the unifying cry of self-government.

Independence came first to the Gold Coast (renamed Ghana) in 1957. The next year, President de Gaulle angrily accepted Guinea's vote to follow suit.[2] At the same time, the other colonies that had been carved out of FWA and FEA chose federation with France, allowing Paris continuing control of foreign affairs, internal security, and defense. In 1960, the logjam broke as the remaining 11 French-speaking colonies became independent. The same year, Nigeria ended its colonial relationship with Britain to become a regional magnet. For the next 20 years, the march to independence continued, and by the end of 1980, only Namibia, on the southwest coast of Africa, remained in a dependent status (see Figure 6.4); South Africa, despite UN resolutions, refused to give up its controlling interest over the former German colony it had inherited as a mandate after World War I. Finally, in 1990, even this dependency ended, as a general agreement on regional relations in southern Africa was reached.

Independence throughout the region had been achieved. But if this was a time for celebration, it was also a time of great concern because there was never a consensus on future directions within each state, let alone within regions or the continent as a whole. Older animosities that sometimes had been kept under wraps by the colonial power burst forth. Opposing local, national, and supranational forces threatened the stability of the fragile new states. Furthermore, the

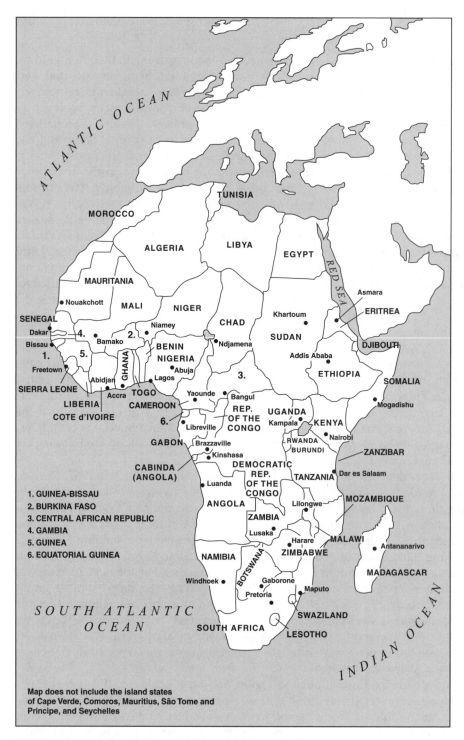

FIGURE 6.4 Political Map of Africa, 2002

Text visible within the map image:

ATLANTIC OCEAN

TUNISIA

MOROCCO

ALGERIA   LIBYA   EGYPT

MAURITANIA   RED SEA

Nouakchott   Asmara

SENEGAL   MALI   NIGER   Khartoum   ERITREA

Dakar   Niamey   CHAD   Addis Ababa   DJIBOUTI

Bissau   Bamako   SUDAN

4.   2.   Ndjamena

5.   BENIN   ETHIOPIA

1.   NIGERIA   SOMALIA

Freetown   Abuja   3.

SIERRA LEONE   Lagos   Mogadishu

LIBERIA   Abidjan   TOGO   Yaounde   Bangui

COTE d'IVOIRE   Accra   CAMEROON   UGANDA

GHANA   6.   REP.   Kampala   KENYA

Libreville   OF THE   RWANDA   Nairobi

GABON   CONGO   BURUNDI

Brazzaville   ZANZIBAR

Kinshasa   DEMOCRATIC   Dar es Salaam

CABINDA   REP.   TANZANIA

(ANGOLA)   OF THE   MOZAMBIQUE

Luanda   CONGO

ANGOLA   Lilongwe

ZAMBIA   MALAWI   Antananarivo

Lusaka   Harare

NAMIBIA   ZIMBABWE   MADAGASCAR

BOTSWANA

Windhoek   Gaborone   Maputo

Pretoria

SOUTH ATLANTIC   SWAZILAND

OCEAN   SOUTH AFRICA   LESOTHO

INDIAN OCEAN

1. GUINEA-BISSAU
2. BURKINA FASO
3. CENTRAL AFRICAN REPUBLIC
4. GAMBIA
5. GUINEA
6. EQUATORIAL GUINEA

Map does not include the island states
of Cape Verde, Comoros, Mauritius, São Tome and
Principe, and Seychelles

196

economic dimension was no more secure than the political, as local economies remained vulnerable to both domestic and international interests. The former colonial states were independent, but their governments lacked the sustained support of the people or, in some cases, the international community. Without such support, unity and economic well-being were unlikely.

GOVERNMENT

To understand African government in the early 2000s, one must realize that there has been an incredible compression of major political events. People who are now middle-aged and elderly grew up in the heyday of colonial rule, lived through World War II and the nationalist rush to independence, and finally, have experienced the instabilities of the postindependence years. The scholar Ali Mazrui quoted former Tanzanian President Julius Nyerere as saying that while some countries are trying to reach the moon and beyond, many Africans are still trying to get to town.[3] Today, such traditional institutions and values as the extended family and communal ownership of property are under attack while a new set of institutions and beliefs are not yet in place.

Instead of rule by the people, African independence has usually resulted in the continued rule of the few, though the new elites are indigenous, not foreign. The urban community, not the majority in the countryside, gets the bulk of state-run programs. In the cities, it is the small middle and upper classes that benefit from government. Despite a long history of group participation in decision making in many societies, pronouncements in the decades after independence were usually made by and for the few. The result was too often an elite driven by self-interest and even greed, while the many were disregarded. A view of politics as a means of extraction and personal enrichment, fostered under the experience of colonial rule, continued into independence, often with devastating results, as corruption among elected and appointed officials became commonplace.

Political solutions tried elsewhere in the Other World have faced opposition and indifference from societies in Africa. A major problem for the social elites is that the people have little faith in them. Although a few traditional authorities such as Chief Gatsha Buthelezi of the Zulu people in South Africa exercise considerable political influence, such examples are rare. Almost all African states comprise many ethnic groups, and traditional authorities may be unsuccessful in reaching out to those who owe them no special allegiance. Moreover, few of these authorities have real political power. They may also carry the baggage of colonial days, when their functions were usually altered by their European overlords, thus leading to the loss of respect from their subjects.

By the early 1980s, competitive political party systems in Africa were a rarity. This fact would have surprised earlier generations because, in many cases, the political party was in the forefront of the march to independence, and in doing so, gained mass support. Some parties managed to gain the grudging blessing of the colonial rulers, who looked fondly to their own political parties as models.

As the twentieth century ended, there were two schools of thought regarding African political systems. One was stated by Susan Rice, Assistant Secretary of State for African Affairs, in an address to the African Affairs Association in late 1997:

> Africa stands at a crossroads. . . . There is now more reason for optimism about Africa's future than at any time since the wave of independence over 30 years ago. . . . Democracy is ascendant. . . . Economic growth is also increasing. . . . Regions of stability are . . . emerging throughout the continent . . . [I]n many countries . . . reconciliation is supplanting confrontations as the means of bridging differences rooted in the past.[4]

The other was summarized by Judith Matloff, reporter for the *Christian Science Monitor,* as she wrapped up almost six years in the region in early 1998:

> I'd like to leave Africa saying that it had turned a corner into peace and prosperity and that most of the countries were on the right track. But that would be myopic and downright dishonest. The poverty and lack of education are so endemic, the access to arms so easy, and the democratic institutions so fragile that it's unlikely that the world's poorest continent will change overnight.[5]

Phrases such as African Renaissance and Africa's second independence are bandied about, but others see scarce improvement. Analysts come up with very different assessments of perceived democratic trends in the region. And Westerners often see Africa as cut from one piece of cloth, not as distinct states. Through the media, it is usually the wars, the poverty, the human rights abuses, and thus, the resignation that stand out. As far-removed states back off, the international lending institutions and nongovernmental aid agencies have become more prominent. Such institutions and agencies, however, have a long way to go. United Nations Secretary General Kofi Annan, from Ghana, elected to a second term and also awarded the Nobel Peace Prize in 2001 for the UN's peacekeeping efforts, bemoaned both divisive and draining colonial systems and more recent African leaders who had too often resorted to "heavy centralization of political and economic power and the suppression of political pluralism."[6] Centralized and personalized forms of government, patterns of corruption, ethnically based decisions, and human rights abuses, asserted Annan, were all too common.

Pan-Africanism and Regional Cooperation

This chapter highlights some, but by no means all of the conflicts in sub-Saharan Africa in the early 2000s. Guinea-Bissau, Chad, Congo (Brazzaville), Namibia, Lesotho, Zambia, Burundi, Kenya, and Uganda are among the states not prominently mentioned in these pages that have been beset by instability and violence. In several cases where opposing forces initially have been unwilling to seek solutions except through the gun, there have been attempts by outside individuals, countries, or organizations to stop the fighting. The notion of a common heritage, common values, and a common future kindles interest among those grown weary

United Nations Tragedy: The wreckage of a UN plane shot down while on a peacekeeping mission in the Congo.
SOURCE: *Emmit B. Evans, Jr.*

by the upheavals. After all, pan-African congresses had been held during early decades of this century.

Back in the early 1960s, there was a struggle between more militant governments who wanted to work for continental fusion and Mother Africa, and those who, having just gained independence, did not wish to be swallowed up by some larger entity. Antagonistic blocs of countries formed. Trying to stem the hostilities, 30 African states met in the Ethiopian capital of Addis Ababa in May 1963. The result was the creation of the Organization of African Unity (OAU), the principles of which included

1. National independence over continental unity,
2. Nonintervention in the affairs of another state,
3. The sanctity of national boundaries,
4. The responsibility of Africans for peacefully solving their own problems,
5. The adoption of a nonaligned or neutralist stance, and
6. Equality of all sovereign states.

Support for liberation movements was agreed to in a resolution, but it was not a principle on which the organization was founded.

In the ensuing years, OAU membership swelled as more than three dozen colonies became independent. Annual meetings of heads of state and foreign ministers were held, often amid great pomp and ceremony, to promote political, economic, and cultural cooperation. But, as in the UN, hard decisions involving action were in short supply. The acrimony of the early years was papered over, only to reignite over a number of issues in the late 1970s. By the mid-1980s, the OAU was so deeply in debt that its day-to-day operations were in jeopardy.

In the last decade, financial problems and coming to grips with the traditional unwillingness to intervene "in the affairs of another state" have been stumbling blocks. In any case, as we know from the Balkan region in East Europe, regional intervention is difficult and perilous. The OAU was all but invisible in the civil wars in Somalia and Rwanda in the first half of the 1990s and has played a peripheral role in other trouble spots since then, preferring rather to cede responsibility to smaller entities. Equivocation on the "noninterference issue" remains, despite support for collective action by national leaders at a 1993 OAU conference.[7]

Given its mixed and often disappointing record, the OAU has undertaken an ambitious and far-reaching program of reform. Beginning in 2002, the body will change its name to the African Union and undertake steps over a number of years that, if successful, will lead to much closer cooperation and eventual integration among the member states. One factor inhibiting progress in the OAU has been the requirement that all major decisions be unanimous; reaching agreement on matters of substance among dozens of disparate states has been notoriously difficult. The reforms are to introduce some majority voting, a permanent legislative body, and, eventually, a common currency similar to the European Union's new euro. It remains to be seen if the new reforms can stay on track and make a real difference in the continent's ongoing political and economic problems.

Smaller geographical organizations have been somewhat more active, albeit not always successful, in political-military matters. The Economic Community of West African States (ECOWAS) played an important role in the long-festering conflict in Liberia in the early 1990s and again in Sierra Leone later in the decade. In both cases, Nigerian soldiers were instrumental in curbing the fighting. Similarly, the Southern African Development Community (SADC), under its Chair, South African President Nelson Mandela, tried to broker a cease fire in the 1998 Congo war (see Central Africa section), but achieved minimal results.

Especially in economic matters, SADC has been the most important and successful of the regional entities, with numerous linkages established. South Africa and its former President Mandela, however, by their very prominence, have produced a wariness or even hostility from some of the other members. The economic clout of South Africa is both a hope and a concern for other member states. Leaders such as Zimbabwe President Robert Mugabe appear to resent being upstaged by the charismatic Mandela. There is still much SADC can do to help the region's southern tier of countries, but national sensitivities and personalities loom large. Otherwise, the more than 200 additional organizations for regional cooperation have simply not been very effective.

African Relations with Outside Powers

Over the last century, Africa's relations with outside powers have gone through several stages and may now be entering a new one. As the earlier discussion in this chapter suggested, the colonial powers consolidated their control over most of the continent in the 1890s. At least through World War II, the United States, the Soviet Union, and China did not challenge the domination of the existing order. Even the advent and pursuit of the cold war did not at first change this order. The Other World, and especially Africa, was not seen as a major theater of competition. Conflicts might flare around the perimeter of the Soviet Union and even to a limited degree in Latin America, but Africa was a backwater.

As African states began to achieve independence in the late 1950s, however, this situation began to change. The U.S.-Soviet rivalry became global, and soon the Chinese entered the maneuvering. In addition, the French continued their strong economic and military presence in the region. For 20 years the jousting continued unabated.

By the 1980s, this foreign competition began to ebb. The superpowers and China became more selective in their involvements. The ideological orientation of any one state was not viewed as very important. The Soviet Union was the largest supplier of military aid to the region, but then, under Mikhail Gorbachev, it reduced military material bound for Mozambique, helped broker the Cuban pull-out from Angola, played a supportive role in achieving Namibia's independence, and withdrew its commitment to what had been its closest ally in the region, Ethiopia.

The Western influence had been much in evidence economically. France was the country that had long had close relations with its former colonies. By the mid-1990s, this had changed. Almost all of the first generation of African postindependence leaders who embraced France passed from the scene. More important, in late 1993, France greatly reduced its support for the common currency used in almost all of French-speaking Africa. These former colonies thus became more vulnerable to the shifts in world markets. Furthermore, France later decided to withdraw its garrisons from the continent. (For relations with the United States, see Sub-Saharan Africa and the United States in the Flashpoints section.)

ECONOMICS AND NATURAL RESOURCES

It has already been suggested that African physical geography, including temperature, rainfall, coastlines, rivers, soils, and the like, created difficult conditions for its peoples. Moreover, foreigners exploited the natural habitat in many parts of the region. For instance, the colonial powers instituted cash crops and the export of livestock, which in turn meant widespread clearing of the land and sometimes depletion of the soil. Similarly, Europeans carving up the continent created or heightened local rivalries, which resulted in conflicts that also affected the landscape. The decline of large areas of present-day Africa has been caused more by human than natural factors. Exploding populations, the movement from countrysides to cities, devastating civil wars, and the shift from a nomadic to a sedentary way of life have major ramifications.

Economic patterns established in Africa a century ago continue to have great relevance today. The search for legitimate trade in the decades after the abolition of slavery resulted in the introduction of such cash crops as cocoa, coffee, tea, cotton, ground nuts, and palm oil, as well as renewed exploration for minerals. Gradually, a shift from subsistence farming to exports took place. In almost all cases, the colonies depended on no more than three crops or minerals for almost all of their earnings. Thus was Africa gradually drawn into the global capitalist system, albeit as a minor player. This pattern remains true today.

After independence, the future at first looked promising. Some countries followed the Western model of letting free enterprise dominate the economy; others chose to have the state play the major role. In either case, the 1960s and early 1970s was a period of growth throughout the continent. Unlike Asia, most of the countries were feeding themselves; unlike Latin America, most of the land was either communally owned or run by small farmers. Foreign investment was forthcoming and commodity prices were high.[8]

With the first oil price shock in 1973, this rosy picture began to change. Only a few African states had appreciable amounts of oil; others were forced to spend more of their precious capital and then to borrow money at high rates of interest to secure oil for industry. By the late 1970s, prices had peaked and were beginning to fall for both agricultural products and minerals. Deindustrialization resulted from declining domestic demand brought on by reduced income and shortages of foreign exchange. Poor maintenance and lack of spare parts, the protection of inefficient basic industries, and political considerations accelerated the economic decline. Drought became more pronounced in the Sahel region south of the Sahara. Sub-Saharan Africa's total debt, which had been $6 billion in 1970, rose to $125 billion by 1987.

By the early or mid-1980s, stagnation had been replaced by economic decline. Governments were living way beyond their means. African per capita income began to decline. Millions who had only barely been eking out a living now fell deeply into poverty and, in some cases, faced starvation.

These problems give a sense of the enormity of the economic disaster Africa is weathering. By 1990, 325 million people, or 62 percent of the region's population at the time, minus South Africa, were living in absolute poverty.[9] Per capita income hovered in the $300-a-year range (U.S. dollars). Ten years later, only the population figure had changed.

How can this situation be altered? For more than a decade, the answer most often given by foreign governments and international lending agencies is privatization. That is, outside help, including additional loans and the restructuring or even writing off of outstanding loans, will only be made available to African countries if they agree to major policy reforms that substitute market forces for state-directed economies.

Reforms focusing on currency devaluations, reductions in government expenditures, and limits in domestic credit were begun by the International Monetary Fund (IMF) in the early 1980s. The World Bank, noting that little had been accomplished, added other "structural adjustments." It sought to increase producer prices, reduce or eliminate subsidies and trade restrictions, improve education and health systems, pay far more attention to the environment, encourage foreign investment, and champion small producers. A domestic bicycle industry or low-cost local roads for nonmotorized vehicles were looked on favorably. Above all, it emphasized private enterprise.

By the mid-1990s, more than two dozen countries in Africa adopted major economic policy reforms. These states embraced the reforms or capitulated to

Western prescriptions. Outside criticisms of these programs included the reduction in the quality and quantity of government services; the introduction of user fees, which disproportionately hurt the poor; and the increased cost of basic food-stuffs and transportation.

Structural adjustment at the national level may be inadequate unless the Western countries open their markets, pay decent prices for African goods, and curtail or suspend debt repayments. Any benefits for African states are likely to take years, if not decades, whereas adverse effects of reform are instantaneous. If discontent rises, government instability and repression will be the likely results. The IMF and World Bank argue that states taking the plunge have done better than those that have not. That is small consolation to millions of individuals who have experienced worsened conditions.

On balance, sub-Saharan African economies at century's end are a bit improved over the beginning of the 1990s, if not over 10 or 20 years earlier than that. "Better fiscal policies, greater trade liberalization, and more-realistic foreign exchange rates in sub-Saharan Africa have helped lead to the rising per capita income—an average of 1 to 1.5 percent a year the past two years,"[10] though economic growth was not as strong in 1997 as 1996. Note also that population growth is 2.7 to 2.8 percent annually. The World Bank estimates that a 6 percent economic growth rate is necessary for real improvement.

There are major problems, specific and general, and the economic turnaround is sputtering. Government debt is simply crushing many states in the region. The following statistic provides just one example: Africa spends four times as much servicing debt as it does on health and education. The region also pays out more in interest on the debt than it receives in trade and other flows. There is a move to provide debt relief to some of the Heavily Indebted Poor Countries (HIPC) and thus better tend to social needs, but the qualifying conditions are stringent and at best will only help a small number of states. Other countries are asking for greater flexibility, especially for hard-hit countries such as Rwanda.

There is good news: Although public monies are declining, they are more than offset by private funds. There is also bad news: The flows only go to a few countries, including South Africa. Furthermore, global economic instabilities, insufficient market shares by small countries to attract major investors, skill deficiencies, inadequate infrastructure, downbeat coverage of Africa by the media, and chance events such as the bombing of two American embassies in East Africa in 1998 were detrimental. Arms purchases, often with kickbacks, "crony companies" that lack competence, payments to security forces or the military, "white elephant" projects, and ruling elites engaging in capital flight exacerbate the financial drain.

Sub-Saharan Africa has great natural resources, much of them untapped. The United States gets almost as much of its foreign oil from the region as it does from the Middle East. In addition to the major petroleum sources along the coast of West Africa, there are also promising prospects in Chad and Sudan. Similarly, natural gas in commercial amounts appears to exist in Angola, Congo, Equatorial Guinea, Gabon, Ghana and Cameroon. New resources used in the

Divided Highway Ends: The main road between Malindi and Lamu, Kenya.

SOURCE: *Emmit B. Evans, Jr.*

Western high-technology industry are being exploited in Africa, but not always for the benefit of the people as a whole. The risks of investing in natural resource extraction are great, but so are the potential profits. Corruption, weak environmental protection (which permits groundwater contamination and unknowing populations coming into contact with uranium waste), and lax miner safety are some of the hazards to be overcome. Overfishing by European fleets is another reality. Although foreign access fishing agreements bring in hundreds of millions of dollars, which help service the debt, the payments come at the price of depriving millions of local inhabitants of a vital food source.

CASE STUDIES

SOUTH AFRICA

The key point about South Africa is that although blacks outnumbered whites by five to one, political power remained with the minority until 1994. Over the generations, white domination wore many faces. At the turn of the twentieth century, the British defeated the Afrikaners in a bloody civil war. The Afrikaners were a people whose ancestors came mainly from the Netherlands beginning in the seventeenth century. For the next few years there were four separate states, with Great Britain in charge of them all; then in 1910, the four fused into one Union of

South Africa, and London became all but invisible. Fearing for the future of blacks in the country, a forerunner to the African National Congress (ANC) arose two years later. However, it could do nothing to prevent the Land Act of 1913, which prevented blacks from owning land in most areas and from owning quality land in all parts of the country. Another important date is 1948, the year that the Afrikaner-backed National party won the whites-only national elections. The newly elected party formally instituted a policy of apartheid, or separate racial development. From then on, blacks (and to a lesser extent, Indians) and those of mixed race, called coloreds, were treated as inferior beings. Brute force, including the arrest of the leaders, legislation, and custom enshrined the new order. For the next 36 years, despite nonviolent protests and occasional acts of sabotage, the status quo of white domination and black subordination prevailed.

Significant resistance to apartheid increased through the 1960s and 1970s. Beginning in late 1984, disturbances became more widespread, and violence by both the state and opponents of apartheid intensified. Arrests numbered in the thousands. A year later, the government declared a state of emergency in much of the country. Authorities tried to keep order by imposing controls on dissidents, including the media. The economy began a downward spiral, helped along by damaging strikes. Limited sanctions imposed by several governments, including the United States, and the loss of many foreign companies were also detrimental. Nevertheless, the white ruling class held firm.

In the late 1980s, the South African government tried both the carrot and the stick to impose its will. The authorities offered minor reforms, and relations improved with some surrounding black-run states; however, several thousand people died because of political unrest, and a second emergency decree resulted in tens of thousands of additional arrests. A change of direction seemed impossible.

Change did come, however, and it came rapidly. There are several explanations for the shift. First, Frederik W. de Klerk, succeeding P. W. Botha as prime minister and head of the National party in 1989, gradually moved his forces in a different direction, including calls to prepare a new constitution and share power.

At the same time, the situation fundamentally improved in neighboring Namibia and Angola. South African leaders perceived that the abating U.S.-Soviet confrontation would lessen the threat of communism within their own borders. Many in the country also noticed democratization in other parts of the world. Both the South African government and the ANC saw a military solution to the internal unrest as unlikely. In addition, the economy continued to sag, and Western powers warned that tougher sanctions were a possibility. Demands for change came from all directions.

The winds struck with gale force. Nelson Mandela, jailed in the early 1960s for promoting the violent overthrow of the government, was dramatically released by Prime Minister de Klerk in 1990, along with other dissidents. The government also lifted the 30-year ban against the ANC, the Pan-African Congress, the South African Communist party, and many other organizations. Over the next few months the government rescinded the state of emergency throughout the country, curbed the secretive state security system, reduced the military budget, and ended political censorship. It also repealed the Separate Amenities Act, thus opening public hospitals, restaurants, libraries, buses, and parks to all.

The first half of 1991 shook apartheid to its roots. Its pillars—the Lands Acts, Group Areas Act, and Population Registration Act—were repealed, and the Internal Security Act was severely amended. It took three more years of maneuvering, however, before the ultimate goal of one person, one vote was achieved. The ANC and the rival Zulu-based Inkatha movement, led by Chief Gatsha Buthelezi, clashed, resulting in thousands of deaths. There were divisions among the whites as well, with a small minority refusing to consider any changes. But in late April 1994, the people of South Africa, including millions of black citizens, went to the polls for the first time in the country's history.

As expected, the ANC was the big winner, receiving 63 percent of the vote as Nelson Mandela became president. Because they did not receive two-thirds of the vote, the victorious party had to work with non-ANC members in Parliament in the writing of a new constitution. The National party finished second and became the official opposition. In addition, de Klerk became one of two vice presidents. The Inkatha Freedom party finished third. In a bid to form a government of unity and reconciliation, Mandela offered a number of cabinet positions to members of the other two parties. Buthelezi became the Home Affairs minister.

Many people predicted that given the struggle that preceded the election, the following months would be ones of upheaval. It did not work out that way. There were growing pains, yes, but both in political circles and throughout the country there was relative tranquility based on a foundation of gradual change. The move from international outcast to liberal democracy in one year was phenomenal. Although some complained that Mandela was moving too slowly to institute reforms, most were supportive of the pace and direction of change. Racial strife gradually eased. Economic growth caught up with population growth for the first time in a decade. There were a number of strikes, but they did not divide the country or undermine the ANC. Finally, in late 1995, orderly local elections took place throughout the country.

Of course, South Africa still faces very serious problems. Gaining political power is a lot different than gaining economic power. Major economic disparities along racial lines continue as poverty cuts deeply across the black majority while a majority of the wealth remains in white hands.

> For many the situation has not yet changed much—the landless; the homeless; the black African majority, more than 40 percent of whom live in absolute poverty; women and children, who are the majority of those living in deprivation, especially in rural areas; and the growing numbers of those who are unemployed, underemployed or living on less than $1 a day.[11]

Land reform or redistribution is a deeply felt issue by many landless farmers. The government promulgated its land restitution program in 1995, but was hesitant to promote widespread change for fears of alienating white farmers and undermining the agricultural sector. The 1 million homes that the government, with private-sector backing, committed itself to building by 1999, were not completed.

There are also disagreements with traditional authorities over what to do with tribal lands.

Economic growth is not keeping up with population growth and formal unemployment is running at least 30 percent. The national currency has been in rapid decline, while foreign investments have only been a fraction of the amounts expected. University tuition has climbed, and many who looked to the new government to set things right have been acutely disappointed. Credit, especially for the poor, has been hard to come by and global competition for foreign assistance is intense.

Many dimensions of South African poverty are closely tied to race. For instance, "only 3 percent of whites—but 18 percent of blacks—[in the country] are not expected to survive to age 40."[12]

Another major problem is dealing with South Africa's past. The Truth and Reconciliation Commission, headed by Archbishop Desmond Tutu, was created by a parliamentary act in 1995. It was to delve into the dark corners of the apartheid years. The Commission's goal was to bring the past to closure by inviting those who had transgressed to testify in public. Toward that end, the Commission had the power to grant amnesty to those who gave an account of their crimes and who could show that the struggle over apartheid was behind their acts. It was not necessary for the perpetrator to show remorse. There were confessions of terrible acts of murder, mutilation, and terror. It was clear that some atrocities were known and often planned by those at the very apex of the government. There were other atrocities committed in support of the revolution. In the end, some refused to testify and others claimed the effort was nothing more than a witch hunt. It was also clear that many South Africans were not reconciled and ready to forgive. For all that, it was a remarkable attempt to put the past in the past.

Since the end of apartheid, political violence has abated somewhat, but criminal violence has increased. The crime wave transcends race, ethnicity, and class. The murder rate is several times that of the United States, and rape has been an especially severe problem. Lawlessness, though, is nothing new in South Africa. How can the country "restore an ethic of lawfulness" after the ANC encouraged people to long defy the white authorities? (There are also disgruntled white farmers and white police officers, disaffected ANC members, and long-standing ethnic conflicts.) Police corruption and low rates of arrests and convictions have caused many to lose faith in their criminal justice system. A statistic indicates that "two-thirds of Johannesburg's citizens and half of Cape Town's were victims of crime between 1993 and 1997 alone."[13]

After six years of work, a new constitution was inaugurated in 1997. A balance was struck between a strong central government and devolving considerable powers to the states. There are strong statements protecting individual rights. Private property rights are balanced by the need to redress past discrimination. The scaffolding for the 1999 national elections was in place. Those results showed that the ANC had lost none of its popularity, receiving over 66 percent of the vote, just a sliver away from the two-thirds mark that would have allowed it to make certain changes in the constitution if it so wished. Thabo Mbeki succeeded

Mandela as president. In all, 13 parties had seats in the new legislature, with the reconstituted Democratic Party finishing second. The Inkatha Freedom Party again ran third, with the New National Party slumping to fourth. President Mbeki was widely regarded as a very able, experienced administrator, even though he obviously lacked Mandela's international stature and charisma. Mbeki has been unable, however, to control South Africa's mounting economic, social, and health problems, and many are disturbed with his idiosyncratic views on human immunodeficiency syndrome (HIV) and AIDS, which have hit his nation especially hard. (See Africa and AIDS in the Flashpoints section.) Concerns have also been raised over Mbeki's adherence to external and historical reasons to explain his administration's lack of economic progress for his nation. The corruption that has long plagued the politics of much of the continent has now also reached South Africa, where a top parliamentary leader of the ANC was charged with fraud, corruption, and committing perjury in 2001.

What of South Africa's image beyond its borders? Mandela himself is much revered, though he has clashed with the United States over his kind words for Cuba, Iran, Libya, and Syria—countries that gave support to the antiapartheid struggle at a time when the cold war made the United States timid. In southern Africa, there is disquiet over one country so obviously more powerful than the others. The South African military's intervention in neighboring Lesotho in 1998 to deal with unrest there underscored this concern. Zimbabwe President Robert Mugabe has shown his displeasure over being upstaged by Mandela; not surprisingly, therefore, Mandela has not been successful in mediating disputes in the region. Although South Africa has been a champion of a regional common market, some of the other countries are concerned about being in that country's orbit.

NIGERIA

Next to South Africa, Nigeria is viewed as the country in sub-Saharan Africa to have the greatest potential. Recurring political instability and economic mismanagement for the past 30 years, however, have taken their toll.

Nigeria's population of 123 million people is the largest on the African continent. Twenty years ago, the country was an economic powerhouse as well. In 1977, per capita gross domestic product (GDP) was $1,000. Ten years later, the figure had dropped to $370; in 1992 it was $320. For the period 1980 to 1992, Nigeria's economic growth rate was −0.4 percent. In that period, the country slipped from the Other World's middle-income to low-income group. By 2000, per capita income had climbed back to $920, still below the figures for two decades earlier.

A major factor in the decline was the precipitous drop in oil prices. The government and many upwardly mobile people lived way beyond their means during this period. Yet the masses saw little of the new wealth. As the last decade drew to a close, the international debt soared to $35 billion, and the government agreed to begin a very stiff structural adjustment program (see Economics and National Resources section). In this environment, social unrest further undermined foreign investment.

The military government that came to power in a 1985 coup (there have been seven coups since independence in 1960, and many more attempted coups) promised elections and the return to civil rule at the beginning of 1993. Indeed, elections were held, but when the military rulers, who had run the country for all but 12 years since independence, did not like the results, they simply annulled them. Since then, strikes and even riots, additional instability in the military, rule by decree, summary executions of the regime's opponents, and a seemingly never-ending economic downdraft have occurred. The election victor, billionaire Mashood Abiola, went to jail, was placed in solitary confinement, sentenced to death, and finally had that sentence commuted. The military, now under the control of General Sani Abacha, ushered in five years of brutal rule while defying global condemnations. In March 1995, an attempt to overthrow the government failed. Its leaders, including a former head of state, were to be put to death, but after national protests, the sentences were commuted to life imprisonment. General Abacha, who rapidly became a billionaire, also attempted to head off further criticism by belatedly promising a return to civilian rule by late 1998.

Before 1995 ended, nine other dissidents, including Ken Saro-Wiwa, a prominent author and playwright, were executed. The government charged that they had fomented strife that led to the murder of several rivals in a major oil-producing area. Saro-Wiwa had protested that the production had resulted in serious pollution in the area. He also railed against the refusal of the corrupt government to give even a fraction of the riches to his poor Ogoni people living in the oil-rich coastal sector. Worldwide condemnation followed the hangings, with none other than South African President Nelson Mandela calling for a worldwide oil embargo. Under the best circumstances, however, it is difficult to get approval for such a global action and even more difficult to enforce it. Nigeria, for instance, is the fifth-largest foreign supplier of oil to the United States and owes over $30 billion to Europe and Japan.

The whole chaotic situation came to a head in 1998. In the spring, several high-ranking military officers from Abiola's part of Nigeria were arrested for allegedly planning a coup; the leaders were sentenced to death. Then in June, Abacha died of a heart attack. A month later, Abiola, still in prison, also died. With the despised head-of-state and his main nemesis gone, the question simply was "What now for Nigeria?"

Abacha's replacement, General Abdusalami Abubakar, gradually moved in a new direction. Many political prisoners were released from jail and the officers' sentences were commuted. A start was made to face up to the omnipresent corruption, with several leading figures including Abacha's security advisor arrested. Most important, national assembly and then presidential elections were held in February 1999. Olusegun Obasanjo was chosen to lead the new civilian government that formally took power three months later. Obasanjo had headed a military regime in the late 1970s before voluntarily yielding power to an elected civilian government. More recently, he had been jailed from 1995 to 1998 on a dubious claim that he was plotting to overthrow Abacha. Although some felt that the newly elected Obasanjo was too close to the military leaders he was replacing, others thought he was the right man for the troubled times in the troubled country.

Sweeping poverty as well as ethnic and regional tensions are deeply rooted. British colonial rulers favored Muslim northerners because they were seen as more obedient and conservative than southerners. After independence, northerners continued to rule at the national level, whether the country was under civilian or military rule. Yet the oil and the major financial, commercial, and industrial centers are in the south. Again the hope was that President Obasanjo would be able to quell the country's long-time divisions; despite good intentions and promising pronouncements, this goal has proved elusive. Deadly ethnic clashes have continued, some involving government troops and most pitting northern Muslims against southern Christians.

Nigeria has vast oil reserves; it is the world's sixth largest producer of oil, with revenues running $30 billion a year. The country also has many minerals, fertile land, and more than 30 universities. Nigeria, however, also has a run-down infrastructure (the nickname for the National Electric Power Authority, or NEPA, is Never Expect Power Again). Oil refineries have closed and the country is actually importing fuel. Agriculture is in a sorry state, and even the industrial base is stunted. Millions are homeless or live in substandard structures, and millions more are downwardly mobile with per capita income continuing to drop. Legions of young people without steady employment are forced to exist by their wits. Smuggling is big business, with perhaps half of the world's heroin passing in and out of the country. Then there is the 75,000 member military, some of whom stand accused of serious abuses of power. What is to become of them? In December 2001, Nigeria's Minister of Justice was assassinated by gunmen invading his home, another indication of Nigeria's ongoing instability.[14] Ethnic violence continued into 2002, and in January of that year, suspicious explosions rocked an army munitions depot in Lagos, causing over 1,000 civilian deaths in the ensuing panic. As the 40th anniversary of independence has come and gone, Nigeria is trying to get back on track. It will not be an easy task.

ZIMBABWE

Zimbabwe became independent in 1980 after a lengthy struggle to end white-minority rule. In the 1997 edition of *The Other World*, the country was considered a relative success story because economic growth had more than kept pace with population growth, family planning programs had made great strides, and ethnic disputes between the majority Shona and minority Ndebele had faded. Literacy rates were among the highest on the continent, racism had been contained, there was a good healthcare system, a thriving tourism industry, a police force that no longer generated fear, a functioning infrastructure, and environmental issues were being successfully met. Finally, there was a reasonable level of political stability.

The downside, always present, has worsened in the last five years. The economy has continued to slump, with inflation and interest rates rising. Many foreign investors are leaving because of what they believe are ruinous government policies; unstable or even collapsed banks; a declining stock market; falling prices for such domestic commodities as gold, other minerals, and tobacco; a high debt load; and tax increases that many claim line the pockets of President Robert Mugabe's supporters or favorites. Unions have risen up in opposition, as have students who claim government corruption. The press, one of the few institutions willing to speak out against the ruling elite, has suffered threats and torture; in late 2001, the president threatened journalists who criticized the violent, lawless actions of his supporters. Minorities, especially gays, are chastised by the president himself. In early 1998, rising prices led to food riots. The local currency had to be propped up by the International Monetary Fund.

The president's supporters become fewer and fewer. Charges of favoritism, luxurious living for the few, and crony capitalism are widespread. *The London Times* reported that "after a relatively slow start from independence in 1980, the Nigerian model has been adopted with alacrity; senior politicians take control of state contracts and licensing, violate all procedures, and pass on the right to politically well-connected businessmen."[15] There are bitter feuds within the almost one-party state. Public support has plummeted. The country continues to have one of the highest HIV-positive rates in Africa.

As in South Africa, probably the most volatile issue is land ownership. Until recently, 4,500 white farmers owned more than 70 percent of the country's most fertile land, leaving the 7 million black farmers to engage in mainly subsistence farming. In the midst of rising discontent, President Mugabe announced that he intended to seize millions of acres of white-owned land and undertake a radical land reform program; he further stated the government would not compensate those who stood to lose their property and livelihood. Poor blacks began squatting on the land in 1997. Calls for international financial assistance to put the plan into effect have met a cool reception. White resistance to any shift in its economic dominance is fierce. Many blacks, however, say they will be patient no longer.

Zimbabwe's involvement in the Congo war of 1998 was another unanticipated financial cost. The expanded war also brought the cool relationship between Mugabe and South African President Nelson Mandela into the open. The latter urged a cease fire, but this was dismissed by the Zimbabwe president.

At the outset of 2002, the earlier promise of a stable, tolerant democratic regime in Zimbabwe seemed thwarted. Mugabe's supporters continued intimidation and attacks against his political opponents, white settlers, and blacks who worked on their farms. New measures designed to suppress opposition groups and the press were introduced before the 2002 presidential election. In March 2002, President Mugabe won reelection in a vote widely denounced by outside observers as unfair; he promptly had his major opponent arrested on charges of treason. Many feared that Mugabe, eager to cling to power, had become one of the "Big Men" who littered the history of Africa's post-independence leadership.

ANGOLA

Angola's history has been highlighted by first, a very harsh colonial government, then a bitter struggle for independence, which was attained in 1975, and since then an almost constant civil war. Abundant resources include diamonds, oil, rich soil, and fish off the coast. The resources, however, especially the diamonds and oil, only exacerbate the tensions and the stakes in the never-ending battle for control of the government and of the country's riches.

The brief statement regarding Portuguese rule is that, in the late sixteenth century, they were the first European power to come to sub-Saharan Africa and the last to leave, and then only when opposition became too strong, both on the battlefield and back in Lisbon. The ensuing battles from 1975 to 1991 between the Popular Movement for the Liberation of Angola (MPLA) and National Union for the Total Independence of Angola (UNITA) took some 300,000 lives. In addition, starvation afflicted more than a half million people; one-half of the country's export earnings went for the war; the economy, even with oil revenue and considerable outside assistance, remained in tatters; and refugees numbered in the hundreds of thousands. With the cold war still going strong, 50,000 Cuban fighters entered on the MPLA side and a lesser number of South Africans supported UNITA. The Soviet Union and the United States lent their support in important but less overt roles as they supplied intelligence and weapons to the warring parties.

In 1991, a peace treaty was signed in Angola, officially ending the 16-year-old civil war. The agreement called for the former enemies to build a unified armed force, promote a multiparty political system and market economy, and plan for elections monitored by a UN observer force. When the votes were counted a year later and the MPLA claimed victory, UNITA refused to recognize the results, claiming it had lost because of fraud and ballot stuffing.

In the succeeding two years, thousands more were killed in renewed fighting. Another treaty was signed in November 1994. This time 7,000 UN peacekeepers monitored the cease fire, and the opposition force was to have a share of the power. Again there were hopes that the contestants would be able to come together in a grand coalition, but again it was not to be.

The on-again, off-again war continued to wreak havoc on the country, drain the economy, and cause tens of thousands of people to flee to refugee camps in neighboring Congo and Zambia. Although the MPLA is not blameless, it is UNITA that has been hit by international sanctions for routinely violating the 1994 agreement, including not fully carrying out the demobilization of its forces. The number and intensity of the clashes increased and intensified during 1998–2001 as the Angolan government of national conciliation collapsed. Generally, the MPLA forces through this period were able to gain the upper hand over UNITA, but the civil war looked to be far from resolution. The UN finally pulled its peacekeeping mission, acknowledged there was no more peace to keep. Even in the Congo war (see Central Africa section), MPLA and UNITA back different sides. With the death of long-time UNITA leader Jonas Savimbi in a government ambush in February 2002, many hoped that this decades-old civil war could finally end. Meanwhile, the great mineral wealth is being squandered, while doctors, nurses, teachers, and the police wait to be paid.

✳ FLASHPOINTS ✳

AFRICA AND AIDS

Recent estimates indicate that approximately 71 percent of the world's total HIV/AIDS cases afflict sub-Saharan Africans.[16] In other words, approximately 35 million of the people suffering from AIDS are African, with several million new cases reported in the region each year. Ninety percent of the world's AIDS deaths have been in Africa, an appalling total of 17 million people, according to a 2001 United States Institute of Peace report. Because 9 of the 10 countries with the highest infection rates are in Africa, these grim statistics will not improve on a regional basis any time soon.[17]

Unlike other parts of the world, 50 percent of HIV-positive adults are women. UN AIDS officials have thus reluctantly decided that women infected with HIV should consider feeding formula instead of breast milk to their babies. In 1997, more than a half-million infants—90 percent of the world's total—were born to HIV-positive mothers. Throughout the region, more than 8 million children are orphans because of AIDS.

Although statistics from different sources are not always congruent, the numbers are overwhelming. Dealing with the epidemic is also overwhelming. There is little money for tests, drugs, or directed support networks. Even in South Africa, health services are totally inadequate to provide treatment for AIDS. The costly combinations of drugs that help keep the virus in check among infected people in the north can barely be considered in the south, where other problems press the population every day. President Mbeki of South Africa, where one in four women in their twenties is infected with HIV, has caused much controversy with his challenges of accepted scientific studies on the relationship of HIV and AIDS, claiming instead that poverty and imperialism are causes of the disease. His administration's policies have also hindered modern treatment of AIDS in his country.

Can anything be done to combat the disease? Many major international conferences have been held to address just this issue, including a UN conference in Durban, South Africa, in July 2000 and a special OAU meeting in April 2001. On the positive side, access to the expensive drug treatments is improving, and a Fall 2001 ruling from the World Trade Organization (WTO) relieved desperate nations of patent infringements in making or acquiring generic substitute drugs. *Education* is the one word most often offered, and in Uganda the education is broad and multisectoral. According to the *Human Development Report 1997*, the East African country's relative success has been based on *providing political leadership, empowering communities, mobilizing employers*, and *addressing socioeconomic issues*, including urbanization, migration, poverty, and gender disparity.[18] There is no magic bullet, but a multifaceted approach can produce encouraging results, and finally, the global community has mobilized resources to cope with this urgent epidemic.

SLAVERY AND HUMAN TRAFFICKING

Slavery, both historical and modern, remains one of the most controversial, sensitive, and compelling subjects in sub-Saharan Africa. Questions about the impact of the historical slave trade on present-day Africa continue under hot debate. Was the European and American slave trade, which robbed West and Central Africa of millions of its young, able inhabitants over the course of several centuries, so devastating economically and psychologically that it has contributed materially to Africa's current state of underdevelopment? Should those areas in Europe and the Americas that benefited from slave labor hundreds of years ago, now all relatively rich, pay reparations to the victimized nations today? Many argue that the former slave-holding nations should not only apologize for these abominations against humanity, but also pay substantial sums to try to set things right. Others contend that the historical slave trade was a regrettable but distant chapter of the past, perpetrated by ancestors long since gone, which has little relevance to the pressing issues of a new millennium. Questions also arise around the Arab-based slave trade in East Africa.

These issues arose in proposals and debates at the UN conference on racism and xenophobia held at Durban, South Africa, in 2001. The United States boycotted the conference, in part because of the controversial slavery reparations proposal, but also because of a proposal from the Arab delegation equating Zionism, the movement for the state of Israel as a Jewish homeland, with racism. Ultimately, the conference proceeded with much acrimony and little resolution of the slavery issue. Condemnations of slavery were adopted that fell far short of a call for direct reparations; a redistributive cause whose time is not likely to come.

Aside from the debate over historical slavery, a few regions of Africa suffer from various forms of modern slavery and human trafficking. In Sudan and Mauritania, the two nations most often cited, traditional forms of chattel, or ownership, slavery persist into the twenty-first century. Usually, this slavery takes the form of wealthier Arab owner holding poorer black Africans in bondage, sometimes through generations and sometimes as a result of capture in war. Both governments deny the existence of such slavery and deem it formally illegal, but human rights activists insist that tens of thousands of slaves are held in the two nations. Furthermore, testimonials of escaped and liberated slaves confirm the practice. International awareness and outrage against the practice, perhaps less brutal than historical slavery but nonetheless invidious, is on the rise. Organizations such as the American Anti-Slavery Group in Boston are agitating and taking action against modern African slavery; other groups and concerned individuals, using a controversial approach, are raising funds to buy slaves' freedom directly from their masters.

Another form of modern African slavery exists in West Africa, in which youths, usually boys from the more deprived nations such as Benin or Togo, sign fraudulent work contracts and become indentured or bonded laborers, usually with no pay, in large agricultural enterprises in the better-off West African nations such as Ghana. The good news about modern slavery in Africa is the heightened publicity, exemplified in the extensive coverage of the decrepit slave ship turned away from several West African ports in the summer of 2001, and the resultant calls for action from many quarters across the globe to abolish these anachronistic, inhumane practices once and for all.

HORN OF AFRICA

Sudan, Ethiopia, Eritrea, and Somalia—four different countries, all poor, with four different histories that affect one another—comprise the Horn of Africa. All have known war recently, and in one the fighting continues. Drought, soaring populations, and depleted natural resources are endemic to the Horn of Africa. Ethiopia is one of the oldest countries in the world and Eritrea is among the newest; both are carving out new directions. Sudan and Somalia, however, seem involved in upheaval without end.

From the 1890s until independence in 1956, Sudan was formally under joint Anglo-French control. In 1958, a coup brought a change of regime and ushered in an era of unrest and military uprisings, the most recent of which occurred in 1989. Alleged plots, such as one resulting in the arrest of military officers and civilians alike in the summer of 1991, are even more common. The sudden changes at the top have had little effect on the on-again, off-again civil war, which has raged for 35 years. The opposing forces comprise 16 million people in the mainly Muslim north and 7 million in the non-Muslim south. The northern-based government, dominated by Islamic fundamentalists, has imposed itself on an evermore hostile south. Both sides have used food as a weapon. To make things more complicated and more terrible, those opposing the government have now split into two groups and spend as much time fighting each other as the common enemy; there are divisions in the north also. The warring factions have varying ethnic support. One side wants independence, while the other supports autonomy within Sudan. In 1993, the United States added Sudan to its list of countries that aided terrorism, claiming that the government is helping individuals and groups bent on destabilizing other states in Africa and beyond, but now the regime, once the home of Osama bin Laden, is providing some intelligence to the United States in the war on terrorism. The tragedy in Sudan rivals that in Central Africa, but has received much less attention by the media or the nation-states of the world.

There are hopes for a brighter tomorrow. In 1998, a new constitution was adopted which, if lived up to, could usher in a federal, multiparty democracy. The south of the country was granted the right to hold an internationally supervised referendum on independence, although deep economic and political problems would remain. At the same time, a cease-fire was proclaimed, but implementation remains spotty at best. Finally, there is the politics of oil. More than 3.5 billion barrels of high-quality crude has been discovered in the southern part of the country, and a $1.2 billion pipeline is being built over nearly 1,000 miles of extremely harsh terrain to get the product moving toward global markets. The oil is in production, but its proceeds and strategic location apparently fuel the ongoing civil war rather than improving the lives of all Sudanese citizens.

Because of inhospitable terrain and no obvious exportable economic resources, Ethiopia was able to keep its independence and its monarchy until conquered by Italy in 1935. Six years later, the British drove the Italians out and restored Emperor Haile Selassie to power. In seeking to enlarge his diverse state and alter the country's landlocked status, the emperor, with British approval, in 1952 claimed the former Italian colony of Eritrea. He did not, however, receive the Eritreans' approval. A military coup in 1974 swept away the old Ethiopian order. A self-proclaimed Marxist government asked the Soviet Union to replace the United States as the primary outside power. In trying to consolidate its control, the government of President Mengistu Haile Mariam became ever more dictatorial. Eritrean nationalism then burst forth. Over the years, two guerrilla fighting units succeeded in pushing the central government out of most of the provinces. Other ethnic groups' increasing discontent further weakened President Mengistu's hold in other parts of the country. The Soviet Union and its allies ended their economic and military aid.

The end came in the spring of 1991 with the collapse of the central government and the flight of Mengistu. Two million people had died under his reign. In the following months, representatives of 27 ethnic and political groups, including the Ethiopian People's Revolutionary Democratic Front (EPDRF) and the Eritrean People's Liberation Front (EPLF), met to work out the future of the country. Meles Zenawi of the EPDRF headed a transition government. More attention began to be paid to the rural poor as Zenawi balanced state and private ownership. Despite new programs, food shortages continued as population growth outstripped grain production by ever-widening amounts.

Despite a new constitution in 1994, which promised democracy and the right of ethnic groups to secede if they wished, several major parties boycotted 1995 elections, claiming their members had been harassed and even jailed when they tried to campaign. The fissures deepened in succeeding years, with human rights groups claiming thousands were arbitrarily arrested, imprisoned, and, in some cases, summarily executed. The media was also tightly controlled. Most observers, however, agree that internal political conditions are much improved over the pre-1991 era.

With Ethiopia's consent, Eritrea invoked its right to self-determination in 1993. Following almost 30 years of war in which 250,000 people were killed, it became the first territory in Africa to secede successfully from another African country. In a referendum, 99.8 percent of the approximately 1.1 million Eritreans voted for independence. Transitional institutions were established, and EPLF leader Issaias Aferweki was elected president by the new National Assembly. The country's population is nearly equally divided between Muslims and Christians. The government has received very high marks for its political sensitivity and economic programs, which focus on small-scale peasant agriculture and a general emphasis on self-reliance, not Western aid. Relatively fertile soil on the high plateau; promising resources of gold, oil, and fish; land reform; upgrading of the rights of women; a lack of crime and corruption; and optimism about the future all created a counter to the discouraging events of surrounding countries.

In mid-1998, again in early 1999, and in May 2000, the two states waged a border war, complete with planes, tanks, and considerable casualties, belying the stated friendship between the two countries' leaders, Meles Zenawi and Issaias Aferweki. Rebellions by Eritrea had gone on since the early 1960s, when the actual annexation by Ethiopia had taken place. For the next 30 years there was minimal cooperation between the national government and its embittered province. Nevertheless, the leadership of both entities worked together to overthrow the hated Mengistu government. But the fraternal relations could not survive the peace.

On one level, this conflict was simply a disagreement over who owned a border area that had been drawn by Italy in 1885. There was much more than that, however. Eritrea had long used the Ethiopian currency, but now introduced its own. In addition, Eritrea's independence meant that Ethiopia was again a landlocked country and dependent on its neighbor for imports and exports; as relations worsened, Ethiopia said it would look to Djibouti and Kenya instead for better trade relations, thus threatening a major source of income for Eritrea. There was even talk of Ethiopia attempting to take back one of two ports it had given up only a few years before. Ethiopia also began to go on a crash industrial program in Tigre, a province adjacent to Eritrea. Again, Eritrea, which had looked to its neighbor for cheap labor and raw materials, felt threatened. Meles, who is Tigran himself, feared he might be replaced by someone from a different ethnic group if he appeared weak. Then as the fighting intensified, there were a half million Eritreans in Ethiopia who, human rights observers claimed, were victimized, and a lesser number of Ethiopeans on the other side of the border who were also seen as innocent pawns. So much for the hoped-for zone of stability. After the renewed fighting in May of 2000, the two nations agreed to a cease-fire including UN peacekeepers in a buffer zone; as of late 2001, this agreement remained in place.

Southern Italian Somaliland and northern British Somaliland were fused at independence in 1960. Nine years later, Mohammed Siad Barre seized power and became a ruthless president for the next 22 years. Even though the overwhelming majority of the people are from the same ethnic group, competing clans and subclans formed the basis for challenges to Barre and each other.

The 1970s and 1980s were also a time of U.S.-Soviet rivalries around the world. In the Horn of Africa, the United States first backed Ethiopia, while the U.S.S.R. supported Barre's version of socialism. In the late 1970s, a new Marxist government in Ethiopia led to the superpowers switching sides, both supplying their beneficiaries with weapons. Despite Barre's deplorable human rights record, the United States continued to funnel military and economic aid to Somalia until the late 1980s.

In 1991, Barre was finally ousted and a struggle for power between different individuals and subclans or lineages began. Life in much of the interior, which was never easy, became harder as famine took its toll. In the months that followed, the UN hesitated. As pictures of starving children filled television screens, however, the world body began to supply food to hundreds of thousands of people. With provisions being hijacked or blocked at the capital of Mogadishu, UN observers, and then U.S. troops, arrived to assist. Gradually, the mission's objective changed from ending starvation to establishing a measure of peace and security to the country by ending the struggle for power. Later it was hoped that the UN could rebuild the infrastructure, the economy, and finally the government itself. This change in objective involved the UN as a participant in the conflict.

By 1993, there were 25,000 American military personnel, thousands of other UN peacemakers, and countless private parties, all attempting to provide assistance. In October of that year, 18 U.S. Army Rangers lost their lives in a futile attempt to capture a Somali leader who was accused of fomenting strife. The international community beat a measured retreat and within two years all military personnel were gone, though a few relief agencies braved the dangers and stayed. Some saw the operation as saving great numbers of lives and offering hope during a time of misery; others believed that UN members came too late and got too enmeshed in local politics and in "nation building."

Since then, there was no operating government in Somalia until Fall 2000, when negotiations led to the possible beginnings of a return to law and order. Success is far from assured, however, as rival warlords maintain their armed militias outside government control. Dozens of clans and subclans functioned on their own and owed no allegiance to anyone claiming to represent the entire country. Certainly the self-declared Republic of Somaliland in the north was economically advancing and owed nothing to leaders further south, though its own independence remains unrecognized abroad. In late 1997, rival Somali factions agreed to form a government, but by the next year fierce fighting again erupted; four years later, fighting broke out over leadership succession in the break-away region of Puntland on the Ethiopian border. Both floods and drought have taken their toll as the world became donor-fatigued and turned its attention elsewhere, but concerns over international terrorism might refocus attention on Somalia.

CENTRAL AFRICA

Without a doubt, events in Central Africa at century's end were the most tumultuous, the most complicated, and the most dangerous in all of sub-Saharan Africa. Personal rivalries, ethnic antagonisms, cross-border conflicts, and precolonial and colonial currents mix in unpredictable ways. In the Democratic Republic of the Congo (formerly Zaire), the third largest country on the continent, the last few years have witnessed the overthrow of a president who had ignominiously ruled since the 1960s, a successor who barely clung to power amidst charges of incompetence, an assasination leading to a young, untried president, and a war in which troops from several surrounding countries joined local forces. One humanitarian nongovernmental organization (NGO), the International Rescue Committee, estimates that 2.5 million people have died as a result of the civil war in rebel-held Eastern Congo in the last three years.[19] In Rwanda, a terrible 1994 civil war that took hundreds of thousands of lives has been followed by continuing bitter ethnic hostilities across borders, with no clear end to the upheavals and the killings in sight. Neighboring countries including Angola, Burundi, Uganda, Sudan, and Zimbabwe, already struggling with major political and economic problems, have been pushed to the limit by convulsions emanating from Congo and Rwanda. Even the United States and France, longtime players in the middle of the region, have remained reluctantly engaged, sometimes in competition with each other and sometimes supporting a common cause. Amidst all the swirls, there is the fear that the turbulence could lead to boundary changes on a scale not seen for more than a hundred years.

Although Congo is one of the largest countries in sub-Saharan Africa, Rwanda is one of the smallest. It is also one of the most tortured states in the region. In 1993, few people in the United States had ever heard of Rwanda, let alone knew anything about it. In 1994, Rwanda gained its "15 minutes of fame" in the world media as between 500,000 and 1 million people, mostly Tutsi, died in terrible massacres. They were the victims of one of the worst cases of genocide that the world had seen since World War II.

At one level, the killings were a continuation of the ethnic rivalry between the Hutu and the Tutsi people that had gone on since the fifteenth century. It also involved differences between the more militant Hutu in the north of Rwanda and their more moderate counterparts to the south. The

Tutsi, although only 15 percent of the population, were wealthier and had for many generations been in charge.

Mass killings occurred periodically from the 1950s until the early 1970s. Ethnic conflict was one way of describing the situation; class conflict was another. A struggle for land in this densely populated country and children made orphans by the fighting and AIDS, who were thus cannon fodder for the recruitment, were indirect explanations of the building tensions.[20]

In late 1993, there were warnings at the UN that a simmering three-year-old civil war might erupt into something much worse. A fragile peace accord was foundering on the makeup of a transitional government. There was a small peacekeeping force already in Rwanda, but after the failure of the UN experience in Somalia, its mandate was very narrow. It was in this atmosphere that the presidents of Rwanda and Burundi were killed when their plane mysteriously crashed in April 1994 on a flight from Tanzania, where they had been discussing how to resolve the conflicts in the two neighboring countries.

What ensued was a terrible massacre in which both Tutsis and moderate Hutu were slaughtered. Astoundingly, at this critical time, the UN Security Council delayed and then refused to allow those peacekeepers who remained in the country to try to stop the killings.

After weeks of only token opposition, the Rwandan Patriotic Front (RPF), a Tutsi-dominated organization, some of whose members had been living in neighboring Uganda for more than a generation, engaged government forces and gradually pushed them back. With international action at a standstill, France, which had backed the Hutu-led government four years before, now sent 2,500 troops to act as a buffer. Ultimately, more than 2 million Rwandans who feared Tutsi retribution for earlier massacres fled the country.

From one grisly chapter to another, the mass exodus created appalling conditions at refugee camps in neighboring countries. Despite belated UN humanitarian assistance, cholera epidemics and dysentery took tens of thousands of additional lives. Ultimately, the camps were shut down and some destitute souls returned to an uncertain future in Rwanda. Others, fearful of returning to Rwanda, continued to live as refugees in Zaire, Burundi, Tanzania, Uganda, and Kenya, where they became grist for those who wanted to continue fighting and ultimately return to their country triumphant.

A Rwandan interim parliament was sworn in late in 1994. The RPF, however, continue to be the power in the country, although elements of the Front's army have abused that position. Tens of thousands of Hutu languish in overcrowded, inhumane Rwandan jails, with charges brought against only a small number, with a much smaller fraction convicted and a few actually executed. Despite $2 billion in international aid since 1994, the government barely functions, the infrastructure is in tatters, and many of the farms are unattended. Meanwhile, the exiled Hutu army of the former regime rearms and elements infiltrate into their former homeland. Not a week goes by without some massacre in some part of the country. If anything, the situation has worsened since 1996, when militants returned amidst a million Hutu civilians who finally decided that anything would be better than living in squalid refugee camps or barely surviving deep in the forests of Congo. The raids and the violence have again accelerated, further undermining the resumption of economic activity in large parts of the country. Of course, the wanton killings work both ways. Seven years after the genocidal slaughter, Rwanda has slowly begun to recover.

In the last few years, events in Rwanda have become ever more closely entwined with those of neighboring Congo (both were under Belgian colonial rule). The huge state in the middle of the continent was a prize, with its lush forests, fertile croplands, and prodigious mineral deposits; however, its painful colonial experience as the Belgian Congo made it totally unprepared for independence in 1960. Not surprisingly, chaos resulted, in which racial, ethnic, and ideological conflicts brought the country close to disintegration. Outside states threatened to intervene, but a UN peacekeeping operation, despite many problems, provided the glue that kept the country together. After the UN departure in 1964, however, instability grew again. A year later, General Joseph Mobutu staged a coup and began to put his mark on the country, a mark that has become all-pervasive.

Thirty years later, Congo was going back in time. It was a country where political and economic conditions had gotten about as bad as they could get. The general had become President Sese Seko Mobutu who ran a "kleptocracy," government by theft. Although Mobutu was a billionaire who maintained several residences in Europe, the World Bank declared Congo bankrupt in 1994. Massive corruption including diamond smuggling, hyperinflation, and hunger were three of the people's problems. Mobutu's promoting tensions and divisions among the country's 250 ethnic groups to ensure his own longevity in office was another. Because of the disintegration of the government infrastructure, civil servants and soldiers were not paid and staged mutinies.

Because of the cold war, Congo for many years was the largest recipient of U.S. aid in sub-Saharan Africa. Indeed, Mobutu came to power with the help of the Central Intelligence Agency (CIA), which used the country as a staging area for activities throughout the continent while turning a blind eye to the endemic decay and corruption. Several attempts at democratic reform during the 1990s came to naught, and in the end the malaise was so advanced that a Tutsi-supported revolt, which started along the border with Rwanda in October 1996, swept the country in just seven months. The president, already terminally ill with prostate cancer, fled the country in May 1997 and died in exile four months later.

Congo is such a big country and Mobutu's last years were so chaotic that the central government had little control over what was happening in the eastern provinces many hundreds of miles away. With dissatisfaction already running high, several neighboring countries lent their support to bring down the Congo president. Rwanda and Uganda were the most prominent of the interveners, each responding to local Tutsi pleas to oust Hutu militants from eastern Congo and thus cut off raids that cost lives. In addition, Tutsis living in eastern Congo were refused citizenship and told to leave the country. Laurent Kabila, who is from southern Congo and who had been an underground opponent of Mobutu for three decades, was anointed as the person to lead the rebellion. Disaffected soldiers joined the revolt, with government troops usually fleeing before the advancing army. Toward the end there was very little fighting but much looting by the retreating Congolese forces. With a good deal of international acclaim, Kabila's forces took the capital of Kinshasa and expectations ran high for a better tomorrow.

It was not to be. Initially, Kabila surrounded himself with Tutsi soldiers and military advisors who were seen by the populace in much of the country as an arrogant occupying force. Old scores were settled by the revamped military as massacres of Hutu refugees ensued. The economic situation, if anything, got worse, with unemployment in the capital reaching 75 percent. Charges of corruption, incompetence, and nepotism against the new president surfaced. Journalists critical of the new government were jailed, newspapers were closed, the opposition was suppressed, and activists were jailed. Despite initial support, the people became opposed to the Kabila regime.

Things came to a head in the summer of 1998. The president, playing the Congo nationalist card, dismissed his Tutsi troops and advisors. There were shoot-outs between Tutsi and non-Tutsi soldiers. Most ominously, militant Hutus fought Tutsis in eastern Congo. Kabila either could not or would not control the situation; in fact, Tutsis in Congo and back in Rwanda and Uganda believed that the president was supporting the new attacks upon his recent benefactors. The result was a new Tutsi rebellion against the Kinshasa government. Aided by disaffected soldiers and a disenchanted population, the rebels took control of much of the country and threatened to bring down the government.

At the eleventh hour, Kabila received outside support from Angola, Namibia, and Zimbabwe. The Angolan government feared being undermined by UNITA forces, against whom they had long struggled (see Angola section), joining with the rebels in Congo. Zimbabwe President Mugabe, despite considerable criticism from his own cabinet as well as opposition figures, saw the danger of a Tutsi empire in the middle of Africa. He was indifferent to calls by South African President Mandela for a peaceful resolution of the dispute. Mugabe's country was also owed a considerable sum of money by Congo, money that might not be repaid if the central government fell apart. In fact, all three states lending support to Kabila feared the dismemberment of Congo and the ensuing chaos that would bring. There were even reports of Sudan sending troops to Eastern Congo as payback for Ugandan support for the rebellion against the Khartoum government in their civil war. Congo (Brazzaville) and the Central African Republic signed alliances with Kabila. Elsewhere, the French, although not playing a role in the fighting, worried that a victory by the rebel Tutsis would favor American interests. To make matters complete, there was much Congolese hostility toward both the United States and France; the Congolese believed that the western powers, longtime supporters of the corrupt Mobutu, wanted to divide, destabilize, and recolonize the country to further their own economic interests. The hostility extended to the UN, which had not ordered the invading troops to leave the country. (The UN, in turn, was open to the possibility that Kabila had allowed his troops to massacre civilian Tutsis and then had not permitted the world body to examine the charge.)

The Congo president, by saying his country was threatened by dismemberment by invading Rwandan and Ugandan forces, rose in popularity. The rebels lost the captured territory in the western Congo as quickly as they had gained it a month earlier, but continued to control a wide crescent in the eastern part of the country where the central government had never been strong. Kabila's new allies showed little interest in pursuing the rebels in distant provinces. Attempts to bring all of the warring parties together to resolve the many-tentacled dispute failed. The president himself, trying to expand on his newly found support, promised elections in 1999, though he had not previously supported democratic principles. While dissolution of Congo had been staved off, the deep enmities engendered by the fighting remained. The clashes had been a political and economic drain on all parties. The war showed that Kabila was reliant on others for his future.

In January 2001, President Laurent Kabila was assassinated by a disloyal bodyguard, and his son Joseph Kabila, a 31-year-old army officer with little political or administrative experience, assumed the presidency. Many observers feared that the awful situation would deteriorate even further. On the contrary, the young and untried president showed stability and competence, and he spoke of building a peaceful, democratic future for his country. A failed 1999 cease-fire accord regained momentum. Despite several negotiated cease-fires, peace initiatives and conferences, sometimes boycotted by one or more of the key parties, the efforts of international mediators such as Nelson Mandela, and the presence of UN peacekeeping forces, the civil war seemed far from settled in early 2002. The regions' troubled past appears destined to follow it into the near future. Finally, the OAU principle of nonintervention in the affairs of another state, which had been ignored during the overthrow of Mobutu, had been shunted aside. How this development would play out across sub-Saharan Africa was uncertain.

THE DEVELOPMENT OF AFRICA ON THE INTERNET

It would be correct to point out that Africa is the poorest and least-wired continent with the fewest Internet subscribers. In the UN Human Development Report of 2001, which focuses on high technology and telecommunications, Africa ranked last on virtually every indicator of all the regions of the Other World. Africa Internet users are made up of the region's elite and foreigners. Africa has by far the lowest number of phone lines per capita in the world, computer usage is absolutely minimal, and on-line users number in the low millions, a large majority of whom live in South Africa. Technology costs are high and basic and computer literacy levels are low.

World Wide Web access, however, is growing, cell phones are becoming commonplace in capital cities, and Internet operations have jumped in the past couple of years from a few states to several dozen. The United States Agency for International Development (AID), for instance, is serving as a catalyst to greater Internet connectedness, establishing or supporting programs in those two dozen African states. The Agency is providing technical advice, training, equipment, and business support. The former United States Information Agency, now a part of the State Department, has also sponsored programs aimed at raising Africa's computer and high-technology literacy. Competition is increasing, private companies are proliferating, and thus far anyway, government interference has been kept to a minimum. Jim Rosenthal, hired by AID to bring the Internet to many of the countries, states: "If you don't factor in the Web into your analysis of Africa, you're going to miss something. We're just two years away from large numbers of people in Africa being able to tell their own story, and that has got to impact politics there."[21]

At one end of the spectrum there is the claim that Africa will be "skipping industrialism entirely and leaping directly into the information era."[22] Even if this proves fanciful, there is growing optimism that "Africa in cyberspace" will dramatically increase in the early years of the twenty-first century as technology becomes cheaper and more congruent with the continent's needs. Urban workers who leave their rural homes for months at a time, for instance, may have new means for staying in contact with their families. Their bosses will be able to conduct more sophisticated business operations, finding out when domestic or foreign products will be arriving or slowing orders to avoid overstocking. With electronic communications still in short supply, there is much room to grow.

Mike Jensen, a South African widely acknowledged as the leading authority on Africa's entry into the "wired" world, noted in 2000,

> The development of the Internet is at a critical point in Africa. Web-based services could help accelerate the continent's economic growth and poverty alleviation, but these tools place large de-

mands on an underlying infrastructure that is currently incapable of servicing them.... It will require greater commitment by African leadership to open up the telecommunication sector to ensure that the potential of the Internet is fully exploited.[23]

Progress in Africa's online activities can be monitored on Jensen's data-rich website, www3.sn.apc.org/africa/, which points out that all 54 African capitals are now wired to the Internet.

WEAPONS IN AFRICA

The cold war is over, ending U.S.-Soviet competition in Africa. Americans are no longer backing one side in Somalia while the Soviets back neighboring Ethiopia. The United States no longer supports one side in the Angolan civil war while the Soviet Union embraces a competing group. Has there been an end to the blood-letting in Africa with the end of the U.S.-Soviet conflict? The answer is a stark no, as peace has failed to follow the demise of the superpower rivalry. Today, civil wars in some African nations are waged more for control of valuable resources, such as diamonds in Sierra Leone or col-tan, a mineral found only in the Congo used in computer chip production, than for the political or ideological reasons of the past. Control of the resources provides power and funding for continuing armed struggles.

There is money to be made in African conflicts. Countries as diverse as France, Romania, Egypt, Russia, and South Africa supplied arms to the warring parties in Rwanda during the post–cold war 1990s. In Angola, a cease-fire led to a partial demobilization of soldiers, causing small arms to fall into the hands of civilians. In southern Africa generally, "there is no doubt that the region is flooded with weapons [as] decades of warfare and violent political struggle have given rise to a pervasive gun culture."[24] South Africa has the highest rate of civilian deaths from firearms in the world.

In Sierra Leone and Liberia, local warlords have traded diamonds, timber, iron ore, and agricultural products for small arms. In Rwanda, it was tea for weapons. In Zimbabwe, the commodities were ivory and rhino horns whereas the commodity of choice in Angola was diamonds.[25] As the Somali government disintegrated in the early 1990s, some half-million weapons were spirited to competing factions. Landmines, a focus of much international concern, are present in abundance in Africa, particularly in war-torn nations such as Somalia and Angola. Cheap small arms have also upset traditional balances between ethnic groups on more local levels, as in western Kenya, where raids between the Pokot and Marakwet peoples have become much bloodier with the infusion of AK-47s.

Weapons sometimes jump from one country to another. Foreign mercenaries brought their own arms to Sierra Leone, Angola, and Zaire (now Congo) and attempts have been made to disarm combatants with gun-buyback programs. Cross-border police cooperation between the South African and Mozambican police have had some effect. In 2001, delegates from nearly 180 nations worldwide began negotiating the first international treaty aimed at curbing the illicit trade in small arms, but this process will take time to bear fruit. In the meantime, the bottom line is that light weapons are easily available in great abundance, and innocent civilians are the main casualties in the continuing carnage.

SUB-SAHARAN AFRICA AND THE UNITED STATES

The United States enjoys enduring, deep, and rich connections of culture and heritage with sub-Saharan Africa. Most Africans would probably agree that maintaining close and friendly ties with the United States is crucial to a positive future for Africa. However, most Americans are not well-informed about African affairs, and the American media rarely covers Africa except in times of political or economic crisis or natural disaster. Normally, it is difficult to find hopeful or positive images of Africa in our mainstream media outlets. This contributes to a sense that Africa is a lost cause teeming with corrupt, greedy politicians, endless civil wars, and horrible epidemics and famines, deserving perhaps of humanitarian attention, but a futile case for more foreign aid or direct intervention.

After the cold war, the United States abandoned anticommunism as the linchpin of its African policies and with it went its support for corrupt leaders. Long-time ally Sese Seko Mobutu, president of Zaire (now the Democratic Republic of the Congo), was rebuked for activities that made him one of the richest men on the continent, if not the world, while silencing any potential opposition. On a more positive note, Washington played a major role as mediator in long-festering civil wars in Angola and Ethiopia.

At the end of 1997, Secretary of State Madeleine Albright visited Africa, declaring a "new chapter." A few months later, President Clinton talked of an "African Renaissance" while touring the region. Despite the words, Africa is at the bottom of America's priorities, with U.S. exports to and imports from the region constituting 1 percent of total U.S. foreign commerce. New initiatives are being shaped, however. Perhaps nothing dominated President Clinton's Africa policy as much as working "to accelerate Africa's full integration into the global economy."[26] For countries embracing Washington's prescription for development, special trade preferences in modest amounts of public funds, mainly for the textile industry, have been available through the much-vaunted African Growth and Opportunity Act, passed in 2000. Funds to strengthen democratic institutions also are being made available. Since 1996, the United States also has sponsored the Africa Crisis Response Initiative, which trains and advises indigenous troops in peacekeeping activities.[27] In a related program, Operation Focus Relief provides training and equipment for Nigerian and other forces assigned to peacekeeping duties in Sierra Leone. Finally, Washington is focusing on the African dimension of such global issues as weapons proliferation, drugs, infectious diseases, terrorism, air navigation, and the environment.

In early 1998, then-President Clinton set off on a six-country, 12-day tour of sub-Saharan Africa, the lengthiest period of time a serving U.S. president has ever spent in Africa. The president spoke of what he saw as a "new African Renaissance" in which democracy and economic reform would flourish. His tone was optimistic, although no major new aid pronouncements were made during the trip (U.S. annual aid for the entire region has hovered around $700 million yearly, less than one-quarter the amount contributed to Israel).

The trip also was intended to show that the years in which Africa was merely a cold war sideshow were history. The stops—Ghana, Uganda, Rwanda, South Africa, Botswana, and Senegal—were an unusual mix. In Rwanda, Clinton said the United States and the world were to blame for doing nothing during the 1994 genocide that took up to 1 million lives. The president, in both Uganda and Senegal, stopped just short of a formal apology for slavery in the United States, offering "regrets" for past treatment of African Americans. In South Africa, Clinton acknowledged that Washington had been very late in actively working to end apartheid (though he also said that, although belated, the country finally took a leadership role to end white rule). More generally, the president stated that the cardinal sin of American foreign policy toward the region had been one of neglect.

Greater access to U.S. markets, promotion of private infrastructure projects, and a $30-million initiative to develop transparent and effective judicial systems in several Central African states were promised. U.S. trade with the region was just over $100 billion in 1996, and of that figure, just $15 billion was African exports to this country, and most of that figure was based on oil imports from then-despotic Nigeria. Still, Clinton's going to Africa had major symbolic importance, a statement that Africa mattered to the United States today and would matter more tomorrow.

The United States, after encountering serious problems while intervening in Somalia in 1993, curbed its interest in Africa. Getting bogged down in quagmires that involved revamping police and security forces, reestablishing basic services, rebuilding infrastructure, and creating jobs did not have support in Washington. The Republican Congress was intent on slashing foreign aid, especially to most African states, where no vital American interests were seen to be at stake.

While the Clinton administration paid considerable attention to Africa, arguably with mixed results, many African advocates feared that a Bush administration would neglect the continent. The former Texas governor's remarks during the 2000 presidential campaign were not encouraging; he seemed much more interested in relations with Mexico and the rest of Latin

America than with Africa, and argued against U.S. intervention and involvement in Africa. However, early actions and policies of the Bush administration, under the leadership of Secretary of State Colin Powell, have not ignored Africa, with emphasis on coping with the AIDS crisis and the threats of international terrorism. President Bush had appointed respected former Senator John Danforth to be his Special Envoy to address the issues of the Sudanese civil war well before the events of September 11, 2001. Secretary Powell visited Africa in the Spring of 2001, and later that year made these remarks at the annual dinner of Africare, a prominent U.S. NGO that raises funds and promotes humanitarian causes in Africa: "AIDS could kill a continent. It is a catastrophe. It is a disaster. It is a pandemic of the worst kind."[28] Powell also gave assurance that U.S. focus on international terrorism, the subject of the next Flashpoint, would not distract it from paying attention to Africa's other problems.

SUB-SAHARAN AFRICA AND INTERNATIONAL TERRORISM

After the striking events of September 11, 2001, the attention of the United States and much of the rest of the world was riveted by the vexing phenomenon of international terrorism, but Africa had already seen its awful impact in two related attacks. In early August 1998, powerful bombs exploded adjacent to U.S. embassies in Kenya and Tanzania, and resulted in the deaths of more than 260 people, including 12 American citizens. More than 5,000 were injured.

There is an African proverb which says that "when the elephants fight, it is the grass that gets trampled." This proverb was often applied to the cold war, with the superpowers in the role of elephants and Africa the grass. As some African commentators pointed out, things do not improve for the grass when elephants "make love" instead of fight; things have improved little if any for Africa since the end of the cold war. In this case, it appeared that the terrorist acts had their origin in the Middle East or Afghanistan. The perpetrators were taking vengeance against the United States for its pro-Israel policies and its support for what were seen as despotic governments in the Arab world. More generally, there was a backlash against the intrusion of American and Western culture and values into Islamic countries.

For Kenyans and Tanzanians the price was high. First were the many killed or injured and the ripple effect on their families. Many of the deceased or those seriously hurt were breadwinners. Thousands, therefore, had their lives uprooted. There were the economic impacts such as tourists staying away in droves and many shops and buildings destroyed, which could only be slowly reconstructed, if at all. To add to the bitterness, there was criticism that U.S. servicemen who were deployed in the hours and days after the bombings were indifferent to the plight of the Africans who were injured, focusing only on American casualties.

Two weeks later the United States struck back, launching surprise missile strikes on terrorist bases in Afghanistan and a factory in Sudan, which allegedly produced chemical weapons, although that evidence remains in question. Rancorous relations of several years' standing between Washington and Khartoum now burst open, with the United States claiming that the Sudanese had been involved in terrorist attacks and that it willingly gave sanctuary and support for those planning subversive acts against other countries, including Egypt, Eritrea, Ethiopia, and Uganda. Sudan, for its part, claimed that Washington was supporting rebels in the southern part of the country who had taken up arms to form their own state. Some went even further, claiming that the United States wanted nothing less than to weaken the government and eventually cause it to fall. In the meantime, Kenyans and Tanzanians tried to get on with their lives while Africans in other countries wondered if they would be next.

Sub-Saharan Africa's ties to the crisis of international terrorism are many and appear to be growing. Virtually every African government expressed sympathy and offers of aid to the United States following the September 11 attacks, and several African nations, such as Sudan, once a headquarters for Al-Qaeda operations, were able to provide important intelligence assistance. Some critics fear, though, that closer ties with authoritarian regimes for help in the war on terrorism could have negative consequences later, as they did with anticommunism in the cold war.

Because Africa has many nations with large Islamic populations, it should not be surprising that there are also substantial followings for militant, fundamentalist Islamist groups among the discontented and disaffected, especially youth. Susan E. Rice, Assistant Secretary for African Affairs in the second Clinton administration, wrote in the *Washington Post*:

> What has Africa got to do with Osama bin Laden or terrorist finance networks? This: Africa is the world's soft underbelly for global terrorism. If we intend to win—and not just fight—the war on terror, we cannot view Africa as separate from our comprehensive, global war. . . . Al Qaeda and other terrorist cells are active throughout East, southern and West Africa, as well as North Africa. These organizations plan finance, train and execute terrorist operations in many parts of Africa, not just Sudan and Somalia.[29]

Al-Qaeda presence in Sudan and Somalia is widely acknowledged in intelligence circles. The Khartoum government, which has had difficult relations with Washington over the last decade because of alleged sponsorship of terrorism, previously hosting Osama bin Laden, the ongoing civil war with the black, partially Christian south, and allegations of modern human slavery, has chosen to avoid confrontation with the United States in the war on terrorism and instead to become a source of useful intelligence. Somalia, still highly unstable with little central governmental authority, is reputedly a safe haven for Al-Qaeda operations and might even provide some sanctuary for terrorist fighters escaping from the United States in Afghanistan. With help from Ethiopian authorities on the border, U.S. officials conducted scouting missions in Somalia late in 2001 for possible later actions against terrorist activities there.

In an article entitled "Blood on the Diamonds," *Washington Post* reporter Holly Burkhalter examined the illicit trade links of Al-Qaeda terrorists, some of whom are linked to the 1998 embassy bombings, in securing diamonds at wholesale prices from Sierra Leonan rebels by way of contacts in neighboring Liberia, and then trafficking the diamonds at windfall profits to the world markets in Belgium. Legislative and other efforts to intercept and close down such lucrative terrorist financial dealings are underway.[30] Nigeria experienced deadly riots by extremist Muslims against Christians in northern cities such as Kano following the U.S. bombing of Taliban and Al-Qaeda positions in Afghanistan. Clearly, official positions in African countries are supportive of U.S. efforts to combat international terrorism, but opinions of the people "on the street" in African Islamic nations may not be so favorable to U.S. positions. Whether the attention on Africa resulting from concerns over international terrorism will be good for African interests in the long term remains to be seen, but short-term disruptions are likely.

ENVIRONMENT

In recent years, a whole cottage industry has been formed of experts bemoaning the environmental present and future in Africa.[31] All essentially have said the same thing: that the region's environment is being overwhelmed. This chapter has offered several reasons why more and more countries cannot feed themselves. Civil wars are making whole areas unfit for human habitation. Only minor advances have been made in limiting population growth. Poverty is a scourge, forcing Africans to mutilate their remaining forests, grasslands, and croplands as well as the wildlife. The continent is becoming increasingly urbanized as millions each year migrate to the cities, placing additional stress on these areas.

African food dependency is growing and reports of serious hunger are widespread. Drought, pests, and insects destroy agriculture. New seed varieties, greater use of chemical fertilizers, and better management are offered as remedies, but the first two again increase dependency on fickle sources beyond the continent. Increased demands for food are leading to falling water tables, and rapid soil erosion is reducing the region's grain harvest.

Rising population and growing consumption are raising levels of air and water pollution. The wood burning for heat and cooking has long choked local skies, and coal-burning power plants in South Africa affect the health of crops and humans. Industrialization throughout the continent is growing and with it the attendant ecological problems. As in Eastern Europe and Russia, industrialization and providing jobs threaten to take precedence over air quality.

Industrialization is also affecting water quality, especially on Lake Victoria, the world's second-largest freshwater lake, and other inland waters in East Africa. An invasion of giant water hyacinths, nourished by pollutants, is choking the inland sea, impeding navigation, and modifying aquatic ecology. Some of the ports on the lake have sustained 50 percent declines in trade, and commercially significant fishing has disappeared in certain areas. Hydroelectricity and transportation are in jeopardy. In fact, the whole regional ecosystem is at risk. Uganda is experimenting with chemicals in hopes of finding a solution, and Kenya is importing weevils from Florida, but there is no short-term fix for Lake Victoria's problems. The lack of cooperation between the countries bordering the lake does not help. A worst-case scenario would be the entire shoreline suffocating in the next few years.

Population growth and poverty are also endangering other species on land. Although poaching of some species has been contained in several countries, more land-poor people and rising populations generally are making it ever more difficult for threatened animals and plants to survive.[32] Civil wars take a terrible toll on more than human life; in Eastern Congo, for example, the fabled Mountain Gorillas have suffered devastating losses. Lake Victoria has seen many indigenous species disappear after the introduction of the predatory Nile perch. Since 1977, 40 percent of Kenya's wildlife has disappeared. Including the much-viewed coral reefs, the country's tourist industry earns $400 million a year, though most of the earnings do not go to the local population. In Zimbabwe, however, local governing bodies have been given authority to make decisions concerning wildlife, including the culling of herds and the selling of body parts. Overall, international treaties and private preserves are helping, but the long-term prognosis is not good.

The life-support systems throughout Africa are now at risk. Land degradation from overgrazing, deforestation, and agricultural mismanagement is severe. Fishing off the southwest coast of Africa has declined by more than 50 percent since the early 1970s. Coral reefs adjacent to East Africa are being affected by nearby land clearing and development. Tropical rainforest devastation is continuing, as deliberately set fires to clear vast areas take a heavy toll in Senegal, Congo, and East Africa. Throughout the region, timber has not been harvested on a sustainable basis, and now earnings from the forests have virtually ceased.

Still, as some African writers have noted, all environmental problems do not rest with the Other World, and Africa faces human issues that cannot yield to simple admonitions from the developed nations to protect nature and end pollution. Africa, with a largely preindustrial economy, accounts for less than 4 percent of the world's carbon dioxide emissions from fossil fuels, while the United States alone accounts for nearly a quarter of that total. This statistic has been shown to have a major impact on the environment, particularly air quality and climate change. Africa's capabilities to protect its own environment, given the pressures of conflicts, health issues, and the debt crisis, among other factors, are limited without understanding and substantive assistance from those in the developed world with the means and technology to make a difference.

WOMEN IN AFRICA

As the *Human Development Report 1997* and again in *2000* make clear, women in Africa generally are subject to a double deprivation—first, the deprivation suffered by most people in the region because of the many factors mentioned in this chapter, and second, the difficulties encountered because of their sex. In the 1997 Report's gender disparity index, which focuses on life expectancy, educational attainment, and income, every one of the bottom 15 states of the 146 countries in the gender disparity table is in the region.[33] Again, winds of change are blowing, but historical and contemporary factors will take time to dislodge.

In precolonial Africa, social and economic positions of women varied greatly. For the most part, women's political influence was felt informally. Women's courts, secret societies, and age-grade institutions certainly existed; women had important religious positions, and they also played important roles in markets, but overall, boys and then men were favored.

The colonial period greatly expanded the superior-inferior distinction. The "colonial rulers assumed that men's domination of women was universal,

Under Sail: Traditional fishermen headed home off the east coast of Africa.

SOURCE: *Emmit B. Evans, Jr.*

a God-given fact."[34] Western conceptions of the role and position of women were transported to Africa. Thus, the commercialization of agriculture hurt women as men grew the cash crops and women were relegated to food crops for local use. Among pastoralists, roles were also more clearly delineated. When the moneyed economy came to the rural areas where most people lived, the men often went to the city to work and women took on additional functions (and hours of toil). Schooling and new skills were the province of boys, not girls. The colonial administration often further diminished the role of women at the local level because the "native authorities" became exclusively male.

Women's participation in the move to independence was considerable, but then tapered off after the coveted goal was reached. One exception is Eritrea, where women engaged in combat for liberation and continue to enjoy a small measure of equality. As in other parts of the world, girls today are taught while very young that they are less valuable, hence less wanted, than boys. To marry young, to produce many children, to work far longer hours than men (including unpaid housework) at far lower pay, to have far less formal education, to have less access to credit and other financial services, and to be subservient to men is the norm. Even to open a bank account without a husband's permission may be difficult. One out of 15 women will die during childbirth compared to one in 3,700 in North America. Female genital excision remains common and traditional in large parts of Africa, even if illegal, though some African NGOs and the UN are questioning the practice, and some women are speaking about the health risks associated with the practice. Western development agencies, however, are only now beginning to target women in their programs.[35]

Changing patterns in the role of women are scattered but occurring. More women are demanding family planning advice as a tool to control the size of their families. Women entrepreneurs are becoming more common, which results in greater confidence by the practitioners. More women are also challenging being "second wives" when that means their property rights and their children's rights are abridged. Battered women are beginning to come forward rather than accept their fate; in the Kenyan capital of Nairobi, the first women's shelter has opened. Also in Kenya, through the Greenbelt Movement, women have been the driving force behind the planting of 20 million trees to combat soil erosion, which was threatening rural livelihoods. Such actions empower women, improve self-esteem, and lead to enhanced social and political influence. Most commentators agree that any long-term strategy for the future of Africa that does not consider women prominently is doomed to failure. Women figure strongly as victims in nearly all of Africa's most serious dilemmas; they must now be brought to the forefront in the decision-making processes that will lead to solutions. Minimizing the role of women is something Africa can no longer afford.

SUMMARY

Natural geography and history impede positive change in Africa. Population, health, education, food, energy, and environmental concerns are troubling problems. Politically, the continuing quest for legitimacy, the social diversity and conflict, the intermittent regional and pan-African cooperation, and the lessening international interest in Africa do not bode well for the years ahead. Finally, by many indicators, economic well-being is very uncertain, while dependency on external agencies that prescribe privatization has increased.

As Africa moves into the twenty-first century, there has been no dramatic turnaround for the region; however, politically and economically there are glimmers of hope. In the 1990s, West Africa would have been a good candidate for a "flashpoint." Particularly gruesome civil wars, marred by many atrocities against civilians, raged in Liberia and Sierra Leone. Côte d'Ivoire, long one of the most stable governments in former French West Africa, suffered a violent military coup, and corrupt dictatorships held sway in several other West African nations. In addition to the shift to civilian rule in the important nation of Nigeria described in the Case Studies above, the civil wars abated in both Liberia and Sierra Leone, and some disarmament and rebuilding has begun. Côte d'Ivoire is more stable with a timetable for a return to civilian rule, and both Ghana and Senegal experienced relatively peaceful and significant transfers of power to opposition leaders through free and fair elections.

Among African leaders and scholars, there is a major debate about whether the causes, and thus the implied cures of Africa's current ills are largely external (such as slavery, colonialism, imperialism, and globalization) or internal (such as poor leadership, corruption, and ethnic conflict).[36] President Mbeki of South Africa is considered a strong proponent of the externalist view, while President Obasanjo of Nigeria has made statements along the internalist lines. Although these are useful distinctions for analysis, many would agree that action for Africa is needed on all fronts, both outside and inside the continent.

People in many cases still fear their own governments, but they are also no longer suffering in silence. Literacy is rising, technology is making inroads in the most distant villages, and from Senegal to Nigeria to Kenya to Zimbabwe, the people "will be heard." Despite problems, developments in South Africa are exciting. Some see promise in the development of the African Union. More people are standing up to mismanagement and corruption. Africa has great potential, but there is much to do and there may be little time left to do it.

Review Questions

1. What are the effects of the European Colonial Period, including the earlier slave trade on the current political and economic situation in sub-Saharan Africa?

2. Why do many Africans believe that their own governments and leaders have not served them well? Are there exceptions to this pattern?
3. What parts of Africa continue to suffer episodes of civil war and ethnic violence? What previous civil wars have been resolved in recent years?
4. Why is there a special relationship between the United States and Africa? Why do some Africans fear that their interests have at times been marginalized in U.S. foreign policy?
5. What factors have made the lot of women especially difficult in much of sub-Saharan Africa? Why is the political and economic participation of women vital for Africa's future success?

Key Terms

- **Apartheid**—The policy of racial discrimination and separation practiced by the white Afrikaner regime in South Africa until the coming of majority rule in the 1990s.
- **The Berlin Conference**—The notorious meeting of European imperial powers to divide Africa for colonial exploitation without the participation of Africans. This division is still reflected in today's political map of Africa; see Figures 6.2, 6.3, and 6.4.
- **"The Elephants and the Grass"**—From a Swahili proverb that claims that grass is trampled when elephants fight, with Africa cast in the role of the grass and the Western powers (formerly, also the Soviet Union) and financial institutions in the role of elephants.
- **Externalists and internalists**—Those who explain Africa's problems and possible solutions on the basis of factors outside Africa (external), such as historical slavery, colonialism, the cold war and globalization, as opposed to factors within Africa (internal) such as corrupt leadership, ethnic conflict, and civil war.
- **The Great Lakes Region**—The area that includes much of Central Africa comprising the northeastern part of the Democratic Republic of the Congo, western Kenya, northern Tanzania, southern Uganda, and all of Rwanda and Burundi that has witnessed much ethnic violence, civil war, and refugee problems.
- **The Horn of Africa**—The region of Northwest Africa consisting of Djibouti, Ethiopia, Eritrea, Somalia, and Sudan that has seen much instability, war, and disaster, both natural and man-made.
- **Modern slavery**—The practices of indentured servitude of youths and of chattel (ownership) slavery of black Africans in Sudan and Mauritania.
- **The Organization of African Unity (OAU)**—Founded in 1963, the association of all independent African nations to promote cooperation and solutions to Africa's problems, often accused in the past of ignoring Africa's most pressing issues but now undergoing a process of reform and eventual transformation into the African Union.

- **Pan-Africanism**—The idea, often associated with Kwame Nkrumah, the charismatic first president of Ghana, that African nations and peoples need to unite for their common good and survival; an ideal not yet realized in practice.
- **The politics of extraction**—A concept closely associated with corruption that holds that political power is intended for acquiring material well-being rather than serving the people, as practiced by the colonial powers and allegedly learned by some of Africa's own leaders, such as Mobutu of Zaire, after independence.

Useful Web Sites

http://www.africare.org
http://www.africapolicy.org
http://allafrica.com
http://www.oau-oua.org
http://www.sas.upenn.edu/African_Studies/AS.html

Notes

1. Figures in the last four paragraphs came from the World Watch Institute and Population Action International, *Human Development Report 1997* and *2000* (New York: Oxford University Press, 1997; 2000).
2. "Angrily" is an understatement. With independence, France cut all ties with Guinea and withdrew, taking with them everything from government vehicles to telephones.
3. Mazrui related the anecdote in the 1986 television series, *The Africans.*
4. Susan Rice, "A New Partnership for the 21st Century," address to the African Studies Association, November 14, 1997.
5. Judith Matloff, "African Anthem: Where Life Goes on, No Matter What," *Christian Science Monitor,* 6 January 1998, p. 9.
6. Robert Reid, "Annan: Africans Must Share Blame," *Associated Press,* 16 April 1998.
7. For a fuller discussion on this subject, see Herman J. Cohen, "Conflict Management in Africa," *CSIS Africa Notes,* February 1998, pp. 1–7.
8. Jennifer Seymour Whitaker, *How Can Africa Survive?* (New York: Council on Foreign Relations, 1988), pp. 30–31.
9. Alan B. Durning, "Ending Poverty," in Lester R. Brown et al., *State of the World, 1990* (New York: Norton, 1990), p. 139.
10. David Francis, "World Reaps Benefits of Economic Reform," *Christian Science Monitor,* 10 February 1998.
11. *Human Development Report 1997,* p. 103.
12. *Human Development Report 1997,* p. 43.
13. R. W. Johnson, "A Brutal Brush with Gun Law in South Africa," *The Sunday Times* (London), 6 September 1998.
14. "Nigerian Justice Minister Shot Dead at Home," *The Washington Post,* 25 December 2001.
15. Jan Raath, "Mugabe's Grace and Favours," *The Times* (London), 18 July 1998.
16. *The World Almanac and Book of Facts 2001* (Mahwah, NJ: World Almanac Books, 2001), p. 562. The figure is taken from 1999 UN AIDS data.

17. In Zimbabwe, where as much as 25 percent of all adults may be infected with HIV, average life expectancy, which was 62 in 1993, was expected to be no more than 49 in the year 2000.
18. *Human Development Report 1997*, Box 3.6, p. 68.
19. This staggering figure cannot be verified, since access to the remote areas of the conflict by outside observers has been impossible, and many of the deaths have resulted from disease and famine related to the conflict, rather than from actual combat. Regardless of the exact figure, few Americans are aware of the enormity of this tragedy, a situation that Ted Koppel's ABC *Nightline* program had hoped to correct in September 2001 through a five-part series entitled "Still in the Heart of Darkness." Unfortunately, the last four parts of the broadcast were preempted by the September 11 terrorist attacks, but the series finally aired in late January 2002.
20. Hal Kane, "Leaving Home," in Lester R. Brown et al., *State of the World, 1995* (New York: Norton, 1995), p. 142.
21. Thomas L. Friedman, "Don't Look Now, but He's Busy Wiring Timbuktu," *The International Herald Tribune*, 6 May 1998.
22. Dominic Gates, "Africa Online," quoting John Perry Barlow in *Microsoft Internet Magazine*, 1 March–23 February 1998.
23. Mike Jensen, "Making the Connection: Africa and the Internet," *Current History*; reprinted in ed. E. Jeffress Ramsey, *Global Studies: Africa* (Guilford, Conn.: Dushkin, 2001), p. 196.
24. Michael Renner, "An Epidemic of Guns," *Worldwatch Magazine*, July/August 1998, p. 25. Most of the specifics in this Flashpoint come from the same article.
25. Michael Renner, "Small Arms, Big Impact: The Next Challenge of Disarmament," *Worldwatch Paper 137*, October 1997, p. 34.
26. Susan Rice, Assistant Secretary of State for African Affairs, "U.S.-Africa Policy," address to the National Association for the Advancement of Colored People, 14 July 1998.
27. In 1998, U.S. soldiers joined their Kenyan, Tanzanian, and Ugandan counterparts in Kenya to show that their hypothetical country of Sumang could be returned to calm after upheaval. Small-scale training and exercises involving U.S. troops and African peacekeeping forces continue into the early 2000s.
28. Peter Carlson, "Powell, on Another Front," *The Washington Post*, 7 November 2001, p. C1.
29. Susan E. Rice, "The Africa Battle," *The Washington Post*, 11 December 2001.
30. Holly Barkhalter, "Blood on the Diamonds," *The Washington Post*, 6 November 2001, p. A23.
31. Impressive books, devoted in major part or entirely to African environmental stresses, include Paul Harrison, *The Greening of Africa* (New York: Penguin Books, 1987); *The Third Revolution* (New York: Penguin Books, 1992); and Lloyd Timberlake, *Africa in Crisis: The Causes, the Cures of Environmental Bankruptcy*, new ed. (London and Toronto: Earthscan, 1988).
32. Since 1989, for instance, Kenya's elephant population has grown by some 60 percent to an estimated 25,000. In the same period, Kenya's human population has grown by 6 million, an increase of about 27 percent.
33. *Human Development Report 1997*, Table 2.8, p. 40.
34. Jeff Haynes, *Third World Politics* (Oxford: Blackwell, 1996), p. 166.
35. Such agencies always run the danger of incurring the wrath of members of the local population who will accuse them of meddling in time-honored traditions.
36. For a fine treatment of this debate from an internalist's point of view, see George B. N. Ayittey, *Africa in Chaos* (New York: St. Martin's Press, 1999), particularly the calls for a return to indigenous African consensual democratic practices in chapters 3 and 9.

For Further Reading

Ali, Taisier, and Matthews, Robert. *Civil Wars in Africa.* Toronto: McGill-Queen's University Press, 1999.

Ayittey, George B.N. *Africa Betrayed.* New York: St. Martin's Press, 1992.

———. *Africa in Chaos.* New York: St. Martin's Press, 1999.

Bayart, Jean-Francois. *The State in Africa: The Politics of the Belly.* London and New York: Longman, 1993.

Bratton, Michael. *Democratic Experiments in Africa: Regime Transitions in Comparative Perspective.* Cambridge and New York: Cambridge University Press, 1997.

Davidson, Basil. *The Black Man's Burden: Africa and the Curse of the Nation State.* New York: Times Books, 1992.

Decalo, Samuel. *The Stable Minority: Civilian Rule in Africa.* Gainesville, Fla.: Florida Academic Press, 1998.

Gourevitch, Philip. *We Wish to Inform You that Tommorow We Will Be Killed with Our Families: Stories from Rwanda.* New York: Farrar, Straus and Giroux, 1998.

Hameso, Seyoum. *State, Society and Development: An Assessment of African Experience.* London: TSC Publications, 1997.

Hochschild, Adam. *King Leopold's Ghost.* New York: Houghton Mifflin, 1998.

Kapuscinski, Ryzard. *The Shadow of the Sun.* Translated by Klara Glowczweka. New York: Alfred A. Knopf, 2001.

Khapoya, Vincent. *The African Experience: An Introduction,* 2nd ed. Upper Saddle River, NJ: Prentice Hall, 1998.

Leach, Melissa, and Mearns, Robin, eds. *The Lie of the Land: Challenging Received Wisdom on the African Environment.* Westport, Conn.: Heinemann, 1996.

Mazrui, Ali. *The African Condition.* New York: Cambridge University Press, 1980.

———. *Cultural Forces in World Politics.* Westport, Conn.: Heinemann, 1990.

Roe, Emery, *Except Africa: Remaking Development, Remaking Power.* Somerset, N.J.: Transaction, 1998.

Soyinka, Wole. *The Open Sore of a Continent.* Oxford and New York: Oxford University Press, 1996.

———. *The Burden of Memory, The Muse of Forgiveness.* Oxford and New York: Oxford University Press, 1999.

Young, Crawford. *The African Colonial State in Comparative Perspective.* New Haven and London: Yale University Press, 1994.

CHAPTER 7

Asia

Joseph N. Weatherby

And at the end of the fight is a tombstone white with the name
of the late deceased, and the epitaph drear: "A fool lies here
who tried to hustle the East."

RUDYARD KIPLING, 1892

INTRODUCTION TO ASIA

For almost 2,000 years, Westerners have looked to Asia. Here the West has sought a source for luxury goods including spices, porcelain, tea, and silk. Since early times hardy adventurers like Marco Polo and Vasco de Gamma have risked hardships and death to gain access to the wealth of Asia. During the last four centuries, profit has been the primary motivation for the rise of Western imperialism in Asia. As early as 1687 this aim was clearly expressed in directions sent to the East India Company's British agent in India. The company is quoted as ordering him to "establish such a polity of civil and military power and create and secure such a large revenue . . . as may be the foundation of a large, well-grounded sure English dominion in India for all time to come."[1]

Throughout most of this period, the West has also had good reason to fear the military power of Asia. On many occasions fierce warriors have ridden out of Asia to crush kingdoms, sack cities, and take slaves. Names like Attila the Hun, Genghis Khan, and Tamerlane still strike fear in the hearts of Europeans hundreds of years after their invasions took place. When the adventurer Marco Polo met Kublai Khan in 1275, the Khan's empire stretched from Korea to Hungary.

It was not until the Europeans developed efficient ships and effective guns that the military dominance of Asia was broken. Technology allowed Western imperialists to dominate large parts of Asia for almost 500 years. Hilaire Belloc's nineteenth-century comment about Africa could also be applied to Western imperialism then taking place in Asia. He is quoted as saying, "Whatever happens, we have got the Maxim Gun and they have not."[2]

Much of the story of modern Asia has been one of the Western search of wealth followed by imperialism that was made possible because of superior military technology. Now that technology is being challenged by the emerging powers of Asia.

It is not an understatement to assert that if the nineteenth century belonged to Britain and the twentieth century was American, the twenty-first century is likely to be Asian. Western policymakers are already recognizing this fact of life. In referring to the growing importance of China, United States Deputy Defense Secretary Paul Wolfowitz has put it this way, "I think the right way to think about China is that it's a country that is almost certain to become a superpower in the next half-century, and maybe in the next quarter-century, and that's pretty fast by historical standards."[3]

A brief review of the information contained in Table 7.1 (pages 242–243) does much to illustrate the great variety of conditions in Other World Asia. Such diversity makes it impossible to analyze the region state-by-state. This chapter will briefly discuss geography, then focus on the major states of the area.

GEOGRAPHY

Where Is Asia?

Viewed from space, there is no Asia! Asia is simply a subdivision of a single Afro-Eurasian "island" that stretches from the Cape of Good Hope all the way to Cape Dezhnyova in Russia. Within this great landmass Asia forms the largest part (see Figure 7.1 on page 244).

The separation of the continent of Asia from that of Africa and Europe is more cultural and historic than geographic. To identify Asia, most geographers arbitrarily draw a line along the Ural Mountains of Russia down through the Caspian Sea. The line then takes in Turkish Anatolia and the eastern shores of the Mediterranean and Red seas to include the Arabian Peninsula. This marks the western boundaries of Asia. All the lands east of that line into parts of the Pacific are considered to be Asian.

The Asian Continent is subdivided into five regions: Southwest Asia or Asia Minor, South Asia, Southeast Asia, East Asia, and Russian Asia or Siberia. Here the authors have included Southwest Asia in the chapter on the Middle East and North Africa. Because, as it is defined in chapter 1, Russia is not part of the Other World. Russian Asia is not discussed here. Admittedly, this definition of Asia is subjective. Places like the former Soviet Republics of Central Asia along with Afghanistan, and Pakistan could have been put in several places. Here the former Soviet Asian Republics are discussed as part of the Middle East. Because of Japan's unique history of development, it is not considered an Other World state. For our purposes, Other World Asia includes Afghanistan and Pakistan as part of South Asia. Southeast Asia and East Asia make up the remaining portions of this chapter.

What Is Other World Asia?

Even limited to South, Southeast, and East Asia, the continent is the world's largest. As might be expected, the land is both physically and climatically complex. Here there are high mountain ranges, important passageways, vast deserts, tropics, and important rivers. In terms of human geography, for thousands of years important civilizations have thrived in both China and India. Until about 500 years ago, China was arguably the most advanced civilization in the world.

The Geography of South Asia   Most of South Asia is part of a peninsula that stretches from the Himalayas to the southern borders of India. Only Afghanistan and Sri Lanka are outside of this peninsula. In the north are found the world's highest mountains, with the famous Mount Everest soaring to a height of 29,028 feet. These mountains are part of a continuous highland region stretching west to Switzerland. Here the range includes the Hindu Kush and the Karakorum separating Pakistan, Afghanistan, and India before becoming the Himalayas of Nepal and Butan. The mountain ranges have made travel in this region difficult.

The Great Deccan Plateau of India lies south of these mountains. This large tableland makes up most of the peninsula. The central parts of the plateau have arid conditions. However, below the mountains of the eastern and western Ghats, much of the coastal area has tropical forests.

Both India and Pakistan have great river systems that support some major areas of population. The Ganges is considered to be a sacred river by Hindu Indians. Rising in the Himalayas, the river flows past the great cities of Allahabad and Varanasi for 1,560 miles before joining the Brahmaputra to reach the Bay of Bengal. The Indus headwaters are in Tibet. The river flows for 1,800 miles through Jammu and Kashmir into Pakistan, where it eventually reaches the Arabian Sea. The Indus has a number of hydroelectric and irrigation systems that are a source of power for Pakistan. The control of some of these systems has been a source of conflict between India and Pakistan since they were granted independence in 1947.

The major cities of South Asia are Kabul, Afghanistan (2,590,000); Karachi, Pakistan (11,794,000); and Islamabad, Pakistan (604,000). India, the second most populous state in the world, has a number of great cities including Mumbaj (Bombay) (18,066,000), Kolkata (Calcutta) (12,918,000), Delhi (11,695,000), and Hyderabad (6,842,000).

Southeast Asia: Southeast Asia is the land that lies to the east of India and to the south of China. Most of the climate is tropical monsoon. This means that there is a wet and dry season. The trees are typical of a warm, humid climate, with palm trees and bamboo common. Rice is grown almost everywhere and is a staple in most of Southeast Asian diets.

TABLE 7.1 CHARACTERISTICS OF ASIAN COUNTRIES

Country	Population (Millions)	Population Growth Rate (%)	Infant Mortality Rate (per 1,000 live births)	Population under 15 Years of Age (%)	Life Expectancy (years)	Urban Population (%)	Literacy Rate (%)	Arable Land (%)	Per Capita GDP ($U.S.)
Middle South									
Afghanistan	25.889	3.54	137	42	46	21	32	12	800
Bangladesh	129.194	1.59	67	36	60	24	38	73	1,380
Bhutan	2.005	2.19	107	40	52	7	42	2	1,000
India	1014.004	1.58	58	34	63	28	52	56	1,720
Maldives	0.301	3.06	35	46	62	26	93	10	1,840
Nepal	24.702	2.34	71	41	58	12	27	17	1,100
Pakistan	141.554	2.17	90	41	61	37	38	27	2,000
Sri Lanka	19.239	0.89	16	27	72	23	88	14	2,500
South East									
Brunei	0.336	2.17	22	31	74	72	88	1	1,700
Myanmar (Burma)	41.735	0.64	74	30	55	27	83	15	1,200
Cambodia	12.212	2.27	103	42	57	16	65	13	700
Indonesia	224.784	1.63	55	31	68	40	84	10	2,830
Laos	5.497	2.5	87	43	53	23	57	3	1,260
Malaysia	21.793	2.01	21	35	71	57	83	3	10,300
Philippines	81.16	2.07	33	37	67	58	95	19	3,500
Singapore	4.152	3.54	4	18	80	100	91	2	26,300
Thailand	61.231	0.93	28	24	69	21	94	34	6,100
Vietnam	78.774	1.49	34	33	69	20	94	17	1,770

	Population	Population Growth Rate	Infant Mortality Rate	Population Under 15 Years of Age	Life Expectancy	Urban Population	Literacy Rate	Arable Land	Per Capita GDP
East Asia									
China	1261.932	0.9	41	25	71	32	82	10	3,600
Korea, North	21.688	1.35	24	26	71	60	95	14	1,000
Korea, South	47.471	0.93	7	22	74	81	98	19	12,600
Mongolia	2.616	1.54	63	34	67	63	83	1	2,250
Comparison States									
Japan	126.55	0.18	4	15	81	79	100	11	23,100
Belgium	10.242	0.18	6	18	78	97	99	24	23,400
Italy	57.634	0.09	6	14	79	67	97	31	20,800

SOURCES: Population, Infant Mortality Rate, Population Under 15 Years of Age, Urban Population, Literacy Rate, and Per Capita GDP from *The World Almanac and Book of Facts, 2001*. Population Growth Rate, Life Expectancy, and Arable Land from *CIA World Factbook, 2000*.

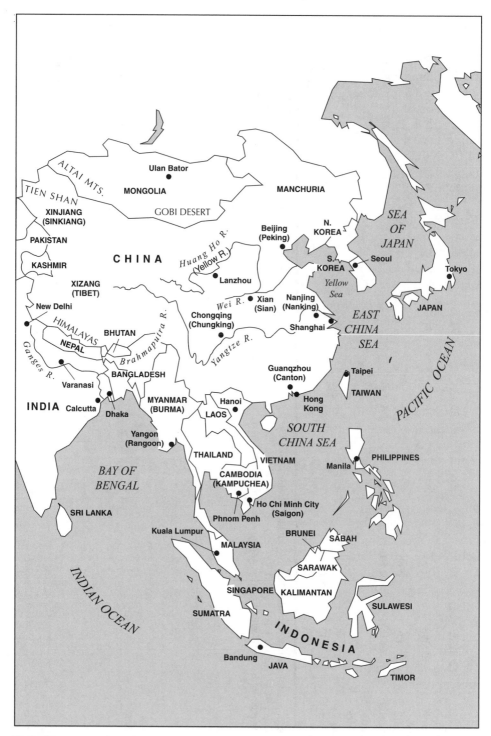

FIGURE 7.1 Political and Physical Characteristics of Other World Asia

The terrain of the region is complex. Mountains separate river valleys, with most people living in the deltas of the region's principal rivers. Southeast Asia has six major river systems: the Brahmaputra, the Irrawaddy, the Salween, the Chao Phraya, the Mekong, and the Hong (Red).

Southeast Asia is a region with large cities. Major Southeast Asian cities include Dhaka (12,317,000) and Chittagong (3,581,000) in Bangladesh, Rangoon (4,196,000) in Myanmar, Bangkok (7,281,000) in Thailand, and Ho Chi Minh City (4,615,000) and Hanoi (3,734,000) in Vietnam. Finally, Singapore is a city with a population of 3,567,000.

East Asia   Other World East Asia is made up of China and Korea. Of these, China is by far the most important. China is the world's most populous and third largest state in area. One out of every four people on the planet is Chinese. China may be divided into six parts: China, the lands to the east and south of the Great Wall; Manchuria; Inner Mongolia; Sinkiang; Tibet; and Taiwan. Today Taiwan is held by the Nationalist Chinese who were driven from the Mainland in 1949. However, most Chinese in both Taiwan and on the Mainland consider Taiwan to be part of "greater" China.

As might be expected, China, as the world's third largest state in area, has a complex geography. Except along the 4,000-mile east coast, high mountains, deserts, and endless forests surround China. All of this has contributed to China's historic isolation from the states to the north and west.

In the west the Tibetan Plateau reaches heights of 12,000 feet. The part called Sinkiang (Xinjiang) is an isolated flat land surrounded by mountains. It is dry land inhabited by Turkic-speaking peoples. Here are located some of the world's highest mountains. Much of this region is underpopulated because it is too cold, too dry, too high, and too remote.

The northeast includes Inner Mongolia and Manchuria. This area has cold, long winters. Manchuria was the site of the puppet-state called Manchukuo. Established by the Japanese in 1932, Manchukuo served as a cover for the Japanese occupation of Manchuria and the later invasion of the Chinese heartland. While it existed, the last surviving member of the Manchu Dynasty, Henry Pu Yi, ruled Manchukuo. With the defeat of Japan in World War II, Manchukuo was abolished and China reestablished control. Today Manchuria is known for agriculture, mining, and manufacturing.

Most people live in the Chinese heartland. Although there are many cities here, most people live in the valleys of China's great rivers, the Huang Ho (Yellow), the Yangtze, and the Xi. Two of these rivers, the Huang Ho and the Yangtze, rise in the same area as the Mekong and Brahmaputra. Finally, the Xi is not important because of its length, which is only about 300 miles. It is an important source of river commerce between the great city of Guangzhou and the Maccao Hong Kong areas. Once known as the Pearl, this river was one of the entry points for European imperialists during the nineteenth century.

About 32 percent of China's 1.2 billion people live in urban areas. It should not be surprising to learn that China has more mega cities than any other Other

World Asian state. The largest and most important cities are in order of size: Shanghai (12,887,000), Beijing (10,839,000), Tianjin (9,146,000), Hong Kong (7,120,000), Chongqing (5,312,000), Shenyang (4,828,000), and Guangzhou (3,893,000). Even the former Portuguese colonial city, Maccao, has a population of 445,594.

Other Asian Names   In Asia there are names that have been used to describe regions or the continent as a whole during different historic periods. Two examples are the Orient and the Far East.

The Orient: In ancient times, the Latin root word referred to the rising of the sun. Gradually the word came to mean eastern lands. At times it could mean anything to the east of Venice. During the eighteenth and nineteenth centuries, Europeans thought of anything along the eastern coast of the Mediterranean to the Pacific to be the Orient. So in old Constantinople (Istanbul), one could cross from "the West to the Orient" while remaining in the city, by crossing the Bosporus Strait. Today, the term "Orient" is usually used to refer to East Asia.

Far East: The Far East is simply a designation given to the general area of East Asia by Western imperialists. Like the terms "Near East" and "Middle East," the Far East designates the distance from the colonial capitals in Europe. Today this term is considered to be offensive to some nationalists.

Religion in Asia

As might be expected in a region so large, Asia has a complex religious heritage. There are at least five major religions or philosophies that have mass appeal. The major sects of Asia are Buddhism, Confucianism, Daoism (Taoism), Hinduism, and Islam. In addition to these major faiths, there are a number of others that are of local importance.

Buddhism   Both a religion and a philosophy, Buddhism was founded by an Indian prince, Gautama, around 550 B.C. Today there are more than 350 million Buddhists worldwide. Buddhism is an acquired rather than a revealed religion like Christianity and Islam. Buddhists view life as a cycle of tribulation. The aim of the believer is to overcome life's suffering through following a series of steps or paths to reach nirvana. To the Buddhist, nirvana is a state of liberation from earthly desires. Buddhists also believe in reincarnation based on one's previous behavior. Although Buddhism began in India, the modern religion has the largest numbers of believers elsewhere. Centers of Buddhist worship are located in Sri Lanka, Tibet, China, and Southeast Asia.

Confucianism   Confucius was born around the same time as Buddha: 551 B.C. He was concerned with how society should be arranged. His ideas of social order have played important parts in the administration of Chinese society for over 2,000 years. Although Confucianism was originally a philosophy, temples and a ritual had developed by the first century A.D. Many emperors even proclaimed Confucianism as a state religion. Confucianism declined because of its association with the old imperial regime. Under Mao, Confucian temples were destroyed and believers severely persecuted. However, in recent years the government of the People's Republic has been more tolerant of this traditional Chinese system of belief. At the present time there are 6.2 million Confucians.

Daoism (Taoism) Founded by Latose in the sixth century B.C., like Confucianism, Daoism was not supposed to be a religion but a way of finding peace in solitude. Later writers developed an elaborate ritual and built temples around what became the Daoist religion. Over time Daoism involved alchemy, magic, ghosts, saints, and gods. One major aim was to find the secret of immortality. Daoism has absorbed practices from both Buddhism and Confucianism. As a native Chinese religion, Daoism has had a great influence on art and literature. Daoists have survived revolution, communism, and the modern world to maintain a small foothold in modern China.

Hinduism Originally a religion of India, Hinduism today has 8 million believers worldwide, making it larger than either Buddhism or Confucianism. Hinduism is one of the world's oldest religions, reaching back 4,000 years. It has no founder, and recognizes numerous traditions and gods, making Hinduism a religion of great diversity. Most Hindus would emphasize that while using different paths, they strive to attain liberation for the soul from a series of lifetimes. The ultimate goal of this cycle reincarnation is to achieve a purity and union with God. One of the features of Hinduism has been the emergence of a caste system that includes four classes: priests, rulers, peasants, and artisans. Sometimes called a fifth class, the untouchables have been discriminated against since early times. Author Stanley Wolpert has described the emergence of the untouchables class in India in the following way, "In all probability the subclass of untouchables emerged in the late Aryan age, recruited first perhaps from those . . . who performed tasks that were considered "unclean" such as the work of tanners, associated with animal carcasses, and that of sweepers, especially among the ashes of cremation grounds."[4] Although officially outlawed in employment in modern India, the caste system still remains a social feature of Hindu life.

Islam The basic ideas of Islam are discussed in some detail in chapter 9. Islam became an important force in South Asia through invasion in the sixteenth century. Traders along the Silk Road spread the religion into China. Today there are 807 million Muslims living in Asia. The most important Muslim majority states are Afghanistan, Bangladesh, Indonesia, and Pakistan. However, there are large Muslim minorities in India, China, and the Philippines.

The Ganges: The river is of great religious significance. Here at Varanasi, Hindus bathe in its sacred waters.

SOURCE: *Earl Huff*

CASE STUDIES

THE PEOPLE'S REPUBLIC OF CHINA: THE DRAGON

THE HISTORY OF OLD CHINA

Many in China place an emphasis on fate. People living in China during the last 175 years would be quick to point out that fate has not been kind to them during this period.

In the preface, a Chinese publication states their frustration in the following way:

> The year 1840, the gate of feudal China was opened by the rumble of gunfire in the Sino-British Opium War, turning the country into a semi colonial and semi feudal society that lasted for more than a century.

Writing about the same subject, the author states further:

> Heavy is the heart whenever looking back to this period of history: The corrupted rulers, the endless wars, the slowly developed economy, the people in deep distress, and the foreign policies humiliating the country and forfeiting its sovereignty . . .[5]

During the nineteenth century, China fought and lost the so-called "Opium Wars." In these conflicts, Chinese authorities attempted to stop the importation of opium, which was being used by British businessmen to pay for their purchases of tea and other luxury goods. In 1860, during one of these conflicts, the British burned the Emperor's Beijing summer palace in retaliation for the Chinese execution of Western hostages.[6] In 1900, a mass movement called the Society of Righteous and Harmonious Fists, or "Boxers," moved against foreign missionaries, businessmen, and diplomats in China. The Chinese leadership attempted to take advantage of the Boxer uprising to oust foreign interests from China. The humiliating defeat of the Boxers resulted in a fatal weakening of the imperial government, resulting in its complete collapse in 1911.

After the empire, China degenerated into a land of warlords and conflict, culminating in the famous civil war between the communists and the nationalists. That war began in 1927 and did not end until the final defeat of the nationalist forces in 1949.

To make matters worse, the Japanese forces took advantage of Chinese disunity to occupy Manchuria in 1931. They established the satellite state called Manchukuo.

In 1937, the Japanese invaded China proper. They did not leave China until the Japanese surrender in 1945.

The civil war between the Chinese communists and nationalists continued until the communists' victory in 1949. Their leader Chiang Kai-shek took the surviving nationalists to the island of Formosa, setting up a dispute over the island's sovereignty that continues to the present day. The civil war and World War II cost untold millions of Chinese lives. These conflicts also set back Chinese economic development for a generation or more.

NEW CHINA UNDER MAO

> We communists never conceal our political views. Definitely and beyond
> all doubt, our future or maximum program is to carry China forward to
> socialism and communism.[7]

In 1949, the Chinese Communists under the leadership of Mao Zedong (Mao Tse-Tung) were able to unify the mainland under one rule for the first time in half a century. Early on, Mao had recognized that the Chinese experience was different from that of Russia. The strength of the party was in the peasants of the countryside, not the urban proletariat! Mao argued that in "semi-colonial and semi-feudal" China, "the broad peasant masses" had simply "risen to fulfill their historic mission to overthrow the rural feudal power." He further stated that, "Every revolutionary comrade should know that the national revolution requires a profound change in the countryside."[8]

With the arrival of Chinese communist rule on October 1, 1949, struggle and pain for the average person in China did not end. During the rule of Mao, at least three traumatic events overshadowed any accomplishments of the regime. These horrible trials of the Chinese people were the Korean War, the Great Leap Forward, and the Cultural Revolution.

China entered the Korean War against the United States when 2.3 million "volunteers" crossed into Korea on October 25, 1950. Using the slogan "Resist America, Aid Korea," the Chinese fought the United Nations (UN) forces to a stalemate along the 38th parallel until a truce was signed in July of 1953.[9]

The human cost of this conflict was terrible for both the Chinese and the Koreans. Geoffrey Stern has put the losses this way:

> In a war of firepower against manpower, the U.S. put Chinese and North Korean deaths at 1.5 million. If this seems incredible, there are Chinese sources which put it even higher.[10]

The Great Leap Forward (1958–1960) was a disaster for the Chinese economy. Mao and the party leadership attempted to bypass the traditional steps of the development process to create a modern industrial and agricultural state overnight. Planners in the cities ordered Chinese farmers to ignore traditional agricultural methods to create communes. Workers in the cities were told to industrialize in ways that were sometimes called "backyard steel mills" by detractors in the West. The result of this misadventure was famine in the countryside and economic disaster in the cities. Mao quietly abandoned this experiment in 1960.

What the Great Leap Forward did to the economy, the Cultural Revolution (1966–1976) did to Chinese civilization. This campaign began as an attempt by Mao to purge China of any opposition. It quickly spread to an attack on intellectuals, teachers, artists, professionals, and progressives not adhering to Mao's authority in the party. Before it ended with Mao's death, the Cultural Revolution had resulted in the imprisonment of thousands and the destruction of China's art and architecture.

CHINA AFTER MAO: THE "KA-CHING" DYNASTY

To get rich is glorious.
DENG XIAOPING[11]

Deng Xiaoping was fond of the story of the black cat and the white cat to illustrate his change in the economic course of China. He would point out that the color of the cat did not matter so long as it caught the mouse. China was opened to the West for development when Deng began what became known as the second revolution in 1978. In 1979, he led a delegation to the United States with the purpose of increasing trade. In an ever-increasing process, Western business interests embraced the opportunity to do business with China.

To be sure, there have been setbacks in this development. The most serious event was the 1989 suppression of the pro-democracy movement in Tiananmen Square. However, China's admission to the World Trade Organization (WTO) and the selection of China to host the Olympic Games both signal that China will be a major economic player during the first half of the twenty-first century.

Deng's rule can be characterized as one that moved the economy away from the old communist dogma and central planning toward a more modern free-market mechanism. However, as the Tiananmen Square tragedy demonstrated, he would not tolerate any political reforms that would set in motion a challenge to the rule of the Communist Party.

China today is a paradox. It is still a state controlled by an aging Communist Party headed by Chairman Jiang Zemin. At the same time China has an economy that is rapidly becoming one of the most "free-wheeling, rough and tumble" capitalist systems in the world! How can these two seemingly contradictory positions be reconciled? The position taken here is that the People's Republic is in the transitional stage of moving from a totalitarian to a one-party authoritarian state. In this case, twenty-first century China is following a course already largely completed on Taiwan. The outcome of this process may be something like fascist Spain during the final years of General Franco's rule. In this case the party will continue to hold on to power by opposing any organization or group that could evolve into a force that could challenge the party organization's grip on power. At the same time the economy will be left largely free to continue to grow at one of the world's fastest rates. Unlike other states in Asia, China is also insulated from world economic downturns because of a huge domestic market with unmet needs.

American companies have been quick to recognize this potential. In a report recently released by the American Chamber of Commerce in the People's

China's Future: Snow is a 5th-grade student who lives 100 miles south of Beijing in Shandong Province.

SOURCE: *Forrest*

Pepsi Street: Shanghai's famous shopping street, the Nanjing Road, is called Pepsi Street by the locals because of the large Pepsi Cola signs that are placed on every lamppost.

SOURCE: *Joe Weatherby*

Republic of China, they point out that of the American firms and businesses doing business in China, 91 percent are optimistic while only 1 percent is slightly pessimistic about the future business prospects in China.[12]

To be sure there are potential sources of unrest. Perhaps the greatest threat to stability is the disparity of income between rural and urban China. However, the euphoria generated by China's admission to the WTO and being selected to host the Olympic Games should buy the authorities time to stabilize the situation before serious problems can develop.

Anyone who has not been in China within the last 10 years cannot imagine the kind of growth that has occurred in places like Hong Kong, Shanghai, and Beijing. Even provincial towns like Suzhou and Taian have their modern high-rise buildings.

What the Chinese citizens want is stability. They are not concerned if the Party remains so long as it provides the kind of environment that will allow them to enjoy the material benefits of the modern world. What they do not want is the kind of uncertainty and chaos that occurred with the collapse of communism in Russia.

INDIA: THE ELEPHANT

Although Vasco de Gamma opened the European route to India, it was the English that were to exercise primary rule over the subcontinent. At first, European penetration of this part of the world was hindered by the previously mentioned Treaty of Tordesillas, which had divided the colonial world between Portugal and Spain. However, after the Protestant Reformation, Holland and

England were no longer restrained from challenging the Portuguese and the Spanish monopoly of Asian trade.

Few could have imagined that when Captain William Hawkins sailed his flagship, *Hector,* to India on the East India Company's first visit, that the English would grow in power until they ruled all of southern Asia! The English presence in the region lasted from the *Hector's* arrival in 1608 until India and Pakistan gained full independence in 1947.[13]

The English arrived in India only a year after the founding of Jamestown in 1607. However, they stayed in India more than 350 years! The British impact on Indian culture is profound. Today India is the world's largest English-speaking nation. Although there are many Indian dialects, English is still the only universally understood language. The schools, universities, hospitals, courts, and even government have an English base.

The British East India Company came to India solely for trade when it established its first factory at Surat in 1612. The first century of British trade in India was accompanied by struggles with both Indian and European leaders. To British thinking, this situation required a military response. This period resulted in the conversion of the East India Company from a mere trading company into the de facto rulers of India. This situation of private company colonial rule was to last until Queen Victoria appointed the first Viceroy of India in 1858.

Under British colonial rule, nineteenth-century India achieved a measure of economic development. In the cities, the emergence of an Indian industrial class was well underway. The British also brought new lands under irrigation, thereby increasing agriculture.

A side effect of this activity was the emergence of a Western-educated Indian middle class. These "new Indians" demanded a greater role in political affairs. In 1885, the self-appointed Indian Congress movement first met to discuss social and political issues. In a manner not unlike the earlier American Continental Congress, these educated Hindu Indians demanded reforms from Britain, not revolution. However, by 1906, a more radicalized national congress was demanding nothing less than self-rule for India. By 1920, even relatively pro-British Indians such as Mohandas Gandhi were openly and actively opposing continued British rule. Gandhi's nonviolent resistance movement provided a base for mass support that complemented the political efforts of the Indian National Congress.

In the same year that the Indian National Congress first demanded self-rule, another organization of nearly equal significance was formed. The Muslim League demanded that the British create a separate Muslim state in Pakistan.

During World War II India did support the British by sending large numbers of troops to fight for the Empire. At the same time, both the Germans and the Japanese tried to foment rebellions in India by attempting to recruit Indian prisoners of war into nationalist armies of liberation. The Japanese movement was called the Indian National Army and was led by Subhas Chandra Bose. The Germans sponsored a movement called the Free Indian Legion. Although these movements may have had as many as 40,000 volunteers, it is believed that no more than 7,000 ever were committed to combat. These nationalist movements

Colonial India: Once elegant buildings from India's imperial past are a backdrop for trade in today's Calcutta.

SOURCE: *Earl Huff*

were discredited by the defeat of fascism and became only a footnote to the history of World War II.[14]

As World War II ended, Britain reluctantly recognized its inability to continue governing South Asia. It announced that it was going to shortly withdraw from the region. In February 1947, amid growing Hindu–Muslim violence, the British Labor government announced a withdrawal date. The Hindus under Mohandas Gandhi and Muslims led by Mohammad Ali Jinnah tried but failed to reach agreement on the establishment of a single Indian state. In August 1947, British India was divided into a Muslim Pakistan and a majority Hindu India. Because large minorities of Hindus and Muslims were caught on the wrong side of the new borders, a population exchange became necessary. During this process, 16 million people were forced to move, while another 500,000 people died in the religious violence that followed independence. This period provokes anger in both India and Pakistan more than 50 years after partition.

The creation of two states did not end communal strife. Just as conflicts between Muslims and Hindus were instrumental in the division of British India into two states, later tensions between the Punjabi of West Pakistan and the Bengalis of East Pakistan resulted in the 1971 creation of a separate state in the east called Bangladesh. Pakistan remains as a Muslim state in the West.

India became free of British rule in 1947. The Chinese mark their independence from colonialism with the establishment of the People's Republic in 1949. At that time most observers would have considered India to be ahead of China. Since that time China has endured major wounds that have resulted in the deaths of millions. Despite these setbacks, why is China economically ahead of "democratic" India today? Several answers should be apparent to the reader. First, China abandoned its state planning in favor of moving toward an open free-market system starting in 1979. India still retains large elements of its creaking, inefficient socialist system. Many of the current leaders still remain hostile to the free competition of the twenty-first century international system. The Prime Minister of India, Atal Behari Vajpayee even called local businessmen in the private sector "crooks" during an Independence Day speech on August 15, 2001.[15]

The Hindu nationalist and former General Secretary of the Bharatiya Janata Party (BJP), K. N. Govindacharya, voices even more anti-internationalist sentiments. He has been quoted as saying that,

> ... as the differences among developed countries had increased in the last five years and the monopoly of the U.S. was on the decline, ... the time had come when nations suffering from the Western concept of globalization should unite ...[16]

Despite talk of economic reform, it should be clear to any reader that the climate for business investment is far better in China than in India. Unlike China, India has also failed to get control of the growth of its population. India's population is increasing at the astounding rate of 50,000 people a day. No developing country will be able to secure economic prosperity for its people without getting that kind of birth rate under control. China has often been criticized for its almost draconian birth control methods. Nevertheless, the government has reduced the Chinese population growth to around 1 percent. At the present time, more than 250 million people in population-growing India still live below the official government's poverty line.[17]

The other great internal problem in India is, like it was in 1947, sectarianism. In recent years, a Hindu movement called the "Saffron Tide," the Hindu color, has come to prominence. The Hindu nationalist BJP party has replaced the old Congress Party as the ruler of India. Like European nationalists of the 1930s, the BJP focuses on "scapegoats" to gain most Hindu support. The more than 100 million Indian Muslims are particularly targeted, but the movement has also singled out Christians and Jews. One of the special targets for BJP attention has been Kashmir. Here the similarities to Serbian activities in Kosovo are frighteningly apparent. As a nuclear power, militant Hindu India could become a major source of conflict in the coming decades.

THE FOUR ASIAN TIGERS: TAIWAN, HONG KONG, SINGAPORE, AND SOUTH KOREA

INTRODUCTION

With one exception, Thailand, the nations of Southeast and East Asia share a common past: colonization by outside powers. Burma, Malaysia, Singapore, Brunei, and Hong Kong were ruled by the British; Indonesia was Dutch; Indochina (Vietnam, Cambodia, and Laos) was French; the Philippines were under Spanish rule, then later under the Americans. In the twentieth century both Korea and Taiwan were occupied by Japan. Typically, boundaries drawn by the colonial powers paid little attention to the ethnic makeup of the lands that they administered, so people with well-established cultural identities were often divided. Just as often, diverse ethnic groups were combined into larger political units. This ethnic mix was often complicated by the addition of large Chinese and Indian minorities who were either transported or encouraged to settle there by the colonial powers. Consequently, when the regions were granted independence, the newly formed states often lacked the sense of nationhood in terms of a nation-state. Cohesion, when it existed, was often nothing more than the common impulse to rid the region of the taint of colonial rule. In the process of forming modern entities, these new Asian nations have strongly opposed any outside pressures as interventions into their rights as sovereign states. The memory of the humiliation of colonial rule dies hard. As author Aeba Takanori has put it,

> The negative perception of foreign control remains as if explosive magma flows within the hearts of the people in these regions.[18]

Thus far, four states have been able to channel a new self-confidence in their ability to compete with the best that the developed world now has to offer. Called the Asian Tigers, these states can serve as models for their neighbors still wallowing in anger and self-pity.

TAIWAN

On the mainland, Taiwan is called Chinese Taipei. This name recalls what is one of the world's longest-lasting disputes; which China rules China? Both the People's Republic of China (communist) and Taiwan (nationalist) officially endorse the concept that Taiwan is part of China. After more than 50 years, they still disagree over who is the legitimate ruler of China.

When 2 million members of the defeated nationalist (Kuomintang) fled from the mainland to China's smallest province, Formosa (Taiwan) in 1949, few observers gave them a chance for long-term survival. The United States, their principal supporter, was braced to abandon the nationalists to their fate. However, when North Korea attacked South Korea in June 1950, the Nationalists received a "new lease on life." The Truman administration recognized that an active nationalist movement could serve as a sufficient threat to the mainland to check Chinese intentions in Korea. The United States placed elements of the Pacific Fleet between the mainland and the nationalists, thus preventing an almost certain communist occupation of the island.

In the half century since the Korean War, Taiwan has not only survived but also prospered. Economically, the Republic of China's development has been remarkable. In 2001, the volume of trade with the United States is second only to Japan. This volume amounts to almost 23 percent of the Republic of China's total exports.[19]

With an economy that produces textiles, clothing, electronics, processed foods, and chemicals, along with agricultural products and fishing, the per capita gross domestic product (GDP) is $16,500 U.S. This means that the average citizen of Taiwan earns as much or more than counterparts in South Africa, Spain, Portugal, or the Czech Republic.

Politically, the Republic of China has evolved from an authoritarian state under martial law headed by the Nationalist Party, to a fairly open democracy where, for the first time, an opposition candidate was elected president in 2000. The new president, Chen Shui-bian, is a fervent nationalist who opposes unification with the mainland. Many members of the defeated Nationalist Party have grown to accept eventual reunification with the mainland. Instead, President Chen has advocated a "no haste, be patient" policy in furthering ties with the mainland. For many businessmen in Taiwan, this new approach has raised fears that the Republic of China would begin to fall behind as the mainland begins an economic takeoff. The head of the American Chamber of Commerce in Taipei, Richard Henson, is quoted as putting the concerns of foreign business investors this way,

> . . . AmCham can comprehend the short term reasons for the administration's "no haste, be patient" economic policy which limits investment in the mainland, it views this approach as destructive to Taiwan's long-term health and vitality, and a lack of economic viability directly leads to questions regarding political viability and national security . . .[20]

For their part, the officials of the People's Republic continued to insist that the only solution to the half century dispute was agreement of the adoption of a "one China two systems policy" similar to the one implemented in Hong Kong.

Despite President Chen's opposition to this solution, polls in 2001 indicated that 51 percent of the people of Taiwan favored the eventual implementation of a one China two systems plan. It must be said that the same poll also found that 78 percent of those asked favored the status quo.[21] The conclusion to be drawn is that as the mainland moves toward economic parity and democratic political maturity, more and more Taiwanese will be receptive to eventual unification.

In this potentially explosive situation, the United States attempted to play an important role in resolving this conflict. In 1949, the Nationalists talked of retaking the mainland. In 2001, they talked of defensive engagement with the mainland. The American role was to reassure the Taiwanese that they would remain militarily strong enough to deter an attack, but not so strong to discourage more talk of independence. The main American hope was that economic integration would, over time, heal the bad feelings and suspicions on both sides, leading to a peaceful settlement.

The alternative to a peaceful evolution is almost too serious to contemplate. The leaders of the United States, the People's Republic, and the Republic of China have each made the danger of the situation abundantly clear. President Jiang Zemin has said,

> Let me once again appeal to the Taiwan authorities to put the national interest first, conform to the tide of history, and unequivocally accept the one China principal.[22]

Xiong Guangkai, Deputy Chief of the General Staff of the Chinese People's Liberation Army (Mainland China) has said that the right to use force is, "aimed at deterring those hostile forces attempting to disrupt China's sovereignty and territorial integrity."[23]

On a trip to Panama, the President of the Republic of China (Taiwan), Chen Shui-bian was quoted as saying that, "Beijing's cherished 'one country two systems' formula aims to annihilate the Republic of China and that the 23 million people of Taiwan will never accept it."[24]

President George Bush stated on a Cable News Network (CNN) broadcast that while he supported a one China policy uniting China and Taiwan, the United States would do whatever it took to defend Taiwan from attack. In the same interview, he was quoted as saying, "We need a peaceful resolution. . . . Our nation will help Taiwan defend herself . . ."[25] The American ability to balance the twenty-first century interests of the People's Republic of China and the Republic of China promises to be very interesting indeed.

HONG KONG

The story of Hong Kong is one of the most interesting in Asia. When it was ceded to Great Britain by the Treaty of Nanjing in 1842, Hong Kong was a barren island. Prior to the British arrival, fishermen and pirates had mainly used the harbor. When it became British, Hong Kong's future was assured. Author Trea Wiltshire has described the British arrival in the following way,

> When Hong Kong became one of the spoils of the Opium War, merchant princes such as William Jardine and John Dent were quick to relocate.

Later the author states,

> The secure base enabled the merchants to form banks that would service these rapid developments of the colonial island and its Treaty Port Sisters. It also provided a convenient headquarters for the fledgling consular services that took root in each of the coastal outposts and for the British Army and Navy.[26]

The growth of Hong Kong as a British colony was accelerated by two events. In 1860, Kowloon and Stone Cutters Island were ceded to the colony by China's signing the Beijing Convention. In 1898, the New Territories, a large area adjacent to Kowloon, was leased to the colony for 99 years. The additions of land allowed the inhabitants to expand past the limits of Hong Kong Island.

During the twentieth century the colony prospered as a door to China until the Japanese occupation during World War II. The British reoccupied the colony in 1945.

It has been said that the greatest postwar event contributing to the growth of capitalist Hong Kong was the communist victory over the mainland in 1949. Why can this be viewed as a positive event in Hong Kong? Simply stated, the communist victory ended the dominance of Shanghai as China's window to the outside world.

Local Market: Abundant produce is displayed in this market in Asia.
SOURCE: *Joe Weatherby*

After 1949, China's isolation allowed Hong Kong to become the "transship-ment point" for most goods and services passing to and from China. Hong Kong became one of the world's leaders in container shipping, and the manu-facture of clothing, toys, calculators, radios, travel goods, handbags, and artifi-cial flowers.

In the 1980s it became clear to the British that the lease on the new territories would not be renewed when it ended in 1997. After months of negotiation, the Chinese and the British agreed to Hong Kong's return to Chinese sovereignty un-der a new arrangement called "one China two systems." Under this arrangement, sovereignty would be transferred from Britain to China, but a great deal of auton-omy would remain in the hands of the Hong Kong people for 50 years.

Thus far, the People's Republic has kept its part of the bargain. In August 2001, the U.S. State Department's report to Congress stated,

> Hong Kong under Chinese sovereignty has remained one of the freest
> cities in Asia with the Hong Kong government committed to advancing
> Hong Kong's distinct way of life.[27]

At the beginning of the twenty-first century, the average income of Hong Kong residents is around $25,000 U.S.[28] This figure is higher than it was at the transfer of power in 1997. It is also higher than the $21,000 average income in the former mother country, Britain.

There are concerns about the long-term future of Hong Kong. The economic explosion that has occurred in Shanghai during the last 10 years threatens to eventually make that city the business center of China. However, as Hong Kong remains particularly advantaged in the race to capitalize on the resources of China, it will continue to remain a major Asian Tiger for a long time to come.

SINGAPORE

According to Dorthy Perkins, the name Singapore literally means "the lion city" when translated into Indian Sanskrit.[29] Modern Singapore is one of the Asian tigers. Situated at the end of the peninsula of Malaysia, this city-state of 3 million people is one of the world's most important trading centers. Because of its location at the mouth of the Strait of Malacca, which leads from the Indian Ocean, Singapore is called the Gateway to the Pacific.

Although the area now called Singapore had been a trading town in early times, it was only a loosely populated island when the Malacca Sultanate ceded it to the British East India Company in 1819. It was then that the company representative, Sir T. Stamford Raffles, founded the city of Singapore. In 1824, the trading post came under the control of the British government. It was to remain a British colony until 1942 when the Japanese captured it. The British reoccupied the island with the defeat of Japan in 1945. Singapore gained full independence from Britain in June 1959.

When the British first established it as a trading post, few could have guessed that a century and a half later Singapore would be one of the world's most important commercial centers. Today, this multicultural city-state has a per capita income of $26,300 U.S. This makes the 4 million residents the second most prosperous people in Asia after Japan.

The key to Singapore's success is more than just strategic geography. The political system is noted as paternalistic. Although a republic with free elections, the government keeps a tight hold on public order. Considering the diversity of Singapore's society both ethnically and religiously, this kind of control is understandable. The People's Action Party has swept every election since 1959. After recent elections, Mr. Low Khiang, one of only two incumbent opposition lawmakers elected to parliament, was quoted as saying, "We don't pretend to be able to form the alternative government."[30]

Political stability and continuity has allowed business to flourish: 81.5 percent of Singapore's exports go to the United States. This is a higher ratio than China, Hong Kong, Taiwan, or Japan.[31]

Singapore, not the United States or Japan, is the model for development currently being followed by the People's Republic of China. The Chinese hope to avoid the chaos of post-Communist Russia by keeping a tight hold on politics while letting a free-market economic system develop.

SOUTH KOREA

Like the other "tigers," Korea experienced both European and Asian colonial rule during nineteenth and twentieth centuries. In 1900, Tsar Nicholas II ordered his troops into Northern China and Korea.[32] The Russian hold on these territories was strengthened by their participation in putting down the Boxer Rebellion in

China. However, Russia lost everything when they were defeated in the Russo-Japanese War of 1904.

Japanese colonial rule was consolidated by 1910 when they annexed Korea. Korea was not to see the end of Japanese rule until their final defeat in World War II. At the Yalta Conference held in February 1945, the Allied Powers agreed to a number of secret provisions regarding Asia that were not made public until 1947. Among the Asian agreements was Russia's commitment to declare war on Japan within three months of the defeat of Japan. In return, Russia would also get footholds in Manchuria and Korea to the 38th parallel. Hans Margenthau has graphically pointed out the continuing role that Korea has played in the great power struggle for Asia.

> The rivalry between Japan and Russia for control of Korea ended with the defeat of Russia in the Russo-Japanese War of 1904–1905. Japanese control of Korea, thus firmly established, was terminated with the defeat of Japan in World War II. From then on, the United States replaced Japan as a check upon Russian ambitions in Korea. China, by intervening in the Korean War, resumed its traditional interest in the control of Korea.[33]

The Korean War lasted from 1950 to 1953. Although the first great military conflict of the cold war, it ended in a stalemate with the opposing parties stretched along the 38th parallel in essentially the same place that they were before the war began. The war did firmly divide North and South Korea into the separate states that exist today.

1953 saw South Korea completely devastated both socially and economically. The struggle on both fronts to become an important player in East Asia has been difficult for the South. With the exception of its military power, the communist North is almost a complete failure.

Today South Korea ranks fourth among the Asian tigers. However, considering the recent past, fourth is an impressive accomplishment. With an average income of $12,600 U.S., Koreans can boast that their earnings exceed those of both China and India in Asia, Argentina and Brazil in the Americas, and Bulgaria and Croatia in Europe. Korea is third of the Asian states exporting products to the United States. Despite the global economic slowdown that occurred after the September 11 attack in New York and Washington, South Korea expects to continue to have both growing shipbuilding and automobile industries.

As South Korea enters the twenty-first century, two potential problems loom on the horizon. First, there is the economic threat coming from China in the market for low-cost goods. To compete, Korea must follow the examples of Japan, Taiwan, and Singapore by moving into the fields of high technology where their higher labor cost can be utilized effectively.

The second problem is in the often-hostile relations that the South has with North Korea. This conflict is one of the world's most dangerous flashpoints. However, there have been some halting moves on both sides aimed at improving relations. There have been recent exchanges that allowed families to get together after more than 50 years. Nevertheless, the 38th parallel remains one of the most militarized borders existing today. It is clearly in the interest of both parties to move toward a normalization of relations, possibly leading to eventual reunification.

Everyone is familiar with the difficulties that have come with German reunification. The differences between North and South in Korea are far greater than those that existed between East and West Germany. Whether this conflict can be resolved in the foreseeable future is impossible to predict.

✳ FLASHPOINTS ✳

AFGHANISTAN

The lands that currently make up Afghanistan have been a crossroads of conflict since ancient times. It was here historic figures including Alexander the Great, Cyrus and Darius the Great, Ghengis Khan, and Tamerlane all fought for control of this important crossroads of Asia. The region has been important more because it was an area surrounded by contending states rather than having value itself. As a buffer area, Afghanistan has always had a strategic importance.

During the nineteenth century, both the Russians and the British repeatedly were involved in Afghan intrigues. Frederick Hartmann emphasized the buffer status of nineteenth-century Afghanistan this way:

> Afghanistan has played such a role ever since British power was expanded up to its southern borders in India and the Russians established a common frontier with the Afghans on the north. There is an old Afghan saying that defines the role of mountainous Afghanistan, "this goat separating the lion from the bear."[34]

Rouhollah Ramazani has made a similar comment:

> Russia's direct agreements (usually after territorial conquest) with the Northern Tier states in the 19th Century largely provided the basis for her present long boundaries with these states. Furthermore, her direct negotiations with Great Britain as in the case of Afghanistan, and her collaboration with Great Britain as in the case of Iran and Turkey, were influential in defining the boundaries of these latter states with each other.[35]

This nineteenth-century great power competition between Russia and Britain in Central Asia was called "the Great Game." During the twentieth century, Britain, Russia, Germany, Iran, China, Pakistan, India, and the United States all played their part in the destabilization of Afghanistan.

Afghanistan maintained the status of a buffer state during the cold war. Both the United States and the Soviet Union vied for influence by extending aid to the Afghans. In 1973, King Zahir Shah was overthrown by the

Afghan military. A military government headed by General Mohammad Daud Khan ruled until 1978.

In 1978, a coup d'etat brought a Marxist government to power in Afghanistan. Splits within the Afghan Communist Party over both Islam and socialist reforms soon threatened the very survival of the Marxist revolution. It was this volatile situation that caused the Soviets to intervene on the night of December 24, 1979. The Afghan prime minister was killed, and in his place the Soviets installed Babrak Karmal. Soviet forces eventually swelled to around 120,000 before their withdrawal in 1989.

The Soviet intervention provoked open civil war. A number of loosely organized resistance fighters calling themselves the *mujahedeen* ("holy warriors") were able to tie down the Soviet military for a decade. Soviet policy throughout much of the Other World was subjected to harsh criticism until the "new thinking" of Mikhail Gorbachev brought a Soviet withdrawal, coupled with military and economic support for the last Soviet-installed government, led by former Afghan secret police chief Najibullah. Tainted by its association with the Soviets, that government failed to establish legitimacy either at home or abroad. More than 5 million refugees fled Afghanistan, most settling in Pakistan near the Afghanistan border.

A stalemate, which had characterized the final years of Soviet intervention, continued for a time after the Soviet withdrawal. The combatants, however, looked for support to outside states such as the former Soviet Union, China, the United States, Pakistan, Saudi Arabia, and Iran. Given the drastic changes that had occurred in the international environment, such support soon diminished as other priorities emerged. In April 1992, the Najibullah government collapsed, and several *mujahedeen* rebel groups entered Kabul, the capital. In the months and years that followed, the nine *mujahedeen* factions that had waged war against the old Soviet-installed governments increasingly turned their weapons on one another. A 10th faction appeared in early 1995. The new faction, known as the Taliban, or "Seekers," was originally made up of students of Islam from the southeastern city of Kandahar. Its avowed aim was to end Afghanistan's internal conflicts and lawlessness and to institute an Islamic government in that state. With covert support from Pakistan, the Taliban gained control of 8 of Afghanistan's 28 provinces within a few months. Within the next few years they extended their control to Kabul and most of the remainder of Afghanistan. In an effort to reform society to conform with their version of Islamic law, they proceeded to ban all music except for religious songs, and eventually banned movies, television, and videocassettes. Severe restrictions were also placed on women's clothing and activities. Meanwhile, armed resistance continued in the countryside.

Although unrest and a fitful civil war continued for years after the Taliban gained control of most of the country, it was the terrorist attack on

New York's World Trade Center that propelled Afghanistan from the shadows to the "center stage" of world events. Western analysts deduced that the attack on the United States was either mounted or supported by the wealthy Saudi Arabian, Osama bin Laden's Al-Qaeda terrorist organization. Both Al-Qaeda and bin Laden received sanctuary by the Afghan Taliban.

In the aftermath of the attack, U.S. President George Bush was unequivocal in stating to the states of the world, "We have found our mission and our moment," then declaring, "Either you are with us or you are with the terrorists."[36]

When the Taliban government refused to meet the American demands to turn over bin Laden and the Al-Qaeda leadership along with several Americans and Europeans being held for allegedly preaching Christianity, American and British forces aided opposition forces in the country to carry out a military campaign in Afghanistan. This campaign resulted in a total Taliban defeat in December 2001. Even before the Taliban government collapsed, there were moves to end more than 20 years of civil war with the establishment of an interim council that would serve until more permanent political arrangements could be made. Meeting in Bonn, Germany, under United Nations sponsorship, most of the rival Afghanistan factions agreed to take steps that if successfully implemented could lead the country toward a peaceful future.

The Bonn agreement provided for a series of steps that could eventually result in an acceptable post-Taliban government.

- An interim council was selected to rule Afghanistan for six months.
- A majority Pashtun leader, Hamid Karzai, would be head of state.
- A Loya or tribal assembly would select a transitional government to rule for two years.
- A general election would be held and a constitution written.
- A supreme court would be established.
- A multinational peace-keeping force would be sent to police Kabul.

Any foreign aid scheduled for Afghan reconstruction would be dependant on the tribes honoring their agreement. In this way, the leadership would have to honor their commitments to the rebuilding package. If the agreement was violated, the foreign aid would be the glue that would hold Afghanistan together until an established government could be put in place.

Both the conflict in Afghanistan and the prospects of an eventual establishment of regular government reflect the artificial nature of the Afghan state. Although Afghanistan has had a form of independence since Ahmad Shah unified the tribes in 1747, the current borders are largely the result of the nineteenth-century rivalries of Russia and Britain. Again, author Rouhollah Ramazani addresses this point.

End of Empire: Regimental plaques on the Khyber Pass, Pakistan.
SOURCE: *Richard Kranzdorf*

> In the case of Afghanistan and Iran, Great Britain assisted through arbitration in providing a basis for their present boundary. And in the case of Afghanistan and the part of India that is now Pakistan, Great Britain established the controversial Durand Line which cuts between ethnically related tribal groups.[37]

Afghanistan is surrounded on all sides by neighbors that are hostile to each other. In the past, all of these states have attempted to exploit the tribal and religious differences that already existed because of the arbitrary way that Afghanistan was shaped in the first place. It can be said that "the Great Game" in Central Asia still continues, only with different players.

In the new great game currently called the War on Terrorism, the participants are Russia, China, the United States, the United Kingdom, India, Pakistan, Iran, and the former Soviet States of Central Asia. To complicate matters, there are also nongovernmental terrorist movements like Al-Qaeda that are major players that have found safe haven in Afghanistan. Whether these outside parties can ever unite the internal forces to build a terrorist-free peaceful Afghanistan that eventually evolves into a modern Afghan nation remains to be seen. Many others have tried and failed to bring stability to this part of the world. The reader should not forget the warning that Rudyard Kipling issued 100 years ago to outsiders that venture into this part of the world.

> One sword-knot stolen from the camp will pay for all the school expenses of any Kurrum Valley scamp who knows no word of moods and tenses. But, being blessed with perfect sight picks off our mess-mates left and right.[38]

KASHMIR (JAMMU AND KASHMIR)

Kashmir has been called the "Switzerland of Asia." This area is probably the most beautiful spot in Asia. Here, there are lush valleys and shimmering lakes surrounded by the rugged mountains of the Karakorums and the Himalayas. It was to this region that the British colonials sent their families during the fever-ridden hot months in India. Like middle-class Americans who relocated to the mountains during the polio epidemics, the English believed that Europeans were safer from the tropical diseases common during the hot seasons if they were in the cool climate of Kashmir. Srinagar became the de facto British capital of India during the summer months.

Kashmir had been a Muslim state since the Mogul empire overran it in 1586. When the British occupied the area in 1846, they recognized Kashmir as a semi-independent state but placed a Hindu prince in charge. Hindus continued to rule locally under British tutelage until British withdrawal from South Asia in 1947.

When India and Pakistan were created out of old British India, most semi-independent states had to choose between joining India or Pakistan. At first the *maharaja* of Kashmir attempted to keep his state neutral, but large portions of the Muslim population revolted, forcing him to flee to India. Once in India, the Hindu *maharaja* declared Kashmir to be Indian against the will of the majority Muslim population. Indian troops were rushed to Kashmir to secure India's claim.

The result was the start of a conflict that continues to the present time. After three wars, Pakistan occupies about one-third and India two-thirds of Kashmir. In the 1980s, Muslim separatists renewed their fight for linking Kashmir with Pakistan. The result has been the continuation of a low-intensity war between the Muslim population, supported by Pakistan, and India for almost 20 years. The conflict has ended the tourist trade and devastated the region. Now that both India and Pakistan have nuclear weapons, the small area of Kashmir constantly threatens to ignite a major conflict in South Asia.

CHINA'S BORDERS

China has long argued that it is not bound by the so-called unequal treaties and agreements forced on it by the imperialist powers during the nineteenth and early twentieth centuries, when a weakened China made numerous territorial concessions. Although China later resolved by force of arms the exact location of its border with India, the "proper" location of its northern borders with the former Soviet republics remained largely unresolved until late 1994, when Presidents Jiang Zemin and Boris Yeltsin met in Moscow to sign agreements that delineated the final 34-mile segment of their disputed border. Perhaps more important, the agreement does not bind all the states of the former USSR. The border issue may yet be complicated by disorder within those states, by a desire for political unity between some of China's minority nationalities and their ethnic kin north of the border, or by a more militant leadership in either China or Russia.

As noted earlier, the regions over which China has historically exercised sovereignty have enlarged or diminished with the power of its central authority. Consequently, it is possible for it to assert a historic connection to vast regions beyond its current borders. As the twenty-first century begins, perhaps the most volatile region lies in the South China Sea, a major waterway and a likely site of large deposits of underwater oil and gas. Today, China claims sovereignty over about 80 percent of the South China Sea and has forcefully asserted its claim, first, by seizing control of the Paracel Islands at the conclusion of the Vietnam War and, second, following a brief naval conflict with Vietnam in 1988, by occupying and fortifying several of the Spratly Islands, a chain of hundreds of islands, reefs, and atolls located between Vietnam and the Philippines. Vietnam continues to claim part of the Spratlys, called the Nansha Islands by the Chinese. Taiwan, the Philippines, Malaysia, and Brunei also claim all or part of the chain. Following a 1995 confrontation with a Filipino naval vessel, the Chinese ministry reaffirmed its "action to safeguard its sovereignty over the Nansha Islands" and assured the world community that its actions would "not affect the freedom and safety of foreign vessels or foreign aircraft to navigate through international sea lanes under international laws."[39]

Though located farther from the Spratlys than any of the other claimants, China is better able to assert its claims because of its relative power. Significantly, after receiving Chinese assurances regarding freedom of navigation, the larger world community, including the United States, seems to have adopted a hands-off policy on the Spratly dispute.

DEVELOPMENT VERSUS ENVIRONMENTAL DESTRUCTION

Despite its recent economic difficulties, a trip to a local clothing or hardware store leaves little doubt that Asia is at the forefront of development within the Other World. First there was Japan emerging from the destruction of World War II. Then came the "four tigers": Hong Kong, Taiwan, Singapore, and South Korea. More recently Thailand, Malaysia, and Indonesia joined the group of rapidly developing Asian states. Emerging from its Maoist policy of rigid self-sufficiency, China opened its doors to the world and began a process of rapid development that has consistently produced an impressive rate of economic growth. Now another Asian giant, India, has begun to stir. With all the vast differences that exist among these states, there is one significant similarity: Economic growth came at a price—a massive degradation of the environment.

Today, throughout Other World Asia, one can witness the results of policies and activities that place a far lesser priority on preservation of the environment than on rapid economic growth. China now has one of the most polluted capitals in the world. Bangkok and Taipei, with their enormous traffic jams, are also rivals for that title. Even Kuala Lumpur, the smallest Asian capital, is now beset with air pollution and traffic congestion. Acid rain and chemical pollution of both air and water in China, along with rapid deforestation in Malaysia, Myanmar, Thailand, and elsewhere in Asia, are typical of the assault on the environment that is occurring as Other World Asia seeks to achieve the level of economic development demanded by its growing population.

Is this an irreversible process, or is it simply a necessary state in development? There is no certain answer to this question. It may be argued, however, that numerous other states achieved rapid economic development with little regard for environmental implications, then vigorously and generally successfully attacked environment problems. Japan is a prime example. Unfortunately, such a process has generally occurred only after the state concerned was both satisfied with its level of development and convinced that its quality of life was threatened.

THE TRAFFIC IN WOMEN AND CHILDREN IN THAILAND

For years, Bangkok has been a well-known place to have a good time. Men from Europe, the Americas, Japan, and other parts of Asia have joined locals in the bars, bordellos, and discos of the city.

The sex industry is important in Thailand, Malaysia, Indonesia, and the Philippines, and ranges between 2 and 14 percent of the gross domestic product of these states.[40]

Because of the Thai cultural tradition of early marriage, many of the women who are engaged as sex workers are really children between 12 and 16 years old. Most of these women are under the age of 18. In Thailand, because of the fear of acquired immunodeficiency syndrome (AIDS), there is an increasing demand to import women and children from rural areas in Myanmar and China. Some of these women are held against their will. In a CNN report on a police raid that rescued 40 women in Bangkok, a Thai police colonel was quoted as saying, through a translator,

They organized the women and sent them out to work for hotels and massage parlors. Then they were brought back here. Those behind it made a lot of money. At least four of the women were found with chains around their ankles to keep them from running away.[41]

This trafficking in women has caused an explosion of sexually transmitted diseases including AIDS among the poor in Thailand and other parts of Asia. Journalist Loretta Ann Soosayra reports that, "Thailand has one of the highest rates of human immunodeficiency virus (HIV)/AIDS in the region, with one in 60 Thais or one million people carrying the virus."[42]

As long as the rich can exploit the poor there seems little hope that this evil traffic can be halted. As long as there are poor who are vulnerable, there are people in Thailand and elsewhere willing to use their power to fill the demand for this activity. This kind of exploitation of women is bad enough as a social issue. As a public health issue, the spread of AIDS in the poorest parts of Asia threatens to rival the horrors of Africa as a twenty-first century plague on humankind.

FEMALE DISCRIMINATION IN CHINA

The current dramatic imbalance in the number of male and female children in China provides a dramatic illustration of the unintended consequence of a well-intended government policy. Before China sought to combat its overpopulation problem by imposing its one-child-per-family policy in 1979, the ratio of male to female children was about 106 males to 100 females. Various sources now report that, in the years since that policy was initiated, the ratio has grown to between 120 and 130 males to every 100 females, and will result in 90 million men being unable to find a spouse at the end of this century.[43] A policy that appeared to hold the promise of making possible a better life for all Chinese now appears to be leading instead to a severe breakdown in the social order. The abduction and sale of women and a rising level of prostitution may be among the consequences.

The current gender imbalance is the result of both the rigid enforcement of the one-child policy (especially in the countryside) and China's illegal but deeply ingrained fundamental discrimination against women. The latter is based upon the traditional belief that baby girls are less important than boys. Traditionally, that cultural preference for boys resulted in a degree of female infanticide and abandonment or gross neglect of baby girls.[44] Those practices have increased somewhat since the introduction of the one-child policy. In addition, modern technology now provides ultrasound scanners that make sex-selective abortions possible. As might be expected, the number of such abortions has dramatically increased.

There is some indication that the Chinese government now recognizes the severity of the gender problem. The use of ultrasound scanners to determine the sex of a fetus has been restricted, and the State Family Planning Commission is seeking "to eliminate the phenomenon of abandonment or drowning baby girls." Even though doctors are now forbidden by law to disclose the sex of fetuses, numerous private laboratories and clinics still offer such tests. In the case of discrimination against females, as in other forms of discrimination, no quick fix is likely to be sufficient to eliminate cultural traits that have evolved over centuries.

ISLAMIC FUNDAMENTALISM

Although Islamic fundamentalism is a phenomenon usually associated with the Middle East rather than Asia, it has been a major force in the Afghan conflict. There are now indications that it may be spreading even further eastward.

Early in the decade, a rebellion in the northern Sumatran region of Indonesia resulted in several thousand deaths. That area contains the most radical Muslim clergy in the country. Just to the north, in Malaysia, the central government's ruling National Front was defeated in 1990 by the Parti Islam in the state of Kalantan. The government in that state soon banned gambling, alcohol consumption by Muslims, singing groups of men and women together, and so on. In 1992 it replaced the existing secular criminal laws with Islamic law. Although the National Front won an electoral landslide in other regions of Malaysia in the 1995 elections, it was unable to unseat the Parti Islam in Kalantan.

Traditionally, both Malaysia and Indonesia have had secular governments and have been regarded as among the most moderate and tolerant of Muslim states. However, with Muslim majorities of 60 and 80 percent, respectively, they provide fertile ground for the further spread of Islamic fundamentalism. The leaders of both states have recognized its potential force. In 1991, even former President Suharto of Indonesia, who in the past had discouraged Islamic activism, found it prudent to make his first pilgrimage to Mecca. Similarly, Malaysian Prime Minister Mahathir Mohammed, who once ridiculed Islamic law, decided not to oppose its adoption in the state of Kalantan.

For the moment, Islamic fundamentalism is more a potential threat than a current threat to the secular regimes of Asia. The greatest danger to the radicalization of Islam comes from the conflict in Afghanistan politically spilling over into the other Muslim communities in Asia. This explosive situation combines a long-standing grievance against Western colonialism with a broad sympathy for those fellow Muslims who are under attack by non-Muslims.

It is not hard for many people in this part of the world to make the dangerous link that their government's support of the "War Against Terrorism" is a surrender to neocolonial control. The supporters of the radicalization of Islam are continually trying to make that link. If they are successful, the chances for an Islamic upheaval in states like Pakistan, Indonesia, and the Philippines will increase. The Other World will then become a dangerous place indeed. The issue of Muslim terrorism is discussed in chapters 2 and 8.

KOREA: NORTH AND SOUTH

For some time the South had pursued a "sunshine" policy of trying to open doors to North Korea. In June 2000, the first ever summit conference between North and South Korea was held in Pyongyang. In addition, there were three occasions for family visits that allowed Southerners to visit their relatives in the North.

Although North and South Korea share a common language, history, and culture, they remain bitterly divided politically. In recent years, the rapidly industrializing South has vigorously moved toward democracy, first at the national level and then, in 1995, at the local level when local government elections were held for the first time since 1961. In contrast, North Korea remains an authoritarian Marxist state whose secretive and unpredictable leadership presides over a faltering economy and a population facing widespread famine. Faced with a loss of aid and trading partners after the fall of world communism, North Korea's 1994 trade plunged to about one-half its 1990 level.[45] Since then, conditions have worsened. As a consequence, it seems to have concluded that there is no alternative to accepting some modification of its long-standing policy of self-reliance. It has therefore indicated a desire to attract foreign investment and has accepted emergency food shipments from South Korea, Japan, the United States, and the European Union. Despite such aid, a 1998 bipartisan, U.S. congressional fact-finding team estimated that 300,000 to 800,000 people were dying in North Korea annually from starvation and related diseases.[46]

North Korea's leadership also presides over a state that caused international concern when its intention to develop nuclear weapons became known. Although that concern diminished somewhat when, in October 1994, North Korea agreed to halt its nuclear program and accepted an offer by the United States, Japan, and South Korea to replace its huge nuclear reactor with others that produce less plutonium, North Korea may not have frozen its nuclear program.

World concern was also raised by the sudden death in July 1994 of Kim Il Sung, who had led North Korea since its inception in 1945. Although his son, Kim Jong Il, was his chosen successor, there was little evidence that he was firmly in control. Indeed, there was considerable speculation that a power struggle continued within the leadership between those who wished to continue past isolationist policies and those who favored increasing economic and political ties with the outside world. In the years that followed, Kim Jong II secured the leadership of the ruling Workers' Party and apparently came to terms with the country's military. Finally, in July 1998, he was elected to the country's parliament and the following September, elevated to what was described as "the highest post of the state."[47] There seems little doubt, however, that he shares that power with the military leadership. Despite these positive developments, there are indications that some policy changes may be in the works that will limit North Korea's options. It is clear that the Bush administration is not as active as the preceding one in encouraging North/South unification. Also, the post World-Trade-Center-attack world is far different from the one that existed prior to September 11. The North Koreans know that they must tone down the saber-rattling of the past if they are to avoid the negative consequences of being classified as a "state in the terrorist camp." That negative label is one that the North Koreans cannot afford. Their economy is still based on the Soviet heavy industry. What industry they have is old, inefficient, and worn out. In agriculture, the economy is such a failure that North Korea is considered to be a famine state.

At the same time, the economic downturn in Europe, North America, and Asia is making aid to North Korea more difficult to obtain. Even the South Korean "sunshine" policy of opening economic doors to Korea has largely been delayed.

North Korea's foreign policy alternatives are much more restricted than they were in the past. The external economic and political push for helping the North is not as strong as it once was. North Korea's ability to make the West "jump" by making threats will cause negative responses that are more costly than the potential turmoil will be worth.

Still, the border between the North and the South is dangerous. North Korea has the military hardware and technology to cause a great deal of pain to an adversary. Broad economic problems in the North have a potential to cause political instability in a state like the North.

The one bright light on the horizon is the idea that the contacts between the North and the South will have a life of their own. Clearly, the task of unifying the Koreas will be far more difficult than it was in the Germanies. Nevertheless, as North Korea's head delegate to North/South talks, Kim Ryong-Song, was quoted as saying,

> The North and South are one people. We need to respect the basic principles of the June 15 joint accord at all times, and honor the interests of the nation above all.[48]

The road to reconciliation may be long and halting, but if successful, one of the world's most dangerous flashpoints will become history.

SRI LANKA

According to the most recent estimates, the population of Sri Lanka is 74 percent Singhalese, most of whom are Buddhist, and 18 percent Tamil, who are primarily Hindu; almost all the remainder are Muslims.[49] Historically, the island has seen numerous clashes between the Tamils, descended from the dark-skinned Dravidians of southern India, and the lighter-skinned Singhalese. Modern conflict began in the late 1950s when the Buddhist-dominated government made Singhalese the sole official language, began resettling Singhalese in predominantly Tamil areas of the island, and passed legislation viewed by Tamils as discriminatory. Conflict increased in the 1970s and became more violent when the militant Tamil Tiger guerrillas launched their first armed attack in 1978. Since that time violence has escalated as the Tigers and other Tamil separatists have sought the establishment of an independent Tamil state, Tamil Eelam, to be carved from northern and eastern Sri Lanka. Anti-Tamil riots and massacres by both sides have followed.

By the mid-1980s, the Indian government apparently feared that the conflict might threaten the stability of India, where 18 miles away, in the southern Indian state of Tamil Nadu, an additional 50 million Tamils reside. With many Indians urging their government to support the Tamils, the Indian and Sri Lankan governments reached an agreement in July 1986 that provided for greater autonomy in the Tamil regions of Sri Lanka and obliged the Indian army to help enforce the accord. When that agreement broke down a few months later, the Indian army became embroiled in the conflict against the Tamil separatists. Finally, a measure of order was restored and Indian forces withdrew, although violence between the Tamils and Singhalese did not end.

In August 1994, the newly elected government of Chandrika Bandaranaika Kumaratunga promised a renewed effort to reach a peace agreement with the Tamil separatists. In January 1995, her government and the Tamil rebels announced that they had agreed to a truce, ending their 12-year conflict. War erupted again the following April, however, when the Tamil Tigers blew up two naval patrol boats, killing 12 sailors, and a week later shot down two air force transports, killing 97 more people.

The civil conflict has killed an estimated 62,000 people during the last eight years.[50] During this period, the economy has been devastated. In a particularly horrific attack, Tamil rebels attacked the international airport, destroying a major portion of the commercial air fleet.

The current president has argued for giving the Tamils autonomy in their areas. Unfortunately, it has been impossible to gain enough political support for this solution among the majority Singhalese to be seriously considered. Like so many insurgent conflicts, this one seems to have developed a life of its own. As long as a violent minority on both sides is willing to continue the fight, they can experience a veto on the chance for peace.

HISTORIC PLACES IN ASIA

Taprobana

This island appears on some of the earliest maps that still exist in Europe. Fourteenth-century works believed to be based on the calculations of ancient Roman Ptolemy, listed Taprobana as a great island in an inland sea called Indicum Mare. G. R. Crone makes the following evaluations of the Ptolemy map, "He greatly overestimated the size of Taprobana (Ceylon) and overlooked the peninsula of the Indian sub-continent. Or perhaps confused it with Ceylon ... "[51] Today Ceylon is called Sri Lanka.

Cathay (derived from Khitai)

The name Cathay caused one of the early misimpressions that Europeans had of Asia. Cathay is a name for China that is derived from a confederation of Mongolian tribes who ruled China from 947 to 1125 A.D. When Marco Polo visited Beijing, the local people were referred to as the Khitai. When Polo returned to Europe he used the name Cathay to refer to the area that he had seen. For several hundred years European mapmakers thought Cathay and China were two different places. It was not until the first Jesuit missionaries made their trip to East Asia in the seventeenth century that Europeans learned that Cathay and China were the same place.[52]

The Silk Road

Although the routes from China to the West date back to 100 B.C., the actual use of the title "Silk Road" was applied by the German geographer Ferdinand von Richthofen in the 1870s.[53] As early as 50 B.C. the Chinese were engaged in trade of silk and other high-value products with Rome. There were three major routes from the Chinese border to the West. The northern route ran from Xian around the northern edge of the Taklimakan Desert to Kashgar. The southern route went from Xiam between the southern Taklimakan Desert and the Kunlun Mountains to reach Kashgar. There was a third route through Kashmir to India. The Silk Roads not only led to the exchange of goods, they also accelerated the spread of religion. Buddhism, Christianity, and Islam were introduced to China by way of the Silk Road. This route was the one followed by the traveler Marco Polo when he went to China. The Silk Road went into decline as the Chinese government started to limit trade with the West during the seventeenth century. Today isolated towns, oases, and ruins are all that mark the paths of what was once one of the most important paths of communication between East and West.

The Spice Islands

Because of the poor condition of food eaten in the West during the fifteenth and sixteenth centuries, there was a great demand for spices imported from the East.

When the great navigator Vasco de Gamma led the Portuguese around Africa to reach India, one of his objectives was to find a source of spices.

Spices had been traded overland to Europe since the days of the Roman Empire. However, de Gamma's successful voyage allowed Europeans to bypass the Muslim merchant middlemen, which greatly increased profits. The first voyage of Columbus was justified as a way of bypassing the Portuguese and Muslims to gain access to a new source of spices.

At first Europeans found spices along the Indian Malabar coast. It was not until later that the true Spice Islands were located in what today are called the Moluccas. Located near the end of the Indonesian island chain, the Moluccas are most famous for the production of nutmeg.[54]

Xanadu

In his trip across the Silk Road, Marco Polo was taken to the Mongol summer capitol of Xanadu (Shang-tu). Located North of the Great Wall, this Mongolian military camp declined when Kublai Khan moved his court to Cambaluc (Beijing). Today only ruins mark the spot that Europeans, since Polo's visit, have pictured as a mysterious place of adventure and romance.

The Forbidden City

This walled compound located in the heart of Beijing was the home of 24 Chinese emperors between the years 1420 and 1911. The palace contains over 9,000 rooms located in a maze of buildings that are separated by gardens, pavilions, and huge squares. The primary entrance to the city is through a series of gates from Tiananmen Square. A large picture of Chairman Mao Tse-Tung, hanging on the first gate, faces Tiananmen Square. As this picture can be seen from almost anywhere in the Square, it serves as a reminder to passersby that the Communist Party still maintains political control.

The Palace gained the name "Forbidden City" because entry was limited to the imperial household and invited guests for over 500 years. The Forbidden City remained in the hands of the royal family even after the establishment of the Chinese Republic until they were expelled in 1924. Since 1925, the Forbidden City has been open to the public as a museum.

Mt. Tai

Known to the world as Tai Shan, Mt. Tai is the sacred mountain of the East in Chinese religious tradition. Probably the most visited mountain in the world, Mt. Tai is really a monolith with five peaks. It has served as a pilgrimage site for over 2,000 years. The tradition is to begin the climb to the highest point of the mountain from a temple in the city of Tai'an. From the mountain base it is only 6,293 steps to the summit. Along the way there are hundreds of stone monuments interspaced by numerous temples and shrines. This mountain is sacred to Chinese, Tibetans, and Mongolians. Author Paul Devereaux states "the temples originated from all three traditions of Buddhism and also Taoism."[55]

Mt. Tai has been climbed by famous personalities from Confucius to Mao. In the 2,500 years separating these two people, almost every Chinese emperor made the ascent to the summit. Watching the dawn from the top, Chairman Mao is said to have made his statement, "the East is red."

Mt. Tai is the subject of many Chinese metaphors. A good example is a quotation from the *Little Red Book of Chairman Mao.* "All men must die, but death can vary in its significance. The ancient Chinese writer Szuma Chien said, 'Though death befalls all men alike, it may be heavier than Mt. Tai or lighter than a feather.'"[56]

Almost There: Pilgrims stop for a rest during the long climb from the town of Tai'an to the summit of Mt. Tai.

SOURCE: *Joe Weatherby*

Today the climb is still made by thousands of Chinese each year. The swirling fogbanks, colorful temples, and seething masses of pilgrims climbing the steps to the summit gives the whole place a feeling of mysterious beauty. The object of the climb is to visit the celestial pillar and the beautiful temple of the Jade Emperor located at the summit. Many pilgrims spend the night on the mountain to witness the dawn. For them, like visitors for the last 2,000 years, the Asian day begins with the view from Mt. Tai.

SUMMARY

As stated at the beginning of this chapter, Asia is the largest continent. The preceding pages have conveyed something of the geography, religious, political, and historical forces that have shaped the continent. Almost without exception, Asia and Asians have experienced both the good and the bad of Western imperialism. Today the Asian heirs to some of the world's most important civilizations seem determined to control their own destinies. As Asia enters the twenty-first century, China (the dragon), India (the elephant), and the "four tigers" seem resolved to make the new century an Asian one.

Review Questions

1. Briefly outline the tension between India and Pakistan.
2. What is the policy of "one China two systems"?
3. What is the dispute over Taiwan all about?
4. Why can Afghanistan be called an artificial country?
5. Who are the Asian tigers?

Key Terms

- **Great Leap Forward**—A period in the 1950s when the Chinese under Mao attempted to industrialize overnight.
- **Cultural Revolution**—A period under Mao when the party used mob rule to eliminate opposition, and in so doing, destroyed much of the cultural heritage of China.
- **Kashmir dispute**—Conflict between India and Pakistan over the largely Muslim region of Indian Kashmir.
- **Marco Polo**—An early European visitor to China who wrote down his adventures and opened up knowledge of China to Western readers.
- **The Silk Road**—Several land trade routes that were used to carry goods between China, India, and the West.

- **Opium Wars**—A series of nineteenth-century conflicts fought primarily between China and Britain to force China to trade goods in exchange for Western supplies of opium shipped from India.
- **Boxer Rebellion**—A rebellion at the end of the nineteenth and beginning of the twentieth centuries against foreign influence provoking military intervention by eight nations.
- **1949**—Date that Chinese communists drove the Nationalists off of the Mainland to Taiwan. This date is called "Liberation Day" on the Chinese Mainland.
- **Daoism**—One of the three main religions of China, and along with Confucianism, is native to China.
- **Buddhism**—The only major religion of China that was imported from the outside.

Useful Web Sites

http://www.china-embassy.org
http://www.glo.gov.tw
http://www.pak.gov.pk
http://www.indianembassy.org
http://www.singstat.gov.sg

Notes

1. *Who Said What When: A Chronological Dictionary of Quotations* (London: Bloomsbury Publishing, 1988), p. 95.
2. Ibid., p. 200. Also note that the Maxim machine gun was the first truly automatic gun. Adopted in 1884, it was the standard British infantry support weapon until after World War I. It, and other guns like it, ended the horse cavalry as a serious instrument of war. See Eric Morris, Christopher Chant, Curt Johnson, H. P. Willmott, *Weapons and Warfare of the 20th Century* (Secaucus, NJ: 1976), p. 13.
3. Bill Gertz, "China Future Superpower," *Washington Times,* 29 August 2001. Accessed from Lexis-Nexis Academic database.
4. Stanley Wolpert, *A New History of India,* 5th ed. (New York: Oxford University Press, 1997), p. 32.
5. *A Glimpse of Old China,* (Beijing, China: China Pictorial Publishing House, 1995), p. 1.
6. Trea Wiltshire, *Encounters with China: Merchants, Missionaries, and Mandarins* (Hong Kong: Form Asia Books Ltd., 1995), p. 42.
7. Chairman Mao Tse-Tung, *Quotations From Chairman Mao Tse-Tung* (Peking: Foreign Language Press, 1966), p. 24.
8. Chairman Mao Tse-Tung, "Report of an Investigation into the Peasant Movement in Hunan," *Selected Works of Mao Tse-Tung,* vol. I (Peking: Foreign Language Press, 1954), pp. 23–59.
9. Dorthy Perkins, *Encyclopedia of China: The Essential Reference to China: Its History and Culture* (New York: Checkmark Books, 2000), p. 259.
10. For more information on Chinese Losses in Korea see Geoffrey Stern, *Atlas of Communism* (New York: Macmillan Publishing Company, 1991).

11. Quote attributed to Chairman Deng Xiaoping. J. D. Brown, *China: The 50 Most Memorable Trips* (New York: Macmillan Publishing Company, 1998), p. 532.
12. "AmCham-China 2001 White Paper on American Business in China," released by the Consulate General of the People's Republic of China, Houston, Tex., 30 April 2001.
13. For an interesting account of the Portuguese, Dutch, and English struggle to control the trade with India, see Wolpert, op. cit., pp. 135–148.
14. Don McCombs, Fred L. Worth, *World War II: 4,139 Strange and Fascinating Facts* (New York: Wings Books, 1983), pp. 278–279.
15. Edward Luce, "Vajpayee's Troubles: As India's Prime Minister Faces Possible Defeat in Crucial State Elections, There Seems Little Chance that He Will Be Able to Concentrate on Much-Needed Economic Reform," *The Financial Times* (London), Comment and Analysis, 4 September 2001.
16. "Globalization Weakening India's Eco Structure," *The Financial Times of India,* February 25, 2001. Accessed from Lexis-Nexis Academic database.
17. "Sino-Indian Economic Ties," *The Hindu* (India), 25 October 2000. Accessed from Lexis-Nexis Academic database.
18. Aeba Takanori, *Asian Magma and Japan-US. Relations: Journal of Japanese Trade and Industry,* 1 May 2001. Accessed from Lexis-Nexis Academic database.
19. "Taiwan Posts Second Largest Export Reliance on U.S. Among Asia Nations," *Chinese Economic News Service* (Taiwan), 8 October 2001. Accessed from Lexis-Nexis Academic database.
20. Interview with Richard Henson, "AmCham President to China Economic News Service," *Taiwan Economic News,* 24 July 2001. Accessed from Lexis-Nexis Academic database.
21. Poll taken by Power News and RTV and reported under the headline, "Half of Taiwanese Accept Unification with China," reported by *Deutsche Press*–Agentur, Germany, 21 August 2001. Accessed from Lexis-Nexis Academic database.
22. People's Republic President Jiang Zemin, "Jang Urges Taiwan to Discuss One China," wire service release from *Deutsche Press–Agentur,* Germany, 9 October 2001. Accessed from Lexis-Nexis Academic database.
23. Ibid.
24. Oscar Chung, Lilian Wu, "ROC President Lashes Out at One Country Two Systems Formula," *Central News Agency* (Taiwan), 30 May 2001. Accessed from Lexis-Nexis Academic database.
25. "Bush Says U.S. Will Defend Taiwan," *United Press International Dispatch,* 25 April 2001. Accessed from Lexis-Nexis Academic database.
26. Trea Wiltshire, *Encounters with China: Merchants Missionaries, and Mandarins* (Hong Kong: Form Asia Books Ltd., 1995), pp. 170–171.
27. "U.S. State Department Find Hong Kong Autonomy Largely Intact Despite Reservations Over Its Treatment of the Falungong Spiritual Group," *AFX News Ltd.* (AFX Asia), 9 August 2001.
28. *The World Almanac and Book of Facts 2001* (Mahwah, N.J.: World Almanac Books, 2001), p. 777.
29. Perkins, op. cit., p. 466.
30. News Release: "Singapore Government's Grip On Power Leaves Opposition Reeling," *Deutsche Press-Agentur* (Germany), 22 October 2001. Accessed from Lexis-Nexis Academic database.
31. Press Release: "Taiwan Posts Second Largest Export Reliance on U.S. Among Asian Nations." Accessed from Lexis-Nexis Academic database.

32. Elizabeth Heresch, *The Empire of the Tsars: The Splendour and the Fall, Pictures and Documents 1896 to 1920* (Vienna: Stroitel Pub., 1991), p. 54.

33. Hans J. Morgenthau, *Politics Among Nations: The Struggle for Power and Peace*, 5th ed. Revised (New York: Alfred A. Knopf, Inc.), pp. 183–184.

34. Frederick H. Hartmann, *The Relations of Nations*, 5th ed. (New York: Macmillan Publishing Company, 1978), p. 331.

35. Rouhollah Ramazani, *The Northern Tier: Afghanistan, Iran, and Turkey* (New York: D. Van Nostrand Co., Inc., 1966), p. 50.

36. "Seeing the World Anew," *The Economist* (London), 27 October 2001, U.S. Edition Special Report Section.

37. Ramazani, op. cit., p. 50.

38. Quoted by Valerie Pakenham, *Out in the Noonday Sun: Edwardians in the Tropics* (New York: Random House, 1985), p. 194.

39. "News Briefing by the Chinese Foreign Ministry," *Beijing Review*, 5–11 June 1995, p. 19.

40. Loretta Ann Soosaya, "No Thai Miracle Cure for HIV/AIDS," *New Stratis Times Press* (Malaysia), August 2001, p. 4.

41. "Inside Asia," Cable News Network, U.S.A., 8 June 2001. Accessed from Lexis-Nexis Academic database.

42. Soosaya, op. cit., p. 4.

43. See, for example, Bob Herbert, "China's Missing Girls," *New York Times*, 30 October 1997, p. A31; and Graham Hutchings, "Female Infanticide Will Lead to Army of Bachelors," *The Daily Telegraph* (London), 11 April 1997, International Section, p. 17.

44. Herbert, "China's Missing Girls," *New York Times*, p. A31.

45. For more information on family planning see *Los Angeles Times*, 9 July 1995, p. A6.

46. John Pomfret, "Congressional Aides Report High Hunger Toll in N. Korea," *The Washington Post*, 20 August 1998, p. A22.

47. "Kim Elevated to 'Highest Post' of North Korea," *Los Angeles Times*, 6 September 1998, p. A1.

48. "Ministerial Talks to Open October 9 on Mt. Kumgang North Korea," *Korea Times* (Kankook, Ilbo, Korea), 5 November 2001. Accessed from Lexis-Nexis Academic database.

49. The Central Intelligence Agency, *The CIA World Factbook 2001*, The Central Intelligence Agency, Office of Public Affairs, Washington D.C., 2001. Accessed from CIA web site.

50. Celia Drugger, "Sri Lanka's President Desolves Parliament and Calls Elections," *The New York Times*, 11 October 2001, sec. A, p. 8.

51. G. R. Crone, *Maps and Their Makers: An Introduction to the History of Cartography* (New York: Capricorn Books, 1962), p. 22.

52. Dorothy Perkins, *Encyclopedia of China: The Essential Reference to China: Its History and Culture* (New York: Checkmark Books, 2000), p. 58.

53. Ibid., p. 464.

54. John Keay, *The Royal Geographical Society History of World Exploration* (New York: Mallard Press, 1991), p. 52.

55. Paul Devereaux, *Secrets of Ancient and Sacred Places: The World's Mysterious Places* (London: Brock Hampton Press, 1992), p. 170.

56. *Quotations from Chairman Mao Tse-Tung* (Peking: Foreign Language Press, 1966), p. 174.

CHAPTER 8

The Middle East
and North Africa

Joseph N. Weatherby

*My own ambition is that the Arabs should be our first brown
dominion, and not our last brown colony.*

LAWRENCE OF ARABIA, 1919

*Both the East and the West want to corrupt us from within,
obliterate every distinguishing mark of our personality and
snuff out the light which guides us.*

MUAMMAR AL-QADDAFI

There is a saying in the West that the Middle East is a region too important to
the outside world to allow it to be governed by Middle Easterners. The Middle
East has played a pivotal role in world affairs since ancient times. Forming the
land bridge between Asia, Africa, and Europe, the Middle East has the strategic
attention of both the East and the West (see Figure 8.1).

The Middle East is also the birthplace of the world's three great monotheistic
religions: Judaism, Christianity, and Islam. For more than 1,000 years, Islam has
been the religion of 90 percent of the region's inhabitants. The effect of religion on
politics is more pronounced in the Middle East than probably in any other region
in the world.

The twentieth century has witnessed one of the greatest transfers of wealth in
history, as vast supplies of oil have been discovered in both the Arabian Peninsula
and North Africa. This development has prompted the bitter Western comment
that "where there are Middle Easterners, there is oil." In the 1990s, Saudi Arabia,

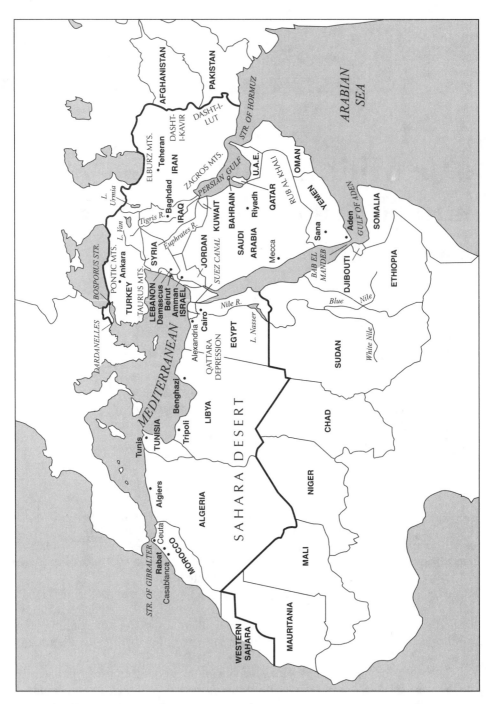

FIGURE 8.1 Political and Physical Characteristics of the Middle East and North Africa

Kuwait, Iran, and Iraq accounted for more than 53 percent of the world's petroleum reserves. This oil is a primary fuel for the industries of Europe, the United States, and Japan. As newspaper headlines indicate, more issues critically important to the future of the United States and the Western world converge in the politics of the Middle East than anywhere else in the Other World.

This chapter offers a brief introduction to the Middle East and North Africa. After a discussion of geography and economics, we trace the history of the Middle East; the story of Islam; and the subsequent rise of nationalism in Egypt, Turkey, Iran, Saudi Arabia, and Israel. The essential aspects of Arab nationalism are also discussed. Finally, the central points of the Arab-Israeli dispute are outlined in the Flashpoints. The data in Table 8.1 illustrate the vast differences in population, wealth, and conditions of life in the North African and Middle Eastern countries.

Although most Americans can point to a map and identify some countries located in the Middle East, few have any idea what nations are actually included in the region. Even scholars fail to agree on the subject. The U.S. Department of Defense states categorically that there is no precise, generally accepted definition of the region variously called the Near East or Middle East.

Because, at times, all the area from the Atlantic coast of Morocco to Afghanistan has been included in this region, no one term seems to describe adequately the whole. The words *Middle East* and *Near East* are inadequate, misleading, and culturally biased. They are misleading because they have been used to describe different places at different times in history. Originally, the Near East referred to the lands of the eastern Mediterranean, and the Middle East described the Indian empire controlled by Britain. The terms converged geographically only during World War II, when the British based their Near Eastern and Middle Eastern operations in Cairo. Because the active involvement of the United States in the region began during this period, Americans have tended to use the term *Middle East,* whereas Europeans continue to use the more traditional designation, the *Near East,* to describe the same area. Even in the absence of this confusion, the terms *Middle East* and *Near East* are culturally biased from the standpoint of inhabitants of the region. Both terms describe the Other World in ways that are meaningful only in reference to the former colonial powers in Europe.

In an effort to avoid these pejorative labels, writers sometimes use the phrases *the Arab world* and *the Islamic world* as substitutes. Unfortunately, these words often confuse as much as they inform. *The Arab world* cannot accurately describe the region as a whole because the phrase ignores 65.6 million Iranians, 65.6 million Turks, and 4.5 million Jews living in Israel. Much of the same problem arises with the use of *Islamic world:* Although Muslims account for most of the area's population, large Christian and Jewish minorities play pivotal roles. This term also implies a religious unity in Islam, which simply does not exist except on the most superficial level.

Despite these concerns, the terms *Middle East* and *North Africa* will be used in this chapter because of their common usage in the United States. The Middle East will be understood to include the Arab states of Arabia and the eastern Mediterranean, Turkey, Israel, and Iran. It will also contain the North African states

TABLE 8.1 CHARACTERISTICS OF MIDDLE EASTERN AND NORTH AFRICAN COUNTRIES

Country	Population (Millions)	Population Growth Rate (%)	Infant Mortality Rate (per 1,000 live births)	Population under 15 Years of Age (%)	Life Expectancy (years)	Urban Population (%)	Literacy Rate (%)	Arable Land (%)	Per Capita GDP ($U.S.)
Middle East									
Bahrain	0.634	1.78	14	30	73	92	85	1	13,100
Iran	65.62	0.83	28	34	70	61	79	10	5,000
Iraq	22.676	2.86	62	42	67	76	58	12	2,400
Israel	5.842	1.67	8	28	79	91	96	17	18,100
Jordan	4.999	3.1	32	38	77	74	87	4	3,500
Kuwait	1.974	3.44	10	29	76	98	79	0	22,700
Lebanon	3.578	1.38	29	28	71	89	92	21	4,500
Oman	2.533	2.46	24	41	72	83	59	0	7,900
Qatar	0.744	3.35	16	26	72	92	79	1	17,100
Saudi Arabia	22.024	3.28	36	43	68	85	63	2	9,000
Syria	16.306	2.58	35	41	68	54	79	28	2,500
Turkey	65.667	1.27	33	29	71	74	82	32	6,600
United Arab Emirates	2.369	1.61	13	30	74	86	79	0	17,400
Yemen	17.479	3.36	67	48	60	24	43	3	740

	Population	Population Growth Rate	Infant Mortality Rate	Population Under 15 Years of Age	Life Expectancy	Urban Population	Literacy Rate	Arable Land	Per Capita GDP
North Africa									
Algeria	31.194	1.74	4.07	15	70	93	100	3	18,000
Egypt	68.36	1.72	66	35	63	45	51	2	2,850
Libya	5.115	2.42	26	36	75	87	76	1	6,700
Morocco	30.122	1.74	49	35	69	55	44	21	3,200
Tunisia	9.593	1.17	30	30	74	65	67	19	5,200
Comparison States									
Canada	31.278	1.02	5	19	79	77	97	5	22,400
Poland	38.646	−0.04	12	19	73	65	99	47	6,800
Italy	57.634	0.09	6	14	79	67	97	31	20,800

SOURCES: Population, Infant Mortality Rate, Population Under 15 Years of Age, Urban Population, Literacy Rate, and Per Capita GDP from *The World Almanac and Book of Facts, 2001.* Population Growth Rate, Life Expectancy, and Arable Land from *CIA World Factbook, 2000.*

of Egypt, Libya, Tunisia, Algeria, and Morocco. This selection may seem arbitrary because it omits Afghanistan, Somalia, the Sudan, and Mauritania, which form transition areas between the Middle East, North Africa, and other adjacent regions.

In the Middle East, one encounters strange-sounding names with a regional significance. The Holy Land, Maghreb, Levant, Judea, Samaria, and the Fertile Crescent are all examples of special places that require more explanation. The *Holy Land* was traditionally associated with pilgrimages and crusades to the sites venerated by Christians because of their association with the life of Jesus. Today, the term also includes sites sacred to Jews and Muslims, most of which are in or near the city of Jerusalem.

The Maghreb is a phrase literally meaning, and by tradition it implies, "The setting sun in the west." This term is used to describe the North African countries of Morocco, Algeria, and Tunisia, and some writers also include Libya and Mauritania. Like the Maghreb, *the Levant* signifies a direction, the eastern point of the compass. The Levant is generally understood to include the present states of Lebanon and Israel.

Judea and *Samaria* are ancient Hebrew names currently applied by the government of Israel to the former Jordanian-held territories on the West Bank of the Jordan River. The old biblical names are used to remind the world that Israel claims a historic right to bring Jewish settlers into these Arab-populated territories. These terms are used by those Israelis who support the expansion of the borders of Israel to include all of the territories that biblical tradition teaches were promised by God to the ancient children of Israel.

The term *Fertile Crescent* is familiar to many in the West because it is the traditional site of the birthplace of Western civilization. It includes the present countries of Israel and Lebanon as well as Syria and Iraq. Some writers say that the Fertile Crescent arches like a bow from the eastern Nile delta to the mouth of the Shatt-al-Arab river in Iraq. Other authorities hold that the western terminus of the bow is Palestine, not the Nile delta. What is important to remember is that this is an area of relatively good agriculture, low population, and a reasonable climate. As in ancient times, this area offers the best hope for the development of a non-petroleum-based economy.

GEOGRAPHY

Western perceptions of the Middle East are simultaneously accurate and misleading. The greatest expanse of desert in the world does exist here, but although there are still camel-mounted Bedouins in parts of the Middle East, most people now live in villages, towns, and cities. Even those Bedouins who have not settled into permanent residences are now likely to be exchanging their "ships of the desert," the camel, for Toyota trucks. Like many parts of the Other World, the Middle East is an area of both variety and dynamic change.

In its simplest form, the Middle East can be divided into three distinct geographic regions: the plains of North Africa and Arabia, the Fertile Crescent, and

The Sahara: Camels gathered around one of the government-prepared watering holes in the Sahara Desert.

SOURCE: *Joe Weatherby*

the northern tier. These areas are surrounded by five seas and five straits and are bisected by two of the world's great river systems.

The Plains of North Africa and Arabia

The vast deserts of the Sahara and the Rub al Khali cover over 95 percent of this region. Because of their immense size, it should not be surprising to learn that the surfaces of these two deserts vary from gravel to rock to sand.

The Qattara Depression, larger than 4,000 square miles, is located near the Mediterranean in Egypt's portion of the eastern Sahara. From time to time, proposals have been made to divert the waters of the Mediterranean over the precipice to the Qattara floor, which is 400 feet below sea level. Engineers estimate that enough falling water could be diverted through generators to create an electric power complex that would rival the Nile's Aswan High Dam. A combination of environmental concerns and a shortage of capital in Egypt has postponed serious consideration of this project for the foreseeable future. There has been another, perhaps more feasible, Qattara proposal to tap an abundant ancient water supply, believed to exist beneath the depression floor, to create a new Nile delta in the desert. Whether the Egyptian government will find the development funds that would be required to attempt either of these ambitious schemes is doubtful at present.

The Rub al Khali of Saudi Arabia is famous for sand mountains that are hundreds of feet high. This desert contains the largest area of sand on Earth. The Rub al Khali is about the size of Texas, extending from Yemen in the East to the United Arab Emirates in the West. For the first time since the ancient caravan routes flourished, Westerners are again penetrating the unknowns of the Rub al Khali, but this time in modern vehicles and engaged in the search for oil.

The remaining 5 percent of the plains of North Africa and Arabia is a transitional territory that includes two distinct areas: desert scrub country and a rich

Mediterranean coastal zone. This zone stretches from the Nile delta westward for most of the length of North Africa and to the Atlantic coast of Morocco as far south as Casablanca. The desert scrub country does contain some soil, moisture, and vegetation, and much of it resembles the high plains of the western United States. The conditions that produce desert scrub occur elsewhere in the Middle East, including southern Turkey, western Iraq, western Iran, and parts of Jordan and Syria. The nomads live in the desert scrub with their ever-migrating herds of sheep and goats.

Most of the residents of the plains live in the narrow coastal zone of the Mediterranean rather than in the deserts. The North African coast of the Atlantic and the Mediterranean generally conforms to what is known as the Mediterranean climate. This climate features hot, dry summers, with brown or dormant vegetation, and cool, wet winters, when the plant life has its growth period. In North Africa, this coastal zone ranges from only a few miles in width in parts of Egypt and Libya to as much as 50 miles in Algeria. In Egypt, the coastal zone and Nile valley and delta combined average 2,700 people per square mile, representing one of the world's densest populations. Remarkably, unlike other high-density areas, such as the Netherlands, the people of Egypt are still largely engaged in traditional Other World occupations including subsistence agriculture (see Box 8.1).

Some of the great cities of both Africa and the Middle East are located in or near the Mediterranean coastal zone. Cairo, with a population of over 9.5 million people, is the largest and most important city on the African continent. Other important North African cities are Alexandria, Egypt (3.5 million); Tripoli, Libya (1 million); Benghazi, Libya (450,000); Tunis, Tunisia (1,700,000); and Algiers, Algeria

---

BOX 8.1   WATER

The greatest shortage in the Middle East is water. Since ancient times, Mediterranean people have used ingenious methods to carry water to the fields. Following are several traditional irrigation methods still used in the region.

> The *qanat* is a tunnel sometimes over 10 miles long that taps the groundwater in the foothills and transports it to the fields in the valleys. This system is used in Iran and other mountainous countries in the northern tier.
> The *shadoof* is an ancient system using a goat-skin bag attached to a pole that is pivoted from the river to the field. This water system is used extensively along the banks of the Nile River in Egypt. The water wheel is a device used to lift and transport water. This system is usually animal-powered.
> The *Archimedes* screw is a portable gear used to raise water from a river or pond to the fields.

(3,700,000). Both Rabat (1,200,000) and Casablanca (3,100,000) are located in the coastal zones of Morocco. Saudi Arabia in the Arabian Peninsula contains the historic cities of Mecca (914,000) and Medina (500,000). The commercial centers of Jedda (1,810,000) and Riyadh (3,324,000) are also located in Saudi Arabia.

These statistics may have more meaning if we compare the size of North African and Arabian cities with those found in the United States. Cairo has 2 million more people than New York City; Alexandria and Casablanca are larger than Houston; Benghazi and Mecca are smaller than San Antonio; Jedda, Rabat, and Riyadh are all larger than San Francisco.

The North African and Arabian plains contain a number of mountains, including the Atlas and Rif mountains of Morocco and the Tell Atlas of Algeria and Tunisia. The highest point in Egypt is the 8,600-foot Jabal Musa (Mount Sinai), located in the southern Sinai. Tradition holds that God gave the Ten Commandments to Moses on Mt. Sinai. The Arabian Peninsula is mountainous in Yemen and Oman. In both places, peaks reach heights of 12,000 feet.[1]

The Fertile Crescent

Perhaps nowhere in the world has so much human history been tied to one single geographic area as in the Fertile Crescent. Everywhere the visitor looks, on the hills or in the valleys, important events in the history of humankind have occurred. Here are the ruins of ancient civilizations, the land of prophets, and the birthplace of Judaism and Christianity. Geographically, the Fertile Crescent includes a narrow coastal zone flanked by the sea on one side and a rather low coastal range of mountains, running north to south, on the other. Along the southern border of Turkey, the Fertile Crescent arches eastward through a gap in the mountains to include the desert scrublands of Syria and Iraq before joining the rich river basins of the Tigris and Euphrates. The region terminates at the northern end of the Persian Gulf.

The coastal zone of the Fertile Crescent is similar in many respects to the coast of California. Although this analogy has limitations apparent to any geographer, it may be useful to consider the following comparisons. If we were to travel the coastal route south from San Francisco to Los Angeles, we would pass through countryside that is similar in many respects to the coastal zone of the eastern Mediterranean, with Beirut being comparable to the Bay Area, Haifa to Monterey and Carmel, the Lebanon Mountains to the California coastal range, the Bekaa valley in Lebanon to the Salinas valley, and Tel Aviv to the area between Santa Barbara and Los Angeles.

With the exception of Beirut, the cities of the eastern Mediterranean do not rival either those of North Africa or the interior of the Fertile Crescent. Tel Aviv has a population of 218,000 and Jerusalem 591,000. Tripoli, the second-largest city in Lebanon, has a population of 245,000 people. The population of Beirut, Lebanon's capital, is 2 million.

The two major cities of the Fertile Crescent are Baghdad, Iraq, and Damascus, Syria. Baghdad, with a climate similar to the southwestern United States, has a

The Souk: Located next to the coral-colored walls of the old kasba, the market, or souk, is the focal point of life in this Moroccan town.

SOURCE: *Joe Weatherby*

population of over 4 million. The population of Damascus is over 2 million. Syria and Iraq are the most important states of the Fertile Crescent. Both are considered to have a good chance to develop well-rounded economies, maintain low population densities, and establish reasonable standards of living. Presently, their problems are mainly political, not geographic or economic.

The Northern Tier

The northern tier is an area of mountains and plateaus linked to a mountain system that stretches from the Alps in the west to the Himalayas in the east. Although Afghanistan and Pakistan are often included in this region, this discussion of the northern tier is limited to Turkey and Iran.

Both countries are located on high plateaus surrounded by mountains. Turkey is situated on a peninsula jutting out into the Mediterranean. Turkey is about the size of Texas and Arkansas combined. The Anatolian plateau, a high, dry region about 3,000 feet above sea level, is located in the center of Turkey. Here, the Turks produce most of their wheat and cereals. Two mountain ranges run east to west along the edges of the plateau. The Pontic Mountains are located on the north and the Taurus Mountains on the south of the peninsula. Eastern Turkey is extremely mountainous along the Iranian border. Mount Ararat, the traditional site of the landing of Noah's ark, is near this border. It is worth noting that Turkey has a long, varied coastal region that includes both a Mediterranean climate along the south and west and a wet area near the Black Sea city of Rise. This city receives as much as 100 inches of rain a year. With such climatic variety in the coastal zone, Turkey raises a number of crops including tea, tobacco, and cotton. Although most people live in villages, Turkey has several large cities. Istanbul, with a population of 9.5 million, is the largest. Ankara, the capital, has a population of 3 million, and Izmir has 2.4 million people.

Nature has played a cruel trick on Iran. Larger than Alaska, Iran consists of a high desert surrounded on all sides by rugged mountains that prevent moisture from penetrating into the interior. The Zagros Mountains run along the length of the eastern shore of the Persian Gulf, and the Elburz Mountains are located along a line parallel to the southern coast of the Caspian Sea. The jewel of the Elburz is a partially snowcapped volcano 18,376 feet high. This volcano, Mt. Damavand, is clearly visible from Tehran. Tehran is built in the foothills of the Elburz and has a setting and climate closely resembling Salt Lake City, Utah.

Most of the interior of Iran consists of two terrible deserts, where some of the world's highest temperatures have been recorded. The Dasht-i-Kavir, or "Salt Desert," and the Dasht-i-Lut, or "Sand Desert," popularly called the "Desert of Death," are largely untraveled even today. The hostile environment in Iran's interior has caused over 70 percent of the country to remain uninhabited. The people of Iran live either along the narrow coastal plain of the Caspian Sea or in scattered urban centers in the north and west. Tehran, the capital, totally dominates these urban centers with a population of over 7.2 million people. The nation's second-largest city, Meshed, has a population of more than 2 million.[2]

Strategic Geography

The Middle East contains two of the world's great river systems: the Nile and the Tigris and Euphrates. The area also has two lesser waterways that are important in the politics of the region: the Suez Canal and the Jordan River.

Flowing 4,037 miles, the Nile is the world's longest river. Rising in Ethiopia and Uganda, it crosses the Sudan, enters Egypt at Lake Nasser, passes through the dam at Aswan, and flows past Cairo to the delta and the Mediterranean. If there is a central feature to Egypt, it is most certainly the Nile, which has been the life-support system for this nation's residents for over 5,000 years. The need to secure the Nile in upper and lower Egypt is as important today as it was when the pharaohs ruled the nation in ancient times. As in the past, today's Egyptian leaders pay particular attention to politics in the Sudan. To the Egyptian, the fate of the Sudan still affects the security of the Nile.

Both the Tigris and the Euphrates begin their journey to the sea in central Turkey. The Euphrates passes through Turkey, Syria, and Iraq, and the Tigris through Turkey and Iraq. The Karun flows from Iran to join with the Tigris and the Euphrates, forming a new river called the Shatt-al-Arab just before reaching the northern shore of the Persian Gulf. It is in this meandering delta of the Shatt-al-Arab near Basra where much of the war between Iraq and Iran was fought during the 1980s. This same area was a strategic objective of American forces during the 1991 war with Iraq.

The Suez Canal has been strategically important since its opening in 1869. One hundred and one miles long, the canal joins the Red Sea with the Mediterranean, saving ships the costly and time-consuming trip around the tip of southern Africa when traveling from the Persian Gulf and points further east to and from Europe. For further information, see the Flashpoints at the end of this chapter.

The Jordan River and its system of lakes and seas are historically significant as the site of many events sacred to Christians and Jews. The Jordan is also politically important because it is the disputed border between Jordan and Israel. The river flows through a valley for about 80 miles between the Sea of Galilee (Lake Tiberias) and the Dead Sea. The Jordan's economic significance is limited. Ranging from 50 to a few hundred feet in width, its potential for irrigation cannot possibly meet the exaggerated hopes for agricultural development of either the Arabs or the Israelis.[3]

No area of the globe is as strategically located as the Middle East. For centuries, it has been the invasion route of Egyptians, Persians, Romans, Christians, and Muslims. Today, its important location as a passageway between Africa, Europe, and Asia is without challenge. Five easily traversed seas surround the Middle East: Arabian, Red, Mediterranean, Black, and Caspian. There are three gulfs of importance: the Gulf of Aden, located at the tip of the Arabian peninsula; the Gulf of Oman, situated between Oman and Iran; and the famous Persian Gulf. Entry and egress to all but two of these bodies of water are controlled by narrow straits: the Straits of Gibraltar, controlling the western Mediterranean; the Dardanelles and the Bosporus, dominating entry to the Black Sea; the Bab el Mandeb, controlling the southern end of the Red Sea and the Suez Canal; and the Straits of Hormuz, which must be passed to enter the Persian Gulf. Strategic straits do not dominate the Arabian Sea, which is part of the Indian Ocean, and the Caspian Sea, which has no outlet.[4]

PEOPLE

A popular misconception is that there is a homogeneous race of people in the Middle East. This notion is fostered by some of the region's religious institutions, whose traditions allude to Arab, Jewish, or even Aryan races. These terms, however, have little meaning in the Middle East today, unless they are limited to linguistic or cultural associations.

Although there are no recognizable groupings about which everyone would agree, authorities acknowledge that the region contains Semitic, Turkish, and Persian-speaking people. Of the Semitic-speaking population, the Arabs are the most numerous. Although there are many dialects, written modern standard Arabic is understood by educated Arabs everywhere. Arabic is spoken from the Atlantic coast of Morocco to the shores of the Persian Gulf. By this definition, approximately 200 million Arabs live in the region. Although there is a single Arab nation in theory only, the common bond of language has meant that unification is an aspiration of many of the region's inhabitants.

The other large Semitic group lives in Israel. Reviving a formerly ritualistic language as a symbol of their nationalism, the more than 4.5 million Jews living in Israel have again made Hebrew a living language.

The ancestors of the 56 million Turkish-speaking people in modern Turkey came to the Anatolian peninsula in the eleventh and twelfth centuries from central Asia. They have lived in a single identifiable state since the Turkish Republic was created from the breakup of the Ottoman Empire following World War I.[5]

Persian is an Indo-European language written with a modified Arabic alphabet. There are about 34 million Persian-speaking Iranians in Iran. Finally, it should be pointed out that the region also contains people who speak different languages, including the Kurds, Armenians, and Greeks.

RELIGION

Two great forces are shaping the character of the modern Middle East. One is the Islamic religion and the other is nationalism.

Islam is the youngest of the three great monotheistic religions that arose in this region; the other two are Christianity and Judaism. Islam has been the dominant religion in the Middle East for more than 1,000 years. Today less than 10 percent of the population is non-Muslim. Thus, to understand the Middle East, it will be necessary to have some knowledge of Islam.

First, however, a distinction should be made between what is often referred to as the popular or folk religion and the formal religion of mosque and church. It is next to impossible to generalize about Middle Eastern folk religions except to point out that the popular practices of Christians, Jews, and Muslims are similar. All have their local saints, sacred places, and symbols. Many of these traditions spill over from one religion to another. For example, people of all religions in the Mediterranean traditionally paint the windows and shutters of their homes blue to ward off the evil eye. The distance between this popular practice and the formal religion of the scholars is often as great as that of the Pentecostal snake handler in the Appalachian Mountains and the pope in Rome. This inquiry will be limited to the formal religious practices of the majority religion, Islam.[6]

Much of the universal appeal of Islam is found in its straightforward simplicity. Unlike Christianity, there are no priests dispensing sacraments, no catechism, and no complicated theology. Islam demands a belief in only one God, called Allah in Arabic. Muslims believe that Mohammed is the prophet of God. The word *Islam* means "submission"; thus, a Muslim is a believer who has submitted to the will of God. This simple theology may be summarized as belief in the oneness of God, the prophecy of Mohammed, judgment day, and life after death.

Islam is more than a religion, as that term is generally understood in the West. It is a way of life, 24 hours a day, 7 days a week, 365 days a year. Muslims do not concern themselves with what is the truth because truth is contained in the profession of faith and the word of God as revealed through Mohammed in the Koran. The great questions of Islam are centered on how a good Muslim should live and relate to others, not what a Muslim should believe in order to enter paradise. Although it is easy to make a profession of faith in Islam, it is difficult to live the life of a good Muslim. As a guide for living, Muslims observe five religious obligations, called the Five Pillars of Islam: professing faith, observing ritual prayer, giving alms, fasting during the month of Ramadan, and making a pilgrimage to Mecca.

The Profession of Faith (Shahadah)

Muslims believe that there is no god but God and that Mohammed is his prophet. The implications of this profession are threefold. First, in contrast to most Christians, who believe that there is one God, expressed as Father, Son, and Holy Spirit, Muslims hold to an uncompromising monotheism: "There is no god but God." Second, Muslims believe that although other prophets, including Jesus, have received revelations, Allah's words as revealed through Mohammed are the final, complete message from God to humankind. Third, Muslims believe that this message is contained, in full, in a book called the Koran.

Prayer (Salat)

Traditionally, Muslims pray at five prescribed periods a day: in the morning before sunrise, noontime, afternoon, sunset, and late evening. The prayer is ritualistic and keeps the believers in constant contact with God. Islam differs from those forms of Christianity in which believers pray through mediators inasmuch as Muslims believe that they have direct access to God.

Alms Giving (Zakat)

Muslims believe that they are obliged to pay a percentage of their income to the poor and needy. They do not believe that poverty is a crime. For Muslims, there is little or no stigma attached to this system of voluntary religious welfare.

Fasting (Sawm)

During Ramadan, the ninth month of the Islamic calendar, all Muslims are called on to observe the fast by abstaining from all food, drink, and other earthly pleasures during daylight hours. This month-long fast, longer than anything practiced in either Christianity or Judaism, teaches Muslims self-denial and moderation.

Pilgrimage to Mecca (Hajj)

If possible, all Muslims are enjoined to visit the Great Mosque in Mecca at least once. Here, facing the Ka'bah and wearing the same ritual white, Muslims from every station in life, from every country in the world, both male and female, pray as equals before God.[7]

North African Door: Popular culture in North Africa holds that either the "hand" door-knocker represents the hand of Mohammed's daughter, Fatima, or that the fingers represent the Five Pillars of Islam.

SOURCE: *Joe Weatherby*

Holy Struggle (Jihad)

Many consider the jihad, or holy struggle, to be almost a "sixth pillar of Islam." This duty, often misunderstood in the West, has two meanings: one inner and one external. The inner meaning calls on Muslims to fight constantly against their own evil inclinations. The external command offers salvation to those Muslims who fight to promote a universal Islamic doctrine. The confusion concerning *jihad* arises because the term has been used in a political manner by some Islamic leaders to further their own purposes. When used in this way, there is some doubt whether it is anything more than a symbolic gesture.[8]

The Growth of Islam: With over 1,126,325,000 adherents, Islam is one of the fastest growing religions. Located on the docks in Doha, Qatar, this portable mosque serves the needs of local dock workers and fisherman.
SOURCE: *Joe Weatherby*

The Muslim community is governed by a hierarchy of principles expected to guide the faithful in all matters of life. These principles, or authorities, are collectively called the *Shari'ah*, or "the path to be followed." This path includes, in descending order of importance, the Koran, the tradition (*Hadith*) of how Mohammed lived, consensus (*Ijma*) of the religious scholars on issues, and deduction (*Qiyas*) where there is no precedent. Not all Muslim communities accept this hierarchy in its entirety.

The great split in Islam began because of a dispute over how the successor (caliph) to Mohammed should be selected. The Shiia branch of Islam is *centered* in Iran. Shiites believe that the first caliph should have been Ali, the son-in-law of Mohammed, and that successive caliphs should have come exclusively from the descendants of Ali. Sunnis, who make up approximately 80 percent of the world's Muslim population, believe that the caliphs should have been chosen by election of the faithful from members of Mohammed's tribe. Over the centuries, many other differences have developed between these two branches, and their disputes still color Middle Eastern politics hundreds of years after the original split occurred.[9]

HISTORY

Since the seventh century, the history of the Middle East has been inexorably bound to the history of Islam, which includes at least five distinct periods: the life of Mohammed, the rightly guided caliphs, the Umayyads, the Abbasids, and the Ottomans.

The Life of Mohammed (A.D. 571–632)

Mohammed was born in A.D. 571 in the city of Mecca. Orphaned while young, he was reared by a grandfather who was a leader of the Meccan Quraysh tribe. Mohammed is traditionally believed to have traveled with caravans to other parts of the Middle East as a young man. His visits may have exposed him to other religions. When he was 40 years old, he started receiving revelations commanding him to tell the world that there was one God, that Mohammed was his prophet, and that there would be a judgment day. These revelations were revolutionary ideas that threatened existing society in Mecca. In the summer of 622, opposition from the Meccans forced Mohammed to flee from Mecca 200 miles north to the city of Medina. The date of Mohammed's flight, called the Hijra, marks the beginning of the Islamic calendar. After converting Medina to Islam, Mohammed lived to see not only Mecca but also the entire Arabian Peninsula become Muslim before his death in 632. It should be remembered that Muslims do not ascribe divine qualities to Mohammed. He is considered to have been a human being who, while living a perfect life, served as a messenger from God.

Mosque of Mohammed Ali: Located on the Citadel towering above Cairo, this mosque was begun in 1824. Today, it remains the most imposing landmark in the city.

SOURCE: *Joe Weatherby*

The Rightly Guided Caliphs (632–661)

Mohammed's death left the movement without a clearly designated successor. This vacuum initiated a struggle for power that ultimately led to the Sunni-Shiia split. Although some of the faithful believed that Ali had been designated by Mohammed as his successor, Abu Bakr (the prophet's father-in-law) was chosen to be the caliph. After only two years, Abu Bakr chose Umar to be the caliph, and under Umar's leadership, Islamic armies conquered the Fertile Crescent, Persia, and Egypt. Much of what is familiar to Westerners about Islam, including the veiling of women and the ban on alcohol, was institutionalized during Umar's tenure. Uthman succeeded Umar, who was assassinated in 644, but he too was assassinated 12 years later. Ali was finally selected as the fourth caliph, only to be challenged by the powerful Umayyad family from Mecca. The Umayyads backed another leader named Mu'awiyah. There was a civil war between the Umayyads, who had the support of Muslims in Syria, and the Muslims who supported Ali. Eventually, Ali was assassinated in 661. Shiites still maintain that Ali was the only legitimate successor to Mohammed.

Muslims look with fondness at the period of the first four caliphs as a time when the religion had a purity of purpose that ultimately was lost. Modern Muslims tend to stress the exertions of the period, the justice, and the humanity, and ignore the disturbing reality that three of the four "rightly guided caliphs" were assassinated. Nevertheless, if there ever was a time that Muslims long to return to, it is this one.

The Umayyad Dynasty (661–750)

Under the first Umayyad caliph, Mu'awiyah, the election of leaders was ended in favor of a dynastic approach, and the political capital of Islam became Damascus. During the almost 100 years that the Umayyads ruled, the Islamic faith spread to three continents. However, it was only a question of time until the non-Arab elements of the empire began to believe that they were being treated as second-class members of the Damascus state. In 750, the non-Arab dissidents of the empire arose and ended the Arab domination by destroying the Umayyads. In place of the Umayyads, a new multicultural system was established, called the Abbasid dynasty.

The Abbasid Dynasty (750–1258)

With the rise of the Abbasids, the so-called Golden Age of Islam began. The empire's new capital in Baghdad saw Muslims lead the world in philosophy, literature, mathematics, and medicine. Many developments that were to bear fruit in the explosion of the arts and sciences during the Renaissance in Europe originated in the streets of Abbasid Baghdad. The rule of the Abbasids came to an end in the year 1258, when Mongol armies from central Asia conquered Baghdad. After the fall of the Abbasids, no single power was able to dominate the Middle East until the Ottoman period.

The Ottoman Empire (1453–1918)

Tradition holds that the Ottomans came to Anatolia from central Asia in the early Middle Ages. By the mid-1300s, they were in the process of establishing an empire that would again extend Muslim control to parts of Europe, Africa, and the Middle East. Although it is difficult to generalize about an empire that lasted for over 600 years, it is safe to state that many of the conditions found in the modern Middle East began in the practices of the Ottomans. For example, the Ottomans were able to rule a diverse multicultural empire stretching over much of the Mediterranean world because they established a system of religious and cultural autonomy called the Millet. Sectarian separation was institutionalized and even encouraged by the Ottomans as long as loyalty and taxes were paid to the caliph. This system of religious toleration resulted in the survival of small Christian and Jewish groups, which otherwise would have disappeared. Middle East groups still divide along sectarian lines after the fashion of the Millet.

During the eighteenth and nineteenth centuries, Ottomans were in retreat in the face of increasing Western power. Many of the negative stereotypes that westerners have about the Middle East come from this period of Ottoman weakness. The Ottomans survived the nineteenth century but collapsed with the defeat of the Central Powers in World War I. The subsequent partition of the non-Turkish elements from the empire resulted in the creation of the modern Turkish Republic.

Islam Today

Much has been written in recent years concerning the resurgence of Islam as a unifying force in the Middle East. Although it can be said that Islam is not a form of nationalism, it is clear that Islamic attitudes and symbols are used and manipulated by nationalists in the Middle East to legitimize their respective political objectives.

It is possible to identify certain important attitudes that Muslims have concerning non-Muslims. Islam victoriously entered the world scene over 1,400 years ago and remained so for almost 1,000 years. This long period of dominance has led to a collective mind set that is reflected in the commonly used Muslim expression "Islam dominates and may not be dominated." Thus, for Muslims, some religions may be tolerated, but none will be allowed parity, much less dominance, if there is power to prevent it.

Although some Muslims view the defeats of the recent past with the rationalization that "Islam gains strength with every testing," there is no denying that it is particularly galling to have unbelievers dominating believers after all these centuries. This attitude is reflected in the responses of many people from the Middle East when they come in contact with the outside world. In the nineteenth century, the early military defeats administered by the West were rationalized on the grounds of Middle Eastern technological inferiority. Attitudes eventually evolved into a conspiratorial view of history in which the West was blamed for every problem in the region.

In this century, continuing defeats, both external and internal, have led to a further sense of helplessness that is reflected in an almost irrational rage against anything Western or modern because it is believed to represent colonialism in a new form. This attitude can be seen in a number of ways, including the actions of students studying in the West, Islamic resurgence movements in the region, and the return to conservative Islamic dress by many university-educated women. Although it is difficult to forecast the direction these frustrations will take, it is safe to say that they have a real basis in fact and can only become a major unsettling element in Middle Eastern politics.

It is popular to focus on "Islamic fundamentalism" when referring to the resurgence of Islam in the Middle East. What is often ignored is that fundamentalist movements exist in all major religions. Like their counterparts in Christianity and Judaism, the fundamentalist movements in Islam represent only a fraction of the total number of believers.

Islamic fundamentalist movements have received positive receptions in many parts of the Middle East where the inhabitants have suffered the experiences of colonialism and neocolonialism, social injustice, poverty, and governmental ineffectiveness. These Muslims resent the harsh life, lack of jobs, and the culture of corruption that has created a wide gap between the rich and the poor. The fundamentalist movements offer hope for change and a new sense of worth to an often-bankrupt society tired of experimenting with imported solutions to problems. Fundamentalists have won many friends by taking leading roles in assisting the sick, the widowed, the poor, and the unemployed. They have been active in reforming the schools and universities. They have even been involved in such diverse activities as blood drives and providing financial aid for funerals. All of these fundamentalist movements call for a moral sense of purpose that offers alternative solutions to the ones advocated by the secular nationalists and the traditional Muslim leaders who currently make up the Middle Eastern establishment.

The lesson of the Iranian revolution should now be clear to everyone. The Islamic reformers captured that revolution from secular nationalists because they offered the masses a chance to put an end to the evils of the past. The Iranian revolution should serve as a warning to the establishment in every state of the Middle East. If the injustices of the past are not addressed, there will be a rise in militant Islamic fundamentalist movements throughout the region.

In part, the Islamic resurgence has occurred because Islam avoided the stigma of failure that accompanied the secular philosophies. In the twentieth century, capitalism, socialism, Marxism, and secular nationalisms have all been tried, and each has ended in failure. Only Islam offers hope for a renewal of Middle Eastern society without the taint of defeat, corruption, or association with colonialism. In whatever form it takes, Islam is today, as it has always been, the central factor in the lives of millions of people.[10]

THE COLONIAL EXPERIENCE

For the better part of 1,300 years, Christians from Europe have fought Muslims from the East. During the last 200 years, this traditional conflict has been worsened by the impact of Western colonialism. It began with the French invasion of Egypt in 1798. Although this occupation was cut short by the British victory over the French fleet at the battle of Aboukir Bay,[11] it signaled a growing European interest in the area. Soon Britain, France, Italy, and Spain pursued their imperial objectives. Germany and Russia were absent only because their ambitions were frustrated by the British and the French. The British began their imperial adventure on the periphery of the Middle East by developing a series of strategic colonies on the shores of the Persian Gulf. By the opening of the Suez Canal in 1869, Britain controlled colonies stretching from Aden, at the mouth of the Red Sea, across southern Arabia all the way to India. Later the British leased the Ottoman island of Cyprus and used it as a naval base to check the Russian attempts to enter the Mediterranean.

The British military occupied Egypt in 1882 because of a fear that the Egyptian government would not pay debts owed to foreign investors. This occupation was considered to be temporary, but the British did not leave Egypt until 1956. They were also interested in expanding their influence along the Red Sea. After much fighting, the Anglo-Egyptian forces occupied the Sudan in the last decade of the nineteenth century. By this time, Britain was the European country with the most extensive presence in the Middle East. When the Ottoman Empire was disbanded at the end of World War I, the British gained custody of Iraq, Palestine, and Transjordan. Semi-independent, these territories were administered by the British as mandates until the end of World War II. For the most part, British colonies in the Middle East were established as strategic colonies either to protect the lifeline to India or to create a stable environment for business investment.

After their earlier occupation of Egypt, French imperial activity was limited to the establishment of a colony in Algeria in 1830. Throughout the nineteenth century, French settlers expanded this colonial bridgehead until it included a large portion of North Africa. In the twentieth century, these holdings grew to include the southern portion of Morocco. France gained control of Syria and Lebanon as part of the partition of the Ottoman Empire. Regardless of their official status, the French administered these territories as colonies.

Spain and Italy developed imperial ambitions in North Africa during the early part of the twentieth century. Italy began a military occupation of Libya in 1911, when the territory was taken from the Ottomans. Building on several ancient enclaves, the Spanish joined the French in the partition of Morocco by occupying the northern portion in 1912. Although established largely for prestige purposes, these colonies proved difficult to pacify completely and expensive to maintain. It is doubtful whether these colonies ever justified the blood and treasure required to hold them.

Although Germany never actually controlled any territory in the Middle East, it did play an active political role as a participant in the great power struggles of the nineteenth and twentieth centuries. Before World War I, it sent military advisors and agents to both the Ottoman Empire and to Persia. It also participated in the planning and partial construction of the Berlin-Baghdad railway. Because the Germans were only in the Middle East in a financial or advisory capacity, and because they were opposed to the British and French, they were the most admired Europeans active in the region.

With the exception of the navy in the war against the Barbary pirates, the United States avoided involvement in the Middle East until the end of World War II. Before President Truman played a leading role in the establishment of the state of Israel, the United States escaped the colonial stigma applied to most other developed countries. Since that time, the United States has been blamed for almost every ill that plagues the region.

During the last 200 hundred years, almost every area in the Middle East has suffered under colonial occupation. Many of these areas fell under European control after World War I. As a result of this experience, the worst forms of imperialism are well remembered. At times, the Western powers have denied that they were officially in the Middle East in an imperial capacity. Nowhere in the Other World was Western imperialism implemented in a more hypocritical or cynical fashion.

GOVERNMENT

By the last quarter of the twentieth century, the countries of the Middle East had received formal independence. The end of colonialism resulted in the creation of one of the most politically complex regions in the Other World, containing democracies, authoritarian civilian states, military-dominated regimes, and monarchies. Morocco, Saudi Arabia, Jordan, and the Arab states of the Persian Gulf are monarchies. Iraq, Libya, and Syria are regimes in which the military plays an important role. Egypt, Tunisia, and Turkey are civilian authoritarian states. Iran is an Islamic republic. In the past, both Israel and Lebanon have been considered Western-style democracies, but a civil war, Palestinian intrigues, Syrian military intervention, and the 1982 Israeli invasion have combined to kill the short-term hope for an independent democracy in Lebanon.

It is important to remember that since independence, few Middle Eastern regimes have demonstrated a sustained commitment to constitutional government. During periods of crisis, decision making has often reverted to informal systems that exist outside the formal mechanisms of government. Thus personalities and politics rather than law dominate the Middle East, as it is understood in the West, where following procedure is more important than winning. Middle Eastern government institutions must be considered as only a part of a greater cultural whole that is involved in political decision making. Traditional social, cultural, and religious institutions still play a disproportionate role in the politics of the region.

ECONOMICS AND NATURAL RESOURCES

It is popular to state that with the exception of petroleum there are no significant mineral deposits in the Middle East. Although it is true that the resources of the region are limited, it is also true that much of the Middle East has not been thoroughly surveyed. Nevertheless, important mineral resources have been found in limited areas. Phosphate deposits are mined in Morocco, the former Spanish Sahara, Tunisia, Jordan, and Egypt. Iron ore is found in both North Africa and Turkey. Some gold has been discovered in Egypt and Saudi Arabia.

Clearly, oil is the great natural resource of the region. The Persian Gulf states provide significant amounts of the oil needed by Europe, Japan, and the United States.[12] What is perhaps more important is the realization that the oil states of the Middle East and North Africa control more than 60 percent of the world's proved reserves of oil and 25 percent of the reserves of natural gas. Because of these resources, this region will play an important economic role in world affairs for a very long time.

There is a vast contrast between oil-rich states with low populations and non-oil-producing states with high populations. For example, the United Arab Emirates per capita gross national product (GNP) is about $17,400 (U.S. dollars); that of the most populated Arab country, Egypt, is only $2,850. This discrepancy is a destabilizing element for the entire region. Iraqi President Saddam Hussein cited economic inequity as a justification for his 1990 invasion of Kuwait:

> The malicious Westerners intentionally multiplied the number of countries with the result that the Arab nation could not achieve the integration needed to realize its full capability. When fragmenting the Arab homeland, they intentionally distanced the majority of the population and areas of cultural depth from riches and their sources.[13]

In an effort to redress some of this economic inequity, Saudi Arabia has donated more than 120 billion dollars in aid to the Other World during the last half-century. This aid has gone to a total of 70 states including 38 in Africa and 25 in Asia. The principal dollar recipients have been friendly, poor Arab states.[14]

The scarcity of water is the most serious impediment to improving agricultural production in the region. In an experiment, the Gulf States and Saudi Arabia have made great strides, at high cost, to start an agricultural industry. There have been calls from some of the poor states to use Arab oil money to make the non-oil-producing states breadbaskets for the region. This pan-Arab agricultural vision for the present is still a dream.

Turkey, with a better supply of water than the Arab states, does have a well-developed agricultural system. The Turks rank among the top 20 nations in the world in the production of wheat, potatoes, barley, olives, tomatoes, sunflower seeds, cotton, tea, and wool. Iran produces wheat and grapes, and Egypt is famous for its high-quality cotton and oranges. Grain products and oranges are also produced in the Levant.

CASE STUDIES
ON MIDDLE EASTERN NATIONALISM

Despite their diversity, the countries of the Middle East underwent similar experiences that shaped their attitudes toward the outside world. All of them felt the humiliation of Western colonialism in one form or another. As was the case elsewhere in the Other World, reaction to the colonial experience served as a spark that ignited the fires of nationalism. Much of the force of Middle Eastern nationalism has centered on a resistance to Western colonialism.

Over the years, the competing nationalism of the Turks, Iranians, Egyptians, and Israelis has resulted in irredentist claims against one another. When one looks at the territorial aspirations of Turks, Kurds, Iranians, Iraqis, Israelis, Palestinians, Jordanians, Egyptians, and Libyans, it becomes obvious that if all of their hopes are to be realized, the people of the Middle East will have to stack countries on top of one another. Reaching a satisfactory solution for these competing nationalistic objectives is one of the great political problems of the twentieth century.

The traditional goal of Middle Eastern nationalism has been to achieve independence. Certainly, here, as elsewhere in the Other World, there is no agreement about what independence means or how it can be realized. The case studies in this chapter demonstrate that Middle Eastern nationalists have used a variety of approaches to achieve their objectives. Some have totally rejected the political and religious institutions of the past, as in Turkey, whereas others have sought independence by returning to what they believe to be the traditions of early Islam, as in Saudi Arabia and Iran. Finally, some nationalists have sought to chart a middle course similar to that of Egypt.

Although included in this discussion, the experience of Israel cannot readily be identified with other nationalism in the region. Israel is a settler state based on Western traditions. The Israeli experiment, however, is interesting because the Zionist form of nationalism is becoming more sectarian and Middle Eastern in its point of view.

In chapter 2, nationalism was described as it has developed in the West. Among the features discussed were exclusivity and suspicion of others. Nationalism also supported the establishment and maintenance of the modern nation-state. We will see from the case studies in this chapter that this process also occurred in the Middle East. Some Middle Eastern nationalism, however, is moving in new directions, making it difficult to categorize in traditional terms. Some nationalistic movements no longer identify with the state boundaries that currently exist. They favor a new unification through supranational units like the Levant or the Maghreb.

Many of the new nationalists view their own governments as illegitimate, and they almost repudiate those goals of their fathers 40 or 50 years ago. At that time, nationalistic efforts were directed at the overthrow of the colonial rule of Britain and France. Some Palestinians, who occasionally refer to opposition to Israel, the United States, and the Arab establishment, have articulated this changed attitude.

They are voicing opposition to Arab governments of both left and right, and they are hoping to use the Palestinian revolution as a catalyst to spread change to all of the states of the Middle East. Recently, this point was forcefully made by the popular dissident Saudi cleric Sheik Hamoud al-Shuaibi. When asked about Arab governments that cooperate with the United States, he replied, "I don't specify any person or group of persons. But everyone who supports America against Islam is an infidel, someone who has strayed from the path of Islam."[15]

Middle Eastern nationalistic sentiments are primarily products of the urban centers. In much of the countryside, people still have loyalties similar to those found in prenationalistic Europe. To these people the first contact with the authority of the state is often a point of contention and not an expression of loyalty. The villagers' contact with the government is limited to paying taxes and watching the state take their village sons away to the army. In many of the rural areas, the values of the central government have little or no legitimacy.

Traditional nationalism has failed to fulfill regional aspirations, so it is being either modified or discarded. In the past, nationalistic goals included political unity and freedom from both colonial and neocolonial domination. Arab nationalism also hoped to establish a classless society, a democratic political system, and an effective challenge to Israel. After years of formal independence, these stated goals remain unfulfilled dreams.

TURKEY

Emerging from the Ottoman defeat of World War I, Turkish nationalism drew on the struggles and writings of the previous 50 years to create a movement based on the unifying aspects of the Turkish language and Turkish identification. This idea succeeded in ways in which the similar Young Turk movement had failed. In the nineteenth century, the Young Turks failed because the multinational character of the old Ottoman Empire rendered the appeal of being Turkish ineffective. Modern Turkish nationalists succeeded because the geographic limits of the new Turkish republic coincided with areas where people identified with being Turkish instead of Ottoman.

The new movement was led by a military hero named Ataturk (Mustafa Kemal). He was determined to break Turkey out of the backwardness of the Ottomans by creating a modern, secular Eastern European republic that could compete on equal terms with any country in the West. At the time, Ataturk's revolution was expected to be as significant as those of his contemporaries: Hitler, Mussolini, and Lenin. Seventy years after the founding of modern Turkey, Ataturk's reforms are not considered as revolutionary as they once were. Since the 1950s, Turkish nationalism has abandoned some of its more controversial themes. For example, Islam is a resurgent force in what was once considered to be a secular state. Nevertheless, as they have done for a half-century, Turkish nationalists still turn away from the Middle East and look toward Europe for their future. We should remember that the central feature of Turkish nationalism has been the rejection of the failed institutions and solutions of the past to create an entirely new system.

Throughout the second half of the twentieth century, Turkish politics continually revolved around heated disputes between competing civilian forces, often interrupted by military takeovers. After the passions of the moment cooled, the military would return to the barracks until the next time. During this period the military even removed Suleyman Demirel, the seven-time prime minister, from office on two occasions.

In domestic affairs, Turkey is a state with a population that is 99 percent Muslim. In practice, it is becoming more religious every day. Since 1997, the army and secular politicians have moved aggressively against militant Islamic movements. Politically active Muslims have been purged from the army and the civil service.

Most Turks still support the move to Westernize the country. They fear fundamentalist movements like those that developed in Iran and Afghanistan. They do not want to see a civil war like the one that is taking place in Algeria. However, they are equally concerned that the government crackdown on Muslim militants could go too far.

In foreign affairs a number of obstacles block the Turkish dream of full membership in the European Union. These international roadblocks include issues involving Cyprus, Kurdistan, and Armenia.

CYPRUS

In 1974, an Athens-supported *coup d'etat* overthrew the multicultural government of Cyprus in an attempt to link the island to Greece. This action provoked a Turkish military intervention. The Turkish victory divided the island between Greek and Turkish Cypriots.

The Turks justify their action by pointing out that the London treaties of 1959 and 1960 allowed Turkish action. The treaties also prohibited Cyprus from joining any other state or group of states without the consent of all the interested parties, including Turkey.[16]

KURDISTAN

Kurdish aspirations for independence pose threats to several states including Turkey, Iran, Iraq, and Syria. In the case of Turkey, there have been low-intensity conflicts with the Kurds taking place for years. Many Turks are fearful that any American attempt to topple the government of Iraq will lead to the establishment of a Kurdish state in northern Iraq. If that event were to occur, that conflict would almost certainly spread to eastern Turkey. However, the Turkish parliament has recently passed a number of measures designed to support the effort to join the European Union. These constitutional reforms include limiting the death penalty and relaxing prohibitions on Kurdish language broadcasts. These reforms are among the requirements that the European Union (EU) has obliged Turkey to meet.[17]

ARMENIA

Although the so-called Armenia massacres occurred 100 years ago, Armenians across Europe and North America are still bitter. They provide a vocal minority opposition to Turkish attempts to join the EU.

TURKISH ECONOMIC REALITIES

The Turkish agricultural and labor sectors are far out of sync with those in Europe. Almost 40 percent of the Turkish population is engaged in agriculture, as opposed to less than 5 percent for Europe as a whole. Turkey exports labor to Europe. Under the free movement of labor policies of the European Community (EC), low-cost Turkish labor could flood the rest of Europe.

As the twenty-first century begins, two opposing nationalists' visions of the future are contending for power in Turkey. Governmental establishment represents one: the residents of the cities and the university-educated elites who support the secular nationalist principles of the republic that Ataturk founded. They defend Westernization, want Turkey to remain a member of North American Treaty Organization (NATO), and work for Turkish admission to the European Community. Others, including Islamic traditionalists and rural conservatives, believe that the country has deserted a rich Middle Eastern heritage. These conservatives support efforts to control the excesses of modern Turkish society. Today Turks are deeply divided over the direction that nationalism should take. Should Turkey continue to push for a place in Europe or should Turks return to their traditional place of leadership in the Middle East and Central Asia?

Clearly, the geopolitical picture in the area has changed with the end of the cold war. Turkey is not as critical to Western interest as it once was. This new situation may also offer a new flexibility and independence to the Turks. Now Turkey has the opportunity to decide whether it will continue to follow the Western path taken by Ataturk or whether it will again turn toward the East. In the East, there is the lure of Iraq and Iran, once major Turkish trading partners. Perhaps more important for the future, there are also 60 million Turkish-speaking Muslims in the former Soviet Union looking to Turkey for leadership.

IRAN

Like the Ottomans, the Persian Empire (Iran) was an Islamic monarchy, except that Shiite Islam was the state religion. Iranian nationalism developed during Anglo-Russian interventions in Persia in the early days of the twentieth century. The history of nationalism in Iran can be divided into three periods: the reign of the Pahlavis, the Mossadeq crisis, and the Islamic Republic.

The first Pahlavi, Reza Shah, was an army officer who seized power in 1921 and had himself crowned king (Shah) in 1925. His rule lasted from 1925 to 1941. Reza Shah believed that a modern state, like Turkey, could be created in Iran. Although many proposed changes emulated those of Ataturk in Turkey, Iran was far less Westernized and change came slowly. Unlike Ataturk and Lenin, who destroyed the old to create a new system, Reza Shah wrapped himself in the traditions of the old Persian monarchy to establish his legitimacy. In the late 1930s, he indicated a sympathy for Adolph Hitler that provoked a Russian-British-American intervention in Iran once World War II began. Reza Shah was deposed, and with the approval of the Western powers, his young son, Mohammed Reza, was placed in power.

Mohammed Reza's reign was uneventful until the Iranian oil crisis of 1951. At that time, a popular nationalist leader, Mohammed Mossadeq, formed a political organization known as the National Front. He gained control of the government and then nationalized the British-owned Anglo-Iranian Oil Company. The Western oil powers responded by boycotting Iranian oil. Deprived of oil revenue by 1953, the Iranian economy was in such bad shape that the Shah used this crisis to attempt to have Mossadeq removed. The Shah's action failed and he was forced into exile in Switzerland. In one of the most interesting periods in modern history, supporters of the Shah were persuaded—it is now believed, with CIA help—to stage a counterrevolt.[18] Mossadeq's allies failed to respond effectively, and the Shah was returned to power within days. The downfall of Mossadeq ended the rule of one of the only truly popular, secular nationalist leaders in modern Iranian history. Returned to power, the Shah ruled in an increasingly arbitrary manner until he was forced into exile in 1979.

When the Ayatollah Khomeini assumed power in Iran, he enjoyed the support of both the secular nationalists abroad and the religious nationalists at home. The Western-educated elites who accompanied him on his return flight from exile in France, carried foreign passports. Khomeini's first cabinet was made up of these secular nationalists. Many of these officials expected to bring liberal democratic rule to Iran. Within three years, all of these officials had disappeared from the political scene. Ayatollah Khomeini built his political base among the poor and the dispossessed who also happened to be the religious conservatives. In this way, he was able to shape the Iranian revolution into a struggle that was both religious and class oriented.

Totally reversing the two millennia of Iranian monarchy, the Islamic Republic of Iran has represented, at the very least, a temporary victory for the religious nationalists over the secular nationalists of the 1950s. The leaders make effective use of the symbols of Shiite Islam to maintain their authority over the Iranian people. According to the rhetoric of the regime, this movement represents an attempt by Shiism to gain the leadership of the Islamic world. The progress of the Islamic revolutionary model developed by Iran is being watched with interest by many states of the Other World.

In 1997, a moderate Shiite cleric was elected president, gaining almost 70 percent of the vote. Although this election victory was confirmed in Mohammad Khatami's reelection four years later, the struggle between reformers and traditionalists continues. The reformers look to a more normal relationship with the outside world. Contacts with Europe, but not the United States, have been increased. However, the United States did remove some trade restrictions on Iran in

March 2000. Conservatives have responded to the attempts at reform by occasional arrests and the banning of reformist newspapers. The conflict between reformers and Islamic conservatives remains unresolved.

In foreign affairs, Iran seemed determined to improve relations with the Persian Gulf States, Russia, and Europe. Iran moved to tone down the rhetoric of exporting their revolution to Saudi Arabia and to the rest of the Gulf. In 1997, Iran hosted an Islamic summit attended by 55 Muslim states. Khatami also signaled his desire to improve relations with Europe by calling for a dialogue of civilizations. Both Europe and Japan responded to this initiative by providing 5 billion dollars in loan guarantees for Iranian development projects.

For its part, the United States became increasingly isolated in the Gulf. The U.S. policy of the dual containment of Iraq and Iran seemed to have failed. Changing conditions in this region indicated that American policymakers needed to reassess the situation.

Perhaps the most difficult issue facing U.S.-Iranian relations was the proposal to build an oil pipeline from Kazakhstan across Iran to the Persian Gulf. To block Iranian interests, U.S. policymakers proposed a more expensive route under the Caspian Sea through the politically unstable lands of the Caucasus region to Turkey. As the Caspian oil rush began, events seemed to overtake U.S. foreign policymakers. Oil companies moved to take advantage of what promised to be the greatest oil discovery since that found in the Persian Gulf. The multinational corporations signaled that they would move to retrieve the oil in Kazakhstan by the most expedient route, which was through Iran. The Caspian states used the U.S.-Iranian conflict to pressure both sides to make concessions. Perhaps economic necessities would force the United States and Iran down the path to eventual reconciliation.

The attack on New York may change the Iranian-U.S. relationship in the future. As Shiites, the Iranian government opposed the Sunni government of the Taliban in Afghanistan. This fact of life resulted in the Iranians providing informal support for some of the actions that were taken by the United States there. They were one of the first countries to send aid to the Afghans once the old regime was driven out. Whether this small opportunity for Iranian-U.S. contact is expanded further remains to be seen.

The real test for the long-term success of the Iranian revolution depends on the ability of the Khatami government to make measurable improvements in the lives of most Iranians. Until now, improvements have remained only promises. Unless some accommodations can be made to improve the living conditions of the average Iranian, the intensity of the Islamic revolution cannot be sustained. Although it is unlikely that Iran will return to the monarchy of the Pahlavis, it is likely that the regime will continue to move to establish the Islamic republic as a major power in the Middle East.

EGYPT

Egyptian nationalism emerged as a reaction to Napoleon's invasion in 1798. The national movement is almost as old as the French Revolution. Experiencing both peaks and valleys during the nineteenth century, nationalists later championed the call to end the British occupation of Egypt that had begun in 1882. In the 1920s, a middle-class anti-British political movement called the Wafd emerged to dominate Egyptian politics until the rise of Nasser in 1952.[19]

Probably no man in the history of the modern Middle East has successfully captured the hearts and minds of Other World peoples of all social classes and political philosophies as did Gamal Abdel Nasser. Espousing a militant nationalism of Arab socialism and social reform at home, Nasser also called for independence from foreign domination, opposition to Israel, and Arab unity abroad. He is best remembered by Middle Easterners for his successful challenges to the policies of the United States and the former colonial powers of Western Europe. It is important to note that Nasser's continuing contribution to Egyptian nationalism is symbolic and transcends specific successes or failures of his policies while he was the country's leader. Following Nasser's death in 1970, Anwar el-Sadat assumed control.

Anwar el-Sadat's 11-year rule over Egypt is extolled in the West as an example of what an enlightened Other World nationalist can accomplish. Sadat expelled the Russians in 1972, fought Israel to a standoff in 1973, and then went to Jerusalem to begin a process that resulted in the 1979 peace agreement with Israel. Sadat's assassination in 1981 is still viewed in the West as a great setback to peace efforts in the region. Surprisingly, Egyptians rarely discuss the tenure of Sadat. In Egypt, he is considered to have frustrated the cause of Arab unity by stressing the separateness of Egypt and peace with Israel over the greater good of the Arab people. Sadat's virtual surrender of the Egyptian economy to Western investment raised new fears of a return to neocolonial status. The danger of an erosion of independence, whether direct or indirect, has become central to the thinking of many Egyptian nationalists who were opposed to Sadat.

President Hosni Mubarak sought to develop a nationalism that steered a middle course between the economic excesses of Sadat and the political adventurism of Nasser. He worked hard to end Egypt's isolation in the Arab world. Expelled after the Camp David agreement, Egypt was restored as a member of the Arab League and the league's headquarters was returned to Cairo. The Egyptians continued to honor the peace agreement with Israel. They reestablished diplomatic relations with Russia and remained a close Arab ally of the United States. The thrust of all of these diplomatic efforts was aimed at establishing Egypt as a bridge between competing states in the region.

At the end of the 1990s, Egyptian foreign policy was directed at convincing Israel that no normalization of life would be possible until both the Palestinian situation and the status of Jerusalem were resolved satisfactorily. At the same time, Mubarak tried to convince the Americans that no peace in the Middle East would occur without forceful leadership from the United States. To successfully pursue these often-contradictory policies, Mubarak had to avoid offending the United States while recognizing that the majority of people in Egypt were anti-Israel.

Perhaps Egypt's most disturbing problem was corruption in the government. When President Mubarak assumed power, he promised that he would put an end to the corruption that had flourished under Anwar Sadat. There was great hope that through his leadership, conditions in Egypt would improve; however, the standard of living for the average Egyptian continued to decline while the number of millionaires increased dramatically. According to the *Guardian* (a London newspaper), much of this wealth, in the midst of massive poverty, came through influence peddling in the Mubarak administration.[20] In his study of urban Egypt, Montasser Kamal states the problem of "influence peddling" this way:

> In this model, relationships are predicated largely on a moral economy of exchange between politicians and bureaucrats on the one side and the area's residents on the other. Votes, permits, jobs, money, and power are all exchanged to aggrandize individuals, minimizing any hope for effective participation by the public in governance.[21]

The unfairness of this discrepancy of wealth encouraged the growth of many Islamic groups dedicated to the goal of cleansing Egyptian society of corruption.

The Mubarak administration countered criticism by pursuing a two-pronged domestic policy. First, it unflinchingly maintained tight control over the political life of the country. The National Democratic Party of Mubarak exercised almost total power. The opposition Muslim Brotherhood remained outlawed, and the press remained tightly censored. Rumors were that the government had imprisoned as many as 17,000 members of the political opposition.[22] Politically, Egypt could be said to be a predemocratic authoritarian state run by the army and the government. Political power remained in the hands of the elites who had always enjoyed it.

Second, the government adopted policies that improved the economic situation over what it was during the early days of Mubarak's tenure. Egyptian inflation declined and the budget was balanced. Both foreign and domestic investments were actively encouraged at a time when the government was selling off the old inefficient industries that had been fixtures of the Arab socialism espoused by Gamal Nasser. The central economic question asked in 2002 was how long could economic progress be maintained if the regime relaxed the political side of the system? As long as economic reforms remained vulnerable to the stability of the tightly controlled political system, a long-term positive future for the Egyptian economy remained problematic.

Of all the states of the Middle East, Egypt is the one that authorities speak of in the most pessimistic terms. Beset by a population explosion that is uncontrollable without using unacceptably draconian measures, no Egyptian government can hope to make significant improvements in the lives of the people in the foreseeable future. The question being asked by all who look at Egypt's problems is: How long will the Egyptian masses wait before turning to more radical solutions to their problems? Because Egypt is the most populous Arab state, the direction that it takes will determine the future of much of the Middle East. Is time for Egypt growing short? Egypt's leaders have many problems and few solutions. The miracle is that Egypt continues to limp on, surviving each gloomy forecast.

SAUDI ARABIAN "BEDO-NATIONALISM"

It is popular to speak of the British royal family as "the family business." Perhaps no better example of a family business exists than that of the House of Saud. Since the alliance between a clan chief, Muhammad ibn Saud, and Muhammad ibn Wahhab in 1744, the House of Saud has played the defining role in Arabian politics. Whether in or out of power, Sauds have always been a force to be reckoned with.

The modern story of Saudi Arabia began in 1901, when the famous leader, Abdul-Aziz Ibn Abdul Rahman Al-Saud (Ibn Saud), rode out of desert exile in Kuwait to capture the fortress of Riyadh. From that base he gradually increased his hold on the Arabian Peninsula until he was able to unite all the major tribes and their territories to create the present state of Saudi Arabia (called The Kingdom) in 1932.

In 1933, Ibn Saud rejected British advice and granted a 60-year petroleum concession to Standard Oil of California. When a great pool of oil was discovered this arrangement became one of the most profitable business deals in history. The oil company first evolved into the Arabian American Oil Company (Aramco) and later, under Saudization, into Saudi Aramco.

Ibn Saud's greatness was in his ability to first win military victories, and then consolidate power by linking his family through marriage and alliances to the other major families in the region. This tribal linkage has remained intact to the present day. Furthermore, he was able, in his international politics, to skillfully balance his role as an Arab leader with that of a world leader.

Incense: A resident of Jedda, Saudi Arabia, demonstrates the proper use of an incense burner. Sandlewood is used as fuel for the burner.

SOURCE: *Joe Weatherby*

Using The Kingdom's vast oil wealth, he and his sons were able to wrench the Arabian people out of the Bedouin system into the modern world. All of this was accomplished without sacrificing the region's traditional values. Saudi Arabia became the world's best example of the premise that a state did not have to be Western to be modern! Because of the leadership from the House of Saud, residents of The Kingdom were able to enjoy the benefits of the modern world while remaining true to the religious and cultural traditions of their Bedouin roots.

At first glance the Saudi government is authoritarian. This is to dismiss the complexity of Arabian politics by substituting Western models of government. Politics in Arabia are true to the traditions of that region. The West separates religion from government and focuses on problem-solving strategies. The Kingdom combines religion and government by placing all issues within an Islamic context. These issues are dealt with on the basis of personal relationships backed by family honor.

Although updated many times in this century, The Kingdom is organized around the complex interaction of powerful tribes and families, often having blood ties to the House of Saud. At each level from district to province, there is room for input offered to local leaders through an unstructured meeting called the majlis. In the bedo-democracy of a majlis, the leader is the first among equals. Appointed governors called amirs repeat this process at provincial levels. The national Majlis al-Sura is composed of 90 members who advise the king. The king rules; he does not reign as they do in the English monarchy.

Because of the linkage of the state with Islam, The Kingdom does not have a constitution in the Western sense. The Koran is the constitution of Saudi Arabia. The state does have a basic law that covers many items found in Western constitutions. These provisions include general rules for the organization of the financial system, the eligibility for succession to king, and the organization of the judiciary. The basic law also provides for a citizen's bill of rights, the protection of private property, and the protection from arbitrary punishment.

September 11 exposed a dark side to the Saudi story. A significant number of the terrorists who bombed the World Trade Center that day were Saudis. When the United States traced the plot back to Saudi Osama bin Laden's organization in Afghanistan, it was found there was more Saudi involvement. The question of why Saudis and others from the wealthy Gulf States would actively participate in terrorism needs an answer.

The Arabian Peninsula has been very religious since the time of Mohammad. In the eighteenth century, the Sauds adapted Wahhabism. The Wahhabi interpretation of Islam is probably the most conservative in the Muslim world. For most of this time, Arabia remained isolated and poor. In this environment it was easy for a ruler to impose a conservative system.

The problem started to occur with the discovery of oil in Arabia. This influx of wealth also brought foreigners and other ideas along with their technical expertise. Saudis welcomed the wealth but not the Western ideas on cultural and political issues. To rationalize the contradiction between Wahhabi religious zealotry and opposition to materialism while at the same time acquiring great wealth was a problem. The House of Saud maintained its power by saying one thing abroad while catering to religious conservatives at home. Domestically, the government tolerated no formal political or religious dissent. They established state-supported mosques everywhere. The clerics were required to remain supportive of government policy. Through this strategy the House of Saud was able to walk a fine line between being supportive of the West abroad while maintaining a certain tolerance for the radical elements of Saudi society at home.

Two events have brought this policy into question. First, the Russian war in Afghanistan mobilized large numbers of Saudis to go and fight there. However, when the veterans returned to their homes, many were commuted to adopting a military solution to solve their social problems.

The second problem occurred as a by-product of the Western intervention in the effort to expel Iraq from Kuwait. When the war was over, the Americans did not go home. The fact that America, Israel's greatest supporter, continues to base large numbers of troops inside Saudi Arabia is a source of great resentment to many Saudis.

Working through religious clerics who remain largely outside the state religious establishment, an underground of radicals emerged. These militants often were wealthy and many were Afghan war veterans. All saw that the oil business had corrupted the purity of Islam. Saudi and Gulf leaders were compromising their principles to deal with the West. Typical of the radical clerics who have inflamed these militants is Sheik Hamoud al-Shuaibi. He directs his criticism against America, Israel, and anyone who supports them. The sheik has been quoted as saying, "It is the duty of every Moslem to stand up with the Afghan people and fight against America."[23]

Because the normal political and media outlets are closed to them, the religious militants have coalesced around "house mosque" clerics like Sheik al-Shuaibi who remain outside the official religious establishment.

Although not yet powerful enough in Saudi Arabia to threaten the survival of the government, these militants can cause social unrest if the government attempts to implement the serious crackdown that America would like to see. Saudi Arabia today has a young, potentially volatile population. Whether the Saudi version of Bedo Nationalism can survive the rise of these Muslim militants remains to be seen.

As Saudi Arabia enters the twenty-first century, The Kingdom faces many other challenges. The birthrate is one of the highest in the Middle East. There are far too many guest workers taking jobs that Saudis should be prepared to occupy. The parallel society established for women in the workforce is both costly and inefficient. The Kingdom must broaden the economic base before the oil revenue declines. Finally, Saudi Arabia's geographical location dictates that The Kingdom must be prepared to play a major role in the Gulf long after their American allies have sailed over the horizon.

THE ARABS

The political scientist Karl Deutsch once said, "A nation is a group of people united by a common dislike of their neighbors and a common misconception about their ethnic origins."[24] If one looks at the spirit of the nation from the perspective of the Arabs, it is clear that Deutsch's observation applies to the Middle East.

Arab nationalism is often characterized as xenophobic, negative in international outlook, and dependent on a historical past that is often more myth than fact. Arabs are suspicious of others because of what they perceive to be more than 200 years of lies and deceit by the colonial powers. Throughout the nineteenth century and well into the twentieth, this pattern repeated itself with cynical regularity. For example, the British promised the Arabs independence during World War I, only to carve up the region into colonial mandates when the war was over. Arab nationalists from Gamal Nasser to Saddam Hussein have seen this event as a treacherous act, ensuring that the Arabs would remain a divided people who could be controlled by outsiders. Many Arab nationalists see American support for the state of Israel as a fresh attempt to divide and dominate the Arab people.

The history that forms the basis of Arab nationalism is characterized by the gap between aspiration and reality. The aspiration is the reestablishment of a single, united Arab nation similar to that which existed during the early days of Mohammed. The reality is that this kind of unity has never existed. Even during its early days, the Islamic state was characterized by civil wars and assassinations. In modern times, the aspiration has been to free the Arab people from foreign domination. The reality has been a reliance on foreign influence, aid, and military support to accomplish Arab political goals. For example, Arab opposition to Israel caused nationalists to embrace almost any outside power that was perceived as being willing to aid in this effort. The reality of this approach has been to mortgage Arab sovereignty to external obligations. Finally, the aspiration that oil can be used to achieve Arab economic independence has clashed with the reality that Arab oil must be sold to the West for hard currency. Instead of unifying the Arabs, wealth generated by oil has divided rich and poor Arabs across the region. Although Arab nationalism is a potent force, it has failed to meet the aspirations of those who seek the rebirth of a great, unified Arab nation.

Business: A young bicyclist carries a load of chairs to be sold in the Cairo market.

SOURCE: *Joe Weatherby*

ISRAEL

Israel may be described as a settler state with a European ideology transplanted into the Middle East. This impression may be less true today than it was in the past. Modern Israel is more conservative, militaristic, sectarian, and Middle Eastern than it once was. With U.S. financial aid more important than ever before, Israel reflects many of the same neocolonial fears and suspicions that are found in other Middle Eastern states.

Founded in Basel, Switzerland, in 1897, modern political Zionism is a form of nationalism that calls for the establishment and maintenance of a Jewish state in Palestine. The return to Palestine is based on Jewish traditions that go back 2,000 years. The specifics of this call have been modified to fit the changing needs of the movement. Today, Zionism generally means that the survival of the State of Israel must be guaranteed as a symbol of refuge for Jews everywhere, whether they choose to immigrate or not.

Over the years, two factions of nationalists emerged to contend for power. The Israeli Labor Alignment represented secular nationalists who were interested in the establishment of a modern state with viable borders. These nationalists included some of the great names of Israeli history, such as David Ben Gurion, Golda Meir, and Abba Eban. They represented the ideas of the European founders of Israel, and their party alignments dominated the policies of Israel from the nation's founding until 1977.

In 1977, the demographic changes in the Israeli population tilted politics in favor of non-European Jews. Continuing Palestinian hostilities and new demographics created conditions that brought a conservative coalition, called the Likud, to power. The Likud represented the second direction taken by the Zionists. Their view argued for the creation of a "Greater Israel" or a "Promised Land" that would include those portions of the Middle East that tradition held were promised by God to the ancient Hebrews. In recent years, non-European Jews had experienced Arab domination; they also tended to support Likud's hard-line policies toward the Arabs.

At the beginning of a new century, Israeli nationalism is in a state of transition. No one can predict with certainty the final direction that the movement will take. On the one hand, Israel can pursue the maximalist Likud goal of recovering and then holding all of "the land of Israel." To the outsider this course seems to be not only impractical but also sure to doom the state to entering into an endless cycle of debilitating wars with the Arabs, followed by costly occupations. To many, this is a process in which Israel cannot hope to prevail.

The other nationalist approach is accommodation with Israel's neighbors. This choice is also dangerous and difficult. It involves making painful concessions on issues that are of primary concern to most Israelis. This course is made all the more difficult because it means that Israel will have to give up the most when exchanging "land for peace." It is analogous to sacrificing several chess pawns in order to win the game. Here, winning for Israel is survival as a Jewish state with secure borders and peaceful neighbors. There are indications that some Israelis are willing to give peace a chance. In 1999, elections resulted in a landslide victory for the Labor Party and Ehud Barak. A decorated general, Barak ran on a program of reaching a final peace settlement with the Arabs. This meant the abandonment of some deeply held territorial goals by some nationalists. Barak's peace efforts were overtaken and discredited when the Palestinians flatly rejected them. It is now known that his plan had offered Palestinian statehood, a return of most of the West Bank and Gaza, plus a foothold of some kind in Jerusalem. As a price for this, Palestinians would have had to give up all disputed claims in Israel and agree to a permanent peace.

To the outsider, this plan had possibilities. Israel had won on the battlefield what the Palestinians wanted returned politically. The Palestinians could never militarily conquer Israel, but they could continue a low-intensity conflict indefinitely. The logic was Israel would have to give up the most because Israel had acquired the most. When the Palestinians rejected the plan at the last minute, the Barak government lost credibility with the majority of people in Israel.

The opposition leader General Ariel Sharon was quick to take advantage of the situation. In September 2000, he took several hundred Likud supporters, soldiers, and police to the Temple Mount to demonstrate Israeli sovereignty over the area that is considered to be Islam's third holiest spot. This provoked a Palestinian riot which was suppressed by the Israeli Army. The Second Intifada became a war of increasing ferocity of strike and counterstrike that was still unresolved over a year and a half after the conflict had begun.

If it was his strategy to provoke a conflict, and no one will ever know that, Sharon used the Israeli reaction to the violence to carry him to an early election as prime minister. For the politician who had been forced to resign his office because of the Palestinian massacres in Lebanon at the Sabra and Shatila refugee camps during the 1980s, his election victory was a stunning comeback.

Since his election, Sharon has publicly repudiated all of the previous agreements with the Palestinians going back to Oslo in the early 1990s. For their part, the Palestinian's demand that negotiations must begin where they left off when they rejected Barak's terms.

Both sides are more militant and polarized than they have been for many years. At this point there is little room for any optimism that a real peace can be reached between Israel and the Palestinians in the near future.

LOOKING AHEAD

Trust everybody, but cut the cards.
FINLEY PETER DUNNE

As will be seen in the Flashpoints, many of the region's conflicts are indigenous and based on long-standing cultural and geographic factors. On the surface, each of these issues should stand alone. In the Middle East, however, the Arab-Israeli conflict dominates the politics of the region, and the failure of the parties to re-solve this dispute has affected most of the other conflicts. The perception is left that the settlement of the Arab-Israeli problem is a precondition to the resolution of other important issues in the region.

What are the prospects for peace? Without a solution to the Arab-Israeli dis-pute, the old adage that "the more things change, the more they will remain the same" will continue to be true. Two scenarios illustrate the difficulty in attempt-ing to forecast the future for any political issue in the Middle East.

THE PESSIMISTIC SCENARIO

It is not the big armies that win battles; it is the good ones.
MAURICE DE SAXE, MARSHAL-GENERAL OF FRANCE

Without a settlement to the Arab-Israeli dispute, those parties on both sides who prefer the status quo to peace can be expected to continue their present policies. The status quo benefits those Israeli factions who believe that any settlement will force Israel to make concessions in territory. Palestinians are fearful that the Arab states might be willing to sacrifice the Palestinian nation to regain territory previ-ously lost to Israel. Many Arab leaders continue to use their dispute with Israel as an excuse to prepare for war abroad and to avoid reform at home.

If the deadlock continues, Arabs will accelerate the arms race to achieve qual-itative military parity with the Israelis. This military development will be achieved at the expense of funds that could be made available for social develop-ment. The likely result of this scenario will be the continuation of Arab regimes that are volatile and unstable.

If the Israeli leadership continues to encourage more Jewish settlement in the West Bank and Gaza, the Arabs will resist it with any means available. The contin-uation of the status quo means that bloodshed will continue on both sides. Because of the destructive capability of modern weaponry, there is always a chance that one of these sharp conflicts will escalate into a major war.

THE OPTIMISTIC SCENARIO

God willing, there will be peace.
A PALESTINIAN EXPRESSION

The 1991 Persian Gulf War involved hundreds of thousands of American soldiers. In this conflict, the Arab-Israeli dispute was a secondary but important aspect. As Iraqi rockets slammed into Israeli cities, it became obvious to all that the issues in the Middle East were interrelated. This event shattered the complacency of those in America who had wished to avoid direct involvement in the affairs of the Middle East. Badly frightened at the prospect of a new Vietnam, many Americans became active in attempts to eliminate the conditions that could lead to a new American military involvement in the region. The result was that the United States applied pressure on all of the parties involved to force them to negotiate.

The end of the cold war also freed the hands of those leaders in the West who had used the policy of containing communism as a test for dealing with the governments in the Middle East. For the first time, there was agreement that it was in the interest of Russia, the United States, and the other Western powers to encourage a settlement between Arabs and Israelis. The major powers combined with a majority of other states in the world to encourage the parties of the region to talk seriously about peace. This new atmosphere made it possible for people living in the Middle East to hope for a period of peace and stability. Although Palestinians and Israelis came close but failed to achieve peace in 2000, there may still be some hope. Both the Israelis and Palestinians have nowhere to go. The Second Intifada has no plan B. Eventually the issues dividing the parties will have to be resolved if either party is to survive in peace.

✸ FLASHPOINTS ✸

PALESTINE

At the beginning of the twenty-first century, a twentieth-century problem is still the central feature of Middle Eastern politics. This dispute is between Jews and Arabs over the control of Palestine. Since 1948, the Palestinian focus has been on opposition to the State of Israel. At the same time, Israeli Jews have consistently opposed the creation of a Palestinian state. The result has been a series of Arab-Israeli wars fought in 1948, 1956, 1967, 1973, and 1982. In addition, there have been a number of continuing low-intensity conflicts that are characterized by the cycle of attack and retaliation. Israelis call Palestinian bombers and hijackers "terrorists," Palestinians call the attacks by the Israeli military and settler shootings and bombings acts of "state terrorism."

Before discussing the specifics of the dispute, several assumptions need to be made. First, the leaders on both sides have raised their demands to the heights of irreducible principles. This has had the effect of painting both parties into ideological corners that ensure that peace is impossible without ideological surrender of the other side.

Second, the ongoing conflict has resulted in both sides suffering grievous injuries at the hands of their opponents. Peace requires a new way of thinking where these past injustices are forgiven if not forgotten.

Third, because Israel has been victorious in every war, all of Palestine has fallen to the Jewish state. Israel still controls most of the land. Thus far, Israel has not been prepared to take the draconian step of expelling the millions of Palestinians who live there. Peace will require that Israel give up the most to end the conflict.

Fourth, Israel can win the military battles, but without peace, Israel is in danger of losing the demographic war with the Palestinians. The doomsday scenario is an Israeli evolution into a new South Africa, with a Jewish minority attempting to maintain political control over a majority Palestinian population. Without peace and stability, few Jews on the outside can be expected to move to Israel. The failure to attract American and European Jews to live in Israel could be a demographic time bomb for Israel.

Finally, it will take cooperation between Palestinians and Israelis for either of the two cultures to prosper. Without continued outside aid, neither entity can succeed on its own.

For a year and a half, the low-intensity conflict called the Second Intifada has raged between Palestinians and Israelis. The result has been a triumph for the extremists in both Israel and Palestine. The people who nearly reached an agreement between the two sides in 2000 are no longer heard over the noise of suicide bombers and helicopter gun ships. The losses suffered by both sides in this latest conflict make it difficult for any leader to offer concessions to the other side.

Nevertheless, there is no place for Palestinians and Israelis to go. When the Second Intifada eventually grinds to a halt, the same issues that confronted the peacemakers in 2000 will remain to be resolved. The first of these issues will be land. How much will be returned to the Palestinians and how much needs to be retained for Israel's military security? A complicating factor is the numerous Israeli settlements that are now part of the Palestinian landscape. The basic elements of the land in dispute are seen in Figure 8.2.

The second issue is water. There is not enough water for everyone. The desert is worthless without water. At present, the Israelis take most of the water for their own use, starving many of those Palestinian farmers who remain in the West Bank.

The third issue is refugees. Almost half a million Palestinians either fled or were forced from their homes in 1948. In every war since that time more Palestinians have gone into exile. Their future status was one of the deal breakers in the 2000 negotiations. It is unreasonable to expect Israel to absorb the millions of Palestinians whose families once lived in what is now Israel. However, to obtain peace, a form of compensation that is fair to those who lost their homes and businesses must be found.

The fourth issue involves the repatriation of Palestinians in Israeli jails. This is an explosive issue that is in part driving the Second Intifada. To the Israelis, many of these people are terrorists. To the Palestinians, the prisoners are freedom fighters working to free their homeland. This issue can be resolved. A prisoner release program has been successful in Northland Ireland and it can be in the Middle East.

Fifth is the issue of Jerusalem. Here religion has become mixed with nationalism by both sides. This makes retreat from the stated demands of Israelis and Palestinians almost impossible. The issue is complicated by the size of the area that is the subject of most of the dispute, the Old City. The

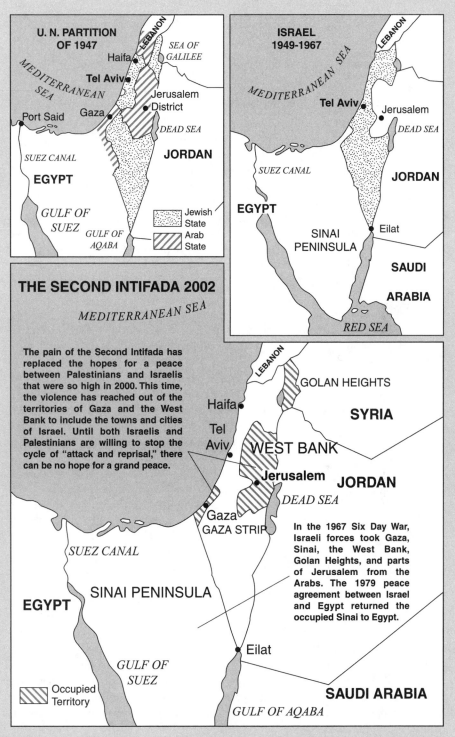

FIGURE 8.2 The Changing Boundaries of Israel: The boundaries of Israel have changed as a result of wars fought with Arab neighbors in 1948, 1956, 1967, 1973, and 1982.

walled portion of the Old City is approximately 1,000 by 1,500 meters. Christian, Jewish, and Muslim holy places are literally stacked one on top of the other. No Palestinian or Israeli leader can negotiate away claims to the Old City. For peace to occur, a way must be found to provide for a Palestinian presence, if only symbolically, in the Old City.

Finally, the creation of a Palestinian state must eventually occur. At present, the terrorists nominally under Palestinian control are so "Balkanized" that a viable state would be impossible. Some solution to the statehood aspirations of the Palestinians must be reached if peace is to be achieved.

The negotiations held in 2000 made a great deal of progress toward a comprehensive peace. It is easy for outsiders to see what needs to be done to achieve a final settlement. However, it will require new thinking by Palestinians and Israelis if the parties are to escape the endless cycle of violence.

THE PALESTINIANS

The Palestinians are an ancient people who trace their origins to the Philistines in the Bible. After the Arab conquest, their sense of national consciousness remained dormant until World War I, when they began again to speak of a Palestinian people. During the negotiations that preceded the creation of the state of Israel, serious proposals were also made in the United Nations (UN) for the creation of a Palestinian state. The Arab side rejected the UN proposal. Unfortunately, any further hope for the establishment of a state that would parallel the one created in Israel was lost with the Arab defeat in the 1948 war. Since that time, all the parties to the Arab-Israeli dispute attempted to manipulate the aspirations of the Palestinians. The Palestinian Liberation Organization (PLO) claimed to represent the interests of the Palestinian people. When the leadership of the PLO agreed to an autonomy agreement, they took a chance that measurable results could be achieved before the opposition to a limited agreement could grow. Many Palestinians, especially those exiled abroad, believed that the current agreement would never lead to Palestinian sovereignty. Furthermore, they charged that limited autonomy permanently surrendered the lands taken from the Palestinian people in 1948. The slow pace of events since the signing of the accord has strengthened the opposition to a settlement with Israel.

The decline of PLO fortunes after 1993 resulted in the corresponding rise of the Islamic fundamentalist organization Hamas. Unlike the PLO, Hamas was opposed to any peace talks with Israel. By active participation in the Intifada, Hamas earned the respect of many Palestinians. Hamas was a "home grown" organization rising out of the occupied territories. Unlike the PLO, Hamas leaders were not intellectuals imported from the Palestinians living abroad. Furthermore, the Hamas opposition to Israel was clear and uncompromising. To a people forced to live under Israeli military occupation for over a quarter of a century, this hard line struck a responsive chord. Facing Hamas, moderate Palestinians were placed in a no-win position. When they moved to compromise with the Israelis and the West, they weakened their position with the Palestinians they claimed to represent. To the chagrin of both the PLO and the Israeli authorities, Hamas has been raised to the status of a major player in Palestinian politics.

It is well known that serious talks came agonizingly close to a peace in 2000. It is also known that the distrust resulting from failure of the peace talks resulted in the Second Intifada. Since that time the militants on both sides have increased their influence. In the case of the Palestinians, the PLO leadership has become increasingly marginalized by the Israeli military attacks on its infrastructure. To Palestinians, the only ones fighting against the Israeli occupation are the militants in Hamas and elsewhere. They have grown in influence to the point that the more moderate Palestinians risk a civil war if they attempt to crack down too hard. Many see these alternatives to the PLO and Yasir Arafat as much worse than what currently exists. A solution to the problem of a lack of effective Palestinian leadership is nowhere in sight.

For their part, the Palestinians have endured a political and social tragedy that colors their politics. They fear that a grand peace may be negotiated by the great powers at their expense. By their often violent actions, the Palestinians ensure that their cause will not be ignored. The result is a Palestinian problem that is influencing issues everywhere in the Middle East.

THE FIRST AND SECOND INTIFADAS

As a result of victory in the 1967 war, Israel gained control of the West Bank and Gaza. Thus, Israel also became responsible for the administration of more than 1.7 million Palestinians. Israeli policy has encouraged Jewish settlement in these territories, which it calls Judea, Samaria, and Gaza, by using the military to control the opposition of the Palestinian majority. The Intifadas represent the emergence of an active Palestinian opposition to the continuation of Israeli military rule.

Begun in 1987, the First Intifada (uprising) was a major change in the Palestinian movement, which before then had been controlled and represented by leaders living in exile. Palestinians in the occupied territories had tended to identify with the politics of Jordan. The early leaders of the Intifada were young, militant, and determined to end Israeli rule in the West Bank and Gaza. This uprising shifted Western attention away from the demands of the Palestinians in exile to focus on the necessity of reaching a settlement with those Palestinians who were living under Israeli occupation. The mass appeal of the Intifada undermined the traditional Palestinian leaders in exile by forcing thousands of people to make a visible commitment to the new, local leadership.

Although the violent images of Jews and Arabs confronting each other in the streets of the West Bank and Gaza dominated television screens around the world, another story emerged from the Intifada. The vast majority of the Palestinians living in the territories were mobilized into a mass movement in resistance to Israeli military rule. The ability of the Palestinians to sustain this effort over an extended period of time forced all parties to take their interests seriously.

After the 1993 agreement was signed with Israel, the Intifada moved into a stage of passive resistance to Israeli rule. By 1998, the autonomy agreement had failed to bring about the promised Israeli withdrawal. While all sides argued over a modest American plan to secure a limited Israeli withdrawal, Israel continued to maintain complete authority over one-third of Gaza and almost 60 percent of the West Bank. In the face of such little progress, Palestinian leader Yasir Arafat renewed his call for statehood. The Israeli Prime Minister responded by warning that any unilateral declaration of Palestinian statehood would end chances for peace. A postponement of the announcement of a Palestinian state combined with a Labor victory in the Israeli elections of 1999 led to the new peace talks that ultimately failed in 2000.

The Second Intifada emerged out of the wreckage of the failed peace talks. Although Sharon's visit to the Jerusalem Temple Mount may have provoked the Second Intifada, any inflammatory event could have started the conflict. A year and a half of fighting later has made the peace proposals victims. Both sides have become more polarized than ever.

To Palestinians, the new Prime Minister, Ariel Sharon, had instigated the conflict. Then, when he repudiated almost 10 years of agreements and indicated that he would not negotiate on the basis of the year 2000 proposals, they saw no incentive to halt the struggle against Israeli occupation.

To Israelis, the renewed bombings demonstrated that the Palestinians had never been interested in peace. For some Sharon supporters, the more radicalized that the Palestinians became, the less need for negotiations. To this end they supported marginalization of the PLO in Palestinian affairs. For the better part of a year the Israeli military targeted Palestinian militants for assassination. When an Israeli cabinet minister was assassinated, the military response was harsh, including the bombing of Palestinian sites by military aircraft, followed by the blockading of Yasir Arafat in his headquarters in the West Bank. His movement in the Palestinian territories was prohibited.

The Bush administration's reactions to the Second Intifada have been less activist than those of his predecessor. Although both President Bush and the Secretary of State have stated that they hope to see the eventual establishment of a Palestinian state, they seem to believe that the time is not right for a "grand peace." Instead, they have advocated a series of incremental steps called the Mitchell Plan.

The Mitchell Plan, proposed by an American select committee headed by former Senator Mitchell, sets out steps that the two sides can take to stop the violence and restore trust in each other.

The Plan calls for the Israelis to pull back to pre-Intifada positions. For their part, the Palestinians must resume their cooperation with Israel to keep the peace. Furthermore, the plan calls for both sides to accept and implement the other agreements made by the parties.

Israel is required by the Plan to halt the building and expansion of Jewish settlements in the West Bank and Gaza. The report also calls on the Israeli military to cease using disproportionate force against the Palestinians.

The Americans believe that the Mitchell Plan offers the parties the best way to save face while backing away from the Second Intifada.

Unfortunately, the conflict on the ground has escalated rather than decreased in violence. Neither Sharon nor Arafat seems to be willing or able to end the violence. Until one side or both become tired of the status quo there seems little interest in actually implementing the Mitchell Plan.

ARMENIA

The Armenians trace their history to the period preceding the fourth century B.C. invasion of Anatolia by Alexander the Great. Armenia is believed to be the oldest Christian state. Since the time of the Romans, it has existed, like Afghanistan and Poland, as a small buffer state surrounded by powerful neighbors. Time after time, Armenians have suffered massacre, partition, and loss of independence. The most recent deprivation occurred during World War I, when it is said that the Ottomans massacred more than a half-million Armenians on the pretext that they had sided with the Russians during the war. In the aftermath of World War I, an independent Armenia made up of portions of eastern Turkey and western Russia was proposed by the League of Nations. The revolution in Russia and the independence of Turkey caused this proposal to be stillborn. Today, only an Armenian republic located in the former Soviet Union remains to remind Armenians of a glorious past.

For over 70 years the former Soviet Union maintained tight control over the national aspirations of its people. The collapse of Soviet centralized power, however, has revived a spirit of nationalism in the region. The 1988 dispute between Armenia and Azerbaijan over the status of Armenians living in the enclave of Nagorno-Karabakh has been difficult to resolve. In September 1991, Armenian nationalists made the situation worse by attempting to proclaim an independent republic in the enclave. If some of the Armenian nationalists living abroad are to be believed, a resurgent Armenia may also attempt to reassert its old claim to parts of eastern Turkey. Any aspiration to a return to Anatolia is certain to cause unrest in Turkey.

THE SIX MUSLIM STATES OF CENTRAL ASIA

The end of the Soviet Union resulted in the emergence of six Muslim states. The newly independent states of Azerbaijan, Turkmenistan, Kazakhstan, Uzbekistan, Kyrgyzstan, and Tajikistan have a combined population of 50 million Muslims. Unlike Slavic Russia, which has cultural connections with Europe, the states surrounding the Caspian and Aral seas can be expected to look to the Muslim south and west for leadership.

This new development has the potential to reshape the political balance of power in the Middle East. Both the northern tier states of Turkey and Iran have moved aggressively into the vacuum left by the collapse of Soviet power, and Turkey has granted recognition to all six republics. Since most of these new states are Turkic-speaking, the Turks have a cultural advantage. Turkey is also a good potential outlet for trade with the six republics because of its close ties with Europe.

Iran has been successful in penetrating parts of the region. Iranian Azerbaijan is separated from former Soviet Azerbaijan by an artificial boundary established in 1813 after a war between the two states. The disadvantage of the Iranian thrust is that Shiism is practiced widely only in Azerbaijan, whereas the other five republics are staunchly Sunni.

Complicating an already confusing environment was the discovery of massive oil reserves in the Caspian region. Experts estimated that the central Asian discovery could be the third largest reserve of petroleum in the world behind the Persian Gulf and Siberia.[25]

The oil rush presented problems for the great powers similar to those played in the "great power game" of the nineteenth century. The Western powers suddenly became interested in these new Muslim states because they possessed something of value.

The major problems centered on getting central Asian petroleum to the West and Japan. Most experts supported building a pipeline from the Caspian region through Iran to the Persian Gulf because it was the most cost-effective route. This plan directly conflicted with the long-term U.S. effort to isolate Iran. The United States proposed a more expensive alternative pipeline, which would run under the Caspian Sea across Azerbaijan to Turkey. Iran and other Caspian states opposed the Turkish pipeline proposal as presenting serious environmental dangers to the region. The United States continued to obstruct the Iranian solution in the face of European moves to implement that plan. One fact remained certain; the discovery of oil had dramatically changed prospects for the new Muslim states of Central Asia.

Finally, the United States intervention into Afghanistan has thrust these Central Asian states into the political spotlight. As America actively courted their support for the war against terrorism, their political importance started to rival their economic potential.

KURDISTAN

Living on the borders of eastern Turkey, western Iran, northern Iraq, and Soviet Armenia, the Kurds present a significant problem in the northern tier. Although they number over 20 million, the Kurds have been unsuccessful in their attempts to create the independent state of Kurdistan. The states with large Kurdish populations, Turkey, Iran, and Iraq, will never agree to the creation of a Kurdish state out of their territories. Moreover, the Kurds have been used by these states as pawns in their own conflicts. For example, during the 1970s, anti-Iraqi Kurds were armed and financed by the Shah of Iran to further Iran's ambitions against Iraq. Still earlier, the Russians had supported Kurdish revolts in Iran to cause trouble for the Shah. During recent years, there have been low-intensity conflicts between Kurds and the authorities in Turkey, Iran, and Iraq. In 1998, the Associated Press reported that Turkey deployed troops in the region after charging Syria with aiding anti-Turkish Kurdish forces.[26]

For the Kurdish dream of independence to be realized, the new state would have to encompass large portions of Syria, Iran, Iraq, and Turkey. Under these conditions, the creation of Kurdistan would destabilize the northern tier. All of the existing powers in the region had opposed the creation of an independent Kurdistan.

In the unrest following the Iraqi defeat in the 1991 Persian Gulf War, Kurds failed in an attempt to break away from the government in Baghdad. Only Western military intervention prevented the Iraqi army from destroying much of the Kurdish population. Since that time, Kurdish leaders have reduced their goals and now envision the eventual creation of an autonomous Kurdish region in northern Iraq. For the moment, it is in the Western interest to keep the Kurdish region alive as a way of putting pressure on Iraq. When the Western dispute with Iraq is resolved, the Kurds are likely to be abandoned again.

THE IRAQI DISPUTES

IRAN

If it is true, as the old saying goes, that "the bones of the Middle East were buried by the dogs of British imperialism," the Iraq-Iran dispute is a case in point. The British that favored the Ottomans over the Persians created the border as the result of a nineteenth-century mediation. The object of this effort was to keep Russia out of the Persian Gulf by giving control of the Shatt-al-Arab River to the British-backed Ottomans. Although the Persians objected to the location of the border on the east bank of the river instead of the usually accepted main channel, it was not until 1975 that Iraq, the Ottoman's successor, agreed to use the navigable channel as the border. In return, the Shah of Iran agreed to stop aiding the Kurdish rebellion against Iraq. After the Shah's demise, Iraq unsuccessfully attempted to restore the old border by invading Iran in 1980. The result was one of the more terrible wars in modern history. When the fighting ended, the battle lines were in approximately the same location as the prewar border. To free troops for service in Kuwait in 1990, the Iraqi authorities conceded all of their major war gains to Iran.

KUWAIT

On August 2, 1990, the Iraqi army invaded Kuwait. This was the latest in a series of disputes between Kuwait and Iraq going back for more than a half-century. These disputes were raised by Iraq as challenges to the historical legitimacy of Kuwait.

Kuwait's history can be traced to the eighteenth century, when the Al-Sabah family gained control. This dynasty has remained in power since that time. During the nineteenth century both the Ottomans and the British attempted to influence the Al-Sabahs. The Iraqi claims rest on the argument that the Al-Sabahs recognized that Kuwait was part of the Ottoman Empire because it was nominally administered from the Iraqi city of Basra. The Iraqis argue that all of the Ottoman Empire that was administered from Basra should be part of Iraq. To them only British intervention during the early years of this century deprived Iraq of Kuwait.[27] During the twentieth century, Kuwait was administered as an independent state under British protection; however, during this period both Saudi Arabia and Iraq claimed parts of its territory.

Although grounded in history, the latest dispute between Iraq and Kuwait was over oil. Because Kuwait controlled the third-largest reserves of crude oil in the world, it was able to influence the world price. The Iraqis charged that Kuwait violated agreements and dumped oil on the world market to harm Iraq. Iraq also disputed the Kuwaiti claims to an oil field on the border of the two countries. Finally, Iraq charged that Kuwait had failed to share its oil wealth with the poor Arab states.[28]

This dispute was complicated by the demographics of Kuwait. With the discovery of oil came thousands of foreign workers. Although denied full citizenship, these workers often prospered, and by August 1990, there were more foreign workers in Kuwait than Kuwaitis. Many of these workers were employed by the state even though they were treated as second-class citizens. The 1990 invasion was welcomed by many of these "guest" workers because Iraq had promised that they would be given full citizenship by the new government.

The allied coalition forces routed the Iraqi army during the 1991 liberation of Kuwait. This victory invalidated most Iraqi claims. In the aftermath of the war, Kuwaiti authorities expelled large numbers of foreign workers. By using these harsh methods, the authorities attempted to reduce the danger that guest workers might again threaten the stability of the regime.[29]

After years of UN-imposed economic sanctions, restrictions on oil sales, and international scrutiny of their every move, the Iraqi authorities remained defiant. They disputed the UN-imposed border settlement, they attempted to frustrate the work of the UN teams sent to destroy the Iraqi weapons of mass destruction, and they reasserted the Iraqi claim to Kuwait. Although these actions provoked occasional military responses, the Iraqi authorities gambled that their sustained pressure on the coalition would eventually force the UN forces to end their sanctions and withdraw from the Persian Gulf region.

Kuwait is a very rich, small nation located in a region noted for poverty. Arab nationalists charge that it has been used as an outpost of Western imperialism. Appealing to the poor of the Middle East, the Iraqis charge that the oil wealth of the Persian Gulf has been stolen from the Arab nations by Kuwait. To many, the massive military response mounted by the United States against the Iraqi invasion confirms the charge that Kuwait is still a colony of the West.

STRATEGIC WATERWAYS AND OIL PIPELINES

THE TURKISH STRAITS

The Dardanelles and Bosporus are narrow straits, 1–4 miles wide, that dominate the Russian-controlled Black Sea. The straits have been a point of conflict between Russia and Turkey for centuries. The continued Turkish control of the Dardanelles and Bosporus is a source of irritation because it has frustrated repeated Russian attempts to gain easy access to the Mediterranean Sea. At present, Russian access to this area is governed by treaty. Should the Turks again attempt to block access, they will provoke a major international conflict.

THE SUEZ CANAL

Opened in 1869, the canal, including the Great Bitter Lake and Lake Timsah, is 101 miles long. It serves as the only direct sea passage from the Mediterranean to the Indian Ocean. Much of the history of the modern Middle East has involved struggles for the control of this strategic waterway. Although the canal is at sea level, requiring no complicated, easily sabotaged system of locks, its location near unstable, hostile neighbors makes its access uncertain at times. For example, in the summer of 1984, an unknown terrorist organization was able to mine parts of the canal and the Red Sea to prevent ships from using the waterway. Because of its importance to Europe, threats to close the Suez Canal always raise the possibility of conflict.

THE PERSIAN (OR ARAB) GULF

The question over name implies a more serious conflict over control of the single most important waterway in the world. It is through the Persian Gulf (Arab Gulf) that two-thirds of the world's oil is exported. The conflict between Kuwait and Iraq raises the possibility of seizure of the Strait of Hormuz by an unfriendly power bent on shutting off oil shipments to the West. Because the United States is committed to keeping the oil flowing from the Gulf, any closure will immediately provoke a great-power intervention, with all of its dangers.

OIL PIPELINES

One of the major problems associated with Middle Eastern oil is getting the product to the consumer. Pipelines are an efficient alternative to ships for the movement of petroleum products from the Persian Gulf and Saudi Arabia to Europe. For many years some pipelines have connected Saudi Arabia with Lebanon and Israel, and others have linked Iraq with the Mediterranean through both Syria and Turkey. The chief problem of relying on pipelines is their vulnerability to sabotage during periods of political instability that often occur in the lands they must cross. For example, the pipeline through Israel has been closed since 1948, and the pipeline from Iraq to the Mediterranean was closed by Syria for the duration of the Iran-Iraq war. Until the political situation in the Middle East changes, the potential of moving oil by pipeline remains an unfulfilled dream.

CYPRUS

Although Greeks outnumber the Turks on Cyprus, mainland Greeks have not formally controlled the island in modern history. From 1571 until 1878, the Ottomans ruled Cyprus as part of their empire. Power then shifted to the British, who stayed until independence was granted in 1960. Attempts were made to establish a Cypriot government that would guarantee a balance of power between Greeks and Turks on the island. This effort finally failed when Greek Cypriot nationalists attempted to move Cyprus into an association with Greece against the will of the Turkish minority. This move provoked the Turkish army's intervention and resulted in a forcible partition of the island in 1974.

During the intervention, 180,000 Greeks fled south and 80,000 Turks fled north. These mass population exchanges caused much bitterness. Since then an additional 60,000 mainland Turks have been resettled in the north by the Turkish government. The island is currently home to 600,000 Greeks and 200,000 Turks. A "green line" patrolled by 1,200 UN peacekeepers separates these two groups.

OPEC AND THE POLITICS OF OIL

In 1901, a Western adventurer, William D'Arcy, received a concession to explore for oil in Iran. At almost the same time, an Armenian, C. S. Gulbenkian, obtained a similar concession in the Ottoman Empire. Less than 50 years later, these concessions had grown into a vast oil cartel controlled by seven Western companies: Exxon, Mobil, Standard Oil of California, Texaco, Gulf, British Petroleum, and Shell. Called the Seven Sisters, these companies gained a virtual monopoly on the production, refinement, and distribution of Middle Eastern oil.

Designed to present a united front when negotiating prices with the oil companies, the Organization of Petroleum Exporting Countries (OPEC) was organized in 1960 by Iraq, Saudi Arabia, Iran, Kuwait, and Venezuela. Subsequently, OPEC membership grew to include Qatar, Libya, Indonesia, Algeria, Nigeria, Ecuador, Gabon, and the United Arab Emirates.

The OPEC cartel was only marginally effective until the October 1973 Middle East war. At that time, the sale of petroleum products was linked by the Arab members of OPEC to the support for their cause against Israel. The selective withholding of oil caused an energy crisis in the West. During the next decade, OPEC oil rose from a pre-1973 price of around $3 a barrel to over $30 a barrel. This oil shock was difficult for the developed world, but it destroyed the hopes for many Other World states that were depending on low-cost energy to finance development. Ignoring 50 years of Western oil cartel exploitation, newspapers in Europe and the United States were filled with articles editorializing on the "evils" of OPEC. Today, more than 20 years after the first oil crisis in the 1970s, Western observers admit that although the economic impact of OPEC has been considerable, it is a political force in the Other World far out of proportion to its size.

In the mid-1980s, OPEC control of the petroleum market loosened. Some members failed to adhere to the cartel's price and production guidelines. The lack of discipline has combined with non-OPEC production increases and Western conservation measures first to stabilize and then to lower dramatically the world price of oil. As the price fell, states desperate to finance the high cost of development became suspicious of other states that exceeded their production quotas. The Iraqi charge that Kuwait cheated on oil production was one of the main reasons for the August 1990 invasion.

In the late 1990s, the oil industry was in disarray. New discoveries in Central Asia, the threat of the removal of sanctions on Iraqi oil exports, and

Black Gold: An oil well display in front of Saudi Aramco headquarters in Dhahran, Saudi Arabia.

SOURCE: *Joe Weatherby*

the dumping of oil products by OPEC members dropped the world price of oil by almost half. The problem for oil producers in the Middle East was to prevent the price of crude from falling further.

The market for oil is in the developed world. As in the days of colonialism, the developed countries will aggressively work to protect such essential resources. Political instability in the Middle East has forced the developed nations to seek alternative sources of energy. With the end of the cold war, there are interesting possibilities for importing oil from Russia. In the short term, there may be more difficulties in utilizing Russian oil sources than possibilities, but vast oil reserves exist in Siberia and the Russians will have to sell a portion on the open market if they have any hope of financing their economic development. If this possibility becomes a reality, it will have serious implications for every state in the region. Like Haiti with sugar and Brazil with rubber, Middle Eastern oil could become just another surplus commodity that is a victim of production elsewhere.[30]

THE ALGERIAN DISPUTE

The rise of Islamic fundamentalism in Algeria has attracted the attention of the West. The problem originated when the secular nationalists, who had ruled Algeria since independence, prevented an Islamic party that appeared to have come to power after the 1992 elections from taking office. Although they had sought power democratically, the Islamic party's slogan had claimed that Muslims voting against them were voting against God. The secular nationalists charged that this kind of campaigning was unfair and justified cancellation of the election results, which provoked an unofficial civil war between the Muslim parties and the secular nationalists. This conflict has killed more than 75,000 people since 1992.

Why have the democratic powers, including the United States and the members of NATO, remained passive in the face of this antidemocratic action taken by the Algerian authorities? This ambivalence is compounded by a similar failure in dealing with the authoritarian rulers in Kuwait, Saudi Arabia, and Egypt. The answer is clear: Western leaders fear that a militant Islamic victory in Algeria can destabilize the friends of the West, not only in Algeria, but also in Morocco, Tunisia, and Egypt. They fear that the West will have to face a militant Islamic threat in North Africa similar to the one that Iran has presented to them in the Persian Gulf and eastern Mediterranean.

Furthermore, an Islamic victory in North Africa could cause a flight of thousands of Moroccan Algerians and Egyptians to the states of southern Europe already shaken by the dispute between Muslims and Christians in Bosnia. Europeans often cite the 1993 prediction by the political scientist Samuel Huntington, who warned that future conflicts in the world would not be over economics or ideology but would be cultural disputes like the current one in Algeria. Large numbers of Muslims moving into Spain, France, and Italy could cause serious internal tensions in those states.

If situations like the one in Algeria are to be effectively handled, the West must learn that Islam is no more monolithic than is Christianity. The Islamic movements in Iran, the West Bank, Egypt, Libya, and Algeria have little in common except broad general principles. They all support the idea of special roles for men and women, oppose secular nationalism imported from the West, reject Western cultural imperialism, and generally support a form of economic populism that aids the poor through the institution of the Mosque. There is little or no common political agenda that crosses state boundaries. It is a mistake for the West to assume that every Muslim in politics is trying to start another Iranian revolution.

Western leaders must learn to stick to the principles that they believe in regardless of who wins an election. To sacrifice support for the values of freedom and democracy abroad to achieve a short-term political goal will ultimately work against Western interests in the Other World. In the case of Algeria, this shortsighted action has actually strengthened popular support for the Islamic militants to the point that they could eventually become a threat to the security of southern Europe.

A CHANGING ROLE FOR SAUDI ARABIAN WOMEN?

The image that Westerners have of Middle Eastern women is stereotypical. It is based on centuries of misunderstanding compounded by the distrust created through political conflicts that have placed Westerners in opposition to actions taken by the Arab world. The result is a constant barrage of misinformation that presents Muslim women in a negative way.

To be fair, women in both the developed and developing worlds have faced difficult struggles to gain a presence outside of the home. For example, it can be said that World Wars I and II emancipated American women. For them, social change only occurred because the United States was locked in desperate struggles for survival. Women were needed for work outside of the home as an essential part of the war effort labor pool. Their arrival in the workforce was due less to the generosity of men than to the necessities of war.

It is impossible to generalize about the status of 100 million women living in the Arab world. Each state and society has different customs and needs. The status of women is changing in Arab states as varied as Egypt and Qatar. In Egypt, schools are being built to meet the special needs of rural women who have been denied an education because of their sex. At the same time, the Emirate of Qatar has granted women the right to vote and to hold public office.

The case of Saudi Arabia can be singled out as an interesting model for change within the intensely conservative context of the Arabian Peninsula. Saudi Arabia is a traditional Muslim state that is in the process of modernizing while, at the same time, attempting to avoid the negative pitfalls often common in Western society. To maintain traditional cultural values while becoming an economically advanced society presents interesting questions as to the role that women should play in this effort. Saudi Arabia may offer an alternative for women caught up in the wrenching changes that are experienced when a traditional society attempts to become technologically advanced.

At present, Saudi Arabia has several problems resulting from the great amount of wealth being injected into the economy through the petroleum industry. First, the society accustomed to a nomadic life of hardship and need is rapidly becoming urban and relatively wealthy. Second, wealth and expansion have created a shortage of skilled labor, while at the same time, allowing Saudi males to treat certain kinds of jobs with disdain. Third, improved medical care has indirectly caused a population explosion. Fourth, an improved educational system has raised expectations in the population. Fifth, The Kingdom's oil wealth has allowed the society to develop expensive duplicate educational, business, and social services for men and women. Finally, these changes have occurred in the most religiously conservative area of the Middle East.

Rapid change has upset many traditional ideas that could eventually threaten the social stability of The Kingdom. Many labor needs are being met by the importation of foreign workers. In 1998, almost one-third of the Saudi workforce was foreign. Foreigners bring new ideas and traditions. Guest workers often become the source of The Kingdom's social problems. Although The Kingdom has actively encouraged the Saudization of labor, many Saudi males still refuse to take lower-level jobs traditionally done by guest workers.

The expenses of financing the Gulf War and postwar Saudi defense programs have combined with changing oil prices to serve as an alert that the "oil party" will come to an end someday. There has been an increasing realization by many in The Kingdom that, like elsewhere in the developed world, both husband and wife may have to enter the workforce if the family is to maintain a decent standard of living. Educated women may be needed to take jobs that have become vacant through Saudization.

This is not to say that Saudi women wish to become Western women; they have a strong commitment to their responsibilities within the home and expect men to be the primary providers. Simply put, when women are needed to become a significant part of the employment pool in appropriate fields such as education, computer science, government service, and medicine, many may opt to bring additional income to the family. In 1998, Crown Prince Abdullah Ibn Abdul Aziz anticipated this future need when laying the foundation stone of a new girls' college when he said, "Our daughters will learn useful subjects and develop their skills and abilities in line with the teachings and sayings of the Prophet Mohammed and our Islamic customs and traditions in an atmosphere of modesty and dignity."[31]

Since 1998, one-quarter of The Kingdom's budget has been allocated to education. There are 123,000 students presently studying in 68 women's colleges belonging to seven universities. In 1996, 13,700 young women graduated from Saudi universities. In 1998, over 5,000 female teachers held advanced degrees.

In a recent move, considered by many to be progress, the Saudi government has begun to issue individual identity cards to female citizens. This seemingly small act gives Saudi women more control over their financial resources because they can now prove their identity at Saudi banks. In fairness, it should be pointed out that Saudi women run more than 1,500 businesses in The Kingdom.[32] They are probably the silent partners in many hundreds more.

The workforce in its current form cannot employ all of these women in their specializations. As needs increase, however, choices for women in The Kingdom can be expected to increase accordingly.

SUMMARY

Geographically, the Middle East and North Africa may be divided into three distinct regions: the plains of North Africa and Arabia, the Fertile Crescent, and the northern tier. The Middle East is an area of contrast, including some of the world's most famous deserts, mountain ranges, and rivers. Oil is the most important natural resource of the region. A scarcity of water limits agricultural development throughout most of the Middle East. The monotheistic religions Judaism, Christianity, and Islam have developed in the Middle East. Today, Islam is the professed religion of 90 percent of the population, and most political activity in this part of the Other World is affected by religion.

Nationalism is a second feature of Middle Eastern politics. Case studies in this chapter describe the various forms of nationalism that have developed in Turkey, Iran, Egypt, Saudi Arabia, and Israel. A brief description of Arab nationalism is also included. These case studies illustrate the directions that nationalists have taken in this part of the Other World.

Review Questions

1. Discuss some of the features of Arab nationalism.
2. List the Five Pillars of Islam.
3. What is the role of oil in Middle Eastern politics?
4. Why is Islam called a way of life?
5. Compare the nationalisms of Turkey, Iran, Egypt, and Israel.

Key Terms

- **Muhammad**—Considered by Muslims to be a human being who lived a perfect life and was a prophet of God.
- **Allah**—The name of God in the Arabic language.
- **Monotheism**—Belief in one God.
- **The Rightly Guided Caliphs**—The first four successors to Mohammad include Abu Bakr, Umar, Uthman, and Ali.
- **1798**—The year of the French invasion of Egypt and considered to be the beginning of the modern European colonial period.
- **Zionism**—Founded in 1897, Zionism is a Jewish form of nationalism calling for the establishment and maintenance of a Jewish state in Palestine.
- **Shah**—Persian word for king.
- **The Ottomans**—Tribe that came to what is now Turkey, in the Middle Ages, and established a great empire that lasted from 1453 to 1918.
- **The Fertile Crescent**—Historic land stretching up the eastern Mediterranean and along the southern border of Turkey to exit through Iraq into the Persian Gulf.

■ **The Suez Canal**—Opened in 1869, the Canal provides a passage from the Mediterranean Sea to the Red Sea.

Useful Web Sites

http://www.israel.org
http://www.iraqi-mission.org
http://www.turkey.org
http://www.idsc.gov.org
http://www.erols.com/lebanon/stat.htm

Notes

1. Madeline Miller, J. Lane Miller, *Harpers Bible Dictionary* (New York: Harper & Row, 1973), p. 688.
2. Population sources: U.S. Department of State, *U.N. Statistical Yearbook,* 42nd ed., 1997; and 1996 *U.N. Demographic Yearbook.*
3. For more information on the politics of water, see Adam Kelliher, "Thrust for Peace Is on Water," *Times* (London), 3 August 1991, p. 6.
4. Lawrence Ziring, *The Middle East Political Dictionary* (Santa Barbara, Calif.: ABC-CLIO Information Services, 1983), p. 415.
5. Lord Kinross, *The Ottoman Centuries* (New York: Morrow Quill, 1977), p. 85.
6. For more information on the Pentecostal Holiness Church, see Ed Housewright, "Faith on a Deadly Scale," *San Francisco Examiner,* 12 March 1995, p. A8.
7. The Ka'bah is a cubelike building located in the courtyard of the Great Mosque in Mecca. According to Muslim tradition, it was the first house of worship built by the prophet Abraham.
8. A. M. Khattab, *A Brief Introduction to Islam* (Perryberg, Ohio: Islamic Center of Greater Toledo, 1983), p. 5.
9. Mark Anderson, Robert Seibert, Jon Wagner, *The Politics of Change in the Middle East: Sources of Conflict and Accommodation* (Englewood Cliffs, N.J.: Prentice Hall, 1993).
10. For more information on fundamentalist Islamic movements, see the Flashpoints on the Palestinians and on Algeria in this chapter.
11. Sometimes called the Battle of the Nile, British Admiral Nelson defeated the French on August 1, 1798. J. R. Hill, *The Oxford History of the Royal Navy* (Oxford, England: Oxford University Press, 1995), p. 111.
12. For pre-1991 Gulf War petroleum export figures, see Richard Teitelbaum, "Where Do We Go from Here," *Fortune,* September 1990, p. 30.
13. Edward Mortimer, Michael Field, "Nationalism, the Steel of the Arab Soul," *Financial Times* (London), 18/19 August 1990, sec. 11.
14. Alfred B. Prados, *Saudi Arabia: Post-War Issues and U.S. Relations,* C.R.S. Issue Brief No. 1B93113, Congressional Research Service, The Library of Congress, Washington, D.C., 1996.
15. Douglas Jehl, "To Some Saudi Clerics, It's Infidels vs. Islam: Harsh Anti-Western Opinions Resonate Among Citizens," *The Dallas Morning News,* 6 December 2001, p. 19A.

16. "Turkey and Europe," *Turkish Daily News,* 16 November 2001. Accessed from Lexis-Nexis Academic database.

17. "Assembly Makes Changes to Boost Bid to Join EU," *The Dallas Morning News,* 4 October 2001, p. 11A.

18. Although never officially acknowledged by the U.S. government, there is little doubt about the CIA involvement in this episode. See Kermit Roosevelt, *Countercoup: The Struggle for the Control of Iran* (New York: McGraw-Hill, 1979), chaps. 11, 12, 13; and R. G. Grant, *MI 5, MI 6: Britain's Security and Secret Intelligence Services* (New York: Gallery Books, 1989), pp. 113–114.

19. Mortimer and Field, "Nationalism, the Steel of the Arab Soul," *Financial Times* (London), sec. 11.

20. David Hirst, "Poised between Control and Chaos," *Guardian* (London), 11 February 1995.

21. Montasser M. Kamal, "Exclusive Governance and Urban Development in Egypt," *The Arab World Geographer* (Toronto, Canada) 3, no. 4 (winter 2000), p. 258.

22. Mark Huband, "Egypt: Pre-Democratic Struggles," *The Financial Times* (London), 13 May 1997, p. 3.

23. Jehr, op. cit.

24. Mortimer and Field, op. cit.

25. Martha M. Hamilton, "The Last Great Race for Oil Reserves?" *The Washington Post,* 26 April 1998, PH 01.

26. "Turkey Issues More Warnings," *The Dallas Morning News,* 5 October 1998, p. 6A.

27. For an interesting account of how the Ottomans, the British, the French, the Germans, and the Russians became involved in the affairs of Kuwait, see William Facey and Gillian Grant, *Kuwait by the First Photographers,* (London, New York: I. B. Taurus Publishers, 1998), pp. 11–16.

28. This charge is countered by Kuwaiti officials who point out that during the last 20 years general assistance aid exceeded $17 billion, or 6 percent of the GNP of Kuwait. This percentage is many times greater than that of any other nation during this period. See Michael Kramer, "Toward a New Kuwait," *Time* 136, no. 27 (24 December 1990): 26–33.

29. For an account of the British-American activities during the 1991 Persian Gulf War, see John Witherow and Aidan Sullivan, *The Sunday Times: War in the Gulf* (London: Sidgwick & Jackson, 1991).

30. Theoretically, the new Siberian wells will enable oil production to be increased dramatically within the next few years. Despite domestic needs, the Russians will have to export a large portion of their production for hard currency that will pay for the machines they need to modernize at home. For an account of joint energy ventures with the West in the former Soviet Union, see "Waiting for the Soviet Dust to Settle," *Dallas Morning News,* 27 August 1991, sect. D; and Elizabeth Shogren, "U.S.-Soviet Drilling Venture Untaps Siberian Black Gold," *Los Angeles Times,* 13 October 1991. For other accounts of competition for OPEC see Gregg Jones, "OPEC Says Rivals Are Acting Piggishly; Massive Output Hurts Prices Cartel Contends," *Dallas Morning News,* 25 November 1995, sec. F, p. 1; and Gregg Jones, "OPEC Nations Struggle with Waning Influence; Role Shifts as Group Turns More Diplomatic," *Dallas Morning News,* 26 November 1995, p. 1.

31. "New Girls' College Being Built Near Riyad," *Saudi Arabia* 15, no. 4 (April 1998).

32. "Saudis Giving Women ID Cards: Badges Bearing Photos an Unprecedented Move Toward Greater Rights," *The Dallas Morning News,* 5 December 2001, p. 6A.

For Further Reading

Al-Munajjed, Mona. *Women in Saudi Arabia Today.* New York: Macmillan, 1997.

Chebel, Malek. *Symbols of Islam.* New York: Assouline/St. Martin's Press, 1997.

Clapp, Nicholas. *The Road to Ubar: Finding the Atlantis of the Sands.* Boston: Houghton Mifflin, 1998.

Cleary, Thomas. *The Essential Koran: The Heart of Islam.* San Francisco: Harper, 1993.

Evron, Yair. *Israel's Nuclear Dilemma.* Ithaca, N.Y.: Cornell University Press, 1994.

Fernea, Elizabeth. *Guest of the Sheik: An Ethnography of an Iraqi Village.* Garden City, N.Y.: Anchor Books, 1965.

Fromkin, David. *A Peace to End All Peace: Creating the Modern Middle East 1914–1922.* New York: Henry Holt, 1989.

Hazelton, Fran, ed. *Iraq since the Gulf War: Prospects for Democracy.* London: Zed Books, 1994.

Hourani, Albert. *A History of the Arab Peoples.* Cambridge, Mass.: Belknap Press, 1991.

Howe, Kathleen Stewart. *Revealing the Holy Land: The Photographic Exploration of Palestine.* Santa Barbara, CA: Santa Barbara Museum of Art.

Kamen, Charles. *Little Common Ground: Arab Agriculture and Jewish Settlement in Palestine 1920–1948.* Pittsburgh: Pennsylvania University Press, 1991.

Lacey, Robert. *The Kingdom: Arabia and the House of Saud.* New York: Avon Books, 1981.

Mahler, Gregory. *Israel: Government and Politics in a Maturing State.* New York: Harcourt Brace Jovanovich, 1990.

Mango, Andrew. *Turkey: The Challenge of a New Role.* New York: Praeger, 1994.

Norwich, John Julius. *Byzantium: The Decline and Fall.* New York: Alfred A. Knopf, 1996.

Nutting, Anthony. *The Arabs: A Narrative History from Mohammed to the Present.* New York: Mentor Books, 1964.

Pampanini, Andrea. *Cities from the Arabian Desert: The Building of Jubail and Yanbu in Saudi Arabia.* New York: Praeger, 1997.

Peretz, Don. *Intifada: The Palestinian Uprising.* Boulder, Colo.: Westview Press, 1990.

Rubinstein, Alvin. *The Arab-Israeli Conflict: Perspectives.* 2nd ed. New York: HarperCollins, 1991.

Shalev, Aryeh. *Israel and Syria: Peace and Security on the Golan.* Boulder, Colo.: Westview Press, 1994.

Sherman, A. J. *Mandate Days: British Lives in Palestine 1918–1948.* UK: Thames and Hudson, 1997.

Singerman, Diane. *Avenues of Participation: Family, Politics, and Networks in Urban Quarters of Cairo.* Princeton: Princeton University Press, 1995.

Smith, Charles. *Palestine and the Arab-Israeli Conflict.* New York: St. Martin's Press, 1992.

Wright, Robin. *In the Name of God: The Khomeini Decade.* New York: Simon & Schuster, 1989.

Yapp, M. *The Near East Since the First World War.* White Plains, N.Y.: Longman, 1991.

Zangeneh, Hamid, ed. *Islam, Iran and World Stability.* New York: St. Martin's Press, 1994.

CHAPTER 9

Prospects for the Future

Dianne Long

If you aim at the stars, you will not lose your direction.
PROVERB

In this concluding chapter, we review the major themes developed that have been presented in the preceding chapters. We also assess how the complex inter-actions of the global community may bring about significant changes in the Other World, and what consequences those changes may have for all the world's people.

THE OTHER WORLD IN THE TWENTY-FIRST CENTURY

To obtain a clear view of the many forces that are in constant interaction in the twenty-first century, it is necessary to divide them, somewhat arbitrarily, into cat-egories that can be examined and discussed. We have chosen several categories, and identified them as follows:

1. Emerging nations in the aftermath of colonialism;
2. The widespread effects of malnutrition and disease;
3. Conflict and the menace of worldwide terrorism; and
4. Social and economic forces and dilemmas.

The Legacy of Colonialism

The legacy of colonialism continues to frustrate the development efforts of Other World countries. This legacy is demonstrated in the lack of national identity, inadequate infrastructure, instability of democratic processes, and continuing economic manipulation and dominance by world powers.

Lack of National Identity   When Britain, France, Germany, and other European powers granted independence to their former colonies, state boundaries were established, but no sense of national identity existed. The political institutions left behind were based on European models created for the convenience of the colonial rulers. The existing political and economic structures were geared to the exportation of goods needed by the mother country, not to internal and sustainable economic development. Ethnic and tribal conflicts remained within new political boundaries and worked against cooperative strategies for entering the modern world.

Inadequate Infrastructure   Today, several decades after independence, most Other World countries still have inadequate infrastructures; low literacy rates; inadequate housing, education, and health facilities; and divisions along caste, tribal, ethnic, religious, and linguistic lines. Many have economies that were once ascending but are now declining. The infrastructure for development simply does not exist sufficiently. Corruption continues and funds terrorist activities that focus on cleansing the developing world of the trapping of the modern industrial state and of the Western values that clash with traditional and fundamental beliefs and customs.

Instability of Democratic Processes   Other World countries responded to colonialism with nationalistic movements united to win independence from foreign exploiters. Sometimes these efforts came early and were successful without prolonged conflict, such as in much of Latin America. For others, the end of World War II marked the close of colonial occupation; foreign flags were lowered from colonial capitals and independence was declared. Yet others currently fight wars of national liberation that persist today. This strife is based on long-held differences in religious belief, social custom, and grudges that have spanned decades. The conflict has worked against nationalization efforts in the main.

Nationalism is a double-edged sword. On the one hand, it can foster national unity by linking the people and culture to the state. On the other hand, it can promote differences between groups and lead to conflict over power and control. Afghanistan is a case in point, as is the former state of Yugoslavia. In both places, differences led to prolonged conflict, war, death, and destruction. Nationalism is a social and psychological force, a development of unity and loyalty to the nation and state that cannot be simply proclaimed or stopped by a leader. Nationalism as it is understood in the West has yet to take firm root in many Other World countries. Instead, we see chronic political instability in much of Asia, Africa, Latin America, and the Middle East. The democratic processes of Western states may be unworkable in Other World countries, where the people remain fragmented, poorly educated, and more concerned about the daily requirements of living than the good of the state. In many cases, democracy and modernism are consciously rejected in favor of traditional and customary approaches. It appears at this juncture that many ex-colonies were ill prepared to continue where their colonial "masters" left off. When the British left India, a bureaucracy had been established that included many Indians. Most other countries, however, were not so lucky. Some had few educated and experienced nationals to assume leadership roles and to help to build a nation.

Military Dominance   In parts of the Other World, the military is viewed as the only institution capable of maintaining public order and serving as a vehicle either for or against change. Although this belief conflicts with Western democratic tradition, the military is sometimes the only force with the technical training, organizational ability, and unity to govern. Furthermore, Other World peoples often view the military as both heroic and modern, whereas civilian society reflects the discredited values of a colonial heritage. For example, the military was used as a force for change by Nasser in Egypt and by the government of Turkey, and military leaders are often elected or appointed to serve as president or to serve in leadership positions in new governments. This pattern of military leadership transformed into governing is common in Africa and in Latin America.

Loyalty in the Face of Change   The Other World is in a state of transition, development, and change at a pace that is unprecedented. Loyalty to existing states has yet to develop. Competing nationalistic movements feed on one another, threatening to disrupt society. We see a pattern emerging that has been repeated in many Other World countries. Colonial status leads to nationalistic movements to repel the colonizers. Independence is followed by a period of increasing internal instability that results in civil war. Eventually, a government emerges to restore at least partial order, by force if necessary. Often the cycle is repeated.

In recent decades, most civil wars have involved assistance from outside states and the involved countries have served as proxies in the global contest between the former Soviet Union and the United States. Resulting conditions were often detrimental to individual citizens if not to the survival of their governments. Anarchy was common. With the end of the Soviet Union as one nation and with the economic and political stability in that part of the world, funding to new nations has dwindled to whatever the West chooses to provide in order to supplement United Nations (UN) and World Bank support. Many policy choices are linked to economic self-interest. The West needs raw materials, particularly oil, for continued production, industrialization, and modernization. Nations without economic links to the West may flounder.

Economic Manipulation and Dominance   The new states are striving for national development and acceptance in the international political and economic community. International governmental organizations such as the Organization of African Unity, the Association of Southeast Asian Nations, the Arab League, and the Economic Community of West African States were created to facilitate regional cooperation and mutual development. A major goal of these and other international organizations is to maximize the economic power of Other World countries as one means of lessening the economic effects of neocolonial practices and fragmentation.

Although the future political organization of the Other World is unclear, the status quo is under attack. Present boundaries and political alignments are inadequate to meet the problems on the horizon in the coming century. Perhaps a rearrangement of priorities will lead to political organizations in the twenty-first century that would be totally unrecognizable to those observing this part of the world today. Only time will tell.

Malnutrition and Disease

Perhaps the most formidable obstacle facing the Other World is providing food for its growing population. Although wars and disease claim many deaths, population continues to increase exponentially in many areas. Any dramatic increase has many corollaries—the need for food, shelter, employment, and educational and health services. There are some hopeful signs that the rate of population growth in some Other World countries is being checked or lowered. In the poorest countries, however, such optimism fails. Even with a lower birthrate, the population of Other World countries will continue to climb because there are so many young women of childbearing age.

Government Choices   There are difficult policy choices most Other World governments have to make. Clearly government can allow population growth to continue unabated and face the resulting social, economic, and political turmoil. Or it can impose population-planning programs that strike at the heart of private family decisions and traditional values—values that place a high premium of life and on bringing future workers into the family. If governments are unable to lower birthrates through voluntary programs by its citizens, more stringent interventions may enter into the health delivery system, including forced abortions and infanticide. The Chinese policy of one-child families has been accompanied by such interventions.

Food Production   Many scholars believe that population explosion is a symptom of underdevelopment. As educational levels and economic development increase, population growth declines. Nevertheless, Other World food production must increase to meet the requirements of the people and to generate needed revenue for building a nation's infrastructure. This is a difficult task, especially for indebted countries, which often export food for hard currencies, leaving their own producers hungry. As one Brazilian said to the author, "Bakers' children go hungry in this country." The dominance of cash crops such as tobacco, sugar, tea, coffee, and other commodities desired in the world can skew the availability of even basic foods. In Cuba, for example, some complain that when there is bread, there are no eggs, and when there are eggs, there is no bread.

Refugees   A corollary of the population problem in the Other World is the dramatic increase in the number of refugees and displaced persons over the past decade or so. It is true that some refugees are the result of war or other conflict, but many, such as those in Somalia, Ethiopia, or the Sudan, have sought food and refuge from drought or famine, either natural or man-made. Some, as in Bangladesh, have become refugees in their own country, and hope is a scarce commodity.

Finding Suitable Farming Methods   The food production problem in many Other World countries is not one of scarcity of land but rather unfavorable climate and the lack of water, resources, and technology to make the land productive. Primitive farming methods, particularly slash and burn, deplete the land's minerals and nutrients. Cutting wood for fuel, clearing forests for pastures, and overgrazing by domesticated animals rob the land of the groundcover needed to retain the rain, if it falls. Desertification increases. Such practices can be changed, but changes occur slowly, if at all. Moreover, it is traditional and simply more profitable in some countries, such as Colombia or Myanmar (Burma), to grow marijuana, coca, opium, or hashish rather than food crops.

Agricultural Planning   One feature of the underdevelopment in the Other World is the absence of effective agricultural planning at any level. What agricultural planning does occur is done by government ministries that have little knowledge of the realities faced by peasants in the rural areas. The problem is to put expertise to practical use in the field. As one observer notes, "The ability of peasant farmers to learn how to use new technology is not in question. But the institutional apparatus for teaching them is in short supply throughout the developing world."[1] Although countries are developing institutional means to bolster food production, they are also sending students to study modern agricultural techniques in the more developed countries.

New Directions   What are the choices for these countries regarding food production? International assistance programs sponsored by the UN, the World Bank, and the U.S. Agency for International Development have proved successful in some instances. In central Java, Indonesia, malnutrition was high until the 1970s, when a new breed of goat was introduced that produces four times the amount of milk as the traditional breed. Fish farming was increased and the cultivation of fresh vegetables encouraged. In parts of Tanzania, new high-yield strains of rice are being sown, and in Sri Lanka the increased cultivation of soybeans and the development of new soy products have resulted in an increase in the daily consumption of calories and proteins.[2]

The Green Revolution   One of the most interesting developments of the 1980s was the green revolution—the explosion of food production capacity—in some Other World countries. Using chemical fertilizers and genetic engineering technology, countries such as India have been able to increase food *production* dramatically, to the extent that net production is theoretically capable of eventually supporting all of the food needs of that country's more than 900 million people. Unfortunately, this development left a sizable proportion of the population still undernourished. Why? It turns out that production is a necessary but insufficient condition for nutritional wellness. The new relative abundance of many foods is not enough; it is also necessary to integrate people into the money economy so that they can purchase goods. People at the subsistence level do not have surplus cash to participate in the marketplace. There is another problem: Even if there are food and consumers with cash to buy, there must also be an elaborate *infrastructure* that successfully sees goods from the point of production through storage and distribution to the point of sale. This requires warehouses; refrigeration; transportation, including roads, rails, or canals; and market outlets. Lacking these elements, there is often significant loss of otherwise consumable products, with consequent malnutrition and starvation. Although agricultural and other technologies have tremendous potential, other social, political, and economic factors also play a major role—a fact often overlooked by international aid agencies, whether public or private. Thus, in some places, there is a return to plowing the land with oxen and to subsistence agriculture. The costs of fertilizer and tractors are too great. Just getting by to feed the family and have enough left over to buy building materials or cloth becomes the norm.

Trade-offs   In addition to outside intervention by aid programs, Other World governments themselves need to intervene with policies for managing agricultural land. There are trade-offs to be made. Cash crops bring in needed dollars and foreign currency needed to build the infrastructure. Food crops may not be suitable to large production, and small production may feed the family but leave the economy weak. If landowners who grow export crops are unwilling to convert to domestic food crops, governments will have to find ways to encourage this change. For example, village agricultural centers could be established where farmers might obtain supplies and expertise and share equipment to maximize production. Above all, farmers have to be convinced that changing their agricultural practices will raise their standard of living, as well as that of their neighbors.

Effects of Food Aid   There is considerable controversy about food aid. Food aid is a Band-Aid measure that satisfies the consciences of the donors and the immediate physical needs of the recipients, but decisively does *not* provide permanent solutions. On the contrary, it can simply postpone the victims' agony unless there is a commitment to developing sustainable solutions that will accommodate the recipients long after the donors have moved on. Rightly or wrongly, this criticism was made of such efforts as Geldof's Live Aid rock festival in London in 1985. It was also a major consideration in the U.S.-led effort to aid Somalia in 1992, where local farmers could not sell food to people who could get it free from international aid agencies just down the street.

Conflict

The twentieth century has taught many lessons. Among the most important is that conflict is a fact of life. Violence and war do not resolve conflict, and militarism is its most frequent corollary. The world must be collectively attentive to the fact that domestic and international conflict may intensify despite the initial euphoria of the post–cold war era. Only the theaters of conflict have changed, along with the drastic decrease in the possibility of a confrontation between the West and the remnants of the former Soviet Union—at least for now.

Many conflicts that ushered in the twentieth century are just now being addressed, and others, long suppressed, are being unleashed. Two world wars only postponed the resolution of some major international conflicts, as did the post–World War II "balance of terror" between East and West. The dam broke in 1989–1990, severely burdening barely tested or trusted mechanisms of conflict management that were unready to assume the role that had been performed by war and nuclear stalemate. Today the world is waging a war against terrorist activity. The developed world is vulnerable to both biological and conventional weapons. The events of September 11, 2001 have brought the issues of safety and security home to citizens who once viewed regional wars as happening "someplace else." The United States and the West moved into an aggressive foreign and defense policy to root out terrorist regimes and actors.

Resolving Conflict   Just as before the cold war, the world is now confronted with two options in approaching these conflicts: (1) cooperation within the framework of international institutions, or (2) unilateral coercive (military) action within and between countries. Until September 11, 2001, the major powers seemed to be gravitating toward the UN and other international bodies as centralized structures within which to confront and resolve old political conflicts. Recent experience with regional wars and terrorism reveals that agreement on conflict resolution direction is difficult. The United States and other industrialized nations of the Other World see terrorism and instability as threatening to their own political and economic lives. However, peoples in the developing areas face desperate choices, and they may now be more prone to take matters into their own hands in both domestic and international or regional conflicts. Historically, their problems were checked by the East-West stalemate, but are now being redefined in ways that appear decidedly disadvantageous from their perspective. Bolstered by inexperience, lack of interest by the major powers, and growing frustration, they will no longer be restrained. Moreover, nonstate actors, who are difficult to hold accountable, are becoming more active.

Collapse of the Old World Order   Whereas the world was approaching the crossroads when this book first appeared in 1987, it is now in the intersection—and there are no traffic lights to regulate the gush of grievances thundering toward collision. For anyone, anywhere, to adopt a fatalistic attitude would be suicidal. Simply stated, the old political and economic world orders have collapsed, accompanied by such major transformations that one authority has referred to them as "sea changes."[3] This description includes but is not limited to an interesting paradox. As the United States and the states of the former Soviet Union literally destroy weapons, arms proliferation among Other World countries is increasing and now includes nuclear, biological, and chemical capabilities. Indeed, as many as 40 countries may have nuclear weapons.

Social and Economic Issues

Changing conditions at the end of the twentieth century have started to affect social issues everywhere. What were formerly Western, value-based issues such as race, gender, religion, and population control are now becoming prominent in the Other World as well. These ideas may be Western-based, but they create tensions in the systems found in the Other World. There, many of these ideas are seen as Western-inspired threats to home, family, society, and religion. In the West, this opposition to rapid change is often linked to the loosely defined concept of family values. In the Other World, however, traditional elders often view these concepts as Western attempts to impose colonialism, divide peoples, and destroy religion through the importation of humanistic values. For instance, in many places the Western interest in Other World population control has been described as genocide. With resistance to Western-inspired social planning linked to colonialism in areas stretching from Latin America through Egypt to India, making measurable change in the social practices of many developing states in the foreseeable future will be extremely difficult.

In economic terms, the loans given by the World Bank and the offer of technological assistance have tied the hands of world leaders. To bring needed funds into a country to support roads, water systems, schools, hospitals and the like, nations have become debtors. As debtor nations, the dominant goal is bringing in dollars and currency to repay loans and interest on debts. Furthermore, economic aid often comes with directives on what projects need to be undertaken, what results are expected, and what methods need to be employed. These economic issues intrude into political and cultural life. The fabric of the society as a whole will need to be addressed.

DECISIONS 2002

There is a vast and growing agenda of issues that the global community must urgently address. Some concerns, such as those discussed above, are more applicable to the Other World, whereas others, such as restructuring the world order, affect everyone. Many problems require the cooperative efforts of all states if conditions are to improve and a more widely acceptable order is to be defined and maintained. This is the case with environmental issues and the economic relations within Other World states, as well as between them and the more industrialized world, which are addressed in the section on a new world order.

Environmental Issues

Environmental issues have recently received considerable attention in Western media. For example, we are cognizant of the acid rain that is destroying forests and lakes in the United States, Canada, and central Europe. We are aware of the hazards resulting from improper disposal of nuclear wastes and the pollution of the marine environment from supertanker oil spills and unprocessed sewage. We are also concerned about the exhaustion of finite resources such as oil. The Other World has environmental problems that are equally devastating: overcrowded cities, lack of sanitation facilities, diseases spread by contaminated water supplies, and desertification resulting from poor land management and the cutting of trees for fuel and pasture. The environmental consequences are too damaging for such practices to continue. The world can be destroyed by the gradual disintegration of the Earth's ecosystem as well as by nuclear war. We can no longer ignore Barry Commoner's laws of ecology. His first law states, "Everything Is Connected to Everything Else"; his second, "Everything Must Go Somewhere."[4] The key question is whether we can continue to survive beyond the twenty-first century if present pollution and resource consumption continue.

Toxic Chemicals   A vast amount of herbicides, insecticides, fungicides, and pesticides is used for agricultural purposes throughout the world. These poisons control weeds, encourage crop growth, and kill off unwanted insects. Unfortunately, they can also enter the food chain. The toxins are manufactured in industrialized states and exported to Other World countries. Although there are some positive consequences, their unregulated use represents a health hazard to agricultural workers and to all consumers who eat food products from the Other World. Some sprays are carcinogenic; some, including DDT, result in the premature death of small animals; and others, such as Agent Orange, which was used by the United States to defoliate the jungles in Vietnam in the 1960s and 1970s, are linked to birth defects in children and miscarriages in women. The effects of the more recent Gulf War are becoming more apparent among the population in Kuwait and soldiers sent to bring stability to the area.

Radioactive Materials   The careless handling of even small amounts of radioactive material can have serious consequences. In late 1983, two employees at a hospital in Juarez, Mexico took a core from a cancer therapy machine in the hospital's warehouse to sell for scrap. Unknown to them, a small hole in the core allowed the 6,000 pellets of radioactive cobalt-60 to spill into their pickup truck as well as into the scrap yard. The pellets became mixed with other junk, which was eventually used by a foundry to make cast iron legs for tables in fast-food restaurants and some 6,000 tons of concrete reinforcing bars. Ultimately, and by accident, the radioactive products were discovered and destroyed, but not before they had been sold throughout Mexico and the United States. Prolonged exposure to such products can cause sterility and death.

In 1986, the near meltdown of the Soviet nuclear reactor in Chernobyl demonstrated to the whole world the dangers of technology that has been pressed beyond its limits in the rush to find alternative energy sources. Reactors in America and elsewhere have also had close calls, especially at Three-Mile Island, Pennsylvania. In 1990, the German government closed several Soviet-designed reactors in eastern Germany for safety reasons, but similar ones elsewhere continue to operate in those countries where they are the *only* electrical energy supply.

Pollution   Air, land, and water pollution are visible in all of the industrialized countries, and efforts made to counteract the environmental effects have met with varying degrees of success. Paradoxically, in many Other World cities, air pollution is often regarded as an indication of economic strength. Factories that belch plumes of smoke into the air represent employment opportunities, economic self-sufficiency, and less dependence on Western economies. Much of the water pollution in the Other World can be traced to poor or nonexistent sewage disposal and to the chemicals in fertilizers that collect in lakes and underground water supplies.

Rainforests   The tropical forests in countries near the Equator are essential to the health of the world's ecosystem. The rainforests, in conjunction with green plants growing on land and on the oceans' surface, act as a natural cleansing system by removing from the atmosphere carbon dioxide produced by the combustion of fossil fuels. Over the last 50 years, many rainforests have been cut down or severely reduced in size. Over half the world's remaining tropical rainforests are now in the Amazon region of Brazil. Some are also found in central Africa, but the forests in West Africa, southern Africa, the Caribbean, North America, and some parts of India are largely gone. In the Amazon alone, over 50 million acres of rainforests, an area about the size of the state of Nebraska, are lost *annually* to logging, the clearing of jungles for farm and grazing land, slash-and-burn agricultural practices, and population resettlement policies that promise impoverished urban refugees newly cleared farmland in the jungles if they will relocate.

As the rainforests are cut back, there is a resulting increase of carbon dioxide in the atmosphere, which scientists fear will result in a gradual warming of the Earth's climate. This greenhouse effect could cause some melting of the polar ice caps, a reduction of regional rainfall, and a change in growing seasons. The rainforests contain a vast variety of trees and undergrowth. When the hardwood trees are cut down for export or simply burned, the undergrowth dies and the rain washes away the topsoil. The resulting erosion makes it unlikely that new growth can survive in place of the old.

The reduction of the rainforests is understandably a concern to environmentalists, particularly those in the industrialized world, where few rainforests still exist. In the Other World, however, the rainforests are considered an untapped source of wealth. As Brazil's foreign debt increases, harvesting hardwoods in the Amazon could be a means of repaying loans through wood exports. Currently, most hardwoods are burned for lack of a market or access to markets. There is a political aspect to this practice as well, as one observer noted, "In many tropical countries where the few have a lot and the many hardly anything, the rainforest is a political asset. The wealthy and powerful abhor land reform—so why not shunt the land-hungry poor into that great green forest, especially if expenses will be underwritten by some international nonprofit lending institution?"[5] This reference

Loss of Rainforest: This area in the Amazon rainforest has been logged off in preparation for rice planting.
SOURCE: *Domingo/Lenderts*

to international nonprofit institutions includes the World Bank, which has provided funds to the Indonesian government to relocate residents of overcrowded Java and Madura to sparsely populated islands. Some rainforests have to be cleared for the new settlements, and a new economy dependent on the further reduction of the wooded areas is created. Much of the hardwood cut in Indonesia is exported to Japan and ultimately sent to the United States as furniture.

Environmental Trends

There is growing international concern about the global environment. In June 1972, the first UN Conference on the Global Environment was held in Stockholm, Sweden. Some 1,200 delegates from 113 countries and 400 international agencies participated, although delegates from the Soviet bloc boycotted the meeting. At the end of the 11-day program, the delegates adopted a 109-point action plan and a "Declaration on the Human Environment." Both were subsequently officially recognized when the UN General Assembly established the UN Environmental Program to act as a prime force and clearinghouse to coordinate multinational efforts to resolve environmental problems.

Since then, other conferences on the international environment have been held, and countries have set up their own agencies for environmental protection. Some countries, however, have been concerned that environmental controls might inhibit their economic development, and international protective measures continue to be favored. If international efforts are to be successful, the industrialized countries must help finance them. In 1972, $100 million was pledged, although actual contributions to the UN Environmental Program were significantly less, mainly because of inflation and other domestic economic problems in the industrialized states.

Despite its reduced budget, the UN Environmental Program is monitoring changing environmental conditions and recommending feasible plans to help countries enact sound environmental policies. Meanwhile, internal environmental movements in Other World countries are gaining strength. Costa Rica has more land under protected status than any other country in Latin America, and "debt swapping" schemes exist in which protection of forest is promised in return for relief from international debt. In Kenya, two nongovernmental organizations planted more trees in a two-year period than the government had in the previous five. In Indonesia, environmental organizations have put pressure on the government to reduce water pollution, regulate mining operations, and reevaluate the wisdom of overcutting hardwood forests.[6] In short, there are critical environmental decisions to be made the world over at the beginning of the twenty-first century.

The most recent effort to address questions about the global environment was held in New York in 1997. The UN Conference on Environment and Development, dubbed the Earth Summit II, brought together world leaders to evaluate progress toward the goals of the Rio summit in 1992. Those goals represented trade-offs among environmental protection, the Other World's need to develop, and the industrialized countries' need to maintain growth and jobs. It was also hoped that the Convention on Biological Diversity would forestall species extinction—the disappearance of more of the planet's animal and plant species.

The Price of Development: A coal-fired power plant near Beijing, China.

SOURCE: *Joe Weatherby*

Only the United States refused to sign because of serious questions about the treaty's provision for sovereign rights over genetic resources.

TOWARD A NEW WORLD ORDER

The world at the beginning of the twenty-first century is a dramatically different place than it was when the first edition of this book was published in 1987. The intervening years have witnessed events that few could have predicted. The events of September 11, 2001, with the destruction of the World Trade Center and part of the Pentagon ended United States innocence of conflict and hatred in the developing world toward Western values and intrusions into other cultures, economies, and governments. The War on Terrorism brought former enemies such as the Soviet Union and the United States together to fight what was considered threats to the civilized world. Prior to this, the collapse of communism produced a surge toward democracy and free-market economic systems in Eastern Europe, Asia, and elsewhere. Faced with increasing demands for national autonomy and a steady erosion of their power, conservative segments in parts of the Soviet empire attempted to launch a coup to return communist values. In the main, their actions discredited their parties, strengthened their reform-minded opponents, and hastened the demise of the states they had hoped to preserve. Today, the remnants of the Soviet bloc are being subjected to numerous disruptive changes as the long dormant forces of religion, nationalism, and ethnicity reemerge and interact with the economic and political change. The world cannot now view terrorism, war, and conflict with a sense of detachment. In an interdependent world, events affecting one part of the world offer both opportunity and danger for people throughout the world.

In many places in Asia, the leaders apparently are unwilling to match their economic reforms with political reforms. In China in June 1989, demands by students and workers for greater democracy were eventually met with a determined and ruthless suppression by elements of the People's Liberation Army (PLA) in Tiananmen Square. That action was followed by similar acts of suppression and by a continuing campaign against "bourgeois democracy." Internally, China remains a rigidly authoritarian state determined to take from the outside world only those things that contribute to its economic development and to resist the importation of the political beliefs and practices that have accompanied such development elsewhere. China's pragmatic leaders realized that the resumption of its traditional role of leadership in Asia and the strengthening of its claim to such a position in the larger world community requires the restoration of the political and economic ties that were damaged, at least temporarily, by its actions in 1989. Thus, it continues to engage in many international activities ranging from the hosting of the 1990 Asian Games and numerous international meetings to diplomatic efforts, such as mending its tattered relations with neighboring states like Russia and Vietnam.

Throughout the 1990s, such efforts appeared to bear fruit as internal order prevailed, foreign investment strengthened, and China's gross domestic product resumed its double-digit rate of growth. Perhaps typical is a statement made by Israel's first ambassador to China, Zev Sofott, a few months after the two states established diplomatic relations in 1992: "China is a big trade partner and its import value topped more than $60 billion dollars last year. We would like to have a small part of that value."[7] Israel was by no means alone in wanting "some of that value." After trying to alter China's human rights performance by threatening to end its most-favored-nation (MFN) trading status, the United States reversed this position and agreed that the two issues would no longer be linked. By the middle of the decade, China again seemed assured of a major role in world affairs, both economically and politically.

In the West, the European states continued their movement toward economic and political integration by ratifying the Maastricht Treaty (1992), creating the European Union (EU), expanding it in 1998, and removing all trade barriers between members. In addition, the EU now has a united Germany as its major economic force. The apparent success of the former European Community (EC) has encouraged many of the former Soviet satellite states to seek a greater role in the economic integration of Europe. Also searching for a role in the common "European home" are the economically and politically troubled states of the former Soviet Union itself. Beyond Europe, the United States fashioned a free-trade agreement with Canada and Mexico (NAFTA) in 1993 and pushed the admission of the Czech Republic, Hungary, and Poland into The North Atlantic Treaty Organization (NATO) (1998). Elsewhere, similar regional trading blocs are taking form in the Other World—for example, the 1992 formation of a free-trade zone by the Association of South East Asian Nations (ASEAN) states and the Asia-Pacific Economic Cooperation (APEC) forum.

These changes have contributed to a new if fitful spirit of cooperation between East and West to a degree unimaginable a few years ago. Former Soviet President Gorbachev spoke of "new political thinking" in seeking accommodation with the West and access to its economy and technology. Former President Bush and his son George W. Bush spoke of a "new world order" to replace confrontation with cooperation as former antagonists jointly use their power and influence to settle international problems. At the same time, these leaders did not shirk from entering into military engagements in Kuwait and in Afghanistan.

As this decade began, it seemed that after over 40 years of immobilization by cold war politics, the concept of collective security might at last fulfill its order-building role assigned by the UN founders. However, there are forces afoot jeopardizing this progress that could plunge the world into a new era of conflict, both "hot" and "cold."

Alternatives to the Old World Order

Certainly, the momentous changes noted above will affect the Other World. Indeed, given such massive changes in the "First" and "Second" Worlds, the term *Third World* is perhaps even less valid now than it was a few years ago. Many of the people living in the less developed regions have long regarded it as an arrogant label devised by the developed states to relegate the people and problems of the less developed countries to inferior status. Today, segments of the East and West seem to be merging into a single developed world, which may interact collectively with the less developed Other World. Although the precise nature and impact of these interactions are still unclear, recent events in Afghanistan, Africa, Eastern Europe, Cambodia, the Pacific Rim, the Persian Gulf, and Palestine may provide some instructive and perhaps disquieting hints.

In each of these regional conflicts, past tendencies of both East and West to seek a political advantage were replaced by a high degree of cooperation in the search for solutions. In each instance their efforts were supported by several Other World states. If this is to be taken as evidence of the emergence of a new world order, what will be its probable nature? One possibility is that in this new era of multipolarity, the great powers will move toward a role that great powers traditionally played in world affairs. It was described nearly a half-century ago by former British diplomat Sir Harold Nicholson:

> It was assumed that the Great Powers were greater than the Small Powers, since they possessed a more extended range of interests, wider responsibilities, and, above all, more money and more guns. Throughout this period the Small Powers were assessed according to their effect upon the relations between the Great Powers: there was seldom any idea that their interests, their opinions, still less their votes, could affect a policy agreed upon . . . [8]

Simply put, such a world order assumes that although all sovereign states are legally equal, those that possess greater power have a greater responsibility to maintain the international political and economic system than do lesser powers. To carry out these responsibilities, the great powers jointly construct and enforce the international system, at times acting as "police," either unilaterally or in concert with other great powers. The effect is to reinforce a status quo that embraces self-interest.

Great-power efforts to bring pressure on the belligerents in Afghanistan, Cambodia, the Middle East, and the Balkans may represent movement toward this model. Should such a model prevail, a few great powers, like the United States, Japan, Russia, China, and the EU, might assume the responsibility for maintaining order throughout the Other World. Such a "condominium of power" has been condemned in the past. Most notably perhaps, China has often warned against great-power hegemony in which major powers impose their solutions to world problems. China seems to be increasingly willing, however, to accept such leadership when it is included among those great powers. Certainly, there is a degree of haughtiness in an order that arrogates to a few states such global responsibilities. Still, as the twentieth century began, such an arrangement would not have been regarded by most states as unreasonable or unusual. It is not altogether impossible that the same attitudes may prevail as the new century begins.

A somewhat less arbitrary scenario would see East and West cooperating within the UN framework to promote international cooperation through the rule of law. As noted above, conditions may now allow the UN Security Council to function in the manner envisioned by its founders. The UN response to the 1990 invasion of Kuwait by Iraq seemed to indicate that such a world order was at least beginning to emerge. At the instigation of the United States, the Security Council quickly condemned the invasion and provided for sanctions against the offending state. With the United States again providing the leadership, several states sent military forces to the region to deal with what former Secretary of State James Baker called the first international crisis of the post–cold war era. A few months later, the Security Council approved the use of military force by member states to restore Kuwait's independence. Significantly, the forces sent to the Persian Gulf remained under the command of their own governments. Although no Soviet units were included in the military force confronting Iraq, the Soviets joined in the demand for the withdrawal of Iraqi troops from Kuwait and the restoration of its sovereignty. They also suggested that the Soviet military might participate in a military action if it were conducted under direct UN command. The EC, China, and Japan joined in the condemnation of the Iraqi action and in varying degrees supported the UN sanctions. With few exceptions, Other World states joined the developed states in supporting the UN sanctions against Iraq. On the surface, at least, collective security seemed to be working.

In Afghanistan, several nations sent military advisors, armies, and weapons, including the United States, Britain, and Russia. There was a united front on acting against terrorism. Whether these efforts will result in the rule of law is another matter. At this writing, the procedures to be used in military tribunals, as well as what other military actions are warranted, are under discussion.

Despite such general support, there is some question about whether the collective security model or the rule-of-law model better describes the effort to confront Iraq. Although most actions were sanctioned by votes in the UN Security Council, the United States clearly took the initiative and provided the bulk of the force and influence that sustained them. It also seemed to view itself as the prime arbiter of its actions. Similarly, other states militarily involved in the region jealously guarded their sovereign right to command their armed forces, thereby complicating collective efforts through the UN. A case can be made that the Other World states that most actively supported the effort felt directly threatened by Iraq's actions; were heavily dependent on the United States, like Egypt; or had their own anti-Saddam Hussein agenda, like Syria. Of the great powers, only the Soviet Union wanted its forces, had they been provided, to be part of UN-directed military efforts.

Perhaps a better illustration of the weakness of the rule-of-law model came later in the Balkans (the former Yugoslavia). In Bosnia, the various military forces sent as "peacekeepers" *did* serve under the direct control of the UN. Under indecisive and divided UN leadership, no state or combination of states (e.g., the EU or NATO) shouldered the responsibility of implementing the UN resolutions, as the United States had done in the Persian Gulf crisis. The result was paralysis, leading to the U.S.-spearheaded NATO intervention in late 1995. That was followed in 1999 by a NATO air assault on Serbia in retaliation for ethnic cleansing in Kosovo.

In short, one may question whether the Persian Gulf or the crises in the Balkans better illustrates the rule of law in international affairs. If, as seems likely, the Balkans is the better example, there seems to be serious reason to doubt whether that model will prevail unless a major power or a group of such powers vigorously leads such enforcement. In such a situation, the difference between the two models we have discussed becomes rather slight and the outlook for an effective UN is remote.

There is, of course, another possibility. In an age when the United States and the former Soviet Union no longer compete with each other for influence in the Other World, major powers may simply ignore that region unless there is a direct threat to their interests. However, the United States no longer possesses the economic preeminence on which its worldwide influence once depended. Although Japan and the EU are active economically, neither seems avidly interested in greater political or military involvement in Other World problems unless they promise to stress their own systems.

China sees itself as a part of the Other World and seems likely to continue its effort to play a leading role. However, it also appreciates its role as a major player on the larger world stage. If its actions in the conflicts discussed above are any indication of its future intentions, it seems likely that China will tend to cooperate with other great powers, at least in the short term. If so, Other World states may indeed receive considerably less attention from the developed states. One positive result would be that Other World states would no longer serve as arenas for proxy conflicts between East and West. In the absence of East-West competition, however, the already small transfer of wealth from the developed world to the Other World may diminish even further.

States are all too often motivated by national interest alone; however, it is hoped that this attitude will not always prevail. It is possible that the developed states may use some of their post–cold war "peace dividend" for an increased effort to solve the many problems that confront the Other World. Unfortunately, there is little evidence now to suggest that this course will occur, as there is little or no political constituency in the developed states to promote it.

Indeed, tendencies in the developed world seem to be toward greater concern with its own interests and less involvement in the problems of the Other World. To overcome a massive government deficit, the U.S. Congress made large cuts in foreign aid to Other World states in 1995 and continued parsimonious actions in subsequent years. As internal problems divert the attention of the former Soviet states from foreign involvement outside Europe, the EU seems intent on a more protectionist course. To the West, the culturally similar states of Eastern Europe are seen as safer and more familiar terrain for investment. In the relatively less developed states of Eastern Europe there are populations whose education, experience, and training are such that investments may be more quickly recouped as those states are slowly integrated economically, culturally, and politically with Western Europe.

Should a new world order emerge in which the UN and the rule of law achieve greater acceptance worldwide, habits of cooperation might develop that could eventually lead to greater joint efforts by the developed states to address the problems of the Other World. However, it is difficult to envision such changes occurring any time soon. It is too soon to tell whether military activities, such as the bombing in Afghanistan, and economic embargo activities, such as the U.S. disturbance of trading with Iraq, will be the primary pattern of bringing the world to order.

NEW INTERNATIONAL RELATIONSHIPS

If the world community is to manage a large and growing number of conflicts, new economic and political relationships must be fashioned. Existing institutions, such as the UN, that can be used to resolve international disputes must be strengthened; new credible and sustainable structures and processes must be created, particularly at the national and regional levels, and all countries must develop the habit of resolving international and domestic conflicts within those frameworks. Unless this task can be accomplished sooner rather than later, the twenty-first century could be a most unpleasant experience for us all.

New Economic Relationships

As noted, the Other World's disadvantageous economic relationship with the industrialized states has contributed to a massive international debt, now approaching $2.5 *trillion.*[9] The disadvantage to emerging states is especially evident in the international trade market: The industrialized states and their multinational corporations control some 80 percent of the global economy. Other World states lack the capital, industrial capacity, technology, and infrastructure to compete with the industrialized countries, which have been honing their economic might for over a century. Because of the need for hard currencies, Other World countries are forced to use their cheap labor to produce goods for export rather than tailor their economies for domestic consumption. This condition means that most Other World countries are almost totally dependent on trade revenues in an international market over which they have little control. To compound the problem, the industrialized states, to protect their economic interests, can increase tariff barriers and impose quotas limiting the amount of goods imported. The question that the industrialized world has to address is this: What economic concessions is it willing to make to help Other World states achieve their economic independence? This question took on new urgency as the once-prosperous "Asian Tigers" experienced their economic slide.

In the 1960s, many Other World countries urged the UN to take a positive step toward the economic rejuvenation of their segment of the world. In the 1970s, the movement for a New International Economic Order (NIEO) took root. Its agenda called for (1) more aid for the Other World from the wealthy states, (2) dispersal of funds through multilateral agencies such as the World Bank instead of country-by-country aid, (3) an increased voice for Other World representatives in the World Bank and International Monetary Fund (IMF) (4), a restructuring or cancellation of debts owed to the industrialized states, (5) some domestic control over multinational corporations, and (6) special trade privileges for Other World countries with the industrialized states.[10] The NIEO advocates argued that Western states must accept responsibility for the economic inequalities in the Other World because they were responsible for the exploitation that came with colonization. Moreover, they argued, the Western countries continue to reap profits because of their control over international pricing mechanisms and neocolonial practices. The Soviet bloc countries supported NIEO demands, but maintained that they should apply only to the Western economies because the Soviet Union and its allies were not part of the colonial experience.

In the 1980s, the General Agreement on Tariffs and Trade (GATT, 1947) supplanted both the UN Conference on Trade and Development (UNCTAD) and the NIEO as the principal mechanism of all international economic activity, including MFN status. Hopes for the NIEO diminished proportionately. Although it is still uncertain whether the Other World will benefit from this change, the GATT did have policymaking authority that the NIEO never had. The GATT was succeeded by the new World Trade Organization (WTO) in January 1995. Although it has a more extensive range of agreements, including intellectual property and global investment rights (Multilateral Agreement on Investment [MAI]), it has no power to enforce.

A new approach was taken by the South Commission, whose report, *The Challenge to the South*, was issued in 1990. It emphasizes the need for cooperation among Other World states and asserts that "responsibility for the development of the South lies in the South, and in the hands of the peoples of the South."[11] Clearly, both cooperation and understanding will be needed from the northern, industrialized countries, although the report represents a major departure from the earlier notion that development of the Other World was the responsibility, indeed the duty, of the North. It does not, however, provide for any institutional framework at a time when the suitability of the "liberal international economic order" (LIEO) to Other World needs is being seriously challenged.

Major changes in the LIEO are on the immediate horizon as this edition goes to press. The global economic crisis beginning in 1998 demonstrated beyond any doubt the reality of the global economy and the interconnectedness of individual economies whether anyone likes it or not. It really is true that if Thailand's economy falters, the impact will be felt in the rest of the so-called Asian Tigers as well as Europe, Russia, and the United States. The LIEO itself is being put to the test, and some, like Kaplan, wonder whether the former Soviet Republics and many Other World countries will ever succeed at capitalism.[12] Where it was expected in the last edition that some, even many Other World countries would form cartels and gain a measure of control over themselves, the opposite now seems more likely. Rich countries and people are buying up Third World assets at bargain prices and some economies are regressing to previous conditions or worse. To suggest that First World economies are impervious to these developments is ridiculous if only because of the massive outstanding debt held by governments and private banks in the United States and Europe. The restructuring of the global economy may not be what the backers of the NIEO wanted, but possibilities include restructuring international debt and outright forgiveness, especially after natural disasters such as the hurricane in Central America (1998).

New Political Relationships

It is indisputable that the cold war is over, and its two former poles, or blocs, are no longer capable of maintaining or returning to the old order. At this writing, the United States is clearly the world's dominant military power and police force. In every other way, however, the world is now more multipolar than at any time in the last half-century, and there is no permanent political or institutional structure to support it. It is precisely the absence of the cold war structure that presents the greatest challenge. What will take its place? A revitalized, reorganized, and strengthened UN? New or revitalized and strengthened regional or international political and economic organizations? Or simply a free-for-all? In 1990, Stanley Hoffmann proposed

> not a world government for which states and peoples are unprepared (and that the managers of the business civilization would not like), but a new experiment in polycentric steering, in which the three major economic powers—plus the (former) Soviet Union . . . and perhaps China— would form a central steering group, and in which regional powers would play comparable roles in their areas.[13]

In this or any other prospective world political structure, there are numerous relevant issues. Among them are power, force, economics, and people—large numbers of people taking to the streets to engage in direct political action.

Power   As anyone who has studied politics and international relations knows, power is a difficult concept to grasp and define. It is very clear that power is taking on a whole new dimension, at least internationally, in the post–cold war era. Alvin Toffler, the futurist, has suggested that above all, power is based on knowledge—even military and economic power are now predicated on knowledge and technology. This is a far cry from the prewar and cold war eras, when international power was defined in terms of nuclear weapon size in megatons, strength of society and economy, and capability and mobility of armies. The United States and the Soviet Union excelled in those power capabilities, as defined in traditional terms, and actually were at *military* parity by the time the Berlin Wall collapsed; both had the ability to "overkill" each other's populations many times over. Perhaps it was a sign of things to come that all that military power had helped neither superpower in Vietnam or Afghanistan, and none was unleashed by either side as the former Soviet Union and communism collapsed. How power is distributed and balanced will be a major issue in constituting any future structure.

The opposite of power, powerlessness, is an old concept with a new face in the post–cold war era. Combined with force, it requires an expansion of the definition of terror. Powerless people and states during the cold war really had no choice but to accept the structure of the global order as defined by the superpowers, a structure that was perceived as disadvantageous from the perspective of power and wealth. That was one of the issues addressed by proponents of the NIEO.

One of the defining characteristics of the post–cold war era, as discussed earlier, is the absence of the bipolar structure and the reemergence of old suppressed hostilities. Thanks to the absence of that structure, the explosion of technology and its availability, states and nonstates—people—are able to use terror to seriously threaten others. This has been amply demonstrated by the Irish Republican Army (IRA) since 1969 and, more recently, by the bombing of the twin towers in New York as well as the United States embassies in Dar es Salaam, Tanzania and Nairobi, Kenya in 1998. None of this was state terrorism.

What needs to be absolutely clear, whether perpetrators are right or wrong, is that states and individual people are now willing and able to threaten and inflict enormous destruction to achieve their goals. Where it was once possible to hold states like North Vietnam and Iran responsible for actions of their citizens, it is no longer. Furthermore, such threats virtually paralyze major powers, which were and are geared for major wars against each other. As has been pointed out, this forces major powers to retreat to their borders behind new "walls" of violence, anarchy, and disease that are every bit as divisive as the old Berlin Wall and the Iron Curtain.

Force   Perhaps the greatest lesson of the twentieth century is that force and the threat of force, military or otherwise, domestic or international, resolves nothing. It can postpone problems, as it has for much of this century, but it cannot eliminate or resolve them. If it is accepted that force is of surprisingly little use as a long-term tool of domestic and foreign policy, it is quite remarkable that there are no structures, institutions, processes, and traditions to take the place of force on any but a short-term basis. Although it may seem that force works in the short term, one of the lessons of history in general, and this century in particular, is that force does not work in the long term and creates wounds that take many years, if not forever, to heal.

Economics   It has always been difficult to disentangle politics and economics at either the domestic or international level. However, it has never been more difficult than it is now, as the nature of state power is redefined and the global economic community takes on a life and inertia of its own. The economic friction and potential battle between the United States, Japan, and China is only one example of the future conflicts that will dominate as the world enters the twenty-first century. In all such cases, the question is this: Who and what will call the shots? Traditional sovereign states? Boards of directors of multinational corporations, isolated from public scrutiny and control? Centralized international, regional, or global organizations?

People   A word on people power is important in light of events in the Philippines, China, Eastern Europe, South Africa, and elsewhere. It cannot and should not be underestimated, as actual events in the past several years demonstrate. Nobody can ever forget the bravery of the young man who stopped a column of tanks from proceeding toward Tiananmen Square in Beijing. Nor can they forget the people of Leipzig who confronted the once formidable East German Army, thereby risking the "Chinese solution" (massacre). And many remember the Sowetans (South Africa), West Bank Palestinians, Rumanians, and others. Given the mixed achievements in these examples, however, the risks are high and the prospects for success are by no means certain and should not be overestimated.

In a related vein, people throughout the world continue to demand public services such as education and medical care. They may be expected to react when such services are threatened by political or economic disarray or by government budget cuts. For example, some voters in Eastern Europe and the former Soviet republics freely elected communists to public office, no doubt in response to major and continuing disruptions in their lives resulting from the shock of free-market reforms. Such actions also provide evidence that the social democratic variation of Marxism is still very much alive, even though Stalinism, or monolithic, dictatorial communism is largely a thing of the past.

SUMMARY

The world has changed drastically during the half-century since World War II, a war that saw the first use of atomic weapons. The UN was born out of that destruction, with the goal of preventing another such catastrophe. Although much has occurred since 1945 and more will take place in the new century, the global community now has the capacity to self-destruct or peacefully coexist. The September 11 tragedy brought us all into a vulnerable space.

The UN Charter was signed by 50 states in 1945. Today, there are approximately 189 members.[14] The expanded membership reflects an international environment that has grown more politically complex and which now has an even greater potential for violent conflict than a half-century ago. At the same time, breakthroughs in communications, transportation, and other technologies have shrunk the world immeasurably, making personal contact easier, more frequent, and almost instantaneous.

Some relationships do not change with time. The inequalities in standards of living persist and are even expanding in many areas of the Other World. Students of the world's condition can note many cruel paradoxes. Medical advances have prolonged the lives of millions, yet tens of thousands die each year from starvation and diseases that accompany malnutrition. There is more widespread awareness now of the fragile nature of the Earth's environment than ever before, although there are now more ways of damaging that environment than ever before. Industrial and technological developments have freed many workers from the drudgery of assembly-line production, yet many more will face a lifetime of illiteracy, poverty, and marginal employment, at best.

The status of the world's states will change over the next half-century. Some will gain more international prestige; others will see their standing diminish; and some, like Czechoslovakia, have disappeared. One hundred years ago, England ruled the seas and governed an empire that extended to every corner of the earth. Today, only the faded remnants of that power remain. The United States will continue to be an international power in the years ahead, even though that power may be redefined. It is unlikely that the Other World will be a cohesive force in the near future, although some states such as China, India, and Brazil are pursuing more prominent leadership roles.

A gloomy scenario for the world in the next century cannot be easily dismissed, on the basis of human actions of the past, although the world and its peoples have demonstrated a remarkable capacity to survive the adversity of natural and human-made disasters.[15] However, a fatalistic outlook that might have been appropriate before is no longer. This is the dawning of a new, exciting, but dangerous age. Increased cross-cultural understanding has helped us grasp our future—a future that does not belong to the Other World or to the First or Second World. The future belongs to all of us; it belongs to the world. The only question is whether we are collectively up to the tasks before us. Shall we survive, perish, or prevail?

ISSUES FOR DISCUSSION

1. Must the United States remain the police officer for the world?

The United States since World War II has acted as a police officer, entering into conflicts in other regions of the world. The nation's rationale originally came from its interests in stopping the spread of communism into other nations and from its desire to protect American companies trading in other areas of the world. Increasingly, the United States has entered into conflicts, primarily in the Middle East and Eastern Europe, where oil and minerals are important. It has continued to engage in political and military activities in the Americas, citing the proximity of these areas to the United States and to the economic ties that exist. Must this pattern continue? Should we wait for the UN peace-keeping forces instead? Will bombing and intervention in another nation's internal affairs bring peace and prosperity?

2. Can we keep other nations from building weapons of mass destruction?

A few nations have nuclear weapons of mass destruction: The United States, France, Britain, Russia, India, Pakistan, and China. Others, including Iran, are suspected of developing them. Is it possible to stop the spread and use of these weapons once they exist? Many think it is not possible to contain the spread because the very existence of such dangerous weapons can be used deliberately or accidentally, destroying populations and environments. Once a number of nations hold these weapons over the head of others for "security," other nations want them too. South Africa is the only state to have built them, tested them, and destroyed them. This is the lonely example of reversing the proliferation of such weapons. Is it possible this strategy can succeed? Or is it flawed in some way?

3. Are we killing our planet with industrialization and modernization?

Industrialized nations and those moving into industrialization are bringing electrification, railroads, roadways, factories, pesticides, herbicides, and other modern systems to their communities. These artifacts of modern life are artificially designed and do not occur naturally in the world. What is not part of nature interferes with nature in some way. The most developed nations produce the greatest pollution to air, waters, and soils. Beijing and Singapore have begun to see the pollution and traffic congestion that rivals what can be found in London, New York, or Frankfort. Trade agreements between countries can step around environmental laws and penalties. Can we find a way to globally protect the planet? Should further industrialization in developing countries be stopped or slowed? Is it desirable even if one is able to do so?

4. Can we care for the children of the world?

Problems of war, drought, disease, and pestilence threaten many in the underdeveloped nations of the world. In some nations, one out of five children is an orphan. Survivors languish with malnutrition, HIV/AIDS, and a host of other ailments and disabilities. Children are the most vulnerable in any social, economic, or political upheaval, because they are dependent upon others for care. Are we able to fulfill our promises to care for children? If we abandon this responsibility, how do we judge our society?

5. Can the world be made safe from terrorism or are we doomed?

With the September 11, 2001, terrorist destruction of the World Trade Center towers in New York City, safety is an issue everywhere in the world. All entry ports into nations are taking extra precautions to scan packages and to question and detain suspicious persons. Some claim that questioning and detaining of persons is equivalent to harassment. Others believe it is necessary. Still others think it is a silly gesture. Nevertheless, we are all taking extra care and hoping for extra safety. Will it work?

Review Questions

1. Must the United States remain the police officer for the world?
2. Can we keep other nations from building weapons of mass destruction?
3. Are we killing our planet?

4. Can we care for our children? Are we able to fulfill our promises to care for all children?

5. Since September 11, all entry ports in nations are taking extra precautions to scan packages and to question and detain suspicious persons. Can safety truly be attained?

Key Terms

- **Nationalism**—A social and psychological force that ties individuals to the welfare of the state.
- **Nationalist movement**—A set of mass participation activities and events that idealizes the state and provides identity for member citizens.
- **International governmental organizations**—Agencies representing the interests of a group of governments, usually economic and political interests.
- **Population explosion**—Dramatic growth in births while increasing life spans.
- **International assistance programs**—Coordinated activities of organizations like the World Bank and The U.S. Agency of International Development that aim at modernization and improvement in quality of life.
- **National infrastructure**—The system of roads, rail, communications and the like used to build the economy.
- **Food aid**—In-kind assistance of agricultural products, usually in times of drought and natural disasters.
- **Cold war**—Cooling of relations between the former Soviet bloc of nations and the Euro-American bloc of nations.
- **Global environment**—The ecosystem of water, land, and natural phenomena we all share in this world.
- **New World Order**—Economic and political cooperation and integration led by powerful nations, like Russia, the United States, and the European Community.

Useful Web Sites

http://www.oneworld.org
http://www.imf.org
http://www.amnesty-usa.org
http://www.afsc.org
http://www.state.gov/www/global

Notes

1. Pierre Crosson, "Agricultural Land: Will There Be Enough?" *Environment* 26 (September 1984): 43.

2. Elaine M. Murphy, *Food and Population: A Global Concern* (Washington, D.C.: Population Reference Bureau, 1984), p. 8.
3. Miles Kahler, "The International Political Economy," *Foreign Affairs* 69 (Fall 1990): 139.
4. Barry Commoner, "The Ecosphere," in *Global Resources,* ed. Martin I. Glassner (New York: Praeger, 1983), pp. 24–25.
5. Peter T. White, "Rain Forests," *National Geographic* 163 (January 1983): 46.
6. Norman Myers, "Third World: Mixed News on the Environment," *Environment* 25 (June 1983): 44–45.
7. *Beijing Review* 55 (May 18–24, 1992): 10.
8. A. Harold Nicholson, "The Old Diplomacy," in *Crisis and Continuity in World Politics,* 2nd ed., ed. George A. Lanyi and Wilson C. McWilliams (New York: Random House, 1973), p. 361. Originally published in Harold Nicholson, *The Evolution of Diplomatic Method* (New York: Macmillan, 1954), pp. 99–107.
9. World Bank, *Global Development Finance* (Washington, D.C.: World Bank, 1999), p. 14.
10. James Lee Ray, *Global Politics,* 7th ed. (Boston: Houghton Mifflin, 1998), pp. 294–296.
11. South Commission, *The Challenge to the South: The Report of the South Commission* (New York: Oxford University Press, 1990).
12. See Robert D. Kaplan, "The Fulcrum of Europe," *The Atlantic Monthly* 282, no. 3 (September 1998): 28–36.
13. Stanley Hoffmann, "A New World and Its Troubles," *Foreign Affairs* 69 (Fall 1990): 120.
14. This number is approximate because Czechoslovakia, East and West Germany, North and South Yemen, North and South Korea, Yugoslavia, the Baltic states, and others have changed their UN status and membership as a result of post–cold war realignments.
15. For a chilling forecast, see Robert D. Kaplan, "The Coming Anarchy," *Atlantic Monthly* 273, no. 2 (February 1994): 44–76.

For Further Reading

Berger, Peter L. *Pyramids of Sacrifice: Political Ethics and Social Change.* New York: Anchor Books, 1976.
Brown, Lester, ed. *State of the World, 1994. A Worldwatch Institute Report on Progress toward a Sustainable Society.* 2nd ed. New York: Norton, 1995.
Council on Foreign Relations. *Foreign Affairs Agenda: The New Shape of World Politics.* Revised ed. New York: Council on Foreign Relations, 1999.
De Soto, Hernando. *The Other Path.* New York: Harper & Row, 1989.
Fukuyama, Francis. *The Great Disruption: Human Nature and the Reconstitution of Social Order.* New York: Free Press, 1999. [Excerpted in *The Atlantic Monthly* 283, 5 (May 1999): 55–80.]
Galli, Rosemary, ed. *Rethinking the Third World.* New York: Crane Russak, 1992.
Gillis, Malcolm, Perkins, Dwight H., Roemer, Michael, and Snodgrass, Donald. *Economics of Development.* 3rd ed. New York and London: Norton, 1992.
Hauchler, I., and Kennedy, P. M., eds. *The Almanac of Development and Peace.* New York: Random House, 1993.
Hughes, Barry B. *World Futures.* Baltimore: Johns Hopkins University Press, 1985.
Kegley, Charles W., and Raymond, G. A. *A Multipolar Peace? Great Power Politics in the 21st Century.* New York: St. Martin's Press, 1994.
Kennedy, Paul. *Preparing for the 21st Century.* New York: Random House, 1993.

Manor, James, ed. *Rethinking Third World Politics*. London and White Plains, N.Y.: Longman, 1991.

Mittelman, James H. *Out from Underdevelopment*. New York: St. Martin's Press, 1988.

Randall, Vicky, and Theobald, R. *Political Change and Underdevelopment*. Durham, N.C.: Duke University Press, 1985.

Thurow, Lester. *Head to Head: The Coming Economic Battle among Japan, Europe, and America*. New York: Warner Books, 1993.

Wright, Robin, and McManus, Doyle. *Flashpoints: Promise and Peril in a New World*. New York: Knopf, 1991.

Index

Racism, colonialism, 26
Radicalism, 67–69
Radioactive materials, 348–49
Rainforests, 349–50
Real Plan, 136–37
Reference materials, guides to, 22
Refugees, 14, 320, 343–44
Regional organizations
    Africa, 198–200
    Latin America, 145–47
    neocolonial practices, 342–43
Religion
    Africa, 187–88
    Asia, 246–47
    Latin America, 113–14
    Middle East, 281, 293–96
    motives for colonialism, 29
Republic of China (Taiwan), 256–58
Resistance movements, 53–54
Roosevelt Corollary, 119, 150
Rub al Khali Desert, 287
Rule of law, 355
Russia
    colonialism in Afghanistan, 262
    colonialism in Korea, 261
    immigration, 32
    oil, 332
    See also USSR, former Soviet Union
Rwanda, 219–21, 227

Sadat, Anwar, 310
Sahara Desert, 185, 287
Sahel, 185
St. Domingue, 30
Salinas de Gortari, Carlos, 129–30, 158–61,
    162–63
Samaria, 286
San Andrés Accords, 160–61
Sandinistas, 125
Sanitation, 9–10
Santa Anna, Antonio López de, 118
Saro-Wiwa, Ken, 209
Saud, House of, 312–14
Saudi Arabia, 19, 287, 311–14
    women, 93
    women's role, 334–35
Scarcity, types of, 82
School of the Americas, 168
Schumacher, E. F., 79–80
Second Intifada, 317, 319, 320, 323–25
    map, 321
Self-interest, 62
Senegal, 227
September 11 attacks

conflicts over inequalities, 84
economies of South America, 138
as terrorism, 54
U.S. military response, 55
Sex industry, 268–69
Shah of Iran, 307–8
Sharon, Ariel, 317, 324
Shiite Muslims, 296, 298, 307–9
Shining Path (Sendero Luminoso), 126
Sierra Leone, 225
Silk Road, 274
Singapore, 260
Slavery, Africa, 190, 214–15, 227
Social class, 77
Socialism, 4
Social structures, 13–16
Social sustainability, 61
Socrates, 1
Somalia, 218–19, 227
    Al-Qaeda organization, 229–30
    weapons, 225
South Africa, 204–8
    environmental issues, 230–31
    organizations, 200
    privatized security, 78
    U.S. on apartheid, 227
    weapons, 225
South Asia, 241
South China Sea, 267
South Commission, 358
Southeast Asia, 241, 245, 255–56
Southern Africa Development Community
    (SADC), 200
South Korea, 260–62, 271–72
Soviet Union. *See* USSR, former Soviet Union
Spain
    colonialism, 29, 31
    empire, 25, 26
    Middle East, 301
    Napoleon resisted, 117
    North African colonies, 33
    unification, 115
Spice Islands, 274–75
Spratly Islands, 267
Sri Lanka, 273
Standards of living, 71–72
Steam engine, 92
Structural adjustment programs, 78, 85, 202–3
Subsistence economies, 19–20, 47, 94
Sudan, 214, 215–16
    U.S. attacks, 229
Suez Canal, 292, 329–30
Sugar economy, 30, 131–32, 139
Sunni Muslims, 296, 298, 307–9